BY THE EDITORS OF CONSUMER GUIDE®

PRESCRIPTION
DRUGS

615
MUL

Copyright ©1986 by Publications International, Ltd. All rights reserved. This book may not be reproduced or quoted in whole or in part by mimeograph or any other printed means, or for presentation on radio, television, videotape or film without written permission from:

Louis Weber, President
Publications International, Ltd.
3841 West Oakton Street
Skokie, Illinois 60076

Permission is never granted for commercial purposes.

Manufactured in the United States of America
10 9 8 7 6 5 4 3 2 1

Library of Congress Catalog Card Number: 86-60087

ISBN 0-517-61056-6

This edition published by:
Beekman House
Distributed by Crown Publishers, Inc.
225 Park Avenue South
New York, N.Y. 10003

Consultant: Peggy Boucher Mullen, Pharm.D.
              Drug Information Specialist, Dynamic Control

Cover Design: Michael Johnson
Cover Photo: Sam Griffith Studio Inc.

Contents

Introduction **5**
What do you know about the drugs you take? Do you know
how they work, what side effects they are likely to cause,
whether you can safely drink alcohol or take other drugs while
using them? The more you know about your prescription
drugs, the lower your risk of suffering allergic reactions, an
overdose, or other drug-induced problems.

Filling Your Prescription **6**
Your prescription shouldn't be a mystery to you; you should be
able to read and understand it. That way, you can be sure
your pharmacist has given you the correct drug and the
correct instructions for taking it. While you're at the pharmacy,
you can also find out whether it's possible to make a money-
saving generic substitution for your prescription.

Administering Medication Correctly **13**
To get the best results from the drugs you take, you must
administer them correctly. Proper administration is economical,
too. These simple guidelines show you how to use liquids and
expensive creams and ointments without waste. There are
even some tips to make swallowing tablets and capsules
easier and for warming eardrops.

Coping with Side Effects **19**
A side effect is any effect other than the one for which you
took the drug. Some side effects are serious and demand
your doctor's attention; others may be expected, unavoidable,
and of little consequence. But which are which? Here you'll
find that out, as well as how to alleviate or avoid some of the
most common minor side effects.

Types of Drugs **27**
You know you're taking a diuretic, but what does a diuretic
do? How does a vaccine work? This primer on the basic
action of drugs will help you understand why you probably
shouldn't be taking decongestants if you have high blood
pressure, why you may feel dizzy after taking nitroglycerin,
and why antibiotics won't cure your cold.

Drug Profiles **38**
Here, arranged alphabetically, are profiles of the most
frequently prescribed drugs in the United States. The drug
profile will tell you if it's more beneficial to take a drug in the
morning, with meals, or on an empty stomach; whether your
drug is likely to make you sleepy or dizzy or more sensitive to
sunlight; and if periodic blood tests, eye examinations, or liver
or kidney function tests are advisable while you're taking the
drug. The information in a drug profile is vital to your comfort
and safety and to the success of your treatment.

Index **232**

CONSUMER GUIDE®

Introduction

The right drug for the right patient in the right dose by the right route at the right time. This rule sums up the decisions made when your doctor gives you a prescription. You've helped make those decisions by giving a complete medical history; you've informed your doctor of any previous allergic reactions you've suffered, any other drugs you may be taking, and any chronic health problems you may have. Once you leave your doctor's office, prescription in hand, you have still more to do as a responsible patient.

You must know how to administer the medication you will be taking. You must understand and comply with your dosage schedule. You must know what to do should side effects occur. You must recognize the signals that indicate the need to call your doctor. All too often, patients leave their doctors' offices without a full understanding of the drug therapy they're about to start, with the result that they do not comply fully with their doctor's prescription. They may stop taking the medication too soon because it doesn't seem to work or because they feel better or because it causes bothersome side effects. They may take the drug improperly or at the wrong time or too often. They may continue drinking alcohol or taking other drugs, perhaps not even realizing that such things as cold pills, oral contraceptives, aspirin, and vitamins could affect the action of the prescribed drug. The end result may be that they do not get better; perhaps they will get worse or they may suffer a dangerous overdose.

PRESCRIPTION DRUGS provides the information you need to take drugs safely. Along with general information on reading a prescription and buying, storing, and using drugs, it provides an introduction to the action of drugs—how drugs work to stop infection, lower blood pressure, or relieve pain. Then it provides detailed information on hundreds of the most commonly prescribed drugs, including how to alleviate certain side effects, whether you should take the drug on an empty stomach or with meals, whether the drug is likely to affect your ability to drive, and whether you can substitute a less expensive, generic drug for a pre-scribed trade name medication. You will discover which side effects are common to some medications and which are danger signals that require immediate attention from your physician.

Of course, this book is not a substitute for consulting your doctor and pharmacist. They are your primary reference sources on the use of drugs. But to assure that you receive the best health care possible, you too must be informed and knowledgeable about the drugs you use.

Filling Your Prescription

While you're having your prescription filled, you should make sure you understand your dosage schedule, what kinds of precautions to take to prevent or reduce side effects, whether you should restrict your diet or drinking habits while taking the drug, which side effects are expected or unavoidable, and which side effects signal a need for a doctor's attention. Your first step in filling your prescription is reading what your doctor has written.

Reading Your Prescription

Prescriptions are not mysterious, and they contain no secret messages. Many of the symbols and phrases doctors use on prescriptions are abbreviated Latin or Greek words, and they are holdovers from the days when doctors actually wrote in Latin. For example, "gtts" comes from the Latin word *guttae,* which means drops, and "bid" is a shortened version of *bis in die,* Latin for twice a day.

You do not have to be a doctor, nurse, or pharmacist to read a prescription, but you should learn how. After all, the prescription describes the drug you will be taking. You should understand what your doctor has written on the prescription blank to be sure the label on the drug container you receive from your pharmacist coincides with the prescription.

The accompanying chart lists the most commonly used symbols and abbreviations on prescriptions. Use it as a guide to read the sample prescriptions that follow.

Common Abbreviations and Symbols Used in Writing Prescriptions

Abbreviation	Meaning	Derivation and Notes
A_2	both ears	*auris* (Latin)
aa	of each	*ana* (Greek)
ac	before meals	*ante cibum* (Latin)
AD	right ear	*auris dextra* (Latin)
AL	left ear	*auris laeva* (Latin)
AM	morning	*ante meridiem* (Latin)
AS	left ear	*auris sinistra* (Latin)
bid	twice a day	*bis in die* (Latin)
c̄	with	*cum* (Latin)

Abbreviation	Meaning	Derivation and Notes
cap	capsule	—
cc or cm³	cubic centimeter	30 cc equals one ounce
disp	dispense	—
dtd#	give this number	*dentur tales doses* (Latin)
ea	each	—
ext	for external use	—
gtts	drops	*guttae* (Latin)
gutta	drop	*gutta* (Latin)
h	hour	*hora* (Latin)
HS	bedtime	*hora somni* (Latin)
M ft	make	*misce fiat* (Latin)
mitt#	give this number	*mitte* (Latin)
ml	milliliter	30 ml equals one ounce
O	pint	*octarius* (Latin)
O₂	both eyes	*oculus* (Latin)
OD	right eye	*oculus dexter* (Latin)
OJ	orange juice	—
OL	left eye	*oculus laevus* (Latin)
OS	left eye	*oculus sinister* (Latin)
OU	each eye	*oculus uterque* (Latin)
pc	after meals	*post cibum* (Latin)
PM	evening	*post meridiem* (Latin)
po	by mouth	*per os* (Latin)
prn	as needed	*pro re nata* (Latin)
q̄	every	*quaqua* (Latin)
qd	once a day	*quaqua die* (Latin)
qid	four times a day	*quater in die* (Latin)
qod	every other day	—
s̄	without	*sine* (Latin)
Sig	label as follows	*signetur* (Latin)
sl	under the tongue	*sub lingua* (Latin)
SOB	shortness of breath	—
sol	solution	—
ss	half-unit	*semis* (Latin)
stat	at once, first dose	*statim* (Latin)
susp	suspension	—
tab	tablet	—
tid	three times a day	*ter in die* (Latin)
top	apply topically	—
ung or ungt	ointment	*unguentum* (Latin)
UT	under the tongue	—
ut dict	as directed	*ut dictum* (Latin)
x	times	—

The first sample prescription is for Darvon Compound-65 (Darvon cpd-65) analgesic. The prescription tells the pharmacist to give you 24 capsules (#24), and it tells you to take one capsule (cap i) every four hours (q̄4h) as needed (prn) for pain. The prescription indicates that you may receive five refills (5x) and that the label on the drug container should state the name of the drug (yes).

Look at the second prescription. It shows you will receive 100 (dtd C) tablets of Lanoxin heart drug, 0.125 mg. You will take three tablets at once (iii stat), then two (ii) tomorrow morning (AM), and one (i) every (q̄) morning (AM) thereafter with (c̄) orange juice (OJ). You may receive refills as needed (prn), and the name of the drug will be on the package (√).

Do remember to check the label on the drug container. If the information on the label is not the same as on the prescription, question your pharmacist. Make doubly sure that you are receiving the right medication and the correct instructions for taking it.

Talking to Your Pharmacist

Once you have read the prescription, its directions may seem clear enough, but will they seem clear when you get home? For example, the prescription for Darvon Compound-65 analgesic tells you to take one capsule every four hours as needed. How many capsules can you take each day—four, six, more? The phrase "as needed" is not clear, and unless you understand what it means, you don't know how much medication you can take per day. What if your prescription instructs you to take "one tablet four times a day"? What does four times a day mean? For some antibiotics, it may mean one tablet every six hours around the clock. For other medications, it may mean one tablet in the morning, one

John D. Jones, MD
Anytown, U.S.A.

DEA#123456789   PHONE#123-4567

NAME *Your Name*

ADDRESS *Anytown, USA.*   AGE 25   DATE 2-15-86

℞   *Darvon Cpd-65*

#24

sig: cap i q 4h prn pain

John D. Jones M.D.

REFILLS *5X*

LABEL *Yes*   MD

at noon, one in the early evening, and one at bedtime. For still others, it may mean one tablet every hour for the first four hours after you get up in the morning. Don't leave the pharmacy with unanswered questions; ask your pharmacist for an explanation of any confusing terms on your prescription.

Your pharmacist is a valuable resource in your health care. He or she should have a record of all the prescription drugs you receive in order to detect any possible life-threatening drug interactions. The pharmacist will be able to tell you if your therapy may be affected by smoking tobacco, eating certain foods, or drinking alcohol, and if the drugs you are taking can cause drowsiness or nausea. He or she can tell you what to expect from the medication and about how long you will have to take it. Of course, people's treatments vary tremendously, but you should know whether you will have to take medication for five to ten days (for example, to treat a mild respiratory infection) or for a few months (for example, to treat a kidney infection).

Your pharmacist should advise you of possible side effects and describe their symptoms in terms you can understand. And the pharmacist should tell you which side effects require prompt attention from your physician. For example, one of the major side effects of the drug Butazolidin is a blood disorder. One of the first symptoms of a blood disorder is a sore throat. Your pharmacist should tell you to consult your physician if you develop a sore throat.

Your pharmacist should also explain how to take your medicine. You should know whether to take the drug before or after a meal or along with it. When you take a drug can make a big difference, and the effectiveness of each drug depends on following the directions for its use. Your pharmacist should describe what "as needed," "as directed," and "take

John D. Jones, MD
Anytown, U.S.A.

DEA #123456789   PHONE #123-4567

NAME _Your Name_   AGE _55_
ADDRESS _Anytown, U.S.A._   DATE _2-15-86_

℞   Lanoxin 0.125
        dtd C
        sig: iii stat, ii tomorrow am.
        then 1q am c̄ or

                    John D. Jones M.D.

REFILLS _Prn_
LABEL   _✓_   MD

with fluid" mean. You may take water with some drugs but not milk. With other drugs, you should take milk. Your pharmacist should tell you how many refills you may have and whether you may need them.

Over-the-Counter Drugs

Drugs that can be purchased without a prescription are referred to as over-the-counter (OTC) drugs, and are sold in a wide variety of settings, such as drug and grocery stores and hotel lobbies. There are no legal requirements or limitations on who may buy or sell them.

Products sold OTC contain amounts of active ingredients considered to be safe for self-treatment by consumers, when labeling instructions are followed.

Many people visit a doctor for ailments that can be treated effectively by taking nonprescription drugs. Actually, prescriptions are sometimes written for such drugs. Your pharmacist will be able to recommend appropriate use of OTC drugs.

If your pharmacist recommends that you not take certain OTC drugs, follow the advice. OTC drugs may affect the way your body reacts to the prescription drugs you are taking. For instance, people taking tetracycline antibiotic should avoid taking antacids or other iron-containing products at the same time; their use should be separated by at least 2 hours. Antacids and iron interfere with the body's absorbtion of tetracycline. Be sure you know what you are taking.

Generic Drugs

One way your pharmacist can help you save money is by dispensing generic drugs. "Generic" means not protected by trademark registration. The generic name of a drug is usually a shortened form of its chemical name. Any manufacturer can use the generic name when marketing a drug. Thus, many manufacturers make a drug called tetracycline.

Usually, a manufacturer uses a trade name as well as a generic name for a drug. A trade name is registered, and only the manufacturer who holds the trademark can use the trade name when marketing a drug. For example, only Lederle Laboratories can call their tetracycline product Achromycin, and only The Upjohn Company can use the trade name Panmycin for tetracycline. Most trade names are easy to remember, are capitalized in print, and usually include the register symbol ® after them.

Many people think that drugs with trade names are made by large manufacturers and generic drugs are made by small manufacturers. But, in fact, a manufacturer may market large quantities of a drug under a trade name; the same manufacturer may sell the base chemical to several other companies, some of which sell the drug generically and some of which sell it under their own trade names. For example, the antibiotic ampicillin is the base for over two hundred different products. However, all ampicillin is produced by only a few dozen drug companies.

Generic drugs are generally priced lower than their trademarked equivalents, largely because they are not as widely advertised. Remember, not every generic is significantly less expensive than its trademarked equivalent. For certain drugs, it's inadvisable to "shop around" for a generic equivalent. Although the Food and Drug Administration has stated that there is no evidence to suspect serious differences between trade name and generic drugs, differences have been shown between brands of certain drugs.

However, for other drugs, consumers may be able to save as much as 75 percent. One hundred capsules of Darvon Compound-65 analgesic may cost $21 to $24. One hundred capsules of the generic equivalent product may cost about $9—a savings of $11 to $13. Pavabid vasodilator may cost $24 per 100 capsules, but if bought generically, the drug may cost as little as $7 per 100 capsules—again, a savings of about $17 per prescription.

In most states, substitution laws allow pharmacists to fill prescriptions with the least expensive equivalent product. If such a substitution law is not yet legal in your state (contact your state pharmacy association to find out), ask your doctor to prescribe drugs by generic names.

How Much to Buy

On a prescription, your doctor specifies exactly how many tablets or capsules or how much liquid medication you will receive. But if you must take a drug for a long time, or if you are very sensitive to drugs, you may want to purchase a different quantity.

The amount of medication to buy depends on several factors. The most obvious is how much money you have or, for those who have a comprehensive insurance program, how much the insurance company will pay for each purchase. These factors may help you decide how much medication to buy. But you must also consider the kind of medication you will be taking.

Medication to treat heart disease, high blood pressure, diabetes, or a thyroid condition may be purchased in large quantity. Patients with such chronic conditions take medication for prolonged periods, and chances are, they will pay less per tablet or capsule by purchasing large quantities of drugs. Generally, the price per dose decreases with the amount of the drug purchased. In other words, a drug that generally costs six cents per tablet may cost four or five cents per tablet if you buy 100 at a time. Many doctors prescribe only a month's supply of drugs, even those that will be taken for a long time. If you wish to buy more, check with your pharmacist.

On the other hand, if you have been plagued with annoying side effects or have had allergic reactions to some drugs, ask your pharmacist to dispense only enough medication on initial prescriptions for a few days or a week to determine whether the drug agrees with you. Pharmacists cannot take back prescription drugs once they have left the pharmacy. You may have to pay more by asking the pharmacist to give you a small amount of the drug, but at least you will not be paying for a supply of medication you cannot take. But, be sure you can get the remainder of the prescribed amount of the drug if it does agree with you. With some drugs, after you have received part of the intended amount, you cannot receive more without obtaining another prescription.

Storing Your Drugs

Before you leave the pharmacy, find out how you should store your drug. If drugs are stored in containers that do not protect them from heat or moisture, they may lose potency.

You can safely store most prescription drugs at room temperature and out of direct sunlight. Even those drugs dispensed in colored bottles or containers that reflect light should be kept out of direct sunlight.

Some drugs require storage in the refrigerator. But the statement "keep in the refrigerator" does not mean that you can keep the drug in the freezer. If frozen and thawed, sugar-coated tablets may crack and some liquid medications will separate into layers that cannot be remixed.

Other drugs cannot be stored in the refrigerator. For example, some liquid cough suppressants will thicken as they become cold, and will not pour from the bottle. Some people keep nitroglycerin tablets in the refrigerator because they believe the drug will be more stable. Nitroglycerin, however, should not be stored in the refrigerator.

Many people keep prescription drugs and other medications in the bathroom medicine cabinet. But this is one of the worst places to keep drugs. Small children can easily climb onto the sink and reach drugs stored above it. Also, the temperature and humidity changes in the bathroom may adversely affect the stability of prescription drugs.

Keep all drugs away from children, and do not keep unused prescription medications. Flush any leftover medication down the toilet or pour it down the sink, and wash and destroy the empty container. Regularly clean out your medicine cabinet and discard all drugs you are no longer using. These drugs can be dangerous to your children, and you might be tempted to take them in the future if you develop similar symptoms. Though similar, the symptoms may not be due to the same disease, and you may complicate your condition by taking the wrong medication.

Definitions of Ideal Storage Temperatures

Cold	Any temperature under 46°F (8°C)
Refrigerator	Any cold place where the temperature is between 36°-46°F (2°-8°C)
Cool	Any temperature between 46°-59°F (8°-15°C)
Room temperature	Temperature usually between 59°-86°F (15°-30°C)
Excessive heat	Any temperature above 104°F (40°C)

Administering Medication Correctly

You must use medication correctly to obtain its full benefit. If you administer drugs improperly, you may not receive their full therapeutic effects. Furthermore, improper administration can be dangerous. Some drugs may become toxic if used incorrectly.

Liquids

Liquids may be used externally on the skin; they may be placed into the eye, ear, nose, or throat; or they may be taken internally.

Before taking or using any liquid medication, look at the label to see if there are any specific directions, such as shaking the container before measuring the dose. If a liquid product contains particles that settle to the bottom of the container, it must be shaken before you use it. If you don't shake it well each time, you may not get the correct amount of the active ingredient. As the amount of liquid remaining in the bottle becomes smaller, the drug will become more concentrated. You will be getting more of the active ingredient with each dose. The concentration may even reach toxic levels.

When opening the bottle, point it away from you. Some liquid medications may build up pressure inside the bottle; the liquid could spurt out quickly and stain your clothing.

If the medication is intended for application on the skin, pour a small quantity onto a cotton pad or a piece of gauze. Do not use a large piece of cotton or gauze as it will absorb the liquid and much will be wasted. Don't pour the medication into your cupped hand; you may spill some of it. If you're using it on only a small area, you can spread the medication with your finger or a cotton-tipped applicator. And never dip cotton-tipped applicators or pieces of cotton or gauze into the bottle of liquid, as this might contaminate the rest of the medication.

Liquid medications that are to be swallowed must be measured accurately. When your doctor prescribes one teaspoonful of medication, he is thinking of a 5 milliliter medical teaspoon. The teaspoons you have at home contain anywhere from 2 milliliters to 10 milliliters of liquid. If you use one of these to measure your medication, you may get too little or too much with each dose. Ask your pharmacist for a medical teaspoon or for one of the other plastic devices for accurately measuring liquid medications. Most of these cost only a few cents, and they are well worth their cost to assure accurate dosages. These plastic measuring devices have another advantage. While many children balk at medication taken from a teaspoon, they often seem to enjoy taking it from a special spoon.

Capsules and Tablets

Many people find it hard to swallow a tablet or capsule. If you're one of them, rinse your mouth with water, or at least wet your mouth, before taking a tablet or capsule. Place the tablet or capsule on the back of your tongue, take a drink of water, and swallow.

If you cannot swallow a tablet or capsule because it is too large or because it "sticks" in your throat, empty the capsule or crush the tablet into a spoon and mix it with applesauce, soup, or even chocolate syrup. But BE SURE TO CHECK WITH YOUR PHARMACIST FIRST. Some tablets and capsules must be swallowed whole, and your pharmacist can tell you which ones they are.

If you have trouble swallowing a tablet or capsule and do not wish to mix the medication with food, ask your doctor to prescribe a liquid drug preparation or a chewable tablet instead, if one is available.

Examples of Drugs that Must be Swallowed Whole

Choledyl tablets	Equanil Wyseals	Tenuate Dospan
Dimetapp Extendtabs	Isordil Tembids	Tepanil Ten-tabs
Donnatal Extentabs	Naldecon	Trinalin
E-Mycin	Tagamet	

Examples of Drugs that Should Be Used Quickly (within 12 Hours) if Crushed or Opened

Combid Spansules	Haldol	Stelazine
Compazine	Mellaril	Thorazine
Elavil	Phenergan	Tofranil
Etrafon	Sinequan	Triavil

Sublingual Tablets

Some drugs, such as nitroglycerin, are prepared as tablets that must be placed under the tongue. To take a sublingual tablet properly, place the tablet under your tongue, close your mouth, and hold the saliva in your mouth and under your tongue as long as you can before swallowing. If you have a bitter taste in your mouth after five minutes, the drug has not been completely absorbed. Wait five more minutes before drinking water. Drinking water too soon may wash the medication into the stomach before it has been absorbed thoroughly.

Eyedrops and Eye Ointments

Before administering eyedrops or ointments, wash your hands. Then, lie down, or sit down and tilt your head back. Using your thumb and forefinger, gently and carefully pull your lower eyelid down to form a pouch.

If you're applying eyedrops, lay your second finger alongside your nose and apply gentle pressure to your nose. This will close off a duct that drains fluid from the eye. If you don't close off this duct, the drops are likely to drain away too soon. Hold the dropper close to the eyelid without touching it. Place the prescribed number of drops into the pouch. Do not place the drops directly on the eyeball; you may blink and lose the medication. Close your eye and keep it shut for a few moments. Do not wash or wipe the dropper before replacing it in the bottle. Tightly close the bottle to keep out moisture.

To administer an ointment to the eye, squeeze a one-quarter to one-half inch line of ointment into the pouch formed as above and close your eye. Roll your eye a few times to spread the ointment. As long as you do not squeeze the ointment directly onto the eyeball, you should feel no stinging or pain.

Be sure the drops or ointments you use are intended for the eye. Also, check the expiration date of the drug on the label or container. Do not use a drug product after that date, and never use any eye product that has changed color. If you find that the medication contains particles that weren't there when you bought it, do not use it.

Eardrops

Eardrops must be administered so that they fill the ear canal. To administer eardrops properly, tilt your head to one side, turning the affected ear upward. Grasp the earlobe and gently pull it upward and back to straighten the ear canal. When administering eardrops to a child, gently pull the child's earlobe downward and back. Fill the dropper and place the prescribed number of drops (usually a dropperful) in the ear, but be careful to avoid touching the ear canal. The dropper can be easily contaminated by contact with the ear canal.

Keep your ear tilted upward for five to ten seconds while continuing to hold the earlobe. Then gently insert a small piece of clean cotton into the ear to be sure the drops do not escape. Do not wash or wipe the dropper after use; replace it in the bottle and tightly close the bottle to keep out moisture.

You may warm the bottle of eardrops before administering the medication by rolling the bottle back and forth between your hands to bring the solution to body temperature. Do not place the bottle in boiling water. The eardrops may become so hot that they will cause pain when placed in the ear, and boiling water can loosen or peel off the label and possibly destroy the medication.

Nose Drops and Sprays

Before using nose drops and sprays, gently blow your nose if you can. To administer nose drops, fill the dropper, tilt your head back, and place the prescribed number of drops in your nose. Do not touch the dropper to the nasal membranes. This will prevent contamination of the medicine when the dropper is returned to the container. Keep your head tilted for five to ten seconds and sniff gently two or three times.

Do not tilt your head back when using a nasal spray. Insert the sprayer into the nose, but try to avoid touching the inner nasal membranes. Sniff and squeeze the sprayer at the same time. Do not release your grip on the sprayer until you have withdrawn it from your nose to prevent nasal mucus and bacteria from entering the plastic bottle and contaminating its contents. After you have sprayed the prescribed number of times in one or both nostrils, gently sniff two or three times.

Unless your doctor has told you otherwise, nose drops and sprays should not be used for more than two or three days at a time. If they have been prescribed for a longer period, do not administer nose drops or sprays from the same container for more than one week. Bacteria from your nose can easily enter the container and contaminate the solution. If you must take medication for more than a week, purchase a new container. Never allow anyone else to use your nose drops or spray.

Rectal Suppositories

A rectal suppository may be used as a laxative or to relieve the itching, swelling, and pain of hemorrhoids. Regardless of the reason for their use, all rectal suppositories are inserted in the same way.

In extremely hot weather, a suppository may become too soft to handle properly. If this happens, place the suppository inside the refrigerator or in a glass of cool water until firm. A few minutes is usually sufficient. Before inserting a suppository, remove any aluminum wrappings. Rubber finger coverings or disposable rubber gloves may be worn when inserting a suppository, but they are not necessary unless your fingernails are extremely long and sharp.

To insert a suppository, lie on your left side and push the suppository, pointed end first, into the rectum as far as is comfortable. You may feel like defecating, but lie still for 20-30 minutes, until the urge has passed. If you cannot insert a suppository, or if the process is painful, coat the suppository with a thin layer of petroleum jelly or mineral oil.

Manufacturers of many suppositories that are used in the treatment of hemorrhoids suggest that the suppositories be stored in the refrigerator. Be sure to ask your pharmacist if the suppositories you have purchased should be stored in the refrigerator.

Vaginal Ointments and Creams

Most vaginal products contain complete instructions for use. If a woman is not sure how to administer vaginal medication, she should ask her pharmacist.

Before using any vaginal ointment or cream, read the directions. They will probably tell you to attach the applicator to the top of the tube and squeeze the tube from the bottom until the applicator is completely filled. Then lie on your back with your knees drawn up. Hold the applicator horizontally or pointed slightly downward and insert it into the vagina as far as it will go comfortably. Press the plunger down to empty the cream or ointment into the vagina. Withdraw the plunger and wash it in warm, soapy water. Rinse it thoroughly and allow it to dry completely. Once it is dry, return the plunger to its package.

Vaginal Tablets and Suppositories

Most packages of vaginal tablets or suppositories include complete directions for use, but you may wish to review general instructions.

Remove any foil wrapping. Place the tablet or suppository in the applicator that is provided. Lie on your back with your knees drawn up. Hold the applicator horizontally or tilted slightly downward and insert it into the vagina as far as it will go comfortably. Depress the plunger slowly to release the tablet or suppository into the vagina. Withdraw the applicator and wash it in warm, soapy water. Rinse it and let it dry completely. Once it is dry, return the applicator to its package.

Unless your doctor has told you otherwise, do not douche two to three weeks before or after you use vaginal tablets or suppositories. Be sure to ask your doctor for specific recommendations on douching.

Throat Lozenges and Discs

Lozenges are made of crystalline sugar; discs are not. Both contain medication that is released in the mouth to soothe a sore throat, reduce coughing, or to treat laryngitis. Neither should be chewed, but should be allowed to dissolve in the mouth. After the lozenge or disc has dissolved, try not to swallow or drink any fluids for awhile.

Throat Sprays

To administer a throat spray, open your mouth wide and spray the medication as far back as possible. Try not to swallow but hold the spray in your mouth as long as you can, and do not drink any fluids for several minutes. Swallowing a throat spray is not harmful. If you find your throat spray upsets your stomach, don't swallow it. Simply spit it out.

Topical Ointments and Creams

Most ointments and creams have only local effects—that is, they affect only the area on which they are applied. Most creams and ointments (especially steroid products, such as hydrocortisone, Aristocort, Kenalog, Lidex, Mycolog, Synalar, Valisone, Vioform-Hydrocortisone) should be applied to the skin as thinly as possible. A thin layer is as effective as a thick layer, and some steroid-containing creams and ointments can cause toxic side effects if applied too heavily.

Before applying the medication, moisten the skin by immersing it in water or by dabbing the area with a clean, wet cloth. Blot the skin dry and apply the medication as directed. Gently massage it into the skin until it has disappeared. You should feel no greasiness after applying a cream. After applying an ointment, the skin will feel slightly greasy.

If your doctor has not indicated whether you should receive a cream or an ointment, ask your pharmacist for the one your prefer. Creams are greaseless and will not stain your clothing. Creams are best to use on the scalp or other hairy areas of the body. If, however, your skin is dry, ask for an ointment. Ointments help keep the skin soft for a longer period.

If your doctor tells you to place a wrap on top of the skin after the cream or ointment has been applied, you may use a wrap of transparent plastic film like that used for wrapping food. A wrap will hold the medication close to the skin and help keep the skin moist so that the drug can be absorbed. To use a wrap correctly, apply the cream or ointment as directed, then wrap the area with a layer of transparent plastic film. Be careful to follow your doctor's directions. If he or she tells you to leave the wrap in place for a certain length of time, do not leave it in place longer. If you keep a wrap on the skin too long, too much of the drug may be absorbed, which may cause side effects. Do not use such a wrap without your doctor's approval and never on a weeping lesion.

Aerosol Sprays

Many topical items are packaged as pressurized aerosol sprays. These sprays usually cost more than the cream or ointment form of the same product. On the other hand, they are useful on very tender or hairy areas of the body where it is difficult to apply a cream or ointment.

Before using an aerosol, shake the can. Hold it upright four to six inches from the skin. Press the nozzle for a few seconds, then release.

Never use an aerosol around the face or eyes. If your doctor tells you to use the spray on a part of your face, apply it to your hand and then rub it into the area. If you get it in your eyes or on a mucous membrane, it can be very painful and it may damage the eyes.

Aerosol sprays may feel cold when they are applied. If this sensation bothers you, ask your pharmacist or doctor whether another form of the same product is available.

Transdermal Patches

Transdermal patches allow for controlled, continuous release of drug. They are convenient and easy to use. For best results, apply the patch to a hairless or clean-shaven area of skin, avoiding scars and wounds. Choose a site (such as the chest or upper arm) that is not subject to excessive movement. It is O.K. to bathe or shower with the patch in place. In the event that the patch becomes dislodged, discard and replace it. Replace a patch by applying a new unit before removing the old one. This will allow for uninterrupted drug therapy; and by changing the site each time, skin irritation will be minimized.

If redness or irritation develops at the application site, consult your physician. Some people are sensitive to the materials used to make the patches.

Coping with Side Effects

Drugs have certain desirable effects—that's why they are taken. The desirable effects of a drug are known as the drug's activity or therapeutic effects. Drugs, however, have undesirable effects as well. Undesirable effects are called side effects, adverse reactions, or, in some cases, lethal effects. An adverse reaction is any undesirable effect of a drug. It can range from minor side effects to toxic or lethal reactions.

Common Minor Side Effects

Side Effect	Management
Blurred vision	Avoid operating machinery
Decreased sweating	Avoid work or exercise in the sun
Diarrhea	Drink lots of water; if diarrhea lasts longer than 3 days, call your doctor
Dizziness	Avoid operating machinery
Drowsiness	Avoid operating machinery
Dry mouth	Suck on candy or ice chips, or chew gum
Dry nose and throat	Use a humidifier or vaporizer
Fluid retention	Avoid adding salt to foods
Headache	Remain quiet; take aspirin or acetaminophen*
Insomnia	Take last dose of the drug earlier in the day*; drink a glass of warm milk at bedtime; ask your doctor about an exercise program
Itching	Take frequent baths or showers or use wet soaks
Nasal congestion	If necessary, use nose drops*
Palpitations (mild)	Rest often; avoid tension; do not drink coffee, tea, or cola; stop smoking
Upset stomach	Take the drug with milk or food*

*Consult your doctor first.

Some side effects are expected and unavoidable, but others may surprise the doctor as well as the patient. Unexpected reactions may be due to a person's individual response to the drug.

Side effects may fall into one of two major groups—those that are obvious and those that cannot be detected without laboratory testing. The discussion of a drug should not be restricted to its easily recognized side effects; other, less obvious side effects may also be harmful.

If you know a particular side effect is expected from a particular drug, you can relax a little. Most expected side effects are temporary and need not cause alarm. You'll merely experience discomfort or inconvenience for a short time. For example, you may become drowsy after taking an antihistamine or develop a stuffy nose after taking reserpine or certain other drugs that lower blood pressure. Of course, if you find minor side effects especially bothersome, you should discuss them with your doctor who may be able to prescribe another drug or at least assure you that the benefits of the drug far outweigh its side effects. Sometimes side effects can be minimized or eliminated by changing your dosage schedule or taking the drug with meals. Consult your doctor or pharmacist before making such a change.

Many side effects, however, signal a serious—perhaps dangerous—problem. And when these side effects appear, you should consult your doctor immediately. The following discussion should help you determine whether your side effects require attention from your physician.

OBVIOUS SIDE EFFECTS

Some side effects are obvious to the patient; others can be discerned only through laboratory testing. We have divided our discussion according to the body parts affected by the side effects.

Ear

Although a few drugs may cause loss of hearing if taken in large quantities, hearing loss is uncommon. Drugs that are used to treat problems of the ear may cause dizziness, and many drugs produce tinnitus, a sensation of ringing, buzzing, thumping, or hollowness in the ear. Discuss with your doctor any problem with your hearing or your ears if it persists for more than three days.

Eye

Blurred vision is a common side effect of many drugs. Drugs such as digitalis may cause you to see a "halo" around a lighted object (a television screen or a traffic light) and other drugs may cause night blindness. Indocin anti-inflammatory (used in the treatment of arthritis) may cause blindness. Librax sedative makes it difficult to accurately judge distance while driving and makes the eyes sensitive to sunlight. While the effects on the eye caused by digitalis and Indocin are dangerous signs of toxicity, the effects caused by Librax sedative are to be expected. In any case, if you have difficulty seeing while taking drugs, contact your doctor.

Gastrointestinal System

The gastrointestinal system includes the mouth, esophagus, stomach, small and large intestines, and rectum. A side effect that affects the gastrointestinal system can be expected from almost any drug. Many drugs produce dry mouth, mouth sores, difficulty in swallowing, heartburn, nausea, vomiting, diarrhea, constipation, loss of appetite, or abnormal cramping. Other drugs cause bloating and gas and some cause rectal itching.

Examples of
Drugs that May Cause Ulcers

Aristocort	Indocin	prednisone
Clinoril	Medrol	reserpine

Diarrhea can be expected after taking many drugs. Drugs can create localized reactions in intestinal tissue—usually a more rapid rate of contraction, which leads to diarrhea. Diarrhea caused by most drugs is temporary.

But diarrhea may signal a problem. For example, some antibiotics may cause severe diarrhea. When diarrhea is severe, the intestine may become ulcerated and begin bleeding. If you develop diarrhea while taking antibiotics, contact your doctor.

Diarrhea produced by a drug should be self-limiting, that is, it should stop within three days. During this time, do not take any diarrhea remedy; drink liquids to replace the fluid you are losing. If diarrhea lasts more than three days, call your doctor.

Examples of
Drugs that May Cause Diarrhea

Actifed-C	erythromycin	oral contraceptives
Aldactazide	Flagyl	Ornade
Aldactone	Haldol	Pavabid
Aldomet	Inderal	penicillins
aminophylline	Indocin	Pronestyl
ampicillin	Keflex	reserpine
Apresoline	K-Lyte	sulfa drugs
Atromid-S	Lanoxin	Tagamet
Benadryl	meprobamate	Talwin Nx
Clinoril	Minipress	tetracycline
Coumadin	Minocin	Thorazine
Diuril	Motrin	Tofranil
Dyazide	Norpace	Zyloprim
Enduron	oral antidiabetics	

As a side effect of drug use, constipation is less serious and more common than diarrhea. It occurs when a drug slows down the activity of the bowel. Drugs such as Librax and Thorazine slow down bowel activity. Constipation also occurs when drugs adsorb moisture in the bowel. And it may occur if a drug acts on the nervous system and decreases nerve impulses to the intestine—an effect produced, for example, by a drug such as Aldomet antihypertensive. Constipation produced by a drug may last several days, and you may help relieve it by drinking at least eight glasses of water a day. Do not take laxatives unless your doctor directs you to do so. If constipation continues for more than three days, call your doctor.

Examples of
Drugs that May Cause Constipation

Actifed-C	Compazine	Librium
Aldomet	Dilantin	Mellaril
Aldoril	Dimetane	Minipress
Benadryl	Dyazide	Pavabid
Bentyl	Flagyl	Percodan
Catapres	Haldol	Stelazine
Clinoril	Inderal	Thorazine
Combid Spansules	Librax	Valium

Circulatory System

Drugs may speed up or slow down the heartbeat. If a drug slows the heartbeat, you may feel drowsy and tired or even dizzy. If a drug accelerates the heartbeat, you probably will experience palpitations (thumping in the chest). You may feel as though your heart is skipping a beat occasionally, and you may have a headache. For most people, none of these symptoms indicates a serious problem. If, however, they bother you, consult your doctor, who may adjust the dosage of the drug or prescribe other medication.

Examples of Drugs that May Cause Fluid Retention*

Apresoline	Librium	oral contraceptives
Aristocort	Medrol	prednisone
Clinoril	Mellaril	Premarin
Combid Spansules	Motrin	Stelazine
Compazine	Nalfon	sulfa drugs
Elavil	Naprosyn	Tolectin
Librax	Norpace	Triavil

*Indicated by a weight gain of two or more pounds a week.

CONSUMER GUIDE®

Some drugs cause edema (fluid retention). When edema forms, fluid from the blood collects outside the blood vessels. Ordinarily, edema is not serious. But if you are steadily gaining weight or have gained more than two or three pounds a week, talk to your doctor.

Drugs may increase or decrease blood pressure. When blood pressure decreases, you may feel drowsy and tired. Or, you may become dizzy and even faint, especially when you rise suddenly from a reclining position. When blood pressure increases, you may feel dizzy, have a headache or blurred vision, or hear ringing or buzzing in your ears. If you develop any of these symptoms, call your doctor.

Nervous System

Drugs that act on the nervous system may cause drowsiness or stimulation. If a drug causes drowsiness, you may become dizzy or your coordination may be impaired. If a drug causes stimulation, you may become nervous or have insomnia or tremors. Neither drowsiness nor stimulation is cause for concern for most people. When you are drowsy, however, you should be careful around machinery and avoid driving. Some drugs cause throbbing headaches, and others produce tingling in the fingers or toes. These symptoms are generally expected and should disappear in a few days to a week. If they don't, call your doctor.

Respiratory System

Side effects common to the respiratory system include stuffy nose, dry throat, shortness of breath, and slowed breathing. A stuffy nose and dry throat usually disappear within days, but you may use nose drops (consult your doctor first) or throat lozenges or gargle with warm salt water to relieve them. Shortness of breath is a characteristic side effect of some drugs (for example, Inderal anti-arrhythmic). Shortness of breath may continue, but it is not usually serious. Barbiturates or drugs that promote sleep may retard respiration. Slowed breathing is expected, and you should not be concerned as long as your doctor knows about it.

Examples of Drugs that May Cause Dizziness

Actifed-C	Dalmane	Nitrostat
Aldactazide	Dimetapp Extentabs	Norpace
Aldactone	Diuril	oral antidiabetics
Aldomet	Enduron	Ornade
Aristocort	Flagyl	Pavabid
Ativan	Keflex	reserpine
Atromid-S	Lomotil	Tagamet
Benadryl	Medrol	Tofranil
Benemid	meprobamate	Triavil
Bentyl	Minipress	Vasodilan
Clinoril	Nitro-Bid	

Skin

Skin reactions include rash, swelling, itching, and sweating. Itching, swelling, and rash frequently indicate a drug allergy, and you should not continue to take a drug if you have developed an allergy to it. Consult your doctor before stopping the drug. Some drugs increase sweating; others decrease it. Drugs that decrease sweating may cause problems in hot weather when the body must sweat to reduce body temperature.

Examples of Drugs that May Cause a Mild Rash

Actifed	Combid Spansules	Norpace
Aldactazide	Compazine	Ornade
Aldactone	Dimetapp Extentabs	penicillins
Aldoril	Diuril	pronestyl
ambenyl	Dyazide	reserpine
ampicillin	Elavil	Stelazine
ativan	Enduron	Tagamet
Atromid-S	Haldol	Thorazine
Benadryl	Indocin	Tofranil
Benemid	Librax	Triavil
Catapres	Librium	Valium
Clinoril	Lomotil	Zyloprim
	Minipress	

If you have a minor skin reaction not diagnosed as an allergy, ask your pharmacist for a soothing cream. Your pharmacist may also suggest that you take frequent baths and dust the sensitive area with a suitable powder.

Another type of skin reaction is photosensitivity (or phototoxicity or sun toxicity)—that is, unusual sensitivity to the sun. Tetracyclines can cause photosensitivity. If, after taking such a drug, you remain exposed to the sun for a brief period of time, say 10 or 15 minutes, you may receive a severe sunburn. You do not have to stay indoors while taking these drugs, but you should be fully clothed while outside and you should use a protective sunscreen while in the sun. Ask your pharmacist to help you choose a protective lotion. Furthermore, you should not remain in the sun too long. Since these drugs may be present in the bloodstream after you

Examples of Drugs that May Cause Photosensitivity

Benadryl	Haldol	sulfa drugs
Compazine	hydrochlorothiazide	tetracycline
Diuril	oral antidiabetics	Thorazine
Enduron	Phenergan	Tofranil

stop taking them, you should continue to take these precautions for two days after therapy with these drugs is complete.

SUBTLE SIDE EFFECTS

Some side effects are difficult to detect. You may not notice any symptoms at all or you may notice only slight ones. Laboratory testing may be necessary to confirm the existence of such side effects.

Kidneys

If one of the side effects of a drug is to reduce the kidneys' ability to remove chemicals and other substances from the blood, these substances begin to accumulate in body tissues. Over a period of time, this accumulation may cause vague symptoms such as swelling, fluid retention, nausea, headache, or weakness. Obvious symptoms, especially pain, are rare.

Liver

Drug-induced liver damage may result in fat accumulation. Often, liver damage occurs because the drug being taken increases or decreases the liver's ability to metabolize other drugs and substances. Liver damage may be quite advanced before it produces any symptoms; therefore, periodic tests of liver function are recommended during therapy with certain drugs.

Blood

A great many drugs affect the blood and the circulatory system but do not produce noticeable symptoms for some time. If a drug lowers the level of sugar in the blood, for example, you probably will not have any symptoms for several minutes to an hour. If symptoms develop, they may include tiredness, muscular weakness, and perhaps palpitations or tinnitus (ringing or buzzing in the ears). Low blood levels of potassium produce dry mouth, thirst, and muscle cramps.

Examples of
Drugs that May Cause Blood Disorders*

Aldactazide	Mellaril	steroids
Apresoline	Minocin	Tagamet
Dyazide	oral contraceptives	Thorazine
Elavil	Orinase	Tofranil
Hygroton	Stelazine	Tolinase
Lasix	sulfa drugs	Zyloprim

*Indicated by a sore throat that doesn't go away in one or two days.

Some drugs decrease the number of red blood cells, which carry oxygen and nutrients throughout the body. If you have too few red blood cells, you have anemia, and you may be pale and feel tired, weak, dizzy, and perhaps hungry.

Some drugs decrease the number of white blood cells, which combat bacteria. Having too few white blood cells increases susceptibility to infection and may prolong illness. If a sore throat or a fever begins after you begin taking a drug and continues for a few days, you may have an infection and too few white blood cells to fight it. Call your doctor.

MANAGEMENT OF SIDE EFFECTS

Consult the drug profiles to determine whether the side effects you are experiencing are minor (relatively common and usually not serious) or major (signs that something is amiss in your drug therapy). If your side effects are minor, you may be able to compensate for them simply. (See table on page 19 for suggestions.) However, consult your doctor if you find minor side effects particularly annoying.

If you experience any major side effects, contact your doctor immediately. Your dosage may need adjustment, or you may have a sensitivity to the drug. Perhaps you should not be taking the drug at all.

Types of Drugs

Prescription drugs fall into a number of groups according to conditions they are prescribed for. In the following pages we will provide you with a better understanding of the types of medications that are prescribed for different conditions. We'll describe the intended actions of drugs and the therapeutic effects you can expect from different types of common medications.

CARDIOVASCULAR DRUGS

Anti-Anginals

The chest pain known as angina occurs when there is an insufficient supply of blood, and consequently of oxygen, to the heart. Anti-anginal drugs cause a sudden drop in blood pressure and cause an increased amount of oxygen to enter certain parts of the heart. They are used to relieve or prevent angina. Nitroglycerin is the most frequently prescribed anti-anginal.

Anti-Arrhythmics

If the heart does not beat rhythmically or smoothly (a condition called arrhythmia), its rate of contraction must be regulated. Anti-arrhythmic drugs, including Inderal, Norpace, Pronestyl, and quinidine sulfate, prevent or alleviate cardiac arrhythmias. Dilantin (phenytoin), most frequently used as an anticonvulsant in the treatment of epilepsy, can act as an anti-arrhythmic agent when it is injected intravenously.

Antihypertensives

Briefly, high blood pressure is a condition in which the pressure of the blood against the walls of the blood vessels is higher than what is considered normal. High blood pressure, or hypertension, is controllable, and by controlling it other diseases can be prevented. Drugs that counteract or reduce high blood pressure can effectively prolong a hypertensive patient's life.

Several different drug actions produce an antihypertensive effect. Some drugs block nerve impulses that cause arteries to constrict; others slow the heart rate and its force of contraction; others reduce the amount of a certain hormone in the blood that causes blood pressure to go up. The mainstay of antihypertensive therapy is often a *diuretic,* a drug that reduces body fluids (see below). Examples of antihypertensive drugs include Aldomet, Aldoril, Apresoline, Catapres, Diupres, Dyazide, Hydropres, Inderal, Lopressor, Minipress, Ser-Ap-Es, and Tenormin.

Diuretics

Diuretic drugs, such as Aldactazide, Aldactone, Diuril, Dyazide, Enduron, Esidrix, hydrochlorothiazide, HydroDIURIL, Hygroton, and Lasix, promote the loss of water and salt from the body. They also lower blood pressure by increasing the width of blood vessels. Because many antihypertensive drugs cause the body to retain sodium and water, they are often used concurrently with diuretics. Most diuretics act directly on the kidneys, but there are different types of diuretics, each with different actions. Thus, therapy for high blood pressure can be individualized for each patient's specific needs.

Thiazide diuretics are the most popular water pills available today. They are generally well tolerated and can be taken once or twice a day. Thiazide diuretics are effective all day, whereas some diuretics have a shorter duration of action. And since patients do not develop a tolerance for their antihypertensive effect, they can be taken for long periods.

However, a major drawback to thiazide diuretics is that they often deplete potassium. This depletion can be compensated for with a *potassium supplement,* such as K-Lor or Slow-K. Potassium-rich foods and liquids, such as bananas, apricots, or orange juice, can also be used to correct the potassium deficiency. *Salt substitutes* are other sources of potassium.

Loop diuretics, such as Lasix, act more vigorously than thiazide diuretics. They promote more water loss but also deplete more potassium.

To remove excess water from the body but retain its store of potassium, manufacturers developed *potassium-sparing diuretics.* Potassium-sparing diuretics, such as Aldactone, are effective in the treatment of potassium loss, heart failure, and hypertension. Potassium-sparing diuretics have been combined with thiazide diuretics in medications such as Aldactazide and Dyazide. Such combinations enhance the antihypertensive effect and reduce the loss of potassium. They are among the most commonly used antihypertensive agents.

Digitalis

Drugs derived from digitalis (for example, digoxin or Lanoxin) affect the heart rate but are not strictly anti-arrhythmics. Digitalis slows the rate of the heart but increases the force of contraction. Thus, digitalis acts as both a heart depressant and a stimulant and may be used to regulate erratic heart rhythm or to increase heart output in heart failure.

Anticoagulants

Drugs that prevent blood clotting are called anticoagulants, or blood thinners. Anticoagulants fall into two categories.

The first category contains only one drug, heparin. Heparin must be given by injection so its use is generally restricted to hospitalized patients.

The second category includes oral anticoagulants, principally derivatives of the drug warfarin. Warfarin may be used in the treatment of conditions such as stroke, heart disease, or abnormal blood clotting. It is also used to prevent the movement of a clot, which could cause serious problems. Use of warfarin after a heart attack is controversial. Some physicians believe that anticoagulants are not helpful beyond the first month or two following a heart attack.

Persons taking warfarin must avoid using many other drugs (including aspirin) because their interaction with the anticoagulant could cause internal bleeding. Patients taking warfarin should check with their pharmacist or physician before using any other medications, including over-the-counter products for coughs or colds. In addition, they must have their blood samples checked frequently by their physician.

Antilipidemics

Drugs used to treat atherosclerosis (arteriosclerosis, hardening of the arteries) act to reduce the cholesterol and triglycerides (fats) that form plaques on the walls of the arteries. Among the drugs that reduce the amount of fat in the blood is the antilipidemic Atromid-S. Use of these drugs is in question; following a special low-fat diet and a good exercise program may be just as beneficial.

Vasodilators

Vasodilating drugs cause the blood vessels to widen. They are used in the treatment of stroke and diseases characterized by poor circulation. Hydergine, used to reduce the symptoms of senility, and Pavabid, used in therapy after a stroke, are two examples of vasodilating drugs. Presently, neither has been proven effective, and both are expensive.

Beta Blockers

Beta blocking drugs block the response to nerve stimulation to slow the heart rate and reduce high blood pressure. They are used in the treatment of angina, hypertension, and arrhythmias. Propranolol (Inderal) and metoprolol (Lopressor) are beta blockers.

DRUGS FOR THE EARS

For an ear infection, a physician usually prescribes an antibiotic and a steroid—for example, Cortisporin otic suspension. The antibiotic attacks infecting bacteria, and the steroid reduces inflammation and pain. Often, a local anesthetic, such as benzocaine or lidocaine, may be prescribed to relieve pain.

DRUGS FOR THE EYES

Almost all drugs that are used to treat eye problems can be used to treat disorders of other parts of the body as well.

Glaucoma is one of the major disorders of the eye—especially for people over age 40. It is caused by increased pressure within the eyeball. Although sometimes treated surgically, glaucoma often can be resolved and blindness prevented through the use of eyedrops. Two drops frequently used are epinephrine and pilocarpine. Pilocarpine is a *cholinergic* drug. Cholinergic drugs act by stimulating the body's parasympathetic nerve endings. These are nerve endings that assist in the control of the heart, lungs, bowels, and eyes. Epinephrine is an *adrenergic* agent. Drugs with adrenergic properties have actions similar to those of adrenalin. Adrenalin is secreted in the body when one must flee from danger or resist attack or combat stress. Adrenalin increases the amount of sugar in the blood, accelerates the heartbeat, and dilates the pupils.

Antibiotics usually resolve eye infections. Steroids can be used to treat eye inflammations as long as they are not used for too long. Pharmacists carefully monitor requests for eyedrop refills, particularly for drops that contain steroids, and may refuse to refill such medication until you have revisited the doctor.

GASTROINTESTINAL DRUGS

Antinauseants

Antinauseants reduce the urge to vomit. Perhaps the most effective antinauseant is a *phenothiazine derivative* such as Compazine. Compazine antinauseant is often administered rectally and usually alleviates acute nausea and vomiting within a few minutes to an hour.

Antihistamines are also commonly used to prevent nausea and vomiting, especially when those symptoms are due to motion sickness.

Anticholinergics

Anticholinergic drugs—for example, Bentyl—slow the action of the bowel and reduce the amount of stomach acid. Because these drugs slow the action of the bowel by relaxing the muscles and relieving spasms, they are said to have an *antispasmodic* action.

Anti-ulcer Medications

Anti-ulcer medications are prescribed to relieve the symptoms and promote healing of a peptic ulcer. The antisecretory ulcer medication Tagamet works by suppressing the production of excess stomach acid. Another anti-ulcer drug, Carafate, works by forming a chemical barrier over an exposed ulcer—rather like a "bandage"—thus protecting the ulcer from stomach acid. These medications provide sustained relief of ulcer pain and promote healing.

Antidiarrheals

Diarrhea may be caused by many conditions, including influenza and ulcerative colitis, and can sometimes occur as a side effect to drug therapy. Narcotics and anticholinergics are used in the treatment of diarrhea because they slow the action of the bowel to check diarrhea. A medication such as Lomotil antidiarrheal combines a narcotic with an anticholinergic.

HORMONES

A hormone is a substance produced and secreted by a gland. Hormones stimulate body functions. Hormone drugs are given to mimic the effects of naturally produced hormones.

Thyroid Drugs

Thyroid hormone was one of the first hormone drugs to be produced synthetically. Originally, thyroid preparations were made by drying the thyroid glands of animals and pulverizing them into tablets. Such preparations are still used today in the treatment of patients who have reduced levels of thyroid hormone production. However, a synthetic thyroid hormone (Synthroid) is also available.

Drugs such as propylthiouracil and radioactive-iodine therapy are used to slow down thyroid hormone production in patients who have excessive amounts of the hormone.

Diabetic Drugs

Insulin, which is secreted by the pancreas, regulates the level of sugar in the blood and the metabolism of carbohydrates and fats.

Insulin's counterpart *glucagon* stimulates the liver to produce glucose, or sugar. Both insulin and glucagon must be present in the right amounts to maintain a proper blood sugar level in the body.

Treatment of diabetes (the condition in which the body is unable to supply and/or utilize insulin) may involve an adjustment of diet and/or the administration of insulin. Glucagon is given only in emergencies (for example, insulin shock when the blood sugar must be raised quickly).

Oral antidiabetic drugs, including Diabinese, Orinase, and Tolinase, induce the pancreas to secrete more insulin by acting on small groups of cells within the pancreas that make and store insulin. Oral antidiabetics are used by diabetics who cannot follow a diet program or do not need to use insulin. These drugs cannot be used by insulin-dependent (juvenile-onset) diabetics, those who can only control their diabetes with injections of insulin.

Steroids

The pituitary gland secretes *adrenocorticotropic hormone* (ACTH), which directs the adrenal glands to produce glucocorticoids such as hydrocortisone and other steroids. Steroids help fight inflammation, and ACTH may be injected to treat inflammatory diseases.

Oral steroid preparations (for example, Medrol and prednisone) may also be used to treat inflammatory diseases such as arthritis or to treat poison ivy, hay fever, or insect bites.

Steroids also may be applied to the skin. Kenalog, Lidex, and Vioform-Hydrocortisone are steroid hormone creams or ointments.

Sex Hormones

Although the adrenal glands secrete small amounts of sex hormones, these hormones are produced mainly by the sex glands. *Estrogens* are the female hormones responsible for secondary sex characteristics such as development of the breasts, maintenance of the lining of the uterus, and enlargement of the hips at puberty. Testosterone (also called androgen) is the corresponding male hormone. It is responsible for secondary sex characteristics such as beards and enlarged muscles. Progesterone is produced in females and prepares the uterus for pregnancy.

Testosterone causes retention of protein in the body, thereby producing an increase in muscle size. Athletes sometimes take drugs called anabolic steroids, similar to testosterone, for this effect, but such use of these drugs is dangerous. Anabolic steroids can adversely affect the heart, nervous system, and kidneys.

Most *oral contraceptives* or birth control pills combine estrogen and progesterone, but some contain only progesterone. The estrogen in birth control pills prevents egg production. Progesterone aids in preventing ovulation, alters the lining of the uterus, and thickens cervical mucus, processes which help to prevent conception. Oral contraceptives, while still used regularly, have many side effects and their use should be discussed with a doctor.

Premarin estrogen hormone is used to treat symptoms of menopause. Provera progesterone hormone is used for uterine bleeding and menstrual problems.

ANTI-INFECTIVES

Antibiotics

Antibacterials are used to treat many bacterial infections. Antibiotics, a specific kind of antibacterial, can be derived from molds or produced synthetically. They have the ability to destroy or inhibit the growth of bacteria and fungi.

When used properly, antibiotics are usually effective. However, antibiotics do not counteract viruses, the major cause of the common cold, and their use in cold therapy is irrational. To adequately treat an infection, antibiotics must be taken regularly for a specific period of time. If a patient does not take an antibiotic for the prescribed period, the infection may not be resolved, and microorganisms resistant to the antibiotic may appear. Antibiotics include aminoglycosides, cephalosporins, erythromycins, penicillins (including ampicillin and amoxicillin), and tetracyclines.

Chemotherapeutics

Another group of drugs used to treat infection, the chemotherapeutics, includes synthetically produced drugs, such as sulfonamides (Gantrisin), nitrofurantoins (Macrodantin), and others.

Some chemotherapeutic agents are used in the treatment of cancer. These *antineoplastics* are, without exception, extremely toxic and cause serious side effects. But to many cancer victims the benefits received outweigh the risks involved.

Antivirals

Antiviral drugs are used to combat virus infections. A new antiviral drug called Zovirax is being used in the management of herpes. Zovirax reduces the reproduction of the herpes virus in initial outbreaks, lessens the number of recurring outbreaks, and speeds the healing of herpes blisters. However, this antiviral drug does not cure herpes.

Vaccines

Vaccines were used long before antibiotics. A vaccine contains weakened or dead disease-causing microorganisms, which activate the body's defense mechanisms to produce a natural immunity against a particular disease such as polio or measles. A vaccine may be used to alleviate or treat an infectious disease, but, most commonly, it is used to prevent a specific disease.

Other Anti-Infectives

Drugs called *anthelmintics* are used to treat worm infestations. Fungal infections are treated with *antifungals,* such as Mycostatin, drugs that destroy and prevent the growth of fungi.

A *pediculocide* is a drug used to treat a person infested with lice, and a *scabicide* is a preparation used to treat a person with scabies.

TOPICAL DRUGS

Dry skin is a very common complaint. The most effective treatment of dry skin is to increase moisture in the air by using a humidifier. Dermatologic problems, such as infection or inflammation are also common ailments. Antibiotics treat skin infections; steroids treat inflammations.

Another common dermatologic problem is acne. Acne can be—and often is—treated with over-the-counter drugs, but it sometimes requires prescription medications. Over-the-counter drugs generally contain agents that open blocked skin pores. Antibiotics such as the tetracyclines, erythromycin, or clindamycin are used orally or applied topically to prevent pimple formation. *Keratolytics,* agents that soften the skin and cause the outer cells to slough off, are also sometimes prescribed. Tretinoin (Retin A), a skin irritant derived from vitamin A, is also used topically in the treatment of acne.

Isotretinoin, also related to vitamin A, is available in an oral form, called Accutane, and is used to treat severe cystic acne that has not responded to other treatment.

CENTRAL NERVOUS SYSTEM DRUGS

Sedatives

All drugs used in the treatment of anxiety or insomnia selectively reduce activity in the central nervous system. Drugs that have a calming effect include Atarax, barbiturates, Equanil, Librium, Miltown, Serax, Sinequan, Tranxene, and Valium. Drugs to induce sleep in insomniacs include

Dalmane, Butisol Sodium, and Seconal. All these drugs have similar action, but those used to induce sleep (called *hypnotics*) are more potent.

Tranquilizers

Psychotics usually receive *major tranquilizers* or *antipsychotic agents.* These drugs calm certain areas of the brain but permit the rest of the brain to function normally. They act as a screen that allows transmission of some nerve impulses but restricts others. The drugs most frequently used are *phenothiazines*—Mellaril, Stelazine, and Thorazine. Haldol, a butyrophenone, has the same effect as Thorazine.

Psychotic patients sometimes become depressed. In such cases *antidepressants* such as Elavil, or *monoamine oxidase inhibitors* are used to combat the depression.

Antidepressants may produce dangerous side effects or interact with other drugs or foods. For example, monoamine oxidase inhibitors greatly increase blood pressure when taken with certain kinds of cheese or other foods or beverages.

Anorectics

Amphetamines are commonly used as anorectics, a category of drugs that is used to reduce the appetite. These drugs quiet the part of the brain that causes hunger. But they also keep people awake, speed up the heart, and raise blood pressure. And after two to three weeks, they lose their effectiveness.

Amphetamines stimulate most people (see above) but they have the opposite effect on a special group of people, hyperkinetic children. Hyperkinesis (the condition of being highly overactive) is difficult to diagnose or define and requires a specialist to treat. When hyperkinetic children take amphetamines or the adrenergic Ritalin, their activity slows down. Why amphetamines affect hyperkinetic children in this way is unknown. Most likely, they quiet these youngsters by selectively stimulating parts of the brain that ordinarily provide control of activity.

Anticonvulsants

Drugs such as Dilantin and phenobarbital can effectively control most symptoms of epilepsy. They selectively reduce excessive stimulation in the brain.

Antiparkinson Agents

Parkinson's disease is progressive, and it is due to a chemical imbalance in the brain. Victims of Parkinson's disease have uncontrollable tremors, develop a characteristic stoop, and eventually become unable to walk. Drugs such as Artane or Cogentin anticholinergics or levodopa are used to correct the chemical imbalance and thereby relieve the symptoms of the disease. They are also used to relieve tremors caused by other drugs.

Analgesics

Pain, of course, is not a disease but a symptom. Drugs used to relieve pain are called analgesics. These drugs form a rather diffuse group. We do not fully understand how most analgesics work. Whether they all act in the brain or whether some act outside the brain is not known. Analgesics may be *narcotic* or *non-narcotic.*

Narcotics are derived from the opium poppy. They act on the brain to cause deep analgesia and often drowsiness. Narcotics relieve coughing spasms and are used in many cough syrups. Narcotics relieve pain and also give the patient a feeling of well-being. They also are addictive. Manufacturers have attempted to produce nonaddictive synthetic narcotic derivatives but have not been successful.

Many non-narcotic pain relievers are commonly used. *Salicylates* are the most commonly used pain relievers in the United States today. And the most widely used salicylate is aspirin. While aspirin does not require a prescription, many doctors may prescribe it to treat such diseases as arthritis.

The aspirin substitute acetaminophen (Tylenol, Phenaphen) may be used in place of aspirin. It, however, cannot relieve inflammation caused by arthritis, and it is much more toxic if overdoses are taken.

A number of analgesics contain codeine or other narcotics combined with non-narcotic analgesics such as aspirin or acetaminophen—for example, Empirin Compound with Codeine, Fiorinal with Codeine, Phenaphen with Codeine, and Tylenol with Codeine. These analgesics are not as potent as pure narcotics, but frequently they are as effective. Because these medications contain narcotics, they have the potential for abuse, and must therefore be used with caution.

Anti-Inflammatory Drugs

Inflammation, or swelling, is the body's response to injury and causes pain, fever, redness, and itching. Common aspirin is one of the most effective anti-inflammatory drugs. Other drugs—Butazolidin, Indocin, Motrin, Nalfon, Naprosyn, Tandearil, and Tolectin—relieve inflammation, but none is more effective than aspirin. Steroids (see above) are also used to treat inflammatory diseases.

Gout, however, is one inflammatory disease that can be treated more effectively with other agents, such as Benemid *uricosuric,* colchicine antigout remedy, or Zyloprim antigout remedy. Gout is caused by excessive uric acid, which causes swelling and pain in the toes and joints. Benemid stimulates excretion of the uric acid in urine; colchicine prevents swelling; and Zyloprim decreases the production of uric acid. Both Benemid and Zyloprim guard against attacks of gout. They do not relieve the pain of an attack as does colchicine.

When sore muscles tense up, they cause pain and inflammation. *Skeletal muscle relaxants*—Equagesic, Norgesic, and Parafon Forte—can relieve the symptoms. Skeletal muscle relaxants often are given with an anti-inflammatory drug such as aspirin. Some doctors believe that aspirin and rest alleviate the pain and inflammation of muscle strain more than skeletal muscle relaxants do.

Local Anesthetics

Other pain-relieving drugs are local anesthetics. Local anesthetics are applied directly to a painful area and relieve such localized pain as a toothache, earache, or hemorrhoidal pain. Local anesthetics do not relieve major, generalized pain and many people are allergic to them. Some local anesthetics, such as lidocaine, are also useful in the treatment of heart disease when given by intravenous or intramuscular injection because they restore the heartbeat to normal.

RESPIRATORY DRUGS

Antitussives

Antitussives control coughs. Dextromethorphan is a non-narcotic that controls the cough from a cold. Another antitussive drug is the narcotic codeine. Most cough drops and syrups must be absorbed into the blood and must circulate through the brain before they act on a cough; they do not "coat" the throat and should be taken with a glass of water.

Expectorants

Expectorants are used to change a nonproductive cough to a productive one, i.e., one that brings up phlegm. Expectorants are supposed to increase the amount of mucus produced. However, no expectorant has been proven effective. Drinking water or using a vaporizer or humidifier is more effective in increasing mucus. Popular expectorant products include Ambenyl and Phenergan Expectorant.

Decongestants

Decongestants constrict the blood vessels in the nose and sinuses to open up air passages. Decongestants can be taken by mouth or as nose drops or spray. Oral decongestants are slow-acting, but do not interfere with the production of mucus or the movement of the cilia of the respiratory tract. They do increase blood pressure. Topical decongestants (nose drops or spray) provide almost immediate relief. They do not increase blood pressure as much as oral decongestants, but they do slow the movement of the cilia. People who use these topical products may also develop a tolerance for them. Consequently, they should not be used for more than a few days at a time.

Bronchodilators

Bronchodilators (agents that relax airways in the lungs) and *smooth muscle relaxants* (agents that relax smooth muscle tissue such as that in the lungs) are also used to improve breathing. Slo-Phyllin and Quibron are commonly used to relieve the symptoms of asthma and pulmonary emphysema. Aminophylline is often given to patients with pulmonary emphysema or chronic bronchitis.

Allergy Medication

Antihistamines counteract the symptoms of an allergy by blocking the effects of histamine, a chemical released in the body that typically causes swelling and itching. For mild respiratory allergies such as hay fever, antihistamines like Benadryl can be used. Benadryl and other antihistamines are slow-acting. For severe allergy attacks injectable epinephrine, which is fast-acting, will often be prescribed.

VITAMINS AND MINERALS

Vitamins and minerals are chemical substances vital to the maintenance of normal body function. Some people have vitamin deficiencies, but most people get enough vitamins and minerals in their diet. Serious nutritional deficiencies, such as pellagra and beri-beri, must be treated by a physician. People who have an inadequate or restricted diet, those with certain disorders or debilitating illnesses, women who are pregnant or breast-feeding, and some others may benefit from taking supplemental vitamins and minerals. However, even these people should consult a doctor to see if a true vitamin deficiency exists.

Drug Profiles

On the following pages are drug profiles for the most commonly prescribed drugs in the United States. These profiles are arranged alphabetically.

A drug profile summarizes the most important information about a particular drug. By studying a drug profile, you will learn what to expect from your medication, when to be concerned about possible side effects, which drugs interact with the drug you are taking, and how to take the drug to achieve its maximum benefit. Each drug profile includes the following information:

Name. Most of the drugs profiled in this book are listed by trade name; those drugs commonly known or prescribed by their generic names (such as insulin, tetracycline, penicillin) are listed generically. All trade name drugs can be identified by an initial capital letter; generics, by an initial lower-case letter. The chemical or pharmacological class is listed for each drug after its name.

Manufacturer. The manufacturer of each trade name product is identified. "Various manufacturers" is listed for generic drugs; most generics are generally available from several different manufacturers.

Ingredients. The components of each drug product are itemized. Many drugs contain several active chemical components and all are included in this category.

Equivalent Products. Products with the same chemical formulation as the profiled drug, including both trade name and generic drugs, are listed as equivalent products. If your prescription is for a product that has equivalents, ask your physician to write your prescription using the generic name. This will enable your pharmacist to fill the prescription with the least expensive equivalent available. Remember, not all drugs have equivalents. For more information about generic and equivalent products, see the section on Generic Drugs, page 10.

Dosage Forms. The most common forms (i.e., tablets, capsules, liquid, suppositories) of each profiled drug are listed, along with the color of the tablets or capsules. Strengths or concentrations are also given. Colors for liquids and suppositories are not included.

Use. This category includes the most important and most common clinical uses for each profiled drug. Your doctor may prescribe a drug for a reason that does not appear in this category. This exclusion does not mean that your doctor has made an error. But if the use for which you are taking a drug does not appear in this category, and if you have any questions concerning the reason for which the drug was prescribed, consult your doctor.

Minor Side Effects. The most common and least serious reactions to a drug are found in this category. Most of these side effects, if they occur, disappear in a day or two. Do not expect to experience these minor side effects, but if they occur and are particularly annoying, do not hesitate to seek medical advice. For advice on how to cope with or relieve some of these side effects, look to the "Comments" section.

Major Side Effects. Should the reactions listed as "Major Side Effects" occur, you should call your doctor. These reactions indicate that something may be going wrong with your drug therapy. You may have developed an allergy to the drug, or some other problem could have developed. Many drugs can cause blood disorders; anti-infective agents may suppress the growth of some infecting microorganisms while allowing others to proliferate wildly; some medications may cause peptic ulcers. If you experience a major side effect, it may be necessary to adjust your dosage or substitute a different drug in your treatment. Major side effects are less common than minor side effects, and you will probably never experience them. But if you do, consult your doctor immediately.

Contraindications. Some drugs are counterproductive when taken by people with certain conditions, i.e., they should not be taken by people with these conditions. These conditions are listed under "Contraindications." If the profiled drug has been prescribed for you and you have a condition listed in this category, consult your doctor.

Warnings. This category lists the precautions necessary for safe use of the profiled drug. For example, certain conditions, while not contraindicating use of the drug, do demand close monitoring. Pregnant women, children under 12, the elderly, people with liver or kidney disease, and those with heart problems must use many drugs cautiously. In some cases, these people will have to have frequent lab tests while taking drugs; in other cases, the doctor will monitor dosages carefully. The "Warnings" category also lists drugs that can interact with the profiled drug. Certain drugs are safe when used alone but may cause serious reactions when taken with other drugs or chemicals, or with certain foods. In this category, you'll also find out whether the profiled drug is likely to affect your ability to drive, whether you are likely to become tolerant to its effects, and whether any laboratory tests are included in the usual course of therapy with the drug.

Comments. While the information in the "Contraindications" and "Warnings" categories reflects that included in the official package inserts, the information in "Comments" is more general and concerns use of the profiled drug. For example, if you can avoid stomach upset by taking the drug with meals, or if you can avoid sleeplessness by taking a drug early in the day, you'll find that information in "Comments." You'll find out how to deal with certain side effects such as dizziness or lightheadedness or mouth dryness. Other information included might concern supplemental therapy: drinking extra fluids while treating a urinary infection or wearing cotton panties while treating a vaginal infection. "Comments" might also include information about the price of the drug, its equivalent products, or methods of administering the drug. This kind of information should guide you in using the profiled drug. Never be reluctant to ask your doctor or pharmacist for further information about any drug you are taking.

Accutane acne preparation

Manufacturer: Roche Laboratories
Ingredient: isotretinoin (13-*cis*-retinoic acid)
Dosage Form: Capsule: 10 mg (pink); 20 mg (maroon); 40 mg (yellow)
Use: Treatment of severe cystic acne
Minor Side Effects: Changes in skin color; conjunctivitis; dry lips and mouth; edema; fatigue; headache; increased susceptibility to herpes simplex virus; increased susceptibility to sunburn; indigestion; inflammation of lips; muscle pain; peeling of palms and soles; rash; thinning of hair
Major Side Effects: Black stools; bruising; burning or tingling sensation of the skin; changes in menstrual cycle; dizziness; hives; increased susceptibility to bone changes; respiratory infections; skin infection; visual disturbances; weight loss.
Contraindications: This drug should not be used by a woman who is, who thinks she is, or who intends to become, pregnant. This drug should not be used by people who are allergic to parabens (a preservative). Consult your doctor immediately if this drug has been prescribed for you and you have either of these conditions.
Warnings: This drug should not be used in conjunction with vitamin A supplements. ● This drug may increase blood fat levels (triglycerides, lipoproteins, cholesterol), especially in overweight or diabetic persons, in persons with increased alcohol intake, and in persons with a family history of high blood fat levels. ● This drug should be used cautiously by women who are breast-feeding. Be sure your doctor knows you are breast-feeding a baby.
Comments: During the course of treatment with this drug, occasionally there may be an apparent increase in skin lesions with crusting. This is usually not a reason to discontinue its use. ● This drug may affect the results of blood and urine tests. ● This drug is usually used only after other acne treatments have failed. ● Store away from light.

acetaminophen with codeine analgesic

Manufacturer: various manufacturers
Ingredients: acetaminophen; codeine phosphate
Equivalent Products: Aceta with Codeine, Century Pharmaceuticals, Inc.; Bayapap with Codeine, Bay Pharmaceuticals, Inc.; Capital with Codeine, Carnrick Laboratories, Inc.; Codap, Reid-Provident Labs., Inc.; Panadol with Codeine, Winthrop Laboratories; Phenaphen with Codeine, A. H. Robins; SK-APAP with Codeine, Smith Kline & French Laboratories; Tylenol with Codeine, McNeil Laboratories
Dosage Forms: Capsule: acetaminophen, 325 mg; codeine phosphate (see Comments) (green/white). Liquid (content per 5 ml teaspoon): acetaminophen, 120 mg; codeine, 12 mg. Tablet: acetaminophen, 300 mg; codeine (see Comments) (all white); acetaminophen, 650 mg; codeine phosphate, 30 mg (white)
Use: Symptomatic relief of mild to severe pain, depending on strength
Minor Side Effects: Constipation; dizziness; drowsiness; dry mouth; flushing; light-headedness; nausea; rash; sweating; urine retention; vomiting
Major Side Effects: Anxiety; bleeding or bruising; breathing difficulties; excitation; fatigue; jaundice; low blood sugar; palpitations; rapid or slow heartbeat; rash; restlessness; sore throat; tremors; weakness
Contraindications: This drug should not be taken by people who are allergic to either of its components. Consult your doctor immediately if this drug has been prescribed for you and you have such an allergy.
Warnings: This drug should be used cautiously by children under 12 and the

elderly; by people who have heart or lung disease, blood disorders, asthma or other respiratory problems, epilepsy, head injuries, liver or kidney disease, colitis, gall bladder disease, thyroid disease, acute abdominal conditions, or prostate disease; and by pregnant or nursing women. Be sure your doctor knows if you fit into any of these categories. • This drug may cause drowsiness; avoid tasks that require alertness. • To prevent oversedation, avoid the use of alcohol or other drugs that have sedative properties. • Because this product contains codeine, it has the potential for abuse and must be used with caution. It usually should not be taken for more than ten days. Tolerance may develop quickly; do not increase the dose without consulting your doctor.

Comments: The name of this drug is followed by a number that refers to the amount of codeine present. Hence, #1 contains 1/8 grain (gr) or 7.5 mg codeine; #2 has 1/4 gr (15 mg); #3 has 1/2 gr (30 mg); and #4 contains 1 gr (60 mg) codeine. • Side effects caused by this drug may be somewhat relieved by lying down. • Avoid use of any other drugs that contain acetaminophen, codeine, or other narcotics. If you have questions about the contents of your medications, ask your pharmacist or physician.

Aceta with Codeine analgesic (Century Pharmaceuticals, Inc.), see acetaminophen with codeine analgesic.

Achromycin V antibiotic (Lederle Laboratories), see tetracycline hydrochloride antibiotic.

Actacin-C expectorant (Vangard Laboratories), see Actifed-C expectorant.

Actamine-C expectorant (H. L. Moore, Inc.), see Actifed-C expectorant.

Actifed-C expectorant

Manufacturer: Burroughs Wellcome Co.

Ingredients: codeine phosphate; pseudoephedrine hydrochloride; triprolidine hydrochloride

Equivalent Products: Actacin-C, Vangard Laboratories; Actamine-C, H. L. Moore, Inc.; Allerfrin with Codeine, Rugby Laboratories; Aprodine-C, Major Pharmaceuticals; Rofed C, Three P Products Corp.; Triacin C, various manufacturers; Trifed C, Geneva Generics, Inc.

Dosage Form: Liquid (content per 5 ml teaspoon): codeine phosphate, 10 mg; pseudoephedrine hydrochloride, 30 mg; triprolidine hydrochloride, 1.25 mg

Use: To suppress coughing or provide symptomatic relief of cough

Minor Side Effects: Blurred vision; confusion; constipation; diarrhea; difficult urination; dizziness; drowsiness; dry mouth; headache; heartburn; insomnia; loss of appetite; nasal congestion; nausea; rash; restlessness; sweating; vomiting; weakness

Major Side Effects: Chest pain; high blood pressure; low blood pressure; palpitations; severe abdominal pain; sore throat

Contraindications: This drug should not be given to premature or newborn infants; nursing mothers; asthmatics; persons allergic to any of its ingredients, to antihistamines, or to codeine or other narcotics; or persons taking monoamine oxidase inhibitors. Consult your doctor immediately if this drug has been prescribed for you and you fit any of these descriptions.

Warnings: This drug should be used cautiously by persons with glaucoma, ulcers, blocked bowels, prostate disease, blocked bladder, high blood pressure, diabetes, heart disease, or thyroid disease; pregnant women; or the elderly. Be sure your doctor knows if you fit any of these categories. • This drug should not be used in conjunction with high blood pressure medication and monoamine oxidase inhibitors; if you are currently taking any drugs of these types, consult your doctor about their use. If you are unsure about the type or contents of your medications, ask your doctor or pharmacist. • This drug may cause drowsiness; avoid tasks that require alertness. • To prevent oversedation, avoid taking alcohol or other drugs that have sedative properties. • Because this product contains codeine, it has the potential for abuse and must be used with caution. It usually should not be taken for more than ten days. Tolerance may develop quickly; do not increase the dosage without consulting your doctor. An overdose usually sedates an adult but may cause excitation leading to convulsions and death in a child.

Comments: Chew gum or suck on ice chips or a piece of hard candy to reduce mouth dryness. • If you need an expectorant, you need more moisture in your environment. Drink nine to ten glasses of water daily. The use of a vaporizer or humidifier may also be beneficial. Consult your doctor. • While taking this drug, do not take any nonprescription item for weight control or cough, cold, or sinus problems without first checking with your doctor.

Adapin antidepressant and antianxiety (Pennwalt Pharmaceutical Division), see Sinequan antidepressant and antianxiety.

Adsorbocarpine ophthalmic solution (Alcon Laboratories, Inc.), see Isopto Carpine ophthalmic solution.

Advil anti-inflammatory (Whitehall Labs.), see Motrin anti-inflammatory.

Akarpine ophthalmic solution (Akorn, Inc.), see Isopto Carpine ophthalmic solution.

AK Sporin H.C. Otic (Akorn, Inc.), see Cortisporin otic solution/suspension.

AK-Sporin Ophthalmic Ointment (Akorn, Inc.), see Neosporin antibiotic ophthalmic solution and ointment.

Ak-Sulf ophthalmic solution and ointment (Akorn, Inc.), see Sodium Sulamyd ophthalmic solution and ointment.

Alatone diuretic and antihypertensive (Major Pharmaceuticals), see Aldactone diuretic and antihypertensive.

Aldactazide diuretic and antihypertensive

Manufacturer: Searle & Co.
Ingredients: spironolactone; hydrochlorothiazide
Equivalent Products: Alzide, Major Pharmaceuticals; Spiractazide, Three P Products Corp.; Spironazide, Henry Schein, Inc.; spironolactone with hydro-

chlorothiazide, various manufacturers (see Comments); Spirozide, Rugby Laboratories

Dosage Form: Tablet: spironolactone, 25 mg and hydrochlorothiazide, 25 mg (white); spironolactone, 50 mg and hydrochlorothiazide, 50 mg (tan)

Use: Treatment of high blood pressure; congestive heart failure; cirrhosis of the liver accompanied by edema or ascites or both; removal of tissue fluid

Minor Side Effects: Cramping; deepened voice; diarrhea; dizziness; drowsiness; dry mouth; fatigue; hairiness; headache; increased urination; itching; loss of appetite; nausea; rash; restlessness; sun sensitivity; vomiting

Major Side Effects: Blood disorders; blurred vision; breast enlargement (in both sexes); bruising; confusion; diabetes; difficulty in achieving erection; elevated blood sugar; elevated calcium; elevated potassium; elevated uric acid; fever; gout; impotence; irregular heartbeat; irregular menses; jaundice; low blood pressure; low potassium; low sodium; lupus erythematosus; muscle spasm; sore throat; stumbling; sudden weight gain; tingling in fingers and toes; weakness

Contraindications: This drug should not be taken by people who are allergic to either of its ingredients or to sulfa drugs. Consult your doctor immediately if this drug has been prescribed for you and you have such an allergy. This drug should not be taken by people who have severe kidney disease, hyperkalemia (high blood levels of potassium), anuria (inability to urinate), or liver failure. Be sure your doctor knows if you have any of these conditions.

Warnings: This drug should be used with caution by people with certain liver diseases, those about to undergo surgery, and pregnant women and nursing mothers. Be sure your doctor knows if you fit any of these categories. • This drug interacts with colestipol hydrochloride, digitalis, lithium carbonate, oral antidiabetics, potassium salts, and steroids. If you are currently taking any drugs of these types, consult your doctor about their use. If you are unsure of the type or contents of your medications, ask your doctor or pharmacist. • Spironolactone has been shown to cause cancer in rats. This has not been shown to occur in people. • Do not take potassium supplements while taking this drug. • This drug may cause lupus erythematosus, breast enlargement, gout, diabetes, and increased blood calcium. It may interfere with thyroid function tests. • Because of its effects on water and salt balance in the body, people taking this drug should have routine blood tests. If you develop signs of such an imbalance—dry mouth, thirst, weakness, confusion, muscle cramps, or lack of urine—call your doctor.

Comments: Unlike many diuretics, Aldactazide diuretic rarely causes potassium loss. Hence, the relatively high price of this drug is justified for persons with low potassium levels. • When taking this drug, as with many drugs that lower blood pressure, you should limit your consumption of alcoholic beverages in order to prevent dizziness or light-headedness. • Persons taking digitalis in addition to this drug should watch carefully for symptoms of increased toxicity (e.g., nausea, blurred vision, palpitations) and notify their doctors immediately if symptoms occur. • If you have high blood pressure, do not take any nonprescription item for cough, cold, or sinus problems without first checking with your doctor. • A doctor probably should not prescribe this drug or other "fixed dose" combination products as the first choice in the treatment of high blood pressure. The patient should receive each of the individual ingredients singly, and if the response is adequate to the fixed dose contained in this product, it can then be substituted. The advantage of a combination product such as this drug is based on increased convenience to the patient. • There are a few "generic brands" of spironolactone with hydrochlorothiazide. Consult your pharmacist; some of them are not generically equivalent to this drug. • This drug must be taken exactly as directed. Do not take extra doses or skip a dose without first consulting your doctor.

Aldactone diuretic and antihypertensive

Manufacturer: Searle & Co.
Ingredient: spironolactone
Equivalent Products: Alatone, Major Pharmaceuticals; spironolactone, various manufacturers (see Comments)
Dosage Form: Tablet: 25 mg (white); 100 mg (tan)
Use: Treatment of high blood pressure and hypokalemia (low blood levels of potassium); removal of fluid from the tissues; diagnosis and treatment of primary hyperaldosteronism
Minor Side Effects: Cramping; diarrhea; dizziness; drowsiness; dry mouth; headache; increased urination; nausea; rash; restlessness; vomiting; weakness
Major Side Effects: Confusion; deepened voice; difficulty in achieving or maintaining an erection; elevated chloride; elevated potassium; enlarged breasts (in both sexes); fever; hairiness; impotence; irregular heartbeat; irregular menses; low salt; postmenopausal bleeding; sudden weight gain; tingling in fingers and toes; uncoordinated movements
Contraindications: This drug should not be used by persons with anuria (no urination), acute renal failure, significant impairment of renal function, or hyperkalemia (high blood levels of potassium). Be sure your doctor knows if you have any of these conditions.
Warnings: This drug should be used with caution by pregnant women, nursing mothers, and people with kidney disease. Be sure your doctor knows if you fit into any of these categories. • When this drug is taken with potassium salts or other diuretics or antihypertensive agents, extreme caution should be used. If you are currently taking any drugs of these types, consult your doctor about their use. If you are unsure of the type or contents of your medications, ask your doctor or pharmacist. Do not take potassium supplements while taking this drug, and ask your doctor how to avoid excess potassium in your diet.
Comments: Unlike many diuretics, this drug does not cause potassium loss. Hence, the relatively high price of this drug is justified for persons with low potassium levels. • This drug causes frequent urination. Expect this effect; it should not alarm you. • While taking this drug, as with many drugs that lower blood pressure, you should limit your consumption of alcoholic beverages in order to prevent dizziness or light-headedness. To avoid dizziness or light-headedness when you stand, contract and relax the muscles of your legs for a few moments before rising. Do this by pushing one foot against the floor while raising the other foot slightly, alternating feet so that you are "pumping" your legs in a pedaling motion. • Persons taking digitalis in addition to this drug should watch carefully for symptoms of increased toxicity (e.g., nausea, blurred vision, palpitations) and notify their doctor immediately if symptoms occur • If you have high blood pressure, do not take any nonprescription item for cough, cold, or sinus problems without first checking with your doctor. • This drug causes cancer in rats, but it has not been shown to cause cancer in people. • There are a couple of "generic brands" of this drug. Consult your pharmacist about these items; some of them are not equivalent to this drug. • Take this drug exactly as directed. Do not take extra doses or skip a dose without consulting your doctor first. • If this drug upsets your stomach, it may be taken with food or milk.

Aldomet antihypertensive

Manufacturer: Merck Sharp & Dohme
Ingredient: methyldopa
Dosage Forms: Tablet: 125 mg (yellow); 250 mg (yellow); 500 mg (yellow).

Oral suspension: (content per 5 ml teaspoon) 250 mg

Use: Treatment of high blood pressure

Minor Side Effects: Bloating; blurred vision; confusion; constipation; decreased sexual ability; diarrhea; dizziness; dry mouth; flatulence; headache; inflamed salivary glands; light-headedness; nasal congestion; nausea; sedation; sore tongue; tremors; vomiting; weakness

Major Side Effects: Anemia; breast enlargement; chest pain; darkening of urine; depression; distention; fever; fluid retention; insomnia; jaundice; liver disorders; liver and urine test abnormalities; loss of appetite; nightmares; numbness or tingling; reduction in number of white blood cells; severe, continuing stomach cramps; slow pulse; sore joints; troubled breathing; unusual body movements

Contraindications: This drug should not be taken by people with active liver disease, such as acute cirrhosis or acute hepatitis or by persons who have had liver reactions from this drug before. Be sure your doctor knows if you have such a condition. This drug should not be taken by people who are allergic to it. Consult your doctor immediately if this drug has been prescribed for you and you have such an allergy.

Warnings: This drug should be used with extreme caution by persons with angina, heart disease, kidney disease, mental depression, Parkinson's disease, or a history of previous liver disease or dysfunction or stroke. Be sure your doctor knows if you have ever had such conditions. You should receive liver function tests periodically as long as you are taking this drug. • This drug should be used cautiously by women who may become pregnant, by pregnant women, and by nursing mothers. • This drug may interfere with lab tests. Be sure your doctor knows you are taking this drug if you are going to have any tests done. • This drug may interfere with the measurement of blood uric acid, so remind your doctor if you have been or are being treated for gout. Also, many patients taking this drug react positively to the Coombs' blood test, indicating destruction of red blood cells or allergy. Often the test is false positive, and no disorder is present, but you should have periodic blood tests as long as you are taking this drug. • This drug should be used with caution in conjunction with other antihypertensive drugs. • This drug should not be taken with amphetamines or decongestants. If you are currently taking any drugs of these types, consult your doctor about their use. Do not take any nonprescription item for weight control or cough, cold, or sinus problems without first checking with your doctor. If you are unsure of the type or contents of your medications, ask your doctor or pharmacist. • This drug may interfere with blood transfusions. If you give or receive blood, be sure to tell the doctor you are taking this drug. • Do not discontinue taking this drug unless directed to do so by your doctor, because high blood pressure can return very quickly. • If you develop a fever or jaundice (yellow eyes or skin) while taking this drug, call your doctor. • This drug may cause drowsiness, especially during the first few days of its use; avoid tasks that require alertness, such as driving or operating machinery.

Comments: Mild side effects (e.g., nasal congestion) are noticeable during the first two weeks of therapy and become less bothersome after this period. • To avoid dizziness or light-headedness when you stand, contract and relax the muscles of your legs for a few moments before rising. Do this by pushing one foot against the floor while raising the other foot slightly, alternating feet so that you are "pumping" your legs in a pedaling motion. • Notify your doctor if any unexplained, prolonged general tiredness occurs. • Occasionally, tolerance to this drug may develop, usually between the second and third month of therapy. Your doctor can deal with this circumstance. • Take this drug exactly as directed. Do not take extra doses or skip a dose without first consulting your doctor. • Intake of alcoholic beverages should be limited while taking this drug.

Aldoril diuretic and antihypertensive

Manufacturer: Merck Sharp & Dohme
Ingredients: hydrochlorothiazide; methyldopa
Dosage Form: Aldoril 15: Tablet: hydrochlorothiazide, 15 mg; methyldopa, 250 mg (salmon). Aldoril 25: Tablet: hydrochlorothiazide, 25 mg; methyldopa, 250 mg (white); Aldoril D30: hydrochlorothiazide, 30 mg; methyldopa, 500 mg (salmon). Aldoril D50: Tablet: hydrochlorothiazide, 50 mg; methyldopa, 500 mg (white)
Use: Treatment of high blood pressure
Minor Side Effects: Bloating; breast swelling; constipation; cramping; decrease in sexual desire; diarrhea; dizziness; dry mouth; gas; headache; impotence; increased urination; light-headedness; loss of appetite; nasal congestion; nausea; sedation; slow pulse; sore tongue; sun sensitivity; tremor; vomiting
Major Side Effects: Anemia; blood disorders; blurred vision; bruising; chest pain; dark urine; depression; elevated blood sugar; fever; fluid retention; hyperuricemia (elevated uric acid in the blood); hypokalemia (low blood potassium); irregular heartbeat; jaundice; joint pain; liver disease; muscle spasm; nightmares; psychosis; rash; sore throat; stroke; tingling in fingers and toes; troubled breathing; weakness
Contraindications: This drug should not be taken by people who are allergic to either of its components or to sulfa drugs. Consult your doctor immediately if this drug has been prescribed for you and you have such an allergy. • This drug should not be used by people with active liver disease (e.g., acute hepatitis or active cirrhosis) or severe kidney disease. Be sure your doctor knows if you have either of these conditions.
Warnings: This drug should be used with caution by persons with liver disease, stroke, anemia, mental depression, Parkinson's disease, allergies, asthma, or kidney diseases, or persons who are on kidney machines. Be sure your doctor knows if you have any of these conditions. • Use of this drug may cause fever, lupus erythematosus, jaundice, liver disease, stroke, low white cell levels, low blood levels of potassium and sodium, calcium retention, diabetes, and gout. If you develop jaundice (yellow skin or dark urine) or body salt imbalance (characterized by thirst, dry mouth, muscle weakness, or cramps), call your doctor. • This drug may affect urine tests, lab tests, and thyroid tests. Be sure your doctor knows you are taking this drug before you undergo any testing. • This drug should be used with caution by pregnant women and nursing mothers. • This drug should be used cautiously with other blood pressure drugs; it also interacts with amphetamine, anesthetics, colestipol hydrochloride, curare, decongestants, digitalis, lithium carbonate, oral antidiabetics, and steroids. If you are currently taking any drugs of these types, consult your doctor about their use. If you are unsure about the type or contents of your medications, ask your doctor or pharmacist. • Many patients react positively to the Coombs' test, which is often done as part of blood transfusions. The positive reaction usually indicates an allergy or destruction of red blood cells. Often, however, the test is false positive and no disorder is present. Have periodic blood tests as long as you take this drug. • If you must have surgery, or are going to give or receive blood, be sure your doctor knows you are taking this drug.
Comments: While taking this drug, do not take any nonprescription item for weight control or cough, cold, or sinus problems without first checking with your doctor. • Mild side effects (e.g., nasal congestion) are most noticeable during the first two weeks of therapy and become less bothersome after this period. • While taking this product (as with many drugs that lower blood pressure), you should limit your consumption of alcoholic beverages in order to prevent

dizziness or light-headedness. • To avoid dizziness or light-headedness when you stand, contract and relax the muscles of your legs for a few moments before rising. Do this by pushing one foot against the floor while raising the other foot slightly, alternating feet so that you are "pumping" your legs in a pedaling motion. • This drug can cause potassium loss. Symptoms of potassium loss include dry mouth, thirst, and muscle cramps. To help avoid potassium loss, take this drug with a glass of fresh or frozen orange juice. You may also eat a banana each day. The use of a salt substitute helps prevent potassium loss. • This drug may interfere with the treatment of diabetes. Be sure your doctor knows you are taking this drug. • Persons taking this product and digitalis should watch carefully for symptoms of increased toxicity (e.g., nausea, blurred vision, palpitations), and notify their doctors immediately if symptoms occur. • Remind your doctor if you have been or are being treated for gout if this drug is prescribed for you. • This drug may interfere with the measurement of blood uric acid. • If you are allergic to a sulfa drug, you may likewise be allergic to this drug. • A doctor probably should not prescribe this drug or other "fixed dose" products as the first choice in the treatment of high blood pressure. The patient should receive each ingredient singly, and if the response is adequate to the fixed dose contained in this product, it can then be substituted. The advantage of a combination product is increased convenience to the patient. • Take this product exactly as directed. Do not take extra doses or skip a dose without consulting your doctor first.

Allerfrin with Codeine expectorant (Rugby Laboratories), see Actifed-C expectorant.

allopurinol gout drug (various manufacturers), see Zyloprim gout drug.

Almocarpine ophthalmic solution (Ayerst Laboratories), see Isopto Carpine ophthalmic solution.

alprazolam antianxiety (various manufacturers), see Xanax antianxiety.

Alzide diuretic and antihypertensive (Major Pharmaceuticals), see Aldactazide diuretic and antihypertensive.

Amaril "D" Spantab adrenergic and antihistamine (Vortech Pharmaceutical, Ltd.), see Naldecon adrenergic and antihistamine.

Amcap antibiotic (Circle Pharmaceuticals, Inc.), see ampicillin antibiotic.

Amcill antibiotic (Parke-Davis), see ampicillin antibiotic.

Amen progesterone hormone (Carnrick Laboratories, Inc.), see Provera progesterone hormone.

aminophylline bronchodilator

Manufacturer: various manufacturers
Ingredient: aminophylline

Equivalent Products: Aminophylline, Rugby Laboratories; Amoline, Major Pharmaceuticals; Lixaminol, Ferndale Laboratories, Inc.; Phyllocontin, Purdue Frederick Company; Somophyllin, Fisons Corporation Pharmaceutical Division; Somophyllin-DF, Fisons Corporation Pharmaceutical Division; Truphylline, G & W Laboratories, Inc.

Dosage Forms: Liquid; Suppository; Rectal solution; Tablet; Sustained-release tablet (various dosages, various colors)

Use: To relieve and/or prevent bronchial asthma; treatment of symptoms of chronic bronchitis and emphysema

Minor Side Effects: Diarrhea; drowsiness; gastrointestinal disturbances (stomach pain, nausea, vomiting); headache; insomnia; irritability; loss of appetite; muscle twitches; nervousness or restlessness

Major Side Effects: Bloody or black, tarry stools; convulsions; difficult breathing; flushing; high blood sugar; low blood pressure; palpitations; rapid or irregular heart rate

Contraindications: This drug should not be taken by people who are allergic to it or similar drugs; or who have an active peptic ulcer. Consult your doctor immediately if this drug has been prescribed for you and you have either of these conditions.

Warnings: Excessive doses of this drug are toxic, so follow your doctor's dosage instructions exactly. • This drug should be used cautiously by people who have heart disease, thyroid disease, liver disease, high blood pressure, or a history of peptic ulcer; and by those who are pregnant or elderly. Be sure your doctor knows if you have any of these conditions. • Some children are unusually sensitive to aminophylline; this drug should be used cautiously by children. • This drug should be used cautiously in conjunction with lithium carbonate, propranolol, cimetidine, diazepam, chlordiazepoxide, certain antibiotics, ephedrine, high blood pressure drugs, certain sedatives, or other xanthines; if you are currently taking any drugs of these types, consult your doctor about their use. If you are unsure of the type or contents of your medications, ask your doctor or pharmacist. • While taking this drug, do not use any nonprescription item for asthma without first checking with your doctor. • Call your doctor if you have severe stomach pain, vomiting, or restlessness, because this drug may aggravate an ulcer.

Comments: While taking this drug, drink at least eight glasses of water daily. • Be sure to take your dose at exactly the right time. • If this drug upsets your stomach, it may be taken with food or milk. • Avoid drinking coffee, tea, cola drinks, cocoa, or other beverages that contain caffeine. • Be sure your doctor knows if you smoke if you are taking this drug. Do not stop or start smoking without informing your doctor.

Aminophylline bronchodilator (Rugby Laboratories), see aminophylline bronchodilator.

Amitid antidepressant (E. R. Squibb & Sons, Inc.), see Elavil antidepressant.

Amitril antidepressant (Parke-Davis), see Elavil antidepressant.

amitriptyline hydrochloride antidepressant (various manufacturers), see Elavil antidepressant.

Amoline bronchodilator (Major Pharmaceuticals), see aminophylline bronchodilator.

amoxicillin antibiotic

Manufacturer: various manufacturers
Ingredient: amoxicillin
Equivalent Products: Amoxil, Beecham Laboratories; Larotid, Beecham Laboratories; Polymox, Bristol Labs; Trimox, E. R. Squibb & Sons, Inc.; Sumox, Reid-Provident Labs., Inc.; Utimox, Parke-Davis; Wymox, Wyeth Laboratories
Dosage Forms: Capsule: 250 mg; 500 mg (various colors). Chewable tablet: 125 mg; 250 mg (various colors). Oral suspension (content per 5 ml teaspoon): 125 mg; 250 mg. Drop (content per ml): 50 mg
Use: Treatment of a wide variety of bacterial infections
Minor Side Effects: Diarrhea; nausea; vomiting
Major Side Effects: Difficult breathing; fever; joint pain; mouth sores; rash; rectal and vaginal itching; severe diarrhea; sore throat; superinfection
Contraindications: This drug should not be taken by pregnant women or by people who are allergic to penicillin. Consult your doctor immediately if this drug has been prescribed for you and you have such an allergy or are pregnant.
Warnings: This drug should be used cautiously by children under 12 and by people who have kidney or liver disease, asthma, severe hay fever, or other significant allergies. Be sure your doctor knows if you have any of these conditions. • Complete blood cell counts and liver and kidney function tests are advisable if you take this drug for a prolonged period of time. • This drug should not be used in conjunction with allopurinol, chloramphenicol, erythromycin, or tetracycline; if you are currently taking any drugs of these types, consult your doctor about their use. If you are unsure of the contents of your medications, ask your doctor or pharmacist. • Severe allergic reactions to this drug (indicated by breathing difficulties and a drop in blood pressure) have been reported, but are rare when the drug is taken orally. • Prolonged use of this drug may allow organisms that are not susceptible to it to grow wildly. Do not use this drug unless your doctor has specifically told you to do so. Be sure to follow directions carefully and report any unusual reactions to your doctor at once.
Comments: This drug is similar in nature to penicillin and ampicillin. • This drug should be taken for at least ten full days, even if symptoms disappear within that time. • The liquid form of this drug should be stored in the refrigerator. Shake well before using. Discard unused portion after 14 days. • Diabetics using Clinitest urine test may get a false high sugar reading while taking this drug. Change to Clinistix, Diastix, Chemstrip UG, or Tes-Tape urine test to avoid this problem.

Amoxil antibiotic (Beecham Laboratories), see amoxicillin antibiotic.

ampicillin antibiotic

Manufacturer: various manufacturers
Ingredient: ampicillin
Equivalent Products: Amcap, Circle Pharmaceuticals, Inc.; Amcill, Parke-Davis; D-Amp, Dunhall Pharmaceuticals, Inc.; Omnipen, Wyeth Laboratories; Pfizerpen A, Pfipharmecs Division; Polycillin, Bristol Labs; Principen, E. R. Squibb & Sons, Inc.; SK-Ampicillin, Smith Kline & French Laboratories; Supen, Reid-Provident Labs., Inc.; Totacillin, Beecham Laboratories
Dosage Forms: Capsule: 250 mg; 500 mg (various colors). Oral suspension (content per 5 ml teaspoon): 100 mg; 125 mg; 250 mg; 500 mg
Use: Treatment of a wide variety of bacterial infections
Minor Side Effects: Diarrhea; nausea; vomiting

Major Side Effects: Abdominal pain; black tongue; bruising; cough; difficult breathing; fever; mouth irritation; rash; rectal and vaginal itching; severe diarrhea; sore throat; superinfection

Contraindications: This drug should not be taken by people who are allergic to penicillin. Consult your doctor immediately if this drug has been prescribed for you and you have such an allergy.

Warnings: This drug should not be used in conjunction with allopurinol, chloramphenicol, erythromycin, or tetracycline; if you are currently taking any drugs of these types, consult your doctor about their use. If you are unsure of the contents of your medications, ask your doctor or pharmacist. ● This drug should be used cautiously by pregnant women, children, and people who have liver or kidney disease, mononucleosis, asthma, severe hay fever, or other significant allergies. Be sure your doctor knows if you have any of these conditions. ● Complete blood cell counts and liver and kidney function tests are advisable if you take this drug for an extended period of time. ● Severe allergic reactions to this drug (indicated by breathing difficulties and a drop in blood pressure) have been reported, but are rare when the drug is taken orally. ● Diabetics using Clinitest urine test may get a false high sugar reading while taking this drug. Change to Clinistix, Diastix, Chemstrip UG, or Tes-Tape urine test to avoid this problem. ● This drug may affect the potency of oral contraceptives. Consult your doctor about using supplementary contraceptive measures while you are taking this drug.

Comments: This drug is similar in nature and action to penicillin and amoxicillin. ● This drug should be taken for at least ten full days, even if symptoms disappear within that time. ● The liquid form of this drug should be stored in the refrigerator. Shake well before using. Any unused portion should be discarded after 14 days. ● Take the drug on an empty stomach (one hour before or two hours after a meal).

Antivert antinauseant

Manufacturer: Roerig
Ingredient: meclizine hydrochloride
Equivalent Product: meclizine hydrochloride, various manufacturers
Dosage Forms: Chewable tablet: 25 mg (pink). Tablet: 12.5 mg (blue and white); 25 mg (yellow and white); 50 mg (green and white)
Use: To provide symptomatic relief of dizziness due to ear infections; or to prevent or relieve dizziness and nausea due to motion sickness

Minor Side Effects: Blurred vision; drowsiness; dry mouth; headache; insomnia; loss of appetite; nervousness; upset stomach

Major Side Effects: Difficult breathing; fever; painful urination; palpitations; skin rash; sore throat

Contraindications: Do not take this drug if you are or may become pregnant. Experimental studies with rats have shown a high association of birth defects with the drug. Consult your doctor immediately if this drug has been prescribed for you and you are pregnant. ● This drug should not be taken by people who are allergic to it. Consult your doctor immediately if this drug has been prescribed for you and you have such an allergy.

Warnings: This drug is not recommended for use by children under 12. ● This drug should be used cautiously by people with asthma, glaucoma, stomach ulcer, urinary tract blockage, or prostate trouble. Be sure your doctor knows if you have any of these conditions. ● This drug may cause drowsiness; avoid tasks that require alertness. ● To prevent oversedation, avoid the use of other sedative drugs or alcohol.

Comments: When used for motion sickness, take this drug one hour before travel, then one dose every 24 hours during travel. ● Although most brands of this drug require a prescription, nonprescription forms are also available. Ask your doctor or pharmacist about them.

Anugard-HC steroid-hormone-containing anorectal product (Vangard Laboratories), see Anusol-HC steroid-hormone-containing anorectal product.

Anusol-HC steroid-hormone-containing anorectal product

Manufacturer: Parke-Davis
Ingredients: benzyl benzoate; bismuth resorcin compound; bismuth subgallate; hydrocortisone acetate; Peruvian balsam; zinc oxide
Equivalent Products: Anugard-HC, Vangard Laboratories; Hemorrhoidal HC, Rugby Laboratories; Rectacort, Century Pharmaceuticals, Inc.
Dosage Forms: Cream: hydrocortisone acetate, 0.5%; bismuth subgallate, 2.25%; bismuth resorcin, 1.75%; benzyl benzoate 1.2%; zinc oxide, 11%; Peruvian balsam, 1.8%. Suppository: benzyl benzoate, 1.2%; bismuth resorcin compound, 1.75%; bismuth subgallate, 2.25%; hydrocortisone acetate, 10 mg; Peruvian balsam, 1.8%; zinc oxide, 11%
Use: Relief of pain, itching, and discomfort arising from hemorrhoids and irritated anorectal tissues
Minor Side Effect: Burning sensation on application
Major Side Effects: Local inflammation or infection at site of application
Contraindications: This drug should not be used by people who are allergic to any of its ingredients. Consult your doctor immediately if this drug has been prescribed for you and you have such an allergy.
Warnings: This drug should be used with caution by pregnant women. Pregnant women should not use the product unnecessarily on extensive areas, in large amounts, or for prolonged periods. • If irritation develops, discontinue use of this drug, and notify your doctor. • This drug should be used with caution by children and infants. • Do not use this drug in the eyes.
Comments: This drug should not be used for more than seven consecutive days, unless your doctor specifically says to do so. • The suppository form of this drug should be stored in a cool, dry place. • If this drug stains your clothing, the stain may be removed by washing with laundry detergent.

AP Creme steroid hormone and anti-infective (T.E. Edwards Co.), see Vioform-Hydrocortisone steroid hormone and anti-infective.

Aphen antiparkinson drug (Major Pharmaceuticals), see Artane antiparkinson drug.

A-poxide sedative and hypnotic (Abbott Laboratories), see Librium sedative and hypnotic.

Apresoline antihypertensive

Manufacturer: CIBA Pharmaceutical Company
Ingredient: hydralazine hydrochloride
Equivalent Products: Azaline, Major Pharmaceuticals; hydralazine hydrochloride, various manufacturers
Dosage Form: Tablet: 10 mg (yellow); 25 mg (deep blue); 50 mg (light blue); 100 mg (peach)
Use: Treatment of high blood pressure

Minor Side Effects: Constipation; diarrhea; difficult urination; dizziness; flushing; headache; loss of appetite; muscle cramps; nasal congestion; nausea; vomiting

Major Side Effects: Anemia; anxiety; blood disorders; bruising; chest pain; confusion; cramping; depression; fever; fluid retention; itching; liver damage; numbness or tingling in fingers or toes; palpitations; rapid heart rate; rash; shortness of breath; sore throat; tenderness in joints

Contraindications: This drug should not be taken by people who are allergic to it; or by those who have coronary artery disease (angina, for example), those who have suffered a heart attack, or those who have mitral valvular rheumatic heart disease. Consult your doctor immediately if this drug has been prescribed for you and you have any of these conditions.

Warnings: This drug may cause angina and heart attacks and should be used cautiously by people in whom coronary heart disease is suspected. Pregnant women, stroke victims, and people who have kidney disease should also use this drug with caution. Be sure your doctor knows if you have, or might have, any of these conditions. • This drug may cause lupus erythematosus, nerve damage, or blood diseases; contact your doctor if any unexplained symptoms of tiredness, weakness, fever, aching joints, or chest pain (angina) occur. • Periodic blood tests are advisable while you are taking this drug. • This drug interacts with other antihypertensive drugs, amphetamines, decongestants, and monoamine oxidase inhibitors; if you are currently taking any drugs of these types, consult your doctor about their use. If you are unsure of the type of your medications, ask your doctor or pharmacist. • This drug may affect your ability to perform tasks that require alertness; avoid driving or operating machinery if the drug makes you dizzy or otherwise impairs your concentration.

Comments: The effects of treatment with this drug may not be apparent for at least two weeks. • Mild side effects (e.g., headache or nasal congestion) are most noticeable during the first two weeks of drug therapy and become less bothersome after this period. • If you experience numbness or tingling in your fingers or toes while using this drug, your doctor may recommend that you take vitamin B_6 (pyridoxine) to relieve the symptoms. • To avoid dizziness or light-headedness when you stand, contract and relax the muscles of your legs for a few moments before rising. Do this by pushing one foot against the floor while raising the other foot slightly, alternating feet so that you are "pumping" your legs in a pedaling motion. • Take this drug exactly as directed. It is best taken with a meal. Do not take extra doses or skip a dose without first consulting your doctor. • Do not stop taking this medication unless your doctor directs you to do so. • While taking this drug, do not take any nonprescription item for weight control or cough, cold, or sinus problems without first checking with your doctor. • Limit your consumption of alcoholic beverages in order to prevent dizziness or light-headedness.

Aprodine-C expectorant (Major Pharmaceuticals), see Actifed-C expectorant.

Aquatensen diuretic and antihypertensive (Wallace Laboratories), see Enduron diuretic and antihypertensive.

Aquazide H diuretic and antihypertensive (Western Research Laboratories, Inc.), see hydrochlorothiazide diuretic and antihypertensive.

Aristocort A steroid hormone (Lederle Laboratories), see Aristocort and Kenalog steroid hormones.

Aristocort steroid hormone (topical)

Manufacturer: Lederle Laboratories
Ingredient: triamcinolone acetonide
Equivalent Products: Aristocort A, Lederle Laboratories; Flutex, Syosset Labs., Inc.; Kenalog, E. R. Squibb & Sons, Inc.; Triacet, various manufacturers; triamcinolone acetonide, various manufacturers
  Dosage Forms: Cream: 0.025%; 0.1%; 0.5%. Ointment: 0.1%; 0.5%
  Use: Symptomatic relief of skin inflammations and irritation caused by certain skin conditions such as eczema or insect bites
  Minor Side Effects: Dryness; increased hair growth; irritation; itching; localized burning; rash
  Major Side Effects: Loss of skin color; secondary infection; skin wasting
  Contraindications: This drug should not be used by people who are allergic to it. Consult your doctor immediately if this drug has been prescribed for you and you have such an allergy.
  Warnings: If irritation develops when using this product, stop using it immediately and call your doctor. • Your doctor will probably monitor your use of this drug closely if you must use it over a large area of skin or under an occlusive dressing, since such measures increase the systemic absorption of the drug and the risk of side effects. • This drug is not for use in the eyes. • If using the spray form on your face, cover your eyes and avoid inhaling any of the spray. • This drug should be used cautiously by pregnant women.
  Comments: If the affected area is extremely dry or is scaling, you may moisten the skin before applying this product by soaking the affected area in water or by applying water with a clean cloth. • The ointment form is preferred for use on dry skin. • Do not use this product with an occlusive wrap of transparent plastic film unless directed to do so by your doctor. If you are using such a wrap, be sure to follow your doctor's directions exactly. Do not leave the wrap in place longer than specified. • Do not use this product more often or for a longer period than your doctor prescribed.

Armour thyroid hormone (USV [P.R.] Development Corp.), see thyroid hormone.

Artane antiparkinson drug

Manufacturer: Lederle Laboratories
Ingredient: trihexyphenidyl hydrochloride
Equivalent Products: Aphen, Major Pharmaceuticals; Tremin, Schering Corp.; Trihexane, Rugby Laboratories; Trihexidyl, Henry Schein, Inc.; Trihexy, Geneva Generics, Inc.; trihexyphenidyl hydrochloride, various manufacturers
  Dosage Forms: Sustained-release capsule: 5 mg (blue with white granules). Syrup (content per 5 ml teaspoon): 2 mg. Tablet: 2 mg; 5 mg (both white)
  Use: Treatment of all forms of Parkinson's disease; prevention of tremors and other symptoms associated with phenothiazine drugs
  Minor Side Effects: Bloated feeling; blurred vision; constipation; dizziness; drowsiness; dry mouth; false sense of well-being; headache; increased sensitivity of eyes to light; mild nausea; nervousness; reduced sweating; weakness
  Major Side Effects: None in most people. However, some people with arteriosclerosis or with a history of abnormal reactions to other drugs may exhibit symptoms of mental confusion, agitation, disturbed behavior, memory loss, palpitations, difficult urination, skin rash, or nausea and vomiting; psychiatric disturbances can result from indiscriminate use leading to overdosage; narrow-angle glaucoma reported.

Contraindications: This drug should not be used by those people who are allergic to it or by anyone with narrow-angle glaucoma, obstructions in the digestive system, stomach ulcers, enlarged prostate gland, urinary tract blockage, achalasia, or myasthenia gravis. Consult your doctor if you have any of these conditions.

Warnings: People treated with this drug should have close monitoring of intraocular pressures at regular, periodic intervals. • Careful and constant long-term observation of people using this drug should be undertaken to avoid allergic and certain other reactions. • This drug should be used with caution by people with heart, liver, or kidney disorders, with thyroid disease or ulcerative colitis, or with high blood pressure. People with any of these conditions should be under close medical observation. If you have any of these conditions, be sure your doctor knows. • Persons over 60 years of age require strict dosage regulation, since they frequently develop increased sensitivity to the action of this type of drug. • This drug should not be taken with antidepressants. If you are currently taking any drugs of this type, consult your doctor immediately about their use. If you are unsure of the type of your medications, consult your doctor or pharmacist.

Comments: This drug is frequently prescribed along with phenothiazine drugs such as Thorazine and Stelazine to reduce the tremors caused by phenothiazines. You should talk with your doctor about waiting before taking this drug to see if you really need it. Many people can take phenothiazine drugs successfully and may not need this drug. • The sustained-release capsule form of this drug is effective over a long time; never take it more frequently than prescribed by your doctor. A serious overdose may result. • Do not stop taking this drug without first consulting your doctor. • Since this drug may cause dryness of the mouth, chew gum or suck on ice chips or a piece of hard candy to reduce this feeling. • Generic brands of this drug are available and vary widely in cost. Consult your doctor and pharmacist. • Certain other drugs, such as Cogentin (Merck Sharp & Dohme) and Kemadrin (Burroughs Wellcome Co.) antiparkinson drugs, have actions similar to those of this drug. • If this drug makes it hard for you to urinate, try to do so just before each dose.

Atarax sedative

Manufacturer: Roerig

Ingredient: hydroxyzine hydrochloride

Equivalent Products: Atozine, Major Pharmaceuticals; Durrax, Dermik Laboratories, Inc.; hydroxyzine hydrochloride, various manufacturers; Hy-Pam (see Comments), Premo Pharmaceutical Labs, Inc.; Vistaril (see Comments), Pfizer Laboratories Division

Dosage Forms: Syrup (content per 5 ml teaspoon): 10 mg. Tablet: 10 mg (orange); 25 mg (green); 50 mg (yellow); 100 mg (red)

Use: Symptomatic relief of anxiety and tension; treatment of itching caused by allergic conditions

Minor Side Effects: Drowsiness; dry mouth

Major Side Effects: Chest tightness; convulsions; difficult breathing; skin rash; sore throat; tremors

Contraindications: Do not take this drug if you are allergic to it or are pregnant. Consult your doctor immediately if the drug has been prescribed for you and you have either of these conditions.

Warnings: This drug should not be used in conjunction with central nervous system depressants, alcohol, or other drugs that have sedative properties; if you are currently taking any drugs of these types, consult your doctor about their use. If you are unsure of the type or contents of your medications, ask your doctor or pharmacist. • This drug may cause drowsiness; avoid tasks that require alertness. • Use of this drug by nursing mothers is not recommended.

Comments: The generic name for Vistaril and Hy-Pam sedatives is hydroxyzine pamoate; although not generically identical, these products are therapeutically equivalent to Atarax sedative and other hydroxyzine hydrochloride products. • Chew gum or suck on ice chips or a piece of hard candy to reduce mouth dryness.

Ativan sedative and hypnotic

Manufacturer: Wyeth Laboratories
Ingredient: lorazepam
Equivalent Product: lorazepam, Quantum Pharmics
Dosage Form: Tablet: 0.5 mg; 1 mg; 2 mg (all are white)
Use: Relief of anxiety, tension, agitation, irritability, and insomnia
Minor Side Effects: Blurred vision; change in appetite; constipation; depression; diarrhea; dizziness; drowsiness; dry mouth; headache; increased salivation; nausea; rash; unsteadiness; weakness
Major Side Effects: Decreased hearing; difficult breathing; difficult urination; disorientation; eye function disturbance; fever; hallucinations; jaundice; menstrual irregularities; mouth sores; palpitations; slurred speech; sore throat
Contraindications: This drug should not be used by people who are allergic to it. Consult your doctor immediately if this drug has been prescribed for you and you have such an allergy. This drug should not be used by people with acute narrow-angle glaucoma or a severe mental disorder. Be sure your doctor knows if you have either of these conditions.
Warnings: This drug should be used cautiously by the elderly; children under 12; pregnant or nursing women; and people with impaired liver or kidney function, or disease of the heart, stomach, or lungs. Be sure your doctor knows if you fit into any of these categories. • This drug may cause drowsiness; avoid tasks that require alertness. • To prevent oversedation, avoid the use of alcohol or other drugs that have sedative properties. • Do not stop taking this drug suddenly without consulting your doctor. If you have been taking this drug regularly, it will be necessary to reduce your dosage gradually. • This drug has the potential for abuse and must be used with caution. Tolerance may develop quickly; do not increase the dose without first consulting your doctor. • Persons taking this drug for long periods should have periodic blood and liver function tests. • This drug is safe when used alone. When it is combined with other sedatives, serious adverse reactions may develop. This drug also interacts with cimetidine, phenytoin, levodopa, lithium, and anticoagulants.
Comments: This drug is currently used by many people to relieve nervousness. It is effective for this purpose, but it is important to try to remove the cause of anxiety as well. • This drug may cause dryness of the mouth. To reduce this feeling, chew gum or suck on ice chips or a piece of hard candy. • Take with food or a full glass of water if stomach upset occurs. • It may take two or three days before this drug's full effects are apparent.

Atozine sedative (Major Pharmaceuticals), see Atarax sedative.

Azaline antihypertensive (Major Pharmaceuticals), see Apresoline antihypertensive.

azatadine and pseudoephedrine antihistamine and decongestant (Schering Corp.), see Trinalin antihistamine and decongestant.

Bactrim and Bactrim DS antibacterials

Manufacturer: Roche Products, Inc.

Ingredients: sulfamethoxazole; trimethoprim

Equivalent Products: Bethaprim SS and Bethaprim DS, Major Pharmaceuticals; Cotrim and Cotrim DS, Lemmon Company; Septra and Septra DS, Burroughs Wellcome Co.; SMZ-TMP and SMZ-TMP DS, Biocraft; Sulfatrim and Sulfatrim DS, various manufacturers

Dosage Forms: Liquid (content per 5 ml teaspoon): trimethoprim, 40 mg; sulfamethoxazole, 200 mg. Tablet: trimethoprim, 80 mg; sulfamethoxazole, 400 mg (green). Double-strength (DS) tablet: trimethoprim, 160 mg; sulfamethoxazole, 800 mg (white)

Use: Treatment of chronic urinary tract infections; certain respiratory infections; middle-ear infections

Minor Side Effects: Abdominal pain; depression; diarrhea; dizziness; headache; loss of appetite; nausea; sore mouth; sun sensitivity; vomiting

Major Side Effects: Anemia; arthritis; bleeding; blood disorders; breathing difficulties; convulsions; difficult urination; fever; fluid retention; hallucinations; itching; jaundice; kidney disease; rash; ringing in the ears; sore throat; tingling in hands or feet; weakness

Contraindications: This drug should not be taken by people who are allergic to either ingredient, by those with folate deficiency anemia, or by those who are pregnant or nursing. Consult your doctor immediately if you have any of these conditions. • This drug should not be used by infants under two months old.

Warnings: This drug should be used cautiously by elderly patients who also take diuretics. • This drug may cause allergic reactions and should, therefore, be used cautiously by people who have asthma, severe hay fever, or other significant allergies. People who have certain vitamin deficiencies or liver or kidney disease should also use this drug with caution. Be sure your doctor knows if you have any of these conditions. • This drug should not be used to treat strep throat. • This drug can cause blood diseases; notify your doctor immediately if you experience fever, sore throat, or skin discoloration, as these can be early signs of blood disorders. • Complete blood cell counts and liver and kidney function tests should be done if you take this drug for a prolonged period. • This drug should not be used in conjunction with barbiturates, cyclophosphamide, isoniazid, local anesthetics, methenamine hippurate, methenamine mandelate, methotrexate, oral anticoagulants, oral antidiabetics, oxacillin, para-aminobenzoic acid (PABA), penicillins, phenylbutazone, phenytoin, or probenecid; if you are currently taking any drugs of these types, consult your doctor or pharmacist.

Comments: This drug should be taken for at least ten full days, even if symptoms disappear within that time. • To be most effective, this drug should be taken at evenly spaced times. Your doctor or pharmacist can help you set up a dosing schedule. • Take this drug with at least one full glass of water. Drink at least nine or ten glasses of water each day. • This drug may cause you to be especially sensitive to the sun, so avoid exposure to the sun as much as possible and use an effective sunscreen that does not contain PABA. • This drug may interfere with blood and urine laboratory tests.

Barbita sedative and hypnotic (Vortech Pharmaceutical, Ltd.), see phenobarbital sedative and hypnotic.

Barophen sedative and anticholinergic (various manufacturers), see Donnatal sedative and anticholinergic.

Bayapap with Codeine analgesic (Bay Pharmaceuticals, Inc.), see acetaminophen with codeine analgesic.

Bay-Ase sedative and anticholinergic (Bay Pharmaceuticals, Inc.), see Donnatal sedative and anticholinergic.

BaySporin Otic (Bay Pharmaceuticals, Inc.), see Cortisporin otic solution/suspension.

Beclovent anti-asthmatic (Glaxo, Inc.), see Vanceril anti-asthmatic.

Beepen VK antibiotic (Beecham Laboratories), see penicillin potassium phenoxymethyl (penicillin VK) antibiotic.

Belix antihistamine (Halsey Drug Co., Inc.), see Benadryl antihistamine.

belladonna alkaloids with phenobarbital sedative and anticholinergic (various manufacturers), see Donnatal sedative and anticholinergic.

Bellalphen sedative and anticholinergic (Columbia Medical Co.), see Donnatal sedative and anticholinergic.

Bellastal sedative and anticholinergic (Wharton Laboratories, Inc.), see Donnatal sedative and anticholinergic.

Benadryl antihistamine

Manufacturer: Parke-Davis
Ingredient: diphenhydramine hydrochloride
Equivalent Products: Belix, Halsey Drug Co., Inc.; Bendylate, Reid-Provident Labs., Inc., Diahist, Century Pharmaceuticals; Diphen, Bay Pharmaceuticals, Inc.; diphenhydramine hydrochloride, various manufacturers; Fenylhist, Mallard, Inc.; Nordryl, North American Pharmacal; Phen-Amin, Scrip-Physician Supply Co.; Robalyn, Three P Products Corp.; SK-Diphenhydramine, Smith Kline & French Laboratories
Dosage Forms: Capsule: 25 mg; 50 mg (both pink/white). Liquid (content per 5 ml teaspoon): 12.5 mg
Use: Treatment of insomnia; motion sickness; Parkinson's disease; or allergy-related itching and swelling
Minor Side Effects: Blurred vision; confusion; constipation; diarrhea; difficult urination; dizziness; drowsiness; dry mouth; headache; insomnia; loss of appetite; nasal congestion; nausea; nervousness; restlessness; sweating; vomiting; weakness; wheezing
Major Side Effects: Changes in menstruation; convulsions; decreased sexual ability; disturbed coordination; fever; low blood pressure; nightmares; palpitations; rash from exposure to sunlight; ringing in ears; severe abdominal pain; shortness of breath; sore throat; tightness in chest; unusual bleeding and bruising
Contraindications: This drug should not be given to infants or taken by nursing mothers. People who are allergic to this drug or similar antihistamines should not use this drug. Consult your doctor immediately if this drug has been

prescribed for you and any of these statements apply to you. • This drug should not be used to treat asthma or other lower respiratory tract symptoms.

Warnings: This drug should be used cautiously by people who have asthma, glaucoma (certain types), ulcers (certain types), enlarged prostate, obstructed bladder, obstructed intestine, thyroid disease, heart disease, or high blood pressure; and by those who are pregnant. Be sure your doctor knows if you have any of these conditions. • Elderly people are more likely than others to experience side effects, especially sedation, with this drug and should use it with caution. • This drug should be used cautiously with aminosalicylic acid, oral anticoagulants, and phenytoin. • This drug should not be used in conjunction with central nervous system depressants or monoamine oxidase inhibitors; if you are currently taking any drugs of these types, consult your doctor about their use. If you are unsure of the type of your medications, ask your doctor or pharmacist. • This drug may cause drowsiness; avoid tasks that require alertness. • To prevent oversedation, avoid alcohol or other sedative drugs.

Comments: Chew gum or suck on ice chips or a piece of hard candy to reduce mouth dryness. • Take only the prescribed amount of this drug. An overdose usually sedates an adult but can cause excitation leading to convulsions and death in a child. • While taking this drug, do not take any nonprescription item for cough, cold, or sinus problems without calling the doctor.

Bendylate antihistamine (Reid-Provident Labs., Inc.), see Benadryl antihistamine.

Bentyl antispasmodic

Manufacturer: Lakeside Pharmaceuticals

Ingredient: dicyclomine hydrochloride

Equivalent Products: Dibent, W. E. Hauck, Inc.; dicyclomine hydrochloride, various manufacturers; Di-Spaz, Vortech Pharmaceutical, Ltd.

Dosage Forms: Capsule: 10 mg (blue). Liquid (content per 5 ml teaspoon): 10 mg. Tablet: 20 mg (blue)

Use: Treatment of gastrointestinal disorders, including peptic ulcer, irritable colon, mucous colitis, acute enterocolitis, and neurogenic colon

Minor Side Effects: Bloating; blurred vision; confusion; dizziness; drowsiness; dry mouth; increased sensitivity to light; headache; insomnia; interference with milk production; loss of taste; nausea; nervousness; reduced sweating; vomiting; weakness

Major Side Effects: Constipation; difficult urination; fever; impotence; palpitations; rapid heartbeat; rash; sore throat

Contraindications: This drug should not be taken by people who have severe ulcerative colitis, severe hemorrhage, obstructed bladder, obstructed intestine, heart disease (certain types), or myasthenia gravis. This drug should not be taken by those who are allergic to it. Consult your doctor immediately if this drug has been prescribed for you and you have any of these conditions or such an allergy.

Warnings: This drug should be used cautiously by people who have hiatal hernia, glaucoma, enlarged prostate, high blood pressure, thyroid disease, liver or kidney disease, or heart disease; or by those who are pregnant. Be sure your doctor knows if you have any of these conditions. • If diarrhea is caused by obstructed intestine, this drug could be harmful. Use of this drug requires careful diagnosis of your condition. • People who have ulcerative colitis should be especially careful about taking this drug, and should never increase the dosage unless told to do so by their doctor. • This drug should not be used in conjunction with amantadine, haloperidol, phenothiazines, or antacids; if you are currently taking any drugs of these types, consult your doctor about their use. If you are unsure of the type or contents of your medications, ask your doctor or pharmacist. • This drug always produces certain side effects, which may include dry mouth, blurred vision, reduced sweating, drowsiness, difficult urination, constipation, increased sensitivity to light, and palpitations. • Avoid tasks that require alertness. • Avoid excessive work or exercise in hot weather. • To prevent oversedation, avoid taking alcohol or other drugs that have sedative properties. Call your doctor if you notice a rash, flushing, or pain in the eye. • In a few instances, infants less than six weeks old have developed breathing problems after being given this drug. In such a situation, you should call your doctor immediately.

Comments: This drug is best taken one-half to one hour before meals. • This drug does not cure ulcers, but may help them improve. • Chew gum or suck on ice chips or a piece of hard candy to reduce mouth dryness. • A product combining Bentyl antispasmodic with phenobarbital is available for persons who are especially nervous or anxious. Despite the phenobarbital content, Bentyl antispasmodic with phenobarbital has not been shown to have high potential for abuse.

Bentyl antispasmodic with phenobarbital (Lakeside Pharmaceuticals, Inc.), see Bentyl antispasmodic.

betamethasone valerate steroid hormone (various manufacturers), see Valisone steroid hormone.

Betapen-VK antibiotic (Bristol Labs), see penicillin potassium phenoxymethyl (penicillin VK) antibiotic.

Betatrex steroid hormone (Savage Laboratories), see Valisone steroid hormone.

Beta-Val steroid hormone (Lemmon Company), see Valisone steroid hormone.

Bethaprim SS and Bethaprim DS antibacterials (Major Pharmaceuticals), see Bactrim and Bactrim DS antibacterials.

Bexophene analgesic (Mallard, Inc.), see Darvon Compound-65 analgesic.

birth control pills, see oral contraceptives.

Bleph-10 Liquifilm ophthalmic solution (Allergan Pharmaceuticals, Inc.), see Sodium Sulamyd ophthalmic solution and ointment.

Blocadren beta blocker

Manufacturer: Merck Sharp & Dohme
Ingredient: timolol maleate
Dosage Form: Tablet: 10 mg; 20 mg (blue)
Use: Treatment of high blood pressure and prevention of heartbeat irregularities following a heart attack
Minor Side Effects: Abdominal pain; blurred vision; bloating; constipation; drowsiness; dry eyes, mouth, or skin; gas or heartburn; headache; insomnia;

loss of appetite; nasal congestion; nausea; slowed heart rate; sweating; tiredness; vivid dreams; vomiting

Major Side Effects: Bleeding or bruising; confusion; decreased sexual ability; depression; diarrhea; difficult urination; dizziness; earache; fever; hair loss; hallucinations; mouth sores; night cough; nightmares; numbness and tingling in the fingers and toes; rash; ringing in the ears; shortness of breath; swelling in the hands or feet

Contraindications: This drug should not be used by people who are allergic to timolol maleate or any other beta blocker. This drug should not be taken by people who suffer from certain types of heart disease or lung disease or anyone who has taken any monoamine oxidase inhibitors within the past two weeks. Consult your doctor immediately if this drug has been prescribed for you and you fit any of these categories.

Warnings: This drug should be used with caution by persons with certain respiratory problems, diabetes, certain heart problems, liver and kidney diseases, hypoglycemia, or thyroid disease. Be sure your doctor knows if you have any of these conditions. • This drug should be used cautiously by pregnant women and by women of childbearing age. • This drug should be used with care during anesthesia and by patients undergoing major surgery. If possible, this drug should be withdrawn 48 hours prior to surgery. • This drug should be used cautiously when reserpine is taken. • This drug is a potent medication, and it should not be stopped abruptly.

Comments: Your doctor may want you to take your pulse every day while you take this medication. Consult your doctor. • Be sure to take your medication doses at the same time each day. • While taking this drug, do not take any nonprescription items for cough, cold, or sinus problems without first checking with your doctor. • The action of this drug is similar to that of Inderal beta blocker (Ayerst Laboratories). • Notify your doctor if dizziness or diarrhea develops.

Brethine bronchodilator

Manufacturer: GEIGY Pharmaceuticals
Ingredient: terbutaline sulfate
Equivalent Product: Bricanyl, Merrell Dow Pharmaceuticals, Inc.
Dosage Form: Tablet: 2.5 mg; 5 mg (white)
Use: Relief of bronchial asthma and bronchospasm associated with bronchitis and emphysema

Minor Side Effects: Anxiety; dizziness; headache; flushing; increased heart rate; insomnia; loss of appetite; muscle cramps; nausea; nervousness; sweating; tremors; vomiting

Major Side Effects: Chest pain; difficult urination; palpitations

Contraindications: This drug should not be taken by people who are allergic to any sympathomimetic amine drug. Consult your doctor immediately if this drug has been prescribed for you and you have an allergy of this type.

Warnings: This drug should be used cautiously by pregnant or nursing women; and people who have diabetes, high blood pressure, thyroid disease, glaucoma, enlarged prostate, Parkinson's disease, heart disease (certain types), or epilepsy. Be sure your doctor knows if you have any of these conditions. • This drug is not recommended for use by children under age 12. • This drug should not be used in conjunction with guanethidine, beta blockers, or monoamine oxidase inhibitors; if you are currently taking any drugs of these types, consult your doctor about their use. If you are unsure of the type or contents of your medications, ask your doctor or pharmacist. • While taking this drug, do not take any nonprescription item for cough, cold, or sinus problems without first checking with your doctor. Do not take any other drug containing a sympathomimetic amine (a decongestant, for example) without consulting your doctor.

Comments: While taking this drug, drink at least eight glasses of water daily.
● Side effects from this drug are usually worse the first week or so of therapy and will lessen in severity after that.

Bricanyl bronchodilator (Merrell Dow Pharmaceuticals, Inc.), see Brethine bronchodilator.

Bristamycin antibiotic (Bristol Labs), see erythromycin antibiotic.

Bromalix antihistamine and decongestant (Century Pharmaceuticals, Inc.), see Dimetapp antihistamine and decongestant.

Bromophen antihistamine and decongestant (Rugby Laboratories), see Dimetapp antihistamine and decongestant.

Brompheniramine Compound antihistamine and decongestant (various manufacturers), see Dimetapp antihistamine and decongestant.

Bronchial expectorant and smooth muscle relaxant (Geneva Drugs Ltd.), see Quibron expectorant and smooth muscle relaxant.

Buff-A-Comp analgesic and sedative (Mayrand Pharmaceuticals, Inc.), see Fiorinal with Codeine analgesic and sedative.

Butal Compound analgesic and sedative (Cord), see Fiorinal analgesic and sedative.

Cafergot migraine remedy

Manufacturer: Sandoz Pharmaceuticals
Ingredients: caffeine; ergotamine tartrate
Equivalent Products: Cafertrate, Henry Schein, Inc.; Ercatab, Cord; Ergo-Caff, Rugby Laboratories; Wigraine, Organon Pharmaceuticals
Dosage Forms: Suppository: caffeine, 100 mg; ergotamine tartrate, 2 mg. Tablet: caffeine, 100 mg; ergotamine tartrate, 1 mg (pink)
Use: To abort or prevent migraine headache
Minor Side Effects: Dizziness; headache; nausea; numbness; vomiting
Major Side Effects: Chest pain; confusion; decreased or increased heart rate; diarrhea; extreme thirst; itching; lack of pulse; localized edema; muscle pain in extremities; stomach pain; tingling in fingers and toes; weakness in legs
Contraindications: This drug should not be used by people with blood vessel disease, heart disease, high blood pressure, malnutrition, severe itching, liver or kidney disease, or infection. This drug should not be used during pregnancy. Consult your doctor immediately if this drug has been prescribed for you and you have any of these conditions. This drug should not be used by people who are allergic to either of its ingredients. Consult your doctor immediately if this drug has been prescribed for you and you have such an allergy.
Warnings: To avoid toxicity, make sure that you stay within the dosage limits recommended. ● This drug should be used cautiously in people with stomach ulcers.

Comments: Cafergot P-B tablets and suppositories have the following ingredients in addition to those of Cafergot tablets and suppositories: Tablet: 0.125 mg l-alkaloids of belladonna and 30 mg sodium pentobarbital (bright green, coated). Suppository: 0.25 mg l-alkaloids of belladonna and 60 mg pentobarbital (sealed in blue aluminum foil). • Other products are available which are similar to Cafergot, but they are not identical. Those products listed above which are identical may differ widely in price. Consult your doctor and pharmacist. • For best results, dosage should start at the first sign of a migraine attack. Learn to recognize the first symptoms of a migraine attack. If Cafergot dosing is delayed for several hours after the beginning of these symptoms, it may not work. • Do not stop taking this drug without consulting your doctor.

Cafergot P-B migraine remedy (Sandoz Pharmaceuticals), see Cafergot migraine remedy.

Cafetrate migraine remedy (Henry Schein, Inc.), see Cafergot migraine remedy.

Calan anti-anginal (Searle Labs), see Isoptin anti-anginal.

Cam-ap-es diuretic and antihypertensive (Camall Company), see Ser-Ap-Es diuretic and antihypertensive.

Capital with Codeine analgesic (Carnrick Laboratories, Inc.), see acetaminophen with codeine analgesic.

Capoten antihypertensive

Manufacturer: E.R. Squibb & Sons, Inc.
Ingredient: captopril
Dosage Form: Tablet: 12.5 mg; 25 mg; 50 mg; 100 mg (white)
Use: Treatment of high blood pressure; heart failure
Minor Side Effects: Dizziness; frequent urination; lightheadedness; loss of taste; swelling; weakness of face, hands, or feet
Major Side Effects: Chest pain; chills; fainting; fast or irregular heartbeat; fever; itching; skin rash; sore throat
Contraindications: This drug should not be taken by people who are allergic to it. Consult your doctor if this drug has been prescribed for you and you have such an allergy.
Warnings: This drug should be used cautiously by people with kidney diseases; blood disorders; elderly people; and women who are pregnant or nursing. Be sure your doctor knows if you fit any of these descriptions. • This drug should be used with caution with other medicines. Inform your doctor if you are taking any cancer medicines, diuretics, antihypertensive drugs, steroids, or potassium supplements. • Because this medicine may initially cause dizziness or fainting, your doctor may start you on a low dose and gradually increase it. • Do not use salt-substitutes or low-salt milk that contain potassium without first checking with your doctor. • Periodic kidney function tests and blood tests are recommended if this drug is prescribed for a long time. • While taking this drug, do not take any nonprescription item for weight control, cough, cold, or sinus problems without first checking with your doctor.
Comments: For maximum effect, take on an empty stomach one hour before meals. Take this drug exactly as directed. Do not take extra doses or skip doses without consulting your physician. • While taking this drug, you should limit

your consumption of alcoholic beverages, in order to minimize dizziness and lightheadedness. Sudden changes in posture may cause dizziness or light-headedness. To relieve this, contract and relax the muscles of your legs for a few moments before rising. Do this by pushing one foot against the floor while raising the other foot slightly, alternating feet so that your legs are in a pedaling motion. • Notify your physician if you develop mouth sores, sore throat, fever, chest pains, or swelling of hands or feet.

captopril antihypertensive (E. R. Squibb & Sons, Inc.), see Capoten anti-hypertensive.

Caquin steroid hormone and anti-infective (Forest Pharmaceutical), see Vioform-Hydrocortisone steroid hormone and anti-infective.

Carafate anti-ulcer

Manufacturer: Marion Laboratories, Inc.
Ingredient: sucralfate
Dosage Form: Tablet: 1 g (pink)
Use: Short-term treatment of ulcers
Minor Side Effects: Back pain; constipation; diarrhea; dizziness; dry mouth; indigestion; itching; nausea; rash; sleepiness; stomach upset
Major Side Effects: None
Contraindications: This drug should not be used by people who are allergic to it. Consult your doctor immediately if this drug has been prescribed for you and you have such an allergy.
Warnings: This drug should be used with caution by pregnant women or nursing mothers. • This drug should not be taken by people who are also taking tetracycline. Consult your doctor if both drugs have been prescribed for you or if you are taking vitamins A, D, E, or K in addition to this drug.
Comments: This drug has only been tested to be effective for short time periods (up to 8 weeks). • Take this drug on an empty stomach at least one hour before or two hours after a meal and at bedtime. • Do not take antacids within 30 minutes before or after taking this drug. • Continue taking this medication for the full time prescribed by your doctor, even if your symptoms disappear.

Cardizem anti-anginal

Manufacturer: Marion Labs.
Ingredient: diltiazem
Dosage Form: Tablet: 30 mg (green); 60 mg (yellow)
Use: Treatment of various types of angina
Minor Side Effects: Constipation; diarrhea; dizziness; drowsiness; fatigue; flushing; gastric upset; headache; increased frequency of urination; indigestion; lightheadedness; nausea; nervousness; weakness
Major Side Effects: Confusion; depression; fainting; hallucinations; low blood pressure; rapid or pounding heart rate; skin rash; swelling of the feet, ankles, or lower legs; tingling of hands or feet
Contraindications: This drug should not be used by people who are allergic to it. Consult your doctor immediately if this drug has been prescribed for you and you are allergic to it.
Warnings: This drug should be used cautiously by people with low blood pressure, certain heart diseases, kidney or liver disease, and by pregnant or

nursing women. Be sure your doctor knows if you have any of these conditions.
• This drug may interact with beta-blockers or digoxin. If you are taking either of these medicines, consult your doctor about their use. • This drug may make you dizzy. Avoid activities that require alertness; and avoid alcohol, which may exaggerate this effect.

Comments: Your physician may want to see you regularly to check your response to the therapy. • This drug must be taken as directed, not just for attacks.

Carmol HC topical steroid (Syntex Laboratories, Inc.), see hydrocortisone acetate topical steroid.

Catapres antihypertensive

Manufacturer: Boehringer Ingelheim Ltd.
Ingredient: clonidine hydrochloride
Dosage Form: Tablet: 0.1 mg (tan); 0.2 mg (orange); 0.3 mg (peach)
Use: Treatment of high blood pressure
Minor Side Effects: Anxiety; constipation; decreased sexual desire; depression; dizziness; drowsiness; dry eyes; dry mouth; fatigue; headache; increased sensitivity to alcohol; insomnia; itching; jaw pain; loss of appetite; nasal congestion; nausea; nervousness; nightmares; vomiting
Major Side Effects: Breathing difficulty; chest pain; cold feeling in fingertips or toes; enlarged breasts (in both sexes); hair loss; heart failure; hives; impotence; jaundice; pain; rash; rise in blood sugar; urine retention; weight gain
Contraindications: This drug should not be used by people who are allergic to it.
Warnings: This drug is not recommended for use by women who are pregnant or who may become pregnant. • This drug should be used cautiously by children. • This drug should be used with caution by persons with severe heart disease, stroke, a recent heart attack, mental depression, or chronic kidney failure. Be sure your doctor knows if you have any of these conditions. • This drug should not be used with alcohol, barbiturates, or other sedatives. If you are currently taking any drugs of these types, consult your doctor about their use. If you are unsure of the type or content of the medications you are taking, ask your doctor or pharmacist. • Tolerance to this drug develops occasionally; consult your doctor if you feel the drug is becoming less effective. Do not stop using this drug without consulting your doctor first. Your doctor will advise you on how to discontinue the drug gradually. • You should receive periodic eye examinations while taking this drug. • This drug can cause drowsiness; avoid tasks that require alertness. • To prevent oversedation, avoid the use of alcohol or other drugs with sedative properties.
Comments: Mild side effects from this drug (e.g., nasal congestion) are most noticeable during the first two weeks of therapy and become less bothersome after this period. • While taking this drug, do not take any nonprescription item for weight control or cough, cold, or sinus problems without first checking with your doctor. • To avoid dizziness or light-headedness when you stand, contract and relax the muscles of your legs for a few moments before rising. Do this by pushing one foot against the floor while raising the other foot slightly, alternating feet so that you are "pumping" your legs in a pedaling motion. • Chew gum or suck on ice chips or a piece of hard candy to reduce mouth dryness. • Take this drug exactly as directed. Do not take extra doses or skip a dose without first consulting your doctor.

Ceclor antibiotic

Manufacturer: Eli Lilly & Co.
Ingredient: cefaclor
Dosage Forms: Capsule: 250 mg (white/purple); 500 mg (gray/purple). Liquid (content per 5 ml teaspoon): 125 mg; 250 mg
Use: Treatment of a wide variety of bacterial infections
Minor Side Effects: Diarrhea; fatigue; heartburn; loss of appetite; nausea; rectal or vaginal itching; mouth sores; vomiting
Major Side Effects: Blood disorders; breathing difficulties; jaundice; kidney disease; rash; severe diarrhea; superinfection; tingling in hands and feet
Contraindications: This drug should not be used by people who are allergic to it or to other antibiotics similar to it. Consult your doctor immediately if this drug has been prescribed for you and you have such an allergy.
Warnings: This drug should be used cautiously by people who are allergic to penicillin or cephalosporin antibiotics or who have other allergies; by women who are pregnant or nursing; and by people with kidney disease. Be sure your doctor knows if you fit into any of these categories. • This drug should be used cautiously in newborn infants. • Prolonged use of this drug may allow organisms that are not susceptible to it to grow wildly. Do not use this drug unless your doctor has specifically told you to do so. Be sure to follow directions carefully and report any unusual reactions to your doctor at once. • This drug should be used cautiously in conjunction with diuretics, oral anticoagulants, and probenecid. • This drug may interfere with some blood tests. Be sure your doctor knows you are taking it. • Diabetics using Clinitest urine test may get a false high sugar reading. Change to Clinistix urine test or Tes-Tape urine test to avoid this problem.
Comments: It is generally believed that about 10 percent of all people who are allergic to penicillin will be allergic to an antibiotic like this as well. • This drug is frequently prescribed for infections that can be adequately treated with penicillin which is less expensive. Ask your doctor if you could take penicillin instead of this drug. You may be able to save money. • This drug should be taken for at least ten full days. • Take this drug with food or milk if stomach upset occurs. • The liquid form of this drug should be stored in the refrigerator. Any unused portion should be discarded after 14 days. Shake well before using.

cefadroxil antibiotic (Mead Johnson Pharmaceuticals; Bristol Laboratories), see Duricef antibiotic.

Cena-K potassium chloride replacement (Century Pharmaceuticals, Inc.), see potassium chloride replacement.

Centrax sedative and hypnotic

Manufacturer: Parke-Davis
Ingredient: prazepam
Dosage Forms: Capsule: 5 mg (light green); 10 mg (aqua); 20 mg. Tablet: 10 mg (light blue)
Use: Treatment of anxiety and its symptoms
Minor Side Effects: Confusion; constipation; depression; diarrhea; dizziness; drowsiness; dry mouth; excess saliva; fatigue; headache; heartburn; loss of appetite; nausea; sweating; vomiting
Major Side Effects: Blurred vision; difficult breathing; difficult urination; double vision; excitement; fever; hallucinations; jaundice; low blood pressure;

menstrual irregularities; mouth sores; rapid, pounding heart rate; rash; slurred speech; sore throat; stimulation; tremors; uncoordinated movements

Contraindications: This drug should not be given to children under six months of age. This drug should not be taken by persons with certain types of glaucoma or a severe mental disorder. This drug should not be taken by a pregnant or nursing woman. This drug should not be taken by people who are allergic to it. Consult your doctor immediately if you have any of these conditions or such an allergy.

Warnings: This drug should be used cautiously by people with epilepsy, respiratory problems, myasthenia gravis, prophyria, a history of drug abuse, or impaired liver or kidney function; and by the elderly or debilitated. Be sure your doctor knows if you fit into any of these categories. • This drug may cause drowsiness; avoid tasks that require alertness. • This drug should not be taken simultaneously with alcohol or other central nervous system depressants. Taken alone, this drug is safe; when it is combined with alcohol or other sedative drugs, serious adverse reactions may develop. • This drug should be used cautiously with phenytoin, cimetidine, and oral anticoagulants. • Do not stop taking this drug without informing your doctor. If you have been taking the drug regularly and wish to discontinue the drug's use, you must decrease the dose gradually, following your doctor's instruction. • This drug has the potential for abuse and must be used with caution. Tolerance may develop quickly; do not increase the dose without first consulting your doctor. • Persons taking this drug should have periodic blood counts and liver function tests.

Comments: This drug currently is used by many people to relieve nervousness. It is effective for this purpose, but it is important to try to remove the cause of the anxiety as well. • This drug may cause dryness of the mouth. To reduce this feeling, chew gum or suck on ice chips or a piece of hard candy. • To lessen stomach upset, take with food or a full glass of water. • The full effects of this drug may not be apparent until it has been taken for two to three days.

Cerespan vasodilator and smooth muscle relaxant (USV [P.R.] Development Corp.), see Pavabid Plateau Caps vasodilator and smooth muscle relaxant.

Cetamide ophthalmic solution and ointment (Alcon Laboratories, Inc.), see Sodium Sulamyd ophthalmic solution and ointment.

Cherapas diuretic and antihypertensive (Kay Pharmacal Co., Inc.), see Ser-Ap-Es diuretic and antihypertensive.

chlordiazepoxide hydrochloride sedative and hypnotic (various manufacturers), see Librium sedative and hypnotic.

Chlordinium sedative and anticholinergic (Lemmon Company), see Librax sedative and anticholinergic.

Chlorofon-F analgesic (Rugby Laboratories), see Parafon Forte analgesic.

Chloroserpine diuretic and antihypertensive (various manufacturers), see Diupres diuretic and antihypertensive.

chlorothiazide diuretic and antihypertensive (various manufacturers), see Diuril diuretic and antihypertensive.

chlorothiazide with reserpine diuretic and antihypertensive (various manufacturers), see Diupres diuretic and antihypertensive.

chlorpromazine hydrochloride phenothiazine (various manufacturers), see Thorazine phenothiazine.

chlorpropamide oral antidiabetic (various manufacturers), see Diabinese oral antidiabetic.

chlorthalidone diuretic and antihypertensive (various manufacturers), see Hygroton diuretic and antihypertensive.

Chlorzide diuretic and antihypertensive (Foy Laboratories), see hydrochlorothiazide diuretic and antihypertensive.

Chlorzone Forte analgesic (Henry Schein, Inc.), see Parafon Forte analgesic.

chlorzoxazone w/APAP analgesic (various manufacturers), see Parafon Forte analgesic.

Choledyl bronchodilator

Manufacturer: Parke-Davis
Ingredient: oxtriphylline
Dosage Forms: Liquid (content per 5 ml teaspoon): 100 mg. Tablet: 100 mg (red); 200 mg (yellow). Sustained-action tablet: 400 mg (pink); 600 mg (tan). Pediatric syrup (content per 5 ml teaspoon): 50 mg
Use: Relief of acute bronchial asthma and reversible bronchospasm associated with bronchitis and emphysema
Minor Side Effects: Central nervous system stimulation; flushing; gastric distress; headache; increased urination; insomnia; irritability; loss of appetite; nausea; nervousness
Major Side Effects: Convulsions; difficult breathing; muscle twitching; palpitations; skin rash; ulcer
Contraindications: This drug should not be used by anyone who is allergic to it, to theophylline, or to caffeine.
Warnings: This drug should be used cautiously by pregnant or nursing women. Women who may become pregnant should use this drug with caution. This drug should be used cautiously by people with high blood pressure; heart, liver, or kidney disease; glaucoma; enlarged prostate; thyroid disease; or stomach ulcer. • This drug should not be used with similar preparations, since adverse reactions, particularly central nervous system stimulation, may occur. Be sure your doctor knows if you are taking such preparations. This drug may interact with clindamycin, erythromycin, lincomycin, troleandomycin, phenobarbital, cimetidine, reserpine, benzodiazepine, lithium, and beta blockers. Ask your doctor or pharmacist if you are unsure of the nature of your medications.
Comments: This drug can cause gastrointestinal distress. It should be taken with food or milk. If you have severe stomach pain, vomiting, or restlessness, call your doctor. • Tolerance to this drug occurs infrequently; it is useful for long-term therapy for bronchospasm. • Be sure to take your dose at exactly the right time. • Do not crush the tablet form. • Drink at least eight to ten glasses of water each day. • Avoid drinking coffee, tea, cocoa, colas, or other beverages that contain caffeine while taking this drug. • Do not use over-the-counter items

for asthma while taking this drug, unless your doctor has told you to do so. •
Your smoking of tobacco may affect this drug's action. Be sure your doctor
knows you smoke if you are taking this drug. Also, do not suddenly stop
smoking without informing your doctor. • This drug may affect the results of
certain blood and urine tests. Tell your doctor you are taking this drug before
any tests.

**Cin-Quin anti-arrhythmic (Rowell Laboratories, Inc.), see quinidine
sulfate anti-arrhythmic.**

**Circanol vasodilator (Riker Laboratories, Inc.), see Hydergine
vasodilator.**

**Clindex sedative and anticholinergic (Rugby Laboratories), see
Librax sedative and anticholinergic.**

Clinoril anti-inflammatory

Manufacturer: Merck Sharp & Dohme
Ingredient: sulindac
Dosage Form: Tablet: 150 mg; 200 mg (both yellow)
Use: Reduction of pain, redness, and swelling due to acute or chronic
arthritis
Minor Side Effects: Abdominal pain; constipation; cramps; diarrhea; dry
mouth; gas; headache; heartburn; indigestion; itching; loss of appetite; nausea;
nervousness; nosebleed; sore mouth; vomiting
Major Side Effects: Chest tightness; chills; depression; dizziness; edema;
fever; gastrointestinal bleeding; headache; hearing loss; high blood pressure;
jaundice; kidney disease; menstrual irregularities; numbness or tingling in
fingers or toes; palpitations; peptic ulcer; psychosis; ringing in the ears; shortness of breath; skin rash; sore throat; swelling of the feet; visual disturbance;
weight gain; wheezing
Contraindications: This drug should not be taken by people who are allergic
to it or to aspirin or other nonsteroidal anti-inflammatory agents. Consult your
doctor immediately if this drug has been prescribed for you and you have such
an allergy.
Warnings: This drug should be used with caution by persons with asthma,
peptic ulcer, certain blood diseases, gastrointestinal bleeding, high blood
pressure, fluid retention, history of gastrointestinal disease, blood clotting
disorders, liver or kidney disease, or certain types of heart disease. Be sure
your doctor knows if you have any of these conditions. • This drug should not be
used by pregnant women, nursing mothers, and children. • Persons using this
drug who experience eye problems should immediately bring these symptoms
to their doctor's attention so that eye tests can be initiated. • This drug interacts
with aspirin, beta blockers, diuretics, phenytoin, and probenecid. People taking
anticoagulants and antidiabetics should be monitored carefully. If you are
currently taking any drugs of these types, consult your doctor about their use. If
you are unsure about the type or contents of your medications, ask your doctor
or pharmacist. • Do not stop taking this drug without informing your doctor. •
This drug may cause dizziness or blurred vision and therefore may impair your
ability to perform hazardous tasks, such as driving or operating machinery.
Comments: This drug is a potent pain reliever and is not intended for general
aches and pains. • Regular checkups by the doctor, including blood tests and
eye examinations, are required of persons taking this drug. • This drug must be
taken with food or milk. Never take this drug on an empty stomach or with

aspirin, and never take more than directed. • In numerous tests, this drug has been shown to be as effective as aspirin in the treatment of arthritis, but aspirin is still the drug of choice for the disease. Because of the high cost of this drug, consult your doctor about prescribing proper doses of aspirin instead. • Do not take aspirin or alcohol while taking this drug without first consulting your doctor. • You should note improvement in your condition soon after you start using this drug; however, full benefit may not be obtained for as long as a month. It is important not to stop taking this drug even though symptoms have diminished or disappeared. • This drug is not a substitute for rest, physical therapy, or other measures recommended by your doctor.

Clinoxide sedative and anticholinergic (Geneva Generics, Inc.), see Librax sedative and anticholinergic.

Clipoxide sedative and anticholinergic (Henry Schein, Inc.), see Librax sedative and anticholinergic.

Codap analgesic (Reid-Provident Labs., Inc.), see acetaminophen with codeine analgesic.

Codoxy analgesic (Halsey Drug Co., Inc.), see Percodan analgesic.

Cogentin antiparkinson drug

Manufacturer: Merck Sharp & Dohme
Ingredient: benztropine mesylate
Dosage Form: Tablet: 0.5 mg; 1 mg; 2 mg (all white)
Use: Treatment of symptoms of Parkinson's disease or control of side effects of phenothiazines
Minor Side Effects: Bloating; blurred vision; constipation; depression; dizziness; drowsiness; dry mouth; headache; increased sensitivity of eyes to light; mild nausea; nervousness; reduced sweating; weakness
Major Side Effects: Difficult urination; hallucinations; involuntary muscular movements; numbness of the fingers; palpitations. Some people with arteriosclerosis or with a history of abnormal reactions to other drugs may exhibit symptoms of mental confusion, agitation, disturbed behavior, or nausea and vomiting; psychiatric disturbances can result from indiscriminate use leading to overdosage; narrow-angle glaucoma has also been reported.
Contraindications: This drug should not be taken by people with narrow-angle glaucoma, intestinal obstructions, stomach ulcers, enlarged prostate gland, urinary tract blockage, myasthenia gravis, achalasia, or by people who are allergic to it. Consult your doctor if this drug has been prescribed for you and you have any of these conditions. Children under the age of three should not use this drug.
Warnings: People treated with this drug should have close monitoring of intraocular pressures at regular, periodic intervals. • Careful and constant long-term observation of people using this drug should be undertaken to avoid allergic and certain other reactions. • This drug should be used with caution by people with heart, liver, or kidney disorders; or with high blood pressure, thyroid disease, or alcoholism. People with any of these conditions should be under close medical observation. This drug should be used with caution by people with glaucoma; obstructive diseases of the intestine or bowel; pregnant women; and by elderly males with possible prostate gland problems. If you have any of these conditions, be sure your doctor knows. • Persons over 60 years of age require strict dosage regulation; they frequently develop increased

sensitivity to this drug. • This drug may cause dizziness or drowsiness; avoid tasks that require alertness.

Comments: This drug is frequently prescribed along with phenothiazine drugs such as Thorazine and Stelazine to reduce the tremors caused by phenothiazines. You should talk with your doctor about waiting before taking this drug to see if you really need it. Many people can take phenothiazine drugs successfully and may not need this drug. • Do not stop taking this drug without first consulting with your physician. • This drug may cause dryness of the mouth; chew gum or suck on ice chips or a piece of hard candy to reduce this feeling. • Because this drug reduces sweating, avoid excessive work or exercise in hot weather. • Certain other drugs, such as Artane (Lederle Laboratories) and Kemadrin (Burroughs Wellcome Co.) antiparkinson drugs, have actions similar to those of this drug. • If this drug makes it hard for you to urinate, try to do so just before each dose.

ColBENEMID uricosuric (Merck Sharp & Dohme), see Benemid uricosuric.

Combagen anticholinergic and phenothiazine (Goldline Labs.), see Combid Spansule anticholinergic and phenothiazine.

Combid Spansule anticholinergic and phenothiazine

Manufacturer: Smith Kline & French Laboratories
Ingredients: isopropamide iodide; prochlorperazine maleate
Equivalent Products: Combagen, Goldline Labs.; Isopro T.D., Rugby Laboratories; Prochlor-Iso, Henry Schein, Inc.; Pro-Iso, Geneva Generics, Inc., various manufacturers
Dosage Form: Capsule: isopropamide iodide, 5 mg; prochlorperazine maleate, 10 mg (yellow/clear with multicolored pellets)
Use: Treatment of intestinal or stomach disorders, including peptic ulcer
Minor Side Effects: Bloating; blurred vision; difficulty ejaculating; dizziness; drooling; drowsiness; dry mouth; fast heart rate; flaking skin; fever; headache; increased sensitivity to light; insomnia; itching; jitteriness; menstrual irregularities; nasal congestion; nausea; nervousness; reduced sweating; restlessness
Major Side Effects: Back pain; blood disorders; bruising; cardiac arrest; constipation; convulsions; difficult breathing; difficult swallowing; difficult urination; enlarged breasts (in both sexes); fluid retention; impotence; involuntary movements of the face, tongue, mouth, or jaw; jaundice; low blood pressure; muscle stiffness; pain in eye; palpitations; rash; sore throat; tremors; uncoordinated movements
Contraindications: This drug should not be used by people suffering drug-induced depression; or who have blood disease, liver disease, jaundice, glaucoma, enlarged prostate, obstructed intestine, or obstructed bladder; or an allergy to the drug or any of its components. This drug may disguise symptoms of brain tumor or obstructed intestine and should not be used by people in whom either condition is suspected. Consult your doctor immediately if this drug has been prescribed for you and you have, or might have, any of these conditions. • This drug should not be used by children under the age of 12.
Warnings: This drug should be used cautiously by pregnant or nursing women; the elderly; and people who have a past history of epilepsy, thyroid disease, myasthenia gravis, jaundice, liver disease, blood disease, or allergy to other drugs. Be sure your doctor knows if any of these conditions apply to you. • This drug interacts with amantadine, anticonvulsants, haloperidol, antacids, other phenothiazines, other anticholinergics, alcohol, and depressants; if you

are currently taking any drugs of these types, consult your doctor about their use. If you are unsure of the type or contents of your medications, ask your doctor or pharmacist. • This drug may cause drowsiness; avoid tasks that require alertness. • To prevent oversedation, avoid the use of alcohol or other drugs that have sedative properties. • This drug may cause discoloration of urine; this is harmless. • This drug may influence the results of thyroid function tests; remind your doctor that you are taking the drug if you are scheduled for a thyroid test.

Comments: The effects of therapy with this drug may not be apparent for at least two weeks. • This drug does not cure ulcers but may help them improve. • Chew gum or suck on ice chips or a piece of hard candy to reduce mouth dryness. • To avoid dizziness or light-headedness when you stand, contract and relax the muscles of your legs for a few moments before rising. Do this by pushing one foot against the floor while raising the other foot slightly, alternating feet so that you are "pumping" your legs in a pedaling motion. • This drug has sustained action; never take it more frequently than your doctor prescribes. A serious overdose could result. • Because this drug reduces sweating, avoid excessive work or exercise in hot weather. • Call your doctor if you notice a rash, flushing, or pain in the eye. • This drug may cause tumors in rats. This effect has not been shown to occur in humans. • If this drug makes it hard for you to urinate, try to do so just before you take each dose. • If you notice fine tremors of your tongue, call your doctor.

Compazine phenothiazine

Manufacturer: Smith Kline & French Laboratories
Ingredient: prochlorperazine
Equivalent Product: prochlorperazine, various manufacturers
Dosage Forms: Liquid concentrate (per ml): 10 mg. Suppository: 2.5 mg; 5 mg; 25 mg. Time-release capsule: 10 mg; 15 mg; 30 mg (all are black/clear with yellow and white beads). Tablet: 5 mg; 10 mg; 25 mg (all yellow)
Use: Control of severe nausea and vomiting; relief of certain kinds of anxiety, tension, agitation, psychiatric disorders
Minor Side Effects: Blurred vision; constipation; diarrhea; dizziness; drooling; drowsiness; dry mouth; fatigue; headache; impotence; insomnia; jitteriness; loss of appetite; milk production; nasal congestion; nausea; photosensitivity; reduced sweating; restlessness; tremors; weakness
Major Side Effects: Asthma; arthritis; blood disorders; breast enlargement; convulsions; difficult urination; eye changes; fever; fluid retention; heart attack; involuntary movements of the mouth, face, neck, and tongue; liver damage; low blood pressure; menstrual irregularities; mouth sores; palpitations; rash; skin darkening; sore throat
Contraindications: This drug should not be taken by people who have blood diseases or severe high or low blood pressure or by those who are suffering drug-induced depression. Consult your doctor immediately if this drug has been prescribed for you and you have such a condition. This drug should not be given to people who are comatose or to children undergoing surgery.
Warnings: This drug should be used cautiously by people with glaucoma; liver, lung, brain, or kidney disease; Parkinson's disease; diabetes; epilepsy; breast cancer; ulcers; or an enlarged prostate gland and by pregnant women and people who have previously had an allergic reaction to any phenothiazine. Be sure your doctor knows if you fit into any of these categories. • This drug may cause drowsiness; avoid tasks that require alertness. To prevent oversedation, avoid the use of alcohol or other drugs that have sedative properties.
• This drug interacts with oral antacids or anticholinergics; if you are currently taking any drugs of these types, consult your doctor about their use. If you are

unsure of the type or contents of your medications, ask your doctor or pharmacist. • When taking this drug, do not take any nonprescription item for cough, cold, or sinus problems without first checking with your doctor. • This drug may cause motor restlessness, uncoordinated movements, and muscle spasms. If you notice any of these effects, the drug should be discontinued or the dosage should be adjusted. Contact your doctor immediately if you notice any such symptoms. • This drug may cause urine to turn pink or red-brown; this is harmless. • Children with acute illnesses should take this drug only under close supervision. Their dosage may need adjustment. • If you take this drug for a prolonged time, it may be desirable for you to stop taking it for a while in order to see if you still need it. However, do not stop taking the drug without talking to your doctor first. You may have to reduce your dosage gradually.

Comments: The effects of this drug may not be apparent for at least two weeks. • Chew gum or suck on ice chips or a piece of hard candy to reduce mouth dryness. • To avoid dizziness or light-headedness when you stand, contract and relax the muscles of your legs for a few moments before rising. Do this by pushing one foot against the floor while raising the other foot slightly, alternating feet so that you are "pumping" your legs in a pedaling motion. • Because this drug reduces sweating, avoid excessive work or exercise in hot weather. • The liquid concentrate form of this drug should be added to 60 ml (2 fluid ounces) or more of water, milk, juice, coffee, tea, or a carbonated beverage, or to pulpy foods (applesauce, etc.) immediately prior to administration. • The capsule form of this drug has sustained action. Never take it more frequently than your doctor prescribes. A serious overdose may result. • If you notice a sore throat, darkening vision, or fine tremors of your tongue, call your doctor. • Some side effects caused by this drug can be prevented by taking an antiparkinson drug. Discuss this with your doctor. • This drug may cause tumors in rats. This effect has not been shown to occur in humans. • This drug may interfere with certain blood and urine laboratory tests.

Condrin-LA antihistamine and adrenergic (Mallard, Inc.) see Ornade Spansule antihistamine and adrenergic.

conjugated estrogens hormone (various manufacturers), see Premarin estrogen hormone.

Constant-T bronchodilator (Geigy Pharmaceuticals), see Theo-dur bronchodilator.

contraceptives (oral), see oral contraceptives.

Cordamine-PA Tabs antihistamine and decongestant (Cord), see Dimetapp antihistamine and decongestant.

Cordilate anti-anginal (Foy Laboratories), see Persantine anti-anginal.

Corgard beta blocker

Manufacturer: E. R. Squibb & Sons, Inc.
Ingredient: nadolol
Dosage Form: Tablet: 40 mg; 80 mg; 120 mg; 160 mg (blue)
Use: Treatment of angina pectoris and high blood pressure
Minor Side Effects: Abdominal pain; bloating; blurred vision; constipation;

drowsiness; dry eyes, mouth, or skin; gas or heartburn; headache; insomnia; loss of appetite; nasal congestion; nausea; slowed heart rate; sweating; vivid dreams; vomiting

Major Side Effects: Bleeding or bruising; confusion; decreased sexual ability; depression; diarrhea; difficult urination; dizziness; earache; fever; hair loss; hallucinations; mouth sores; night cough; nightmares; numbness and tingling in the fingers and toes; rash; ringing in the ears; shortness of breath; swelling in the hands or feet

Contraindications: This drug should not be used by people who are allergic to nadolol or any other beta blocker. This drug should not be taken by people who suffer from certain types of heart disease or lung disease or anyone who has taken any monoamine oxidase inhibitors within the past two weeks. Consult your doctor immediately if this drug has been prescribed for you and you fit any of these categories.

Warnings: This drug should be used with caution by persons with certain respiratory problems, diabetes, certain heart problems, liver and kidney diseases, hypoglycemia, or thyroid disease. Be sure your doctor knows if you have any of these conditions. • This drug should be used cautiously by pregnant women and by women of childbearing age. • This drug should be used with care during anesthesia and by patients undergoing major surgery. If possible, this drug should be withdrawn 48 hours prior to surgery. • This drug should be used cautiously when reserpine is taken. • This drug is a potent medication, and it should not be stopped abruptly.

Comments: Your doctor may want you to take your pulse every day while you take this medication. Consult your doctor. • Be sure to take your medication doses at the same time each day. • While taking this drug, do not take any nonprescription items for cough, cold, or sinus problems without first checking with your doctor. • Notify your doctor if dizziness or diarrhea develops.

Corque steroid hormone and anti-infective (Geneva Generics, Inc.), see Vioform-Hydrocortisone steroid hormone and anti-infective.

Cortan steroid hormone (Halsey Drug Co., Inc.), see prednisone steroid hormone.

Cortef Acetate topical steroid (The Upjohn Company), see hydrocortisone acetate topical steroid.

Cortef steroid hormone (The Upjohn Company), see hydrocortisone steroid hormone.

Cortin steroid hormone and anti-infective (C & M Pharmacal, Inc.), see Vioform-Hydrocortisone steroid hormone and anti-infective.

cortisol steroid hormone (various manufacturers), see hydrocortisone steroid hormone.

Cortisporin ophthalmic suspension

Manufacturer: Burroughs Wellcome Co.
Ingredients: polymyxin B sulfate; neomycin sulfate; hydrocortisone; thimerosal, bacitracin (ointment only)
Dosage Forms: Drop (content per ml): polymyxin B sulfate, 10,000 units;

neomycin sulfate, 0.5%; hydrocortisone, 1%; thimerosal, 0.001%. Ointment (content per gram): hydrocortisone, 1%; bacitracin, 400 units; neomycin sulfate, 0.5%; polymyxin B sulfate, 5000 units

Use: Short-term treatment of bacterial infections of the eye

Minor Side Effects: Blurred vision; burning; stinging

Major Side Effects: Disturbed or reduced vision; eye pain; headache; severe irritation

Contraindications: This product should not be used for fungal or viral infections of the eye or for eye infections with pus. Nor should this product be used for conditions involving the back part of the eye. This drug should not be used by people who are allergic to any of its ingredients or by those with tuberculosis. Consult your doctor immediately if this drug has been prescribed for you and you have any of these conditions.

Warnings: Frequent eye examinations are advisable while this drug is being used, particularly if it is necessary to use the drug for an extended period of time. • This drug should be used cautiously by people with inner ear disease, kidney disease, or myasthenia gravis. • Prolonged use of this drug may result in glaucoma, secondary infection, cataracts, and eye damage. Contact your doctor immediately if you notice any visual disturbances (dimming or blurring of vision, reduced night vision, halos around lights), eye pain, or headache.

Comments: As with all eyedrops, this drug may cause minor, temporary clouding or blurring of vision when first applied. • Discard any unused portion of this drug. • Consult your doctor if symptoms reappear. • This product should be shaken well before using. • Be careful about the contamination of medications used for the eyes. Wash your hands before administering eyedrops. Do not touch the dropper to the eye. Do not wash or wipe the dropper before replacing it in the bottle. Close the bottle tightly to keep out moisture. • See the chapter on Administering Medication Correctly for instructions on using eyedrops.

Cortisporin
otic solution/suspension

Manufacturer: Burroughs Wellcome Co.

Ingredients: hydrocortisone; neomycin sulfate; polymyxin B sulfate

Equivalent Products: AK-Sporin H.C. Otic, Akorn-Inc.; BaySporin Otic, Bay Pharmaceuticals, Inc.; Ortega Otic M, Ortega Pharmaceutical Co.; Otobione Otic, Schering Corp.

Dosage Forms: Solution (per ml): hydrocortisone, 1%; neomycin sulfate, 5 mg; polymyxin B sulfate, 10,000 units. Suspension (per ml): hydrocortisone, 1%; neomycin sulfate, 5 mg; polymyxin B sulfate, 10,000 units

Use: Treatment of superficial bacterial infections of the outer ear

Minor Side Effects: Burning sensation; hives; itching

Major Side Effects: None

Contraindications: This drug should not be used to treat viral or fungal infections. This drug should not be taken by people who are allergic to it. Consult your doctor immediately if you have such a condition or such an allergy.

Warnings: This drug should not be used for more than ten days. • This drug should be used cautiously if there is a possibility that the patient has a punctured eardrum. • This drug should be used cautiously by persons with myasthenia gravis or kidney disease. • Notify your doctor if your skin becomes red and swollen, scaly, or itchy; allergic reactions to neomycin are common.

Comments: To administer eardrops, tilt your head to one side with the affected ear turned upward. Grasp the earlobe and pull it upward and back to straighten the ear canal. (If administering eardrops to a child, gently pull the earlobe downward and back.) Fill the dropper and place the prescribed number of drops in the ear. Be careful not to touch the dropper to the ear canal, as the dropper can easily become contaminated this way. Keep the ear tilted upward for five to ten seconds, then gently insert a small piece of cotton into the ear to prevent the drops from escaping. • Do not wash or wipe the dropper after use. Close the bottle tightly to keep out moisture. • Discard any remaining medicine after treatment has been completed so that you will not be tempted to use the medication for a subsequent ear problem without consulting a doctor. • If you wish to warm the drops before administration, roll the bottle back and forth between your hands. Do not place the bottle in boiling water.

Cotrim and Cotrim DS antibacterials (Lemmon Company), see Bactrim and Bactrim DS antibacterials.

Coumadin anticoagulant

Manufacturer: Du Pont, Inc.
Ingredient: sodium warfarin
Equivalent Products: Coufarin, Bolar Pharmaceutical Co., Inc.; Panwarfin, Abbott Laboratories; sodium warfarin, various manufacturers
Dosage Form: Tablet: 2 mg (lavender); 2.5 mg (orange); 5 mg (peach); 7.5 mg (yellow); 10 mg (white)
Use: Prevention of blood clot formation in conditions such as heart disease
Minor Side Effects: Blurred vision; cramps; decreased appetite; diarrhea; heavy bleeding from cuts; nausea
Major Side Effects: Black stools; coughing up blood; fever; hemorrhage; jaundice; loss of hair; mouth sores; nausea; rash; red urine; severe headache
Contraindications: This drug should not be taken if any condition or circumstance exists in which bleeding is likely to be worsened by taking the drug (such as ulcers or certain surgeries). Be sure that you have given your doctor a complete medical history. • This drug should not be taken by people who are allergic to it or by pregnant women. Consult your doctor immediately if this drug has been prescribed for you and you have either condition.
Warnings: This drug should be used cautiously by people who have any condition where bleeding is an added risk, including those suffering malnutrition; or who have liver disease, kidney disease, intestinal infection, wounds or injuries, high blood pressure, blood disease (certain types), diabetes, menstrual difficulties, indwelling catheters, and congestive heart failure. The drug should be used cautiously by nursing mothers. Be sure your doctor knows if you have any of these conditions. • This drug interacts with alcohol, allopurinol, aminosalicylic acid, anabolic steroids, antibiotics, antidepressants, antipyrine, Bactrim/Septra, barbiturates, bromelains, chloral hydrate, chloramphenicol, chlordiazepoxide, chlorpropamide, cholestyramine, chymotrypsin, cimetidine, cinchophen, clofibrate, dextran, dextrothyroxine, diazoxide, diuretics, disulfiram, ethacrynic acid, ethchlorvynol, glucagon, glutethimide, griseofulvin, haloperidol, indomethacin, mefenamic acid, meprobamate, methyldopa, methylphenidate, metronidazole, monoamine oxidase inhibitors, nalidixic acid, neomycin, oral antidiabetics, oral contraceptives, oxolinic acid, oxyphenbutazone, paraldehyde, phenylbutazone, phenytoin, primidone, quinidine, quinine, rifampin, salicylates, steroids, sulfinpyrazone, sulfonamides, sulindac, thyroid drugs, tolbutamide, triclofos sodium, and vitamin C. If you are currently taking any drugs of these types, consult your doctor about their use. If you are unsure of the type or contents of your medications, ask your doctor or pharmacist.
Comments: Do not start or stop taking any other medication, including aspirin, without checking with your doctor. • Regular blood coagulation tests are essential while you are taking this drug. Many factors—including diet,

environment, exercise, and other medications—may affect your response to this drug, so blood tests will need to be repeated often. If clots fail to form over cuts and bruises, or if purple or brown spots appear under bruised skin, call your doctor immediately. ● Do not increase your dose or take this drug more frequently than your doctor prescribes. ● While taking this drug, avoid drinking alcoholic beverages. ● A change in urine color may or may not be serious; if you notice a change, contact your doctor. ● Be sure all of your health care professionals know you are taking this drug.

Curretab progesterone hormone (Reid-Provident Labs., Inc.), see Provera progesterone hormone.

Cycline-250 antibiotic (Scrip-Physician Supply Co.), see tetracycline hydrochloride antibiotic.

Cyclopar antibiotic (Parke-Davis), see tetracycline hydrochloride antibiotic.

cyproheptadine hydrochloride antihistamine (various manufacturers), see Periactin antihistamine.

Dalmane hypnotic

Manufacturer: Roche Products, Inc.
Ingredient: flurazepam hydrochloride
Dosage Form: Capsule: 15 mg (orange/ivory); 30 mg (red/ivory)
Use: Sleeping aid
Minor Side Effects: Bitter taste in mouth; constipation; depression; diarrhea; dizziness; drowsiness; dry mouth; fatigue; flushing; headache; heartburn; loss of appetite; nausea; nervousness; sweating; vomiting
Major Side Effects: Blurred vision; chest pain; depression; difficult urination; double vision; fainting; falling; jaundice; joint pain; low blood pressure; mouth sores; nightmares; palpitations; rash; shortness of breath; slurred speech; sore throat; stimulation; uncoordinated movements
Contraindications: This drug should not be taken by people who are allergic to it. Consult your doctor immediately if this drug has been prescribed for you and you have such an allergy.
Warnings: This drug should be used cautiously by people with impaired liver or kidney function, lung disease, or myasthenia gravis; the elderly or debilitated; people who are severely depressed; and pregnant women. Be sure your doctor knows if you fit into any of these categories. ● This drug is not recommended for use by people under the age of 15. ● This drug may cause drowsiness; avoid tasks that require alertness. ● Periodic blood counts and liver function tests should be performed if this drug is used over a long period. ● To prevent oversedation, this drug should not be taken with alcohol and other sedative drugs or central nervous system depressants. This drug may interact with cimetidine, oral anticoagulants, disulfiram, isoniazid, and rifampin. If you are currently taking any drugs of these types, consult your doctor about their use. If you are unsure of the type or contents of your medications, ask your doctor or pharmacist. ● This drug has the potential for abuse and must be used with caution. Tolerance may develop quickly; do not increase the dose of the drug without first consulting your doctor. ● This is a safe drug when used alone. When it is combined with other sedative drugs or alcohol, serious adverse reactions may develop. ● This drug should not be stopped suddenly. The dosage should be reduced gradually. Consult your doctor.

Comments: This drug currently is widely used for inducing sleep. It is effective, but eliminating the cause of the insomnia is also important. • This drug should be taken 30 to 60 minutes before retiring. • Take this medication with food or a full glass of water if stomach upset occurs. Do not take it with a dose of antacids since they may retard absorption of the drug. • This drug may cause a feeling of dry mouth. To reduce this feeling, chew gum or suck on ice chips.

D-Amp antibiotic (Dunhall Pharmaceuticals, Inc.), see ampicillin antibiotic.

Darvocet-N analgesic

Manufacturer: Eli Lilly & Co.
Ingredients: propoxyphene napsylate; acetaminophen
Dosage Form: Darvocet-N 50: Tablet: propoxyphene napsylate, 50 mg; acetaminophen, 325 mg (orange). Darvocet-N 100: Tablet: propoxyphene napsylate, 100 mg; acetaminophen, 650 mg (orange)
Use: Relief of mild to moderate pain
Minor Side Effects: Abdominal pain; blurred vision; constipation; dizziness; drowsiness; euphoria; fatigue; headache; light-headedness; loss of appetite; nausea; restlessness; sedation; vomiting; weakness
Major Side Effects: Diarrhea; hives; liver dysfunction; palpitations; rash; ringing in the ears; seizures; sore throat; stomach cramps; troubled breathing
Contraindications: This drug should not be used by persons allergic to either of its ingredients. Consult your doctor immediately if this drug has been prescribed for you and you have such an allergy.
Warnings: This drug should be used cautiously by people with heart, lung, liver, or kidney disease or with blood disorders; it should be used cautiously by pregnant or nursing women. Be sure your doctor knows if you have any of these conditions. • This drug is not recommended for use by children under 12. • This drug has the potential for abuse and must be used with caution. Tolerance may develop quickly; do not increase the dose of the drug without consulting your doctor. • This drug can cause drowsiness; avoid tasks that require alertness. • To prevent oversedation, avoid alcohol and other drugs that have sedative properties. • This drug should be used with extreme caution by patients taking tranquilizers or antidepressant drugs. If you are currently taking any drugs of these types, consult your doctor about their use. If you are unsure of the type or contents of your medications, ask your doctor or pharmacist.
Comments: Aspirin or acetaminophen should be tried before therapy with this drug is undertaken. If aspirin or acetaminophen does not relieve pain, this drug may be effective. • You may want to ask your doctor to prescribe an inexpensive generic brand of propoxyphene hydrochloride instead of the napsylate form. It will be less expensive and the napsylate form is converted to hydrochloride once it is in the stomach. • Side effects from this drug may be somewhat relieved by lying down. • This drug may interfere with certain urine laboratory tests. Tell your doctor you are taking this drug before any urine tests.

Darvon Compound-65 analgesic

Manufacturer: Eli Lilly & Co.
Ingredients: aspirin; caffeine; propoxyphene hydrochloride
Equivalent Products: Bexophene, Mallard, Inc.; Dolene Compound 65,

Lederle Laboratories; Doxaphene Compound, Major Pharmaceuticals; propoxyphene hydrochloride compound, various manufacturers; SK-65 Compound, Smith Kline & French Laboratories

Dosage Form: Capsule: aspirin, 389 mg; caffeine, 32.4 mg; propoxyphene hydrochloride, 65 mg (crimson/light gray)

Use: Relief of mild to moderate pain

Minor Side Effects: Abdominal pain; anxiety; blurred vision; constipation; dizziness; drowsiness; euphoria; headache; indigestion; light-headedness; nausea; restlessness; ringing in the ears; sedation; vomiting; weakness

Major Side Effects: Chest tightness; kidney disease; liver dysfunction; rash; seizures; shortness of breath; sore throat

Contraindications: This drug should not be used by people allergic to any of its ingredients. It may cause allergic reactions and should not, therefore, be taken by people who have asthma, severe hay fever, or other significant allergies. Be sure your doctor knows if you have such a condition.

Warnings: This drug should be used cautiously by pregnant or nursing women, by children under 12, and by persons with diabetes, ulcers, and liver or kidney disease. Be sure your doctor knows if you are pregnant or nursing. • Persons who take this drug in high doses over long periods may develop kidney disease. Follow your doctor's dosage instructions carefully. • This drug may cause drowsiness; avoid tasks that require alertness. • To prevent oversedation, avoid the use of alcohol or other central nervous system depressants or drugs that have sedative qualities. • This drug should not be used in conjunction with alcohol, methotrexate, oral anticoagulants, orphenadrine, probenecid, or sulfinpyrazone. If you are currently taking any drugs of these types, consult your doctor about their use. If you are unsure of the type or contents of your medications, ask your doctor or pharmacist. • This drug has the potential for abuse and must be used with caution. Tolerance may develop quickly; do not increase the dose of this drug without first consulting your doctor. • If your ears feel unusual, or you hear buzzing or ringing, or if your stomach hurts, your dosage may need adjustment. Call your doctor.

Comments: An aspirin or acetaminophen product should be tried before this drug. If aspirin or acetaminophen does not relieve pain, this drug may be effective. • Side effects from this drug may be somewhat relieved by lying down.

Deapril-ST vasodilator (Mead Johnson Co.), see Hydergine vasodilator.

Deconade antihistamine and adrenergic (H. L. Moore, Inc.), see Ornade Spansule antihistamine and adrenergic.

Decongestabs adrenergic and antihistamine (various manufacturers), see Naldecon adrenergic and antihistamine.

Delapav vasodilator and smooth muscle relaxant (Dunhall Pharmaceuticals, Inc.), see Pavabid Plateau Caps vasodilator and smooth muscle relaxant.

Deltamycin antibiotic (Trimen Laboratories, Inc.), see tetracycline hydrochloride antibiotic.

Deltapen-VK antibiotic (Trimen Laboratories, Inc.), see penicillin potassium phenoxymethyl (penicillin VK) antibiotic.

Deltasone steroid hormone (The Upjohn Company), see prednisone steroid hormone.

Depletite anorectic (Reid-Provident Labs., Inc.), see Tenuate anorectic.

Desyrel antidepressant

Manufacturer: Mead Johnson Co.
Ingredient: trazodone
Dosage Form: Tablet: 50 mg (orange); 100 mg (white); 150 mg (orange)
Use: Relief of depression
Minor Side Effects: Bad taste in mouth; blurred vision; constipation; diarrhea; dizziness; drowsiness; dry mouth; headache; insomnia; lightheadedness; loss of appetite; nasal congestion; weight loss or gain
Major Side Effects: Chest pain; decreased sexual desire; disorientation; fluid retention; memory loss; nightmares; numbness; rapid heart beat; seizures; shortness of breath; skin rash; tingling in fingers or toes; tremors; uncoordinated movements
Contraindications: This drug should not be taken by people who are allergic to it; by those with a history of alcoholism; by anyone with liver or kidney disease; or those who have recently had a heart attack. Consult your doctor immediately if this drug has been prescribed for you and you fit any of these categories.
Warnings: This drug is not recommended for use by children under age 18. ● This drug should be used cautiously by people who have certain types of heart disease and by pregnant or nursing women. Be sure your doctor knows if you fit any of these conditions. ● This drug interacts with digoxin, phenytoin, clonidine, and barbiturates. If you are also taking antihypertensive drugs you may require a decreased dose. If you are taking any drugs of these types, consult your doctor about their use. If you are unsure of the type or contents of your medicines, ask your doctor or pharmacist. ● This drug should be used with caution by people who are receiving electroshock therapy or those about to undergo surgery. ● This drug may cause drowsiness; avoid tasks that require alertness. To prevent oversedation, avoid the use of alcohol or other sedative agents.
Comments: Take this medicine exactly as your physician prescribes. Do not stop taking it without first checking with your doctor. ● While taking this drug, do not take any nonprescription item for cough, cold, sinus, or weight problems without first checking with your doctor or pharmacist. ● To minimize dizziness and lightheadedness, take this medicine with food. Chew gum or suck ice chips or hard candy to reduce dry mouth. ● To avoid dizziness or lightheadedness when you stand, contract and relax the muscles of your legs for a few minutes before rising. Do this by pushing one foot against the floor while raising the other foot slightly, alternating feet so that you are "pumping" your legs in a pedaling motion.

Diabinese oral antidiabetic

Manufacturer: Pfizer Laboratories Division
Ingredient: chlorpropamide
Equivalent Product: chlorpropamide, various manufacturers
Dosage Form: Tablet: 100 mg; 250 mg (both blue)

Use: Treatment of diabetes mellitus

Minor Side Effects: Cramps; diarrhea; dizziness; fatigue; headache; heartburn; increased sensitivity to sun; loss of appetite; nausea; stomach upset; vomiting; weakness

Major Side Effects: Anemia; difficult breathing; fluid retention; jaundice; low blood sugar; numbness or tingling of fingers and toes; rash; ringing in the ears; sore throat

Contraindications: This drug should not be used by people with juvenile or insulin-dependent diabetes (see Comments); severe or unstable "brittle" diabetes; diabetes complicated by ketosis and acidosis, major surgery, severe infection, or severe trauma; or severe liver, thyroid, or kidney disease. Be sure your doctor knows if you have any of these conditions. This drug should not be used by pregnant women or women of childbearing age.

Warnings: This drug should be used cautiously by people with Addison's disease. If you have this disease, be sure your doctor knows. • If you have any signs of liver damage, such as jaundice, itching, rash, dark urine, low-grade fever, sore throat, or diarrhea, call your doctor. • This drug should be used cautiously in conjunction with alcohol, antibacterial sulfonamides, anticonvulsants, barbiturates, chloramphenicol, dicumarol, guanethidine, monoamine oxidase inhibitors, oral anticoagulants, oral contraceptives, phenylbutazone, probenecid, rifampin, salicylates, or steroids. If you are currently taking any drugs of these types, consult your doctor about their use. If you are unsure of the type or contents of your medications, ask your doctor or pharmacist. • Use of this drug in combination with certain other drugs may bring about hypoglycemia. When starting this drug, your urine should be tested for sugar and acetone at least three times daily and your doctor should review the results at least once a week. Your doctor may also want you to have frequent laboratory tests of liver function. • This drug should not be used as a substitute for diet regulation, weight control, exercise control, proper hygiene, or prompt care of infection. • It takes from three to five days for complete elimination of this drug from the body. Thus, accidental ingestion of the drug necessitates close supervision for this period, even if recovery seems to have occurred. • It may be necessary for you to use insulin while taking this drug, particularly during the transition period from insulin to this oral antidiabetic.

Comments: Oral antidiabetic drugs, such as this drug, are not effective in the treatment of diabetes in children under age 12. • Studies have shown that a balanced diet and exercise program may be just as effective as this drug. However, drugs of this type allow diabetics more leeway in their lifestyles. Nonetheless, persons taking this drug should carefully watch their diet and exercise program. • During the first six weeks of therapy with this drug, visit your doctor at least once a week. • While taking this drug, check your urine for sugar and ketones at least three times a day. • You will have to be switched to insulin therapy if complications (e.g., ketoacidosis, severe trauma, severe infection, diarrhea, nausea, or vomiting) or the need for major surgery develop. • This drug should be taken at the same time each day. • Ask your doctor how to recognize the first signs of low blood sugar. • Do not use alcohol while taking this drug. Avoid the use of any other drugs, including nonprescription cold remedies and aspirin, unless your doctor tells you to take them. • You may sunburn easily while taking this product. Avoid exposure to the sun as much as possible. • You may retain fluid while taking this drug. Be careful to watch for swollen feet or hands or a rapid weight gain, each of which could be indicative of fluid retention.

Diachlor diuretic and antihypertensive (Major Pharmaceuticals), see Diuril diuretic and antihypertensive.)

Diahist antihistamine (Century Pharmaceuticals, Inc.), see Benadryl antihistamine.

Diaqua diuretic and antihypertensive (W. E. Hauck, Inc.), see hydrochlorothiazide diuretic and antihypertensive.

diazepam sedative and hypnotic (various manufacturers), see Valium sedative and hypnotic.

Dibent antispasmodic (W. E. Hauck, Inc.), see Bentyl antispasmodic.

dicyclomine hydrochloride antispasmodic (various manufacturers), see Bentyl antispasmodic.

diethylpropion hydrochloride anorectic (various manufacturers), see Tenuate anorectic.

digoxin heart drug (various manufacturers), see Lanoxin heart drug.

Dilantin anticonvulsant

Manufacturer: Parke-Davis
Ingredient: phenytoin sodium
Equivalent Products: Diphenylan Sodium, The Lannett Company, Inc.; Ditan, Mallard, Inc.; phenytoin sodium, various manufacturers (see Comments)
Dosage Forms: Capsule: 30 mg (white with pink stripe); 100 mg (white with orange stripe). Flavored tablet: 50 mg (yellow). Liquid (content per 5 ml teaspoon): 30 mg; 125 mg
Use: Control of epilepsy
Minor Side Effects: Bleeding, tender gums; blurred vision; constipation; drowsiness; headache; insomnia; muscle twitching; nausea; vomiting
Major Side Effects: Arthritis; blood disorders; change in facial features; chest pain; confusion; dizziness; gland swelling; gum enlargement; hairiness; liver damage; nervousness; numbness; rash; slurred speech; sore throat; uncoordinated movements
Contraindications: This drug should not be taken by people who are allergic to it. Consult your doctor immediately if this drug has been prescribed for you and you have such an allergy.
Warnings: This drug should be used cautiously by the elderly; people who have impaired liver function; and pregnant women. Be sure your doctor knows if you have any of these conditions. • Diabetics who need to take this drug should check their urine sugar more frequently than usual. • This drug should not be used to treat seizures if they are due to hypoglycemia. Careful diagnosis is essential before this drug is prescribed. • Because the metabolism of this drug may be significantly altered by the use of other drugs, great care must be taken when this drug is used concurrently with other drugs. Be sure that your doctor is aware of every medication that you take. Do not start or stop taking any other medication without first consulting your doctor. This drug interacts with barbiturates, carbamazepine, chloramphenicol, cimetidine, disulfiram, doxycycline, isoniazid, oral anticoagulants, oral antidiabetics, oral contraceptives, phenyl-

butazone, quinidine, steroids, sulfaphenazole, and tricyclic antidepressants; if you are currently taking any drugs of these types, consult your doctor about their use. If you are unsure of the type or contents of your medications, ask your doctor or pharmacist. • The results of certain lab tests may be altered if you are taking this drug. If you need any tests, remind your doctor that you are taking this drug. • Depending on the type of epilepsy being treated, this drug may be used in combination with other anticonvulsants. • This drug may cause low blood pressure, lymph node enlargement, and rash. Consult your doctor if you feel faint or light-headed, notice that your glands are swollen, or develop a rash. • This drug may cause a bone disease. • Do not stop taking this drug suddenly; you may start to convulse.

Comments: Although several generic versions of this drug are available, you should not switch from one to another without your doctor's complete approval and careful assessment. • Take this drug with food or milk. • Do not use this drug to treat headaches unless your doctor specifically recommends it. • Therapy with this drug may cause your gums to enlarge enough to cover the teeth. Gum enlargement can be minimized, at least partially, by good dental care—frequent brushing and massaging the gums with the rubber tip of a good toothbrush. • This drug may cause drowsiness; avoid tasks that require alertness. • To prevent oversedation, avoid the use of alcohol or other drugs that have sedative properties. • If you take phenobarbital in addition to this drug, you may be able to take them together in a single product, Dilantin with Phenobarbital anticonvulsant. Consult your doctor. • The liquid form of this drug must be shaken thoroughly before use.

Dilantin with Phenobarbital anticonvulsant (Parke-Davis), see Dilantin anticonvulsant.

Dilart vasodilator and smooth muscle relaxant (Trimen Laboratories, Inc.), see Pavabid Plateau Caps vasodilator and smooth muscle relaxant.

Dilitrate SR anti-anginal (Reed & Carnrick), see Isordil anti-anginal.

diltiazam anti-anginal (various manufacturers), see Cardizem anti-anginal.

Dimalix antihistamine and decongestant (Mallard, Inc.), see Dimetapp antihistamine and decongestant.

Dimetapp antihistamine and decongestant

Manufacturer: A. H. Robins Company
Ingredients: brompheniramine maleate; phenylephrine hydrochloride; phenylpropanolamine hydrochloride
Equivalent Products: Bromalix, Century Pharmaceuticals, Inc.; Bromophen, Rugby Laboratories; Brompheniramine Compound, various manufacturers; Cordamine-PA Tabs., Cord; Dimalix, Mallard, Inc.; Histatapp TD, Upsher-Smith Laboratories, Inc.; Midatap, Vangard Laboratories; Normatane, Vortech Pharmaceutical, Ltd.; Purebrom TD, Purepac Pharmaceutical Co.; Rotapp, Three P Products Corp.; S/T Decongest, Scot-Tussin Pharmacal Co., Inc.; Tagatap, Tutag Pharmaceuticals, Inc.; Tamine, Geneva Generics, Inc.;

Tri-Phen, Bay Pharmaceuticals, Inc.; Veltap, The Lannett Company, Inc.; Westapp, Western Pharmacal Co.

Dosage Forms: Liquid (content per 5 ml teaspoon): brompheniramine maleate, 4 mg; phenylephrine hydrochloride, 5 mg; phenylpropanolamine hydrochloride, 5 mg. Sustained-release tablet: brompheniramine maleate, 12 mg; phenylephrine hydrochloride, 15 mg; phenylpropanolamine hydrochloride, 15 mg (light blue)

Use: Relief of hay fever symptoms and respiratory congestion

Minor Side Effects: Blurred vision; confusion; constipation; diarrhea; dizziness; drowsiness; dry mouth; headache; heartburn; insomnia; loss of appetite; nasal congestion; nausea; rash; restlessness; sweating; upset stomach; vomiting; weakness

Major Side Effects: Chest pain; difficult urination; high blood pressure; loss of coordination; low blood pressure; palpitations; severe abdominal pain; sore throat; unusual bleeding or bruising

Contraindications: This drug should not be used to treat asthma or other symptoms of the lower respiratory tract. This drug should not be taken by people allergic to it or to certain other antihistamines. If you are allergic to any antihistamine, check with your doctor or pharmacist before taking this drug. This drug should not be taken by pregnant women; people who are using monoamine oxidase inhibitors (ask your pharmacist if you are unsure); or people with enlarged prostate, obstructed bladder, glaucoma, heart disease, or severe high blood pressure. Consult your physician immediately if this drug has been prescribed for you and you have any of these conditions. The tablet form of this drug should not be taken by children under 12 years of age.

Warnings: This drug should be used cautiously by people who have blood vessel disease, high blood pressure, a history of stroke, seizures, diabetes, ulcers, or thyroid disease. Be sure your doctor knows if you have any of these conditions. • Use this drug cautiously with children; overdosage may cause excitation leading to convulsions and death. • This drug may cause drowsiness; avoid tasks that require alertness. To prevent oversedation, avoid the use of alcohol or other drugs that have sedative properties.

Comments: The tablet form of this drug must be swallowed whole. • The tablet form of this drug has sustained action; never increase your dose or take it more frequently than your doctor prescribes. A serious overdose could result. • Chew gum or suck on ice chips or a piece of hard candy to reduce mouth dryness. • While taking this drug, do not take any nonprescription item for cough, cold, or sinus problems without first checking with your doctor.

Diphen antihistamine (Bay Pharmaceuticals, Inc.), see Benadryl anti-histamine.

Diphenatol anticholinergic and antispasmodic (Rugby Laboratories), see Lomotil anticholinergic and antispasmodic.

diphenhydramine hydrochloride antihistamine (various manufacturers), see Benadryl antihistamine.

diphenoxylate hydrochloride with atropine sulfate anticholinergic and antispasmodic (various manufacturers), see Lomotil anticholinergic and antispasmodic.

Diphenylan Sodium anticonvulsant (The Lannett Company, Inc.), see Dilantin anticonvulsant.

dipyridamole anti-anginal (various manufacturers), see Persantine anti-anginal.

Di-Spaz antispasmodic (Vortech Pharmaceutical, Ltd.), see Bentyl antispasmodic.

Ditan anticonvulsant (Mallard, Inc.), see Dilantin anticonvulsant.

Diupres diuretic and antihypertensive

Manufacturer: Merck Sharp & Dohme

Ingredients: chlorothiazide; reserpine

Equivalent Products: Chloroserpine, various manufacturers; chlorothiazide with reserpine, various manufacturers

Dosage Form: Tablet: chlorothiazide, 250 mg; 500 mg; reserpine, 0.125 mg (both pink)

Use: Treatment of high blood pressure

Minor Side Effects: Abdominal pain; colds; constipation; cramping; decrease in sexual desire; diarrhea; dizziness; drooling; dry mouth; flushing; headache; impotence; itching; light sensitivity; loss of appetite; muscle aches; nasal congestion; nausea; nosebleed; restlessness; slow pulse; tremors; vomiting; weight gain

Major Side Effects: Anemia; anxiety; blood disorders; blurred vision; bruising; chest pain; depression; difficult urination; drowsiness; fainting; fluid retention; glaucoma; hearing loss; heart failure; jaundice; muscle spasms; nervousness; nightmares; palpitations; rash; rise in blood sugar; sedation; shortness of breath; sore throat; tingling in fingers and toes; ulcer; weakness

Contraindications: This drug should not be taken by persons allergic to either of its components. Consult your doctor immediately if this drug has been prescribed for you and you have such an allergy. This drug should not be taken by persons suffering from anuria (no urine), peptic ulcer, ulcerative colitis, or severe depression. This drug should not be taken by patients undergoing electroshock therapy. Consult your doctor immediately if this drug has been prescribed for you and you have any of these conditions.

Warnings: This drug should be used cautiously by pregnant women, and persons with kidney disease, liver disease, coronary artery disease, allergies, gout, or asthma. Nursing mothers who must take this drug should stop nursing. Be sure your doctor knows if you fit into any of these categories. • Use of this drug could bring about the appearance of diabetes that has been latent. It could also cause low potassium and sodium levels, gout, high calcium levels, ulcers, colitis, gallstones, or asthma. • Persons taking this drug should have periodic blood and urine tests. • This drug could affect thyroid tests. If you are having such tests, be sure your doctor knows you are taking this drug. • If you are scheduled for surgery, be sure your doctor knows you are taking this drug. • Persons taking this drug and digitalis should watch carefully for signs of increased toxicity (e.g., nausea, blurred vision, palpitations). • This drug should not be taken with amphetamines, colestipol hydrochloride, decongestants, levodopa, lithium carbonate, quinidine, monoamine oxidase inhibitors, or oral antidiabetics. This drug should be used cautiously in conjunction with digitalis, curare, steroids, or other blood pressure drugs. If you are currently taking any drugs of these types, consult your doctor about their use. If you are unsure of the type or contents of your medications, ask your doctor or pharmacist. • This drug may cause drowsiness or depression; avoid tasks that require alertness. To prevent oversedation, avoid the use of other sedative drugs. If you feel continually tired or depressed, consult your doctor. • While taking this product (as with many drugs that lower blood pressure), you should limit your consumption of alcoholic beverages in order to prevent dizziness or light-headedness.

Comments: A doctor probably should not prescribe this drug or other "fixed dose" products as the first choice in the treatment of high blood pressure. The patient should receive each of the ingredients individually, and if response is adequate to the fixed doses contained in this drug, this product can then be substituted. The advantage of a combination product such as this drug is based on increased convenience to the patient. • Take this drug with food or milk. • This drug causes frequent urination. Expect this effect; it should not alarm you. • The effects of therapy with this drug may not be apparent for at least two weeks. • Mild side effects (e.g., nasal congestion) are most noticeable during the first two weeks of therapy and become less bothersome after this period. • This drug can cause potassium loss. Some of the symptoms of potassium loss include dry mouth, thirst, and muscle cramps. Call your doctor if you notice such symptoms. To help avoid potassium loss, take this drug with a glass of fresh or frozen orange juice. You may also eat a banana each day. The use of a salt substitute helps prevent potassium loss. • To avoid dizziness or light-headedness when you stand, contract and relax the muscles of your legs for a few moments before rising. Do this by pushing one foot against the floor while raising the other foot slightly, alternating feet so that you are "pumping" your legs in a pedaling motion. • Take this drug exactly as directed. Do not take extra doses or skip a dose without first consulting your doctor. • While taking this drug, do not take any nonprescription item for weight control or cough, cold, or sinus problems without first checking with your doctor. • Products equivalent to this drug are available and vary widely in cost. Ask your doctor to prescribe a generic preparation; then ask your pharmacist to fill it with the least expensive brand. • Reserpine causes cancer in rats. It has not been shown to cause cancer in people. • If you are allergic to a sulfa drug, you may likewise be allergic to this drug.

Diuril diuretic and antihypertensive

Manufacturer: Merck Sharp & Dohme
Ingredient: chlorothiazide
Equivalent Products: chlorothiazide, various manufacturers; Diachlor, Major Pharmaceuticals; SK-Chlorothiazide, Smith Kline & French Laboratories
Dosage Forms: Liquid (content per 5 ml teaspoon): 250 mg. Tablet: 250 mg; 500 mg (both white)
Use: Treatment of high blood pressure; removal of fluid from tissues
Minor Side Effects: Constipation; cramps; diarrhea; dizziness; headache; heartburn; itching; loss of appetite; nausea; restlessness; sun sensitivity; upset stomach; vomiting
Major Side Effects: Blood disorders; blurred vision; bruising; chest pain; elevated blood sugar; elevated uric acid; fever; jaundice; mood changes; muscle spasm; rash; sore throat; tingling in the fingers and toes; weakness; weak pulse
Contraindications: This drug should not be used by people who are allergic to it or to sulfa drugs, or by people who are suffering a lack of urination. Consult your doctor immediately if this drug has been prescribed for you and you have any of these conditions.

Warnings: This drug should be used cautiously by people who have diabetes, kidney or liver disease, a history of allergy or asthma, or by those who are pregnant. Be sure your doctor knows if you have any of these conditions. • Nursing mothers who must take this drug should stop nursing. • This drug may affect the potency of, or your need for, other blood pressure drugs, antidiabetics, and some surgical muscle relaxants; dosage adjustment may be necessary. • This drug interacts with colestipol hydrochloride, digitalis, lithium, and steroids. If you are currently taking any drugs of these types, consult your doctor about their use. If you are unsure of the type or contents of your medications, ask your doctor or pharmacist. • This drug may affect thyroid and other laboratory tests; be sure your doctor knows that you are taking this drug if you are having any tests done. • This drug may cause gout or high blood levels of calcium. The drug may cause the onset of diabetes that has been latent. • This drug can cause potassium loss. Signs of such loss include dry mouth, thirst, weakness, muscle pain or cramps, nausea, and vomiting. Call your doctor if you experience any of these symptoms. To help prevent this problem you should have blood tests done periodically while taking this drug. To help avoid potassium loss, take this product with a glass of fresh or frozen orange juice, or eat a banana every day. The use of a salt substitute also helps prevent potassium loss. • While taking this product, limit your consumption of alcoholic beverages in order to prevent dizziness or light-headedness. • If you are taking digitalis in addition to this drug, watch carefully for symptoms of increased digitalis toxicity (e.g., nausea, blurred vision, palpitations) and notify your doctor immediately if they occur. • If you have high blood pressure, do not take any nonprescription item for weight control or cough, cold, or sinus problems without first checking with your doctor.

Comments: Try to plan your dosage schedule to avoid taking this drug at bedtime. • To avoid dizziness or light-headedness when you stand, contract and relax the muscles of your legs for a few moments before rising. Do this by pushing one foot against the floor while raising the other foot slightly, alternating feet so that you are "pumping" your legs in a pedaling motion. • This product causes frequent urination. • This drug must be taken exactly as directed. Do not take extra doses or skip a dose without first consulting your doctor.

Diu-Scrip diuretic and antihypertensive (Scrip-Physician Supply Co.), see hydrochlorothiazide diuretic and antihypertensive.

Dolene Compound 65 analgesic (Lederle Laboratories), see Darvon Compound-65 analgesic.

Dolobid anti-inflammatory analgesic

Manufacturer: Merck Sharp & Dohme
Ingredient: diflunisal
Dosage Form: Tablet: 250 mg (peach); 500 mg (orange)
Use: Symptomatic treatment of mild to moderate pain; treatment of osteoarthritis
Minor Side Effects: Bloating; confusion; constipation; diarrhea; dizziness; drowsiness; gas; headache; heartburn; insomnia; loss of appetite; nausea; vomiting
Major Side Effects: Anemia; asthma; blood disorders; blood in stools, urine, or mouth; blurred vision; depression; difficult breathing; fatigue; fluid retention; high blood pressure; itching; jaundice; loss of hair; loss of hearing; numbness or tingling in fingers or toes; rash; ringing in the ears; severe abdominal pain; sore throat; ulcer; weight gain

Contraindications: This drug should not be used by people who are allergic to it or to aspirin or other nonsteroidal anti-inflammatory drugs. Consult your doctor immediately if this drug has been prescribed for you and you have such an allergy. This drug should not be used by pregnant or breast-feeding women. If you have either of these conditions and this drug has been prescribed for you, consult your doctor immediately.

Warnings: This drug should be used cautiously by elderly people; children under 14; people with a history of gastrointestinal disorders; and by people with mental illness, epilepsy, Parkinson's disease, infections, bleeding disorders, kidney or liver disease, high blood pressure, or heart failure. Be sure your doctor knows if you fit into any of these categories. • Nursing women who must use this drug should stop nursing. • The severity of the side effects caused by this drug depends upon the dosage taken. Use the least amount possible and watch carefully for side effects. • This drug may damage the stomach or intestines. Call your doctor if you experience stomach pain or your stools are black and tarry. • If you notice changes in your vision, call your doctor. • If you have headaches while taking this drug, notify your doctor. This drug may cause drowsiness; avoid tasks that require alertness. Side effects are more likely to occur in the elderly. • This drug interacts with aspirin, other anti-inflammatories, probenecid, lithium, phenytoin, anticoagulants, steroids, sulfa drugs, diabetes drugs, and diuretics. If you are currently taking any drugs of these types, talk to your doctor about their use. If you are not sure about the type or contents of your medications, talk to your doctor or pharmacist.

Comments: This drug is not intended for general aches and pains. • Regular checkups by the doctor, including blood tests, are required of persons taking this drug. • This drug may be taken with food or milk immediately after meals, or with antacids (other than sodium bicarbonate). Never take this drug on an empty stomach or with aspirin or alcohol. • If you are taking an anticoagulant ("blood thinner"), remind the doctor. • This drug may cause discoloration of the urine or feces. If you notice a change in color, call your doctor. • It may take a month before you feel the full effect of this drug.

Donnamor sedative and anticholinergic (H. L. Moore, Inc.), see Donnatal sedative and anticholinergic.

Donnapine sedative and anticholinergic (Major Pharmaceuticals), see Donnatal sedative and anticholinergic.

Donna-Sed sedative and anticholinergic (Vortech Pharmaceutical, Ltd.), see Donnatal sedative and anticholinergic.

Donnatal sedative and anticholinergic

Manufacturer: A. H. Robins Company
Ingredients: atropine sulfate; scopolamine hydrobromide; hyoscyamine sulfate; phenobarbital
Equivalent Products: Barophen, various manufacturers; Bay-Ase, Bay Pharmaceuticals, Inc.; belladonna alkaloids with phenobarbital, various manufacturers; Bellalphen, Columbia Medical Co.; Bellastal, Wharton Laboratories, Inc.; Donnamor, H. L. Moore, Inc.; Donnapine, Major Pharmaceuticals; Donna-Sed, Vortech Pharmaceutical, Ltd.; Hyosophen, Rugby Laboratories; Malatal, Mallard, Inc.; Neoquess, O'Neal, Jones & Feldman; Palbar, W. E. Hauck, Inc.; Relaxadon, Geneva Generics, Inc.; Seds, Pasadena Research; Spaslin, Blaine Co., Inc.; Spasmolin, various manufacturers; Spasmophen, The Lannett Com-

pany, Inc.; Spasquid, Geneva Generics, Inc.; Susano, Halsey Drug Co., Inc.; Vanatal, Vangard Laboratories

Dosage Forms: Liquid (content per 5 ml teaspoon): atropine sulfate, 0.0194 mg; scopolamine hydrobromide, 0.0065 mg; hyoscyamine sulfate, 0.1037 mg; phenobarbital, 16 mg. Capsule (green/white); Tablet (white): atropine sulfate, 0.0194 mg; scopolamine hydrobromide, 0.0065 mg; hyoscyamine sulfate, 0.1037 mg; phenobarbital, 16.2 mg. Sustained-action tablet: atropine sulfate, 0.0582 mg; scopolamine hydrobromide, 0.0195 mg; hyoscyamine sulfate, 0.3111 mg; phenobarbital, 48.6 mg (green)

Use: Treatment of bed-wetting; motion sickness; premenstrual tension; stomach and intestinal disorders; urinary frequency

Minor Side Effects: Blurred vision; confusion; constipation; decreased sexual desire; dizziness; drowsiness; drying up of breast milk; dry mouth; headache; insomnia; loss of taste; muscle pain; nausea; nervousness; rapid heart rate; reduced sweating; sensitivity of eyes to sunlight; vomiting; weakness

Major Side Effects: Breathing difficulty; difficult urination; hallucinations; hot and dry skin; impotence; jaundice; palpitations; rash; slurred speech; sore throat

Contraindications: This drug should not be taken by people who have glaucoma, enlarged prostate, obstructed bladder, obstructed intestine, acute hemorrhage, severe ulcerative colitis, liver disease, myasthenia gravis, hiatal hernia, or porphyria; or by those who are allergic to any of the ingredients in this drug. Consult your doctor immediately if the drug has been prescribed for you and you have any of these conditions or such an allergy.

Warnings: This drug should be used cautiously in conjunction with amantadine, haloperidol, antacids, phenothiazines, alcohol, griseofulvin, tranquilizers, oral anticoagulants, steroids, sulfonamides, tetracycline, tricyclic antidepressants, quinidine, digitalis, rifampin, oral contraceptives, chloramphenicol, or phenytoin; if you are currently taking any drugs of these types, consult your doctor about their use. If you are unsure of the type or contents of your medications, ask your doctor or pharmacist. ● Do not use this drug to treat diarrhea caused by an obstructed intestine. ● Despite its phenobarbital content, this drug has not been shown to have high potential for abuse. Nonetheless, be sure to follow dosage instructions carefully. ● This drug should be used with caution by people with kidney, thyroid, or heart disease, or high blood pressure; and by pregnant and nursing women. Be sure your doctor knows if you fit into any of these categories. ● This drug may cause drowsiness; avoid tasks that require alertness. ● To prevent oversedation, avoid taking alcohol or other drugs that have sedative properties.

Comments: This drug is best taken one-half to one hour before meals. ● This drug does not cure ulcers but may help them improve. ● If this drug makes it hard for you to urinate, try to do so just before taking each dose. ● Because this drug may reduce sweating, avoid excessive work or exercise in hot weather.

Doxaphene Compound analgesic (Major Pharmaceuticals), see Darvon Compound-65 analgesic.

Doxy-Caps antibiotic (Barr and Edwards Co.), see Vibramycin antibiotic.

Doxychel antibiotic (Rachelle Laboratories, Inc.), see Vibramycin antibiotic.

doxycycline hyclate antibiotic (various manufacturers), see Vibramycin antibiotic.

Doxy-Lemmon antibiotic (Lemmon Company), see Vibramycin antibiotic.

Doxy-Tabs antibiotic (Barr Laboratories), see Vibramycin antibiotic.

Drize antihistamine and adrenergic (B. F. Ascher & Co., Inc.), see Ornade Spansule antihistamine and adrenergic.

Duraphyl bronchodilator (McNeil Laboratories), see Theo-dur bronchodilator.

Duricef antibiotic

Manufacturer: Mead Johnson Pharmaceuticals
Ingredient: cefadroxil
Equivalent Product: Ultracef, Bristol Laboratories
Dosage Forms: Capsule: 500 mg (white/burgundy). Tablet: 1 g (white). Liquid (content per 5 ml teaspoon): 125 mg; 250 mg; 500 mg
Use: Treatment of bacterial infections
Minor Side Effects: Diarrhea; dizziness; headache; heartburn; nausea; vomiting
Major Side Effects: Difficulty breathing; hypersensitivity reactions such as rash, itching, and fever; severe diarrhea; vaginal itching; superinfection
Contraindications: This drug should not be used by persons who are allergic to it, to other cephalosporin antibiotics, or to penicillin antibiotics (see Comments). Consult your doctor if this drug has been prescribed for you and you have such an allergy.
Warnings: This drug should be used cautiously by persons with kidney disease or a history of colitis and by pregnant or nursing women. Make sure your doctor knows if you fit into any of these categories. • Contact your doctor if you develop diarrhea while taking this medication, especially if it is severe or contains blood. • Diabetics using Clinitest urine test may get a false high sugar reading while taking this drug. Change to Clinistix, Diastix, Chemstrip UG, or Tes-Tape while taking this drug to avoid this problem.
Comments: It is generally believed that 10 percent of all people allergic to penicillin drugs may be allergic to a cephalosporin-type antibiotic such as Duricef. Talk to your doctor or pharmacist about alternative medicines if you have such an allergy. • If stomach upset occurs, take this drug with food or milk. • Finish all of this medication, even if your symptoms disappear after a few days. The drug is usually taken for a full ten days. Stopping treatment early may lead to re-infection. • The liquid form must be stored in the refrigerator and shaken well before using. Discard any unused portion after 14 days.

Durrax sedative (Dermik Laboratories, Inc.), see Atarax sedative.

Dyazide diuretic and antihypertensive

Manufacturer: Smith Kline & French Laboratories
Ingredients: hydrochlorothiazide; triamterene

Dosage Form: Capsule: hydrochlorothiazide, 25 mg; triamterene, 50 mg (maroon/white)

Use: Treatment of high blood pressure; removal of fluid from the tissues

Minor Side Effects: Constipation; diarrhea; dizziness; drowsiness; dry mouth; fatigue; headache; itching; loss of appetite; nausea; restlessness; sun sensitivity; upset stomach; vomiting; weakness

Major Side Effects: Asthma; bruising; elevated blood sugar; elevated uric acid; jaundice; kidney stones; mood changes; muscle cramps or spasms; palpitations; rash; sore throat; tingling in fingers or toes; weak pulse

Contraindications: This drug should not be used by persons with severe liver or kidney disease, hyperkalemia (high blood levels of potassium), or anuria (inability to urinate). Be sure your doctor knows if you have any of these conditions. This drug should not be used routinely during pregnancy in otherwise healthy women, since mother and fetus are being exposed unnecessarily to possible hazards. This drug should not be used by persons allergic to it or to sulfa drugs. Consult your doctor immediately if this drug has been prescribed for you and you have such an allergy.

Warnings: This drug usually does not cause the loss of potassium. Do not take potassium supplements while taking this drug unless directed to do so by your doctor. • This drug should be used cautiously by pregnant women; children; and people with diabetes, allergy, asthma, liver disease, anemia, blood diseases, high calcium levels, or gout. Nursing mothers who must take this drug should stop nursing. Be sure your doctor knows if you fit into any of these categories. • This drug may affect the results of thyroid function tests. Be sure your doctor knows you are taking this drug if you must have such tests. • Regular blood tests should be performed if you must take this drug for a long time. You should also be tested for kidney function. • If you develop a sore throat, bleeding, bruising, dry mouth, weakness, or muscle cramps, call your doctor. • Persons who take this drug with digitalis should watch for signs of increased toxicity (e.g., nausea, blurred vision, palpitations). Call your doctor if such symptoms develop. • If you must undergo surgery, remind your doctor that you are taking this drug. • This drug interacts with curare, digitalis, lithium carbonate, oral antidiabetics, potassium salts, steroids, or spironolactone. If you are currently taking any drugs of these types, consult your doctor about their use. If you are unsure of the type or contents of your medications, ask your doctor or pharmacist.

Comments: This drug causes frequent urination. Expect this effect; it should not alarm you. • This drug may cause the urine to turn blue; this is harmless. • Although the price of this drug is relatively high compared to some other drugs used to treat high blood pressure, the price is justified because it does not cause potassium loss. • Take this drug with food or milk. • Take this drug exactly as directed. Do not skip a dose or take extra doses without first consulting your doctor. • While taking this drug (as with many drugs that lower blood pressure), you should limit your consumption of alcoholic beverages in order to prevent dizziness or light-headedness. • To avoid dizziness or light-headedness when you stand, contract and relax the muscles of your legs for a few moments before rising. Do this by pushing one foot against the floor while raising the other foot slightly, alternating feet so that you are "pumping" your legs in a pedaling motion. • If you are allergic to a sulfa drug, you may likewise be allergic to this drug. Be sure to inform your doctor if you have a sulfa-drug allergy. • When taking this drug, do not take any nonprescription item for weight control or cough, cold, or sinus problems without first checking with your doctor. • Potassium supplements should be avoided while taking this drug unless they are prescribed by your doctor. • A doctor should probably not prescribe this drug or other "fixed dose" products as the first choice in the treatment of high blood pressure. The patient should receive each of the individual ingredients singly, and if the response is adequate to the fixed doses contained in Dyazide, it can be substituted. The advantage of a combination product such as this drug is increased convenience to the patient.

E.E.S. antibiotic (Abbott Laboratories), see erythromycin antibiotic.

Effer-K potassium replacement (Nomax Pharmaceutical, Inc.), see K-Lyte potassium replacement.

Elavil antidepressant

Manufacturer: Merck Sharp & Dohme
Ingredient: amitriptyline hydrochloride
Equivalent Products: Amitid, E. R. Squibb & Sons, Inc.; Amitril, Parke-Davis; amitriptyline hydrochloride, various manufacturers; Emitrip, Major Pharmaceuticals; Endep, Roche Laboratories; SK-Amitriptyline, Smith Kline & French Laboratories
Dosage Form: Tablet: 10 mg; 25 mg; 50 mg; 75 mg; 100 mg; 150 mg
Use: Relief of depression
Minor Side Effects: Agitation; blurred vision; confusion; constipation; cramps; diarrhea; dizziness; drowsiness; dry mouth; fatigue; headache; heartburn; increased sensitivity to light; insomnia; loss of appetite; nausea; peculiar tastes; restlessness; sweating; vomiting; weakness; weight gain or loss
Major Side Effects: Bleeding; convulsions; difficult urination; enlarged or painful breasts (in both sexes); fainting; fever; fluid retention; hair loss; hallucinations; high or low blood pressure; imbalance; impotence; jaundice; mood changes; mouth sores; nervousness; nightmares; numbness in fingers or toes; palpitations; psychosis; ringing in the ears; seizures; skin rash; sleep disorders; sore throat; stroke; tremors; uncoordinated movements
Contraindications: This drug should not be taken by people who are allergic to it; those who have recently had a heart attack; or those who are taking monoamine oxidase inhibitors (ask your pharmacist if you are unsure). Consult your doctor immediately if this drug has been prescribed for you and you fit into any of these categories.
Warnings: This drug is not recommended for use by children under age 12. • This drug should be used cautiously by people who have glaucoma (certain types), heart disease (certain types), high blood pressure, enlarged prostate, epilepsy, urine retention, liver disease, or hyperthyroidism; and by pregnant or nursing women. Be sure your doctor knows if you have any of these conditions. • This drug should be used cautiously by patients who are receiving electroshock therapy or those who are about to undergo surgery. • Close medical supervision is required when this drug is taken with guanethidine or Placidyl hypnotic. • This drug may cause changes in blood sugar levels. • This drug interacts with alcohol, amphetamine, barbiturates, clonidine, epinephrine, oral anticoagulants, phenylephrine, and depressants; if you are currently taking any drugs of these types, consult your doctor about their use. If you are unsure of the type or contents of your medications, ask your doctor or pharmacist. • This drug may cause drowsiness; avoid tasks that require alertness. • To prevent oversedation, avoid the use of alcohol or other drugs that have sedative properties. • Report any sudden mood changes to your doctor.
Comments: Take this medicine exactly as your doctor prescribes. Do not stop taking it without first checking with your doctor. • While taking this drug, do not take any nonprescription item for cough, cold, or sinus problems without first checking with your doctor. Be sure your doctor is aware of every medication you use, and do not stop or start any other drug without your doctor's approval.

• This drug may cause the urine to turn blue-green; this is harmless. • The effects of therapy with this drug may not be apparent for two to four weeks. • Chew gum or suck on ice chips or a piece of hard candy to reduce mouth dryness. • Avoid long exposure to the sun while taking this drug. • To avoid dizziness or light-headedness when you stand, contract and relax the muscles of your legs for a few moments before rising. Do this by pushing one foot against the floor while raising the other foot slightly, alternating feet so that you are "pumping" your legs in a pedaling motion. • Many people receive as much benefit from taking a single dose of this drug at bedtime as from taking multiple doses throughout the day. Talk to your doctor about this.

Elixophyllin SR bronchodilator (Berlex Laboratories, Inc.), see Slo-Phyllin bronchodilator.

Emcodeine analgesic (Major Pharmaceuticals), see Empirin with Codeine analgesic.

Emitrip antidepressant (Major Pharmaceuticals), see Elavil antidepressant.

Empirin with Codeine analgesic

Manufacturer: Burroughs Wellcome Co.
Ingredients: aspirin; codeine phosphate
Equivalent Product: Emcodeine, Major Pharmaceuticals
Dosage Form: Tablet: aspirin, 325 mg; codeine phosphate (see Comments)
Use: Relief of moderate to severe pain
Minor Side Effects: Confusion; constipation; dizziness; drowsiness; euphoria; flushing; headache; indigestion; itching; light-headedness; loss of appetite; nausea; slight blood loss; sweating; vomiting
Major Side Effects: Black, tarry stools; breathing difficulties; jaundice; palpitations; rapid or slow heartbeat; ringing in the ears; skin rash; tremors; ulcers; urine retention
Contraindications: This drug should not be used by people who are allergic to any of its ingredients. Consult your doctor immediately if this drug has been prescribed for you and you have such an allergy.
Warnings: This drug may cause drowsiness; avoid activities requiring alertness, including driving a motor vehicle or operating machinery. • To prevent oversedation, avoid the use of other sedative drugs or alcohol. • This drug should be used cautiously by elderly or debilitated persons; pregnant women; and persons with head injuries, diseases of the abdomen, allergies, thyroid disease, peptic ulcer, liver or kidney disease, coagulation problems, or prostate problems. Be sure your doctor knows if you have any of these conditions. • This drug interacts with alcohol, ammonium chloride, methotrexate, steroids, 6-mercaptopurine, oral antidiabetics, phenytoin, steroids, oral anticoagulants, and gout medications (probenecid, sulfinpyrazone). If you are currently taking any drugs of these types, consult your doctor about their use. If you are unsure of the type or contents of your medications, ask your doctor or pharmacist. • Products containing narcotics (e.g., codeine) are usually not used for more than seven to ten days. This drug has the potential for abuse and must be used with caution. Tolerance may develop quickly; do not increase the dose of this drug without first consulting your doctor.
Comments: For this and other preparations containing codeine, the number which follows the drug name always refers to the amount of codeine present.

Hence, #2 has 1/4 grain (15 mg); #3 has 1/2 grain (30 mg); and #4 contains 1 grain (60 mg). These numbers are standard for amounts of codeine. • Take this drug with food or milk to lessen stomach upset. • If your ears feel strange, if you hear buzzing or ringing, or if your stomach hurts, your dosage may need adjustment. Call your doctor. • Side effects caused by this drug may be somewhat relieved by lying down.

E-Mycin antibiotic (The Upjohn Company), see erythromycin antibiotic.

Endep antidepressant (Roche Laboratories), see Elavil antidepressant.

Enduron diuretic and antihypertensive

Manufacturer: Abbott Laboratories
Ingredient: methyclothiazide
Equivalent Products: Aquatensen, Wallace Laboratories; Ethon, Major Pharmaceuticals; methyclothiazide, various manufacturers
Dosage Form: Tablet: 2.5 mg (orange); 5 mg (salmon)
Use: Treatment of high blood pressure; removal of fluid from the tissues
Minor Side Effects: Constipation; cramps; diarrhea; dizziness; drowsiness; headache; heartburn; itching; loss of appetite; nausea; restlessness; sun sensitivity; vomiting
Major Side Effects: Blood disorders; blurred vision; bruising; chest pain; dry mouth; elevated blood sugar; elevated uric acid; fever; jaundice; mood changes; muscle spasm; shortness of breath; skin rash; sore throat; thirst; tingling in the fingers and toes; weakness
Contraindications: This drug should not be taken by people who have severe kidney disease, or who are allergic to this drug or sulfa drugs. Consult your doctor immediately if this drug has been prescribed for you and you have such a condition or such an allergy.
Warnings: This drug should be used cautiously by pregnant women and by people who have asthma or allergies, kidney or liver disease, or diabetes. Be sure your doctor knows if you have any of these conditions. • Nursing women who must take this drug should stop nursing. • This drug interacts with digitalis, lithium, nonsteroidal anti-inflammatories, oral antidiabetics, and steroids; if you are currently taking any drugs of these types, consult your doctor about their use. If you are unsure of the type or contents of your medications, ask your doctor or pharmacist. • This drug may affect the potency of, or your need for, other blood pressure drugs and antidiabetics; dosage adjustment may be necessary. • This drug must be used cautiously with digitalis; be sure your doctor knows if you are taking digitalis in addition to this drug. Watch for symptoms of increased toxicity (e.g., nausea, blurred vision, palpitations) and notify your doctor if they occur. • If you have high blood pressure, do not take any nonprescription item for weight control or cough, cold, or sinus problems without first checking with your doctor. • While taking this product (as with many drugs that lower blood pressure), you should limit your consumption of alcoholic beverages in order to prevent dizziness or light-headedness. • This drug may influence the results of thyroid function tests; if you are scheduled to have such a test, remind your doctor that you are taking this drug. • This drug may cause gout, high blood levels of calcium, or the onset of diabetes that has been latent; periodic measurement of blood levels of sugar, calcium, uric acid, and potassium are advisable while you are using this drug.

Comments: Try to plan your dosage schedule to avoid taking this drug at bedtime. • This drug causes frequent urination. Expect this effect; it should not alarm you. • To avoid dizziness or light-headedness when you stand, contract and relax the muscles of your legs for a few moments before rising. Do this by pushing one foot against the floor while raising the other foot slightly, alternating feet so that you are "pumping" your legs in a pedaling motion. • To help avoid potassium loss while using this product, take your dose with a glass of fresh or frozen orange juice and eat a banana each day. The use of a salt substitute also helps prevent potassium loss. Signs of potassium loss include dry mouth, thirst, weakness, muscle pain or cramps, nausea, and vomiting. Call your doctor if you notice such symptoms. • This drug must be taken exactly as directed. Do not skip a dose or take extra doses without first consulting your doctor.

Enoxa anticholinergic and antispasmodic (Reid-Provident Labs., Inc.), see Lomotil anticholinergic and antispasmodic.

Equagesic analgesic

Manufacturer: Wyeth Laboratories
Ingredients: aspirin, meprobamate
Equivalent Products: Equazine-M, Rugby Laboratories; Meprogesic Q, Quantum Pharmics; Micrainin, Wallace Laboratories; Tranquigesic, Goldline Laboratories
Dosage Form: Tablet: aspirin, 250 mg; meprobamate, 200 mg (white)
Use: Relief of tension headache, or pain in muscles or joints accompanied by tension and/or anxiety
Minor Side Effects: Abdominal pain; blurred vision; dizziness; drowsiness; fatigue; light-headedness; nausea; vomiting
Major Side Effects: Buzzing in ears; chest tightness; fainting; fever; headache; loss of coordination; mental depression; palpitations; shortness of breath; skin rash; sore throat
Contraindications: This drug should not be used by people who have an allergy or intolerance to aspirin or to the product's other components. Consult your doctor immediately if this drug has been prescribed for you and you have such an allergy.
Warnings: This drug should be used cautiously by pregnant or nursing women; children under 12; and people who have certain blood disorders, asthma or other significant allergies, kidney or liver disease, gout, peptic ulcer, or epilepsy. Be sure your doctor knows if you fit into any of these categories. • This drug interacts with central nervous system depressants, anticoagulants, oral antidiabetics, methotrexate, and gout medications (probenecid, sulfinpyrazone). If you are currently taking any drugs of these types, consult your doctor about their use. If you are unsure of the type or contents of your medications, ask your doctor or pharmacist. • Check with your pharmacist or physician before taking any nonprescription item for cough, cold, or sinus problems while you are taking this drug. • This drug may cause drowsiness; avoid tasks that require alertness. • To prevent oversedation, avoid the use of alcohol or other drugs that have sedative properties. • This drug has the potential for abuse and must be used with caution. Tolerance develops quickly; do not take the drug more frequently than prescribed or increase the dose without first consulting your doctor. • Notify your doctor if your ears feel strange, if you hear buzzing or ringing, if your stomach hurts, or if you get a rash, sore throat, or fever. Your dosage may need adjustment or you may have an allergy to one of the drug's ingredients.

Comments: Take this drug with food or milk to lessen stomach upset. • Do not stop taking this drug suddenly without consulting your doctor. Your doctor may want you to reduce your dose gradually.

Equanil sedative and hypnotic (Wyeth Laboratories), see meprobamate sedative and hypnotic.

Equazine-M analgesic (Rugby Laboratories), see Equagesic analgesic.

Eramycin antibiotic (Wesley Pharmacal Co.), see erythromycin antibiotic.

Ercatab migraine remedy (Cord), see Cafergot migraine remedy.

Ergo-Caff migraine remedy (Rugby Laboratories), see Cafergot migraine remedy.

ergoloid mesylates vasodilator (various manufacturers), see Hydergine vasodilator.

Eryc antibiotic (Parke-Davis), see erythromycin antibiotic.

Erypar antibiotic (Parke-Davis), see erythromycin antibiotic.

EryPed antibiotic (Abbott Laboratories), see erythromycin antibiotic.

Ery-Tab antibiotic (Abbott Laboratories), see erythromycin antibiotic.

Erythrocin antibiotic (Abbott Laboratories), see erythromycin antibiotic.

erythromycin antibiotic

Manufacturer: various manufacturers
Ingredient: erythromycin
Equivalent Products: Bristamycin, Bristol Labs; E. E. S., Abbott Laboratories; E-Mycin, The Upjohn Company; Eramycin, Wesley Pharmacal Co.; Eryc, Parke-Davis; Erypar, Parke-Davis; Ery Ped, Abbott Laboratories; Ery-Tab, Abbott Laboratories; Erythrocin, Abbott Laboratories; Ethril, E. R. Squibb & Sons, Inc.; Ilosone, Dista Products Co.; Ilotycin, Dista Products Co.; Pediamycin, Ross Laboratories; Pfizer-E, Pfipharmecs Division; Robimycin, A. H. Robins Company; RP-Mycin, Reid-Provident Labs., Inc.; SK-Erythromycin, Smith Kline & French Laboratories; Wyamycin, Wyeth Laboratories
Dosage Forms: Capsule; Chewable tablet; Drops; Liquid; Tablet (various dosages and various colors)
Use: Treatment of a wide variety of bacterial infections
Minor Side Effects: Abdominal cramps; black tongue; cough; diarrhea; fatigue; irritation of the mouth; loss of appetite; nausea; vomiting
Major Side Effects: Fever; hearing loss; jaundice; rash; rectal and vaginal itching; superinfection

Contraindications: This drug should not be taken by people who are allergic to it. Consult your doctor immediately if you have such an allergy.

Warnings: This drug should be used cautiously by people who have liver disease and by pregnant or nursing women. • This drug may affect the potency of theophylline; if you are currently taking theophylline, consult your doctor about its use. If you are unsure about the contents of your medications, ask your doctor or pharmacist.

Comments: Take this drug on an empty stomach (one hour before or two hours after a meal). • It is best to take this drug at evenly spaced intervals throughout the day and night. Your pharmacist or physician will help you choose the best schedule. • This drug should be taken for at least ten full days, even if symptoms disappear within that time. • The liquid forms of this drug should be stored in the refrigerator. • Not all erythromycin products are chemically equivalent. However, most produce the same therapeutic effect. Discuss with your doctor or pharmacist which forms of erythromycin are appropriate for you, and then choose the least expensive product among those recommended.

Esidrix diuretic and antihypertensive (CIBA Pharmaceutical Company), see hydrochlorothiazide diuretic and antihypertensive.

Estrocon estrogen hormone (Savage Laboratories), see Premarin estrogen hormone.

Ethon diuretic and antihypertensive (Major Pharmaceuticals), see Enduron diuretic and antihypertensive.

Ethril antibiotic (E. R. Squibb & Sons, Inc.), see erythromycin antibiotic.

Etrafon phenothiazine and antidepressant (Schering Corp.), see Triavil phenothiazine and antidepressant.

Fastin anorectic

Manufacturer: Beecham Laboratories
Ingredient: phentermine hydrochloride
Equivalent Products: Obe-Nix, Holloway, Inc.; Obephen, Mallard, Inc.; Obermine, Forest Pharmaceuticals; Obestin-30, Ferndale Laboratories, Inc.; phentermine hydrochloride, various manufacturers; Phentrol No. 2, Vortech Pharmaceutical, Ltd.; Unifast Unicelles, Reid-Provident Labs., Inc.; Wilpowr, Foy Laboratories
Dosage Form: Capsule: 30 mg (blue/white)
Use: Short-term treatment of obesity
Minor Side Effects: Blurred vision; constipation; diarrhea; dizziness; drowsiness; dry mouth; headache; impotence; increase or decrease in sexual desire; insomnia; nausea; restlessness; unpleasant taste in the mouth; vomiting; weight loss
Major Side Effects: Chest pain; difficult urination; enlarged breasts in men or women; euphoria; fever; high blood pressure; involuntary muscle movements; menstrual irregularities; overstimulation of nerves; palpitations; rapid heartbeat; rash; sore throat; tremors
Contraindications: This drug should not be taken by people who have heart disease (certain types), thyroid disease, glaucoma, or moderate to severe high

blood pressure. People with a history of drug abuse, those allergic to this drug, people who are agitated, and those who are taking or have recently taken a monoamine oxidase inhibitor (ask your pharmacist if you are unsure) should not use this drug. Consult your doctor immediately if this drug has been prescribed for you and you fit any of these categories.

Warnings: This drug has the potential for abuse and must be used with caution. Tolerance to this drug may develop quickly; do not increase the dose without first consulting your doctor. If you feel this drug is no longer working for you, call your doctor. • This drug should be used cautiously by pregnant women and by people with mild high blood pressure, epilepsy, or diabetes. Be sure your doctor knows if you have any of these conditions. • This drug is not recommended for use by children under 12. • This drug interacts with acetazolamide, guanethidine, phenothiazines, sodium bicarbonate, and antidepressants; if you are currently taking any drugs of these types, consult your doctor about their use. If you are unsure of the type or contents of your medications, ask your doctor or pharmacist. • While taking this drug, do not take any nonprescription item for cough, cold, or sinus problems without first checking with your doctor. • Avoid foods rich in tyramine; ask your doctor for a list of such foods. • This drug may mask symptoms of fatigue and impair the ability to perform tasks that require alertness. • Do not take this drug as a stimulant to keep awake.

Comments: The effects of this drug on appetite control wear off; do not take this drug for more than three weeks at a time. One way to get full benefit from this drug is to take it for three weeks, stop for another three weeks, and then resume drug therapy. Consult your doctor about this regimen. • To be effective, therapy with this drug must be accompanied by a low-calorie diet. • To avoid sleeplessness, do not take this drug later than 3:00 P.M. • Ionamin anorectic (Pennwalt Pharmaceutical Division) is not an exact generic equivalent of this drug, but in the body they become identical substances.

Fenylhist antihistamine (Mallard, Inc.), see Benadryl antihistamine.

Fiorgen PF analgesic and sedative (Goldline Laboratories), see Fiorinal analgesic and sedative.

Fiorinal analgesic and sedative

Manufacturer: Sandoz Pharmaceuticals
Ingredients: aspirin; butalbital; caffeine
Equivalent Products: Butal Compound, Cord; Fiorgen PF, Goldline Laboratories; Isollyl, Rugby Laboratories; Lanorinal, The Lannett Company, Inc.; Marnal, Vortech Pharmaceutical, Ltd.; Protension, Blaine Co., Inc.; Tenstan, Halsom
Dosage Forms: Capsule (bright green/light green); Tablet (white): aspirin, 325 mg; butalbital, 50 mg; caffeine, 40 mg
Use: Relief of headache pain associated with tension
Minor Side Effects: Dizziness; drowsiness; gas; insomnia; lightheadedness; loss of appetite; nausea; nervousness; vomiting
Major Side Effects: Chest tightness; difficult urination; jaundice; loss of coordination; palpitations; ringing in the ears; shortness of breath; ulcers
Contraindications: This drug should not be taken by people who have porphyria or by those who are allergic to it. Consult your doctor immediately if this drug has been prescribed for you and you have either condition.
Warnings: This drug should be used cautiously by people who have ulcers, coagulation problems, liver disease, gout, or kidney disease; and by those who are pregnant or nursing. Be sure your doctor knows if you have any of these

conditions. ● Because of the butalbital (barbiturate) content, this drug may be habit-forming; do not take this drug unless absolutely necessary. This drug has the potential for abuse and must be used with caution. Tolerance may develop quickly; do not increase the dose without first consulting your doctor. ● No more than six tablets or capsules of this drug should be taken in one day. ● This drug may cause drowsiness; avoid tasks that require alertness. ● To prevent oversedation, avoid the use of alcohol or other drugs that have sedative properties. ● The safety and effectiveness of this drug when used by children under the age of 12 has not been established. ● This drug interacts with alcohol, aminophylline, theophylline, 6-mercaptopurine, anticoagulants, methotrexate, probenecid, sulfinpyrazone, central nervous system depressants, phenytoin, and antidepressants; if you are currently taking any drugs of these types, consult your doctor about their use. If you are unsure of the type or contents of your medications, ask your doctor or pharmacist.

Comments: Many headaches are believed to be caused by nervousness or tension or prolonged contraction of the head and neck muscles. This drug is reported to relieve these conditions to help control headache. ● Take this drug with food or milk. ● If your ears feel strange, if you hear ringing or buzzing, or if your stomach hurts, your dosage may need adjustment. Call your doctor. ● Since this drug may cause drowsiness, do not drive a motor vehicle or operate machinery.

Fiorinal with Codeine analgesic and sedative

Manufacturer: Sandoz Pharmaceuticals
Ingredients: aspirin; butalbital; caffeine; codeine phosphate
Equivalent Products: Buff-A-Comp, Mayrand Pharmaceuticals, Inc.; Isollyl with Codeine, Rugby Laboratories
Dosage Form: Capsule #1 (red/yellow); #2 (grey/yellow); #3 (blue/yellow): aspirin, 325 mg; butalbital, 50 mg; caffeine, 40 mg; codeine phosphate (see Comments)
Use: Relief of pain associated with tension
Minor Side Effects: Blurred vision; constipation; dizziness; drowsiness; flushing; headache; indigestion; insomnia; loss of appetite; nausea; nervousness; sweating; tiredness; vomiting
Major Side Effects: Abdominal pain; chest tightness; confusion; difficult breathing; jaundice; kidney disease; ringing in the ears; skin rash; sore throat; ulcer
Contraindications: This drug should not be taken by people who are allergic to any of its ingredients. Consult your doctor immediately if this drug has been prescribed for you and you have such an allergy.
Warnings: The use of this drug may be habit-forming, due to the presence of codeine and butalbital. This drug has the potential for abuse and must be used with caution. Tolerance to this drug may develop quickly; do not increase the dose of this drug without consulting your doctor. ● No more than six capsules of this product should be taken in one day. ● This drug should be used cautiously by people who have ulcers, coagulation problems, liver disease, gout, brain disease, porphyria, thyroid disease, gallstones or gallbladder disease, or kidney disease; and pregnant or nursing women. Be sure your doctor knows if you have any of these conditions. ● This drug may cause drowsiness; avoid tasks that require alertness. ● To prevent oversedation, avoid the use of alcohol or other drugs that have sedative properties. ● The safety and effectiveness of this drug when used by children under the age of 12 has not been established. ● This drug interacts with alcohol, ammonium chloride, anticoagulants, methotrexate, oral antidiabetics, oral contraceptives, probenecid, quinidine, steroids, sulfinpyrazone, vitamin C, central nervous system depressants, griseofulvin,

phenytoin, sulfonamides, tetracyclines, and antidepressants; if you are currently taking any drugs of these types, consult your doctor about their use. If you are unsure of the type or contents of your medications, ask your doctor or pharmacist.

Comments: For this and other preparations containing codeine, the number that follows the drug name always refers to the amount of codeine present. Hence, #1 has 1/8 grain (7.5 mg) codeine; #2 has 1/4 grain (15 mg); #3 has 1/2 grain (30 mg). These numbers are standard for amounts of codeine contained in any codeine product. • Many headaches are believed to be caused by nervousness or tension or prolonged contraction of the head and neck muscles. This drug is reported to relieve these conditions to help control headache. • Take this drug with food or milk. • Nausea caused by this drug may be relieved by lying down. • If your ears feel strange, if you hear ringing or buzzing, or if your stomach hurts, your dosage may need adjustment. Call your doctor. • Since this drug may cause drowsiness, do not drive a motor vehicle or operate machinery.

Flagyl antimicrobial and antiparasitic

Manufacturer: Searle & Co.
Ingredient: metronidazole
Equivalent Products: metronidazole, various manufacturers; Metryl, Lemmon Company; Protostat, Ortho Pharmaceutical Corp.; Satric, Savage Laboratories
Dosage Form: Tablet: 250 mg (blue, film coated); 500 mg (blue, film coated)
Use: Treatment of infections of the genital-urinary tract, lower respiratory tract, central nervous system (brain, spinal cord, and nerves), bones, joints, abdomen, intestinal tract, lining of the heart, and skin
Minor Side Effects: Abdominal cramps; change in urine color; constipation; decreased sexual interest; diarrhea; dizziness; dry mouth; headache; insomnia; irritability; joint pain; loss of appetite; metallic taste in the mouth; nasal congestion; nausea; restlessness; vomiting
Major Side Effects: Confusion; convulsions; flushing; hives; itching; loss of control of urine; mouth sores; numbness and tingling in fingers and toes; rash; sense of pressure inside abdomen; superinfection in the mouth or vagina; unexplained sore throat or fever; unusual fatigue; unusual weakness; white furry growth on tongue
Contraindications: This drug should not be used by people with a history of blood disease or with active physical disease of the central nervous system. Be sure your doctor knows if you have such a condition. In patients with trichomoniasis, this drug should not be used during the first three months of pregnancy. This drug should not be taken by people who are allergic to it. Consult your doctor immediately if this drug has been prescribed for you and you have such an allergy.
Warnings: This drug should be used with caution by pregnant women after the first three months of pregnancy and during the first three months of pregnancy if Flagyl is prescribed for a condition other than trichomoniasis. Nursing mothers who must use this drug should consider another method of infant feeding. This drug should be used with caution by those with severe liver disease. This drug should not be taken with anticoagulants or anti-alcoholic drugs. Alcohol should not be consumed when taking this drug because it may cause nausea, vomiting, stomach pains, and headache. If you are currently taking anticoagulants, anti-alcoholic drugs, or alcoholic beverages, consult your doctor about their use. If you are unsure about the type or contents of your medications, ask your doctor or pharmacist. • Total and differential blood tests may be recommended before, during, and after therapy with this drug. • Known

or previously unrecognized vaginal fungal infections may present more prominent signs during therapy with this drug.

Comments: This drug has been shown to produce cancers in mice and rats, but this effect in humans has not been clearly documented. • Do not stop taking this drug earlier than recommended by your doctor. Four to six weeks should elapse before a repeat course of treatment. • If this drug is being used to treat a sexually transmitted disease, your sexual partner may also need to be treated. You should refrain from sexual intercourse, or a condom should be used, while you are taking this product to prevent reinfection. • You should wash your hands before handling food and after using the bathroom. • This drug may cause darkening of the urine. Do not be alarmed. • If numbness or tingling of fingers or toes occurs, call your doctor. • Take this drug with food or milk if it upsets your stomach. • This drug may cause an unpleasant, metallic taste; this side effect is normal and not a cause for alarm.

Flexeril muscle relaxant and analgesic

Manufacturer: Merck Sharp & Dohme
Ingredient: cyclobenzaprine hydrochloride
Dosage Form: Tablet: 10 mg (yellow)
Use: Relief of muscle spasm
Minor Side Effects: Abdominal pain; black tongue; blurred vision; dizziness; drowsiness; dry mouth; fatigue; indigestion; insomnia; muscle pain; nausea; nervousness; sweating; unpleasant taste in the mouth; weakness
Major Side Effects: Confusion; depression; difficult urination; disorientation; hallucinations; headache; increased heart rate; itching; numbness in fingers and toes; rash; swelling of the face and tongue; tremors
Contraindications: This drug should not be taken by people who are taking or have recently (within two weeks) taken monoamine oxidase inhibitors, those who have certain heart or thyroid diseases, and those who are allergic to it. Consult your doctor immediately if this drug has been prescribed for you and you fit any of these categories.
Warnings: This drug interacts with monoamine oxidase inhibitors, alcohol, barbiturates, and other central nervous system depressants; anticholinergics; and some antihypertensives. If you are currently taking any drugs of these types, consult your doctor about their use. If you are unsure of the type or contents of your medications, ask your doctor or pharmacist. • This drug should be used with extreme caution by people who have urinary retention, epilepsy, blood clots, narrow-angle glaucoma, congestive heart failure, arrhythmias, increased intraocular pressure, or thyroid disease. Be sure your doctor knows if you have any of these conditions. • Children below the age of 15 and pregnant women should use this drug with caution. • This drug is not recommended for use by nursing mothers. • This drug may cause drowsiness; avoid tasks that require alertness. • Use of this drug for periods longer than two to three weeks is not recommended.
Comments: This drug is not useful to reduce muscle spasm associated with diseases of the central nervous system or spine, such as cerebral palsy. • This drug should not be taken as a substitute for rest, physical therapy, or other measures recommended by your doctor to treat your condition. • While taking this drug, do not take any nonprescription item for cough, cold, or sinus problems without first checking with your doctor. • Since this drug may cause dryness of the mouth, chew gum or suck on ice chips or a piece of hard candy to reduce this feeling.

Florvite vitamin and fluoride supplement (Everett Laboratories, Inc.), see Poly-Vi-Flor vitamin and fluoride supplement.

fluocinolone acetonide steroid hormone (various manufacturers), see Synalar steroid hormone.

Fluonid steroid hormone (Herbert Laboratories), see Synalar steroid hormone.

Flurosyn steroid hormone (Rugby Laboratories), see Synalar steroid hormone.

Flutex steroid hormone (Syosset Labs., Inc.), see Aristocort and Kenalog steroid hormones.

furosemide diuretic and antihypertensive (various manufacturers), see Lasix diuretic and antihypertensive.

Gamazole antibacterial (Major Pharmaceuticals), see Gantanol antibacterial.

Gantanol antibacterial

Manufacturer: Roche Products, Inc.
Ingredient: sulfamethoxazole
Equivalent Products: Gamazole, Major Pharmaceuticals; Gantanol DS, Roche Products, Inc.; sulfamethoxazole, various manufacturers; Urobak, Shionogi USA
Dosage Forms: Liquid (content per 5 ml teaspoon): 500 mg. Tablet: 500 mg (green). Double Strength Tablet: 1 g (light orange)
Use: Treatment of a variety of bacterial infections, especially of the urinary tract
Minor Side Effects: Abdominal pain; depression; diarrhea; dizziness; headache; insomnia; loss of appetite; nausea; sun sensitivity; vomiting
Major Side Effects: Aching joints and muscles; anemia; bleeding; blood disorders; convulsions; fever; fluid retention; goiter; hair loss; hallucinations; itching; jaundice; kidney disease; loss of fluid; rash; ringing in the ears; sore throat
Contraindications: This drug should not be used by pregnant women at term, or by nursing mothers, or (in most cases) given to infants less than two months old. This drug should not be used by people allergic to it or by those with porphyria. Consult your doctor immediately if this drug has been prescribed for you and you fit these descriptions or have such an allergy.
Warnings: This drug should be used with caution during pregnancy. This drug should be used with caution by persons with kidney disease, liver disease, intestinal or urinary tract blockage, blood disease, bronchial asthma, severe hay fever, or other allergies. Be sure your doctor knows if you have any of these conditions. This drug should not be used for treatment of strep throat. • Complete blood counts and frequent urinalysis should be done in persons receiving this drug for prolonged periods of time. • Report any symptoms of fever or sore throat to your doctor at once; these are early signs of blood disorders. • This drug may cause you to be especially sensitive to the sun. Avoid exposure to the sun as much as possible while taking this medication.

Use a sunscreen that does not contain para-aminobenzoic acid (PABA). Ask your pharmacist for a recommendation. • This drug should not be taken with barbiturates, methenamine hippurate, methenamine mandelate, methotrexate, oral anticoagulants, oral antidiabetics, oxacillin, para-aminobenzoic acid, phenylbutazone, or phenytoin. If you are currently taking any drugs of these types, consult your doctor about their use. If you are unsure of the type or contents of your medications, ask your doctor or pharmacist.

Comments: It is best to take this drug in evenly spaced doses throughout the day. Your doctor or pharmacist will help you choose a dosage schedule. • The liquid form of this product must be shaken well before use. • This drug should be taken with at least a full glass of water on an empty stomach (one hour before or two hours after a meal). Drink at least nine glasses of water each day. • This drug should be taken for as long as prescribed, even if symptoms have disappeared before that time. • This drug may cause thyroid tumors in rats. This has not been shown to occur in humans.

Gantanol DS antibacterial (Roche Products, Inc.), see Gantanol antibacterial.

Gantrisin antibacterial

Manufacturer: Roche Products, Inc.
Ingredient: sulfisoxazole
Equivalent Products: Gulfasin, Major Pharmaceuticals; Lipo Gantrisin. Roche Products, Inc.; SK-Soxazole, Smith Kline & French Laboratories; sulfisoxazole, various manufacturers; Sulfizin, Reid-Provident Labs., Inc.
Dosage Forms: Pediatric suspension, syrup (content per 5 ml teaspoon): 500 mg. Emulsion (content per 5 ml teaspoon): 1 g (Lipo Gantrisin). Tablet: 500 mg (white)
Use: Treatment of a variety of bacterial infections, especially of the urinary tract
Minor Side Effects: Abdominal pain; depression; diarrhea; dizziness; headache; insomnia; loss of appetite; nausea; sun sensitivity; vomiting
Major Side Effects: Aching joints and muscles; anemia; bleeding, convulsions; difficult urination; fever; fluid retention; goiter; hair loss; hallucinations; itching; jaundice; loss of coordination; loss of fluid; muscle pain; rash; ringing in the ears; sore throat; tingling in the hands and feet
Contraindications: This drug should not be taken by people who are allergic to it, or by those who are pregnant and near delivery or nursing. Consult your doctor immediately if this drug has been prescribed for you and you have any of these conditions. In most cases, this drug should not be given to infants under two months of age.
Warnings: This drug may cause allergic reactions and should, therefore, be used cautiously by people who have asthma, severe hay fever, or other significant allergies. People who have liver or kidney disease, intestinal or urinary tract blockage, or porphyria should also use this drug with caution. Be sure your doctor knows if you have any of these conditions. • This drug can cause blood diseases; notify your doctor immediately if you experience fever, sore throat, or skin discoloration, as these can be early signs of blood disorders. Complete blood cell counts and liver and kidney function tests should be done if you take this drug for a prolonged period. • This drug should not be used in conjunction with barbiturates, local anesthetics, methenamine hippurate, methenamine mandelate, methotrexate, oral anticoagulants, oral antidiabetics, oxacillin, para-aminobenzoic acid, phenylbutazone, or phenytoin; if you are currently taking any drugs of these types, consult your doctor about their

use. If you are unsure of the type or contents of your medications, ask your doctor or pharmacist. • This drug may cause you to be especially sensitive to the sun, so avoid exposure to the sun as much as possible and use an effective sunscreen that does not contain para-aminobenzoic acid (PABA).

Comments: This drug should be taken for as long as prescribed, even if symptoms disappear before that time. • Take this drug with at least a full glass of water. Drink at least nine glasses of water each day. • It is best to take this drug in evenly spaced doses throughout the day and night. Your doctor or pharmacist will help you choose a dosage schedule. • The liquid form of this product must be shaken well before use. • This drug is also available as an ophthalmic suspension. • This drug may cause thyroid tumors in rats. This effect has not been shown to occur in humans.

Gerimal vasodilator (Rugby Laboratories), see Hydergine vasodilator.

Glyceryl-T expectorant and smooth muscle relaxant (Rugby Laboratories), see Quibron expectorant and smooth muscle relaxant.

Gulfasin antibacterial (Major Pharmaceuticals), see Gantrisin antibacterial.

G-well pediculocide and scabicide (Goldline Laboratories), see Kwell pediculocide and scabicide.

Gyne-Lotrimin antifungal agent

Manufacturer: Schering Corp.
Ingredient: clotrimazole
Equivalent Product: Mycelex-G, Miles Pharmaceuticals
Dosage Forms: Vaginal cream 1% (per applicator): 5 g. Vaginal tablet: 100 mg
Use: Treatment of monilial infections of the vagina
Minor Side Effects: Redness; stinging sensation; vaginal burning
Major Side Effects: Abdominal cramps; blistering; bloating; irritation; painful urination; peeling of the skin
Contraindications: This drug should not be used by people who are allergic to it. Consult your doctor immediately if you have such an allergy.
Warnings: Although no ill effects from such use have been documented, this drug should be used cautiously during pregnancy. • If irritation occurs, stop using this product and call your doctor.
Comments: If no improvement is evident by the time you have used up your first prescription of this drug, you should see your doctor for rediagnosis. • Do not stop using this drug even if you do not notice improvement of your symptoms. Complete the full course of therapy. • If you have a fungal infection of the vagina, wear cotton panties rather than those made of nylon or other nonporous material while the infection is being treated. • Careful attention to personal hygiene may help prevent subsequent infections. • Apply this product after cleaning the affected area unless directed otherwise by your doctor.

Halcion sedative-hypnotic

Manufacturer: The Upjohn Company
Ingredient: triazolam

Dosage Form: Tablets: 0.25 mg (blue); 0.5 mg (white)

Use: Short-term relief of insomnia

Minor Side Effects: Blurred vision; constipation; dizziness; drowsiness; headache; lethargy; lightheadedness; loss of appetite; nausea; nervousness; relaxed feeling; vomiting

Major Side Effects: Confusion; depression; hallucinations; impaired coordination; memory loss; nightmares; rapid heartbeat; ringing in the ears; tremors; weakness

Contraindications: This drug should not be used by persons allergic to it or by pregnant women. Consult your doctor immediately if this drug has been prescribed for you and you have such a condition.

Warnings: This drug should be used with caution by depressed people; nursing mothers; persons under the age of 18; elderly patients and people with liver or kidney diseases, narrow-angle glaucoma, or psychosis. Be sure your doctor knows if you belong in one of these groups. • Because this drug has the potential for abuse, it must be used with caution, especially by those with a history of drug dependence. Tolerance may develop quickly; do not increase the dose or take this drug more often than prescribed without first consulting your physician. Do not abruptly discontinue taking this drug if you have been taking it for a long time. Your dosage may need to be decreased gradually. • This drug is safe when taken alone; when it is combined with other sedative drugs or alcohol, serious adverse reactions may develop. Avoid the use of alcohol, other sedatives, or central nervous system depressants. If you are currently taking any drugs of these types, consult your doctor about their use. If you are unsure of the type or contents of your medications, ask your doctor or pharmacist. • This drug causes drowsiness; avoid tasks that require alertness.

Comments: Take this drug one-half to one hour before bedtime unless otherwise prescribed. • After you stop taking this drug, your sleep may be disturbed for a few nights.

Haldol antipsychotic agent

Manufacturer: McNeil Laboratories

Ingredient: haloperidol

Dosage Forms: Liquid concentrate (content per ml): 2 mg. Tablet: 0.5 mg (white); 1 mg (yellow); 2 mg (pink); 5 mg (green); 10 mg (aqua); 20 mg (salmon)

Use: Treatment of certain psychotic disorders; certain symptoms of Gilles de la Tourette's syndrome in children and adults; severe behavior problems in children; short-term treatment of hyperactive children

Minor Side Effects: Blurred vision; confusion; constipation; diarrhea; dizziness; drooling; drowsiness; dry mouth; fatigue; headache; heartburn; impotence; insomnia; jitteriness; loss of appetite; menstrual irregularities; milk production; nausea; photosensitivity; restlessness; sweating; vomiting; weakness

Major Side Effects: Aching joints and muscles; blood disorders; breast enlargement (in men and women); convulsions; difficult breathing; difficult urination; eye changes; fluid retention; hair loss; hallucinations; heart attack; involuntary movements of the mouth, face, neck, and tongue; jaundice; liver damage; low blood pressure; mouth sores; palpitations; skin darkening; skin rash; sore throat; tremors

Contraindications: This drug should not be taken by people who are severely depressed, comatose, unconscious, or who have central nervous system depression due to alcohol or other centrally acting depressants, or who have Parkinson's disease. Be sure your doctor knows if you have any of these conditions. This drug should not be taken by people who are allergic to it.

Consult your doctor immediately if this drug has been prescribed for you and you have such an allergy.

Warnings: This drug should be used with caution by pregnant and nursing women. • This drug should not be taken in combination with lithium. • Broncho-pneumonia may result from usage of this drug. • Call your doctor if you feel lethargic, dehydrated, or short of breath, or if you have difficulty breathing. • This drug may impair mental and/or physical abilities required for performance of hazardous tasks such as operating machinery or driving a motor vehicle. • This drug should not be taken with alcohol. • This drug should be taken cautiously by patients with severe heart or blood vessel diseases, with liver disease, anemia, glaucoma, enlarged prostate, ulcers, or kidney disease; by those receiving anticoagulant or anticonvulsant therapy; by those with known allergies or thyroid disease. Be sure your doctor knows if you have any of these conditions or if you are taking any of these drug types, or any of the following: alcohol, oral antacids, anticholinergics, depressants. If you are unsure about the type or contents of your medications, ask your doctor or pharmacist.

Comments: The effects of therapy with this drug may not be apparent for at least two weeks. • This drug has a persistent action; never take it more frequently than your doctor prescribes. A serious overdose may result. • While taking this drug, do not take any nonprescription item for cough, cold, or sinus problems without first checking with your doctor. • This drug may cause dryness of the mouth. To reduce this feeling, chew gum or suck on ice chips or a piece of hard candy. • To avoid dizziness or light-headedness when you stand, contract and relax the muscles of your legs for a few moments before rising. Do this by pushing one foot against the floor while raising the other foot slightly, alternating feet so that you are "pumping" your legs in a pedaling motion. • If this drug upsets your stomach, it may be taken with food or milk. • This drug may cause tumors in rats. This effect has not been shown to occur in humans. • If you notice a sore throat, darkening of your vision, or any fine tremors of your tongue, call your doctor. • If you are taking this drug for a prolonged time, it may be advisable for you to stop for a while to see if you still need it. Talk to your doctor before stopping this drug. It may be necessary for you to reduce the dosage gradually. • Some of the side effects caused by this drug can be prevented by taking an antiparkinsonism drug. Talk to your doctor about this.

HC-Form steroid hormone and anti-infective (Recsei Laboratories), see Vioform-Hydrocortisone steroid hormone and anti-infective.

Hemorrhoidal HC steroid-hormone-containing anorectal product (Rugby Laboratories), see Anusol-HC steroid-hormone-containing anorectal product.

H-H-R diuretic and antihypertensive (Geneva Generics), see Ser-Ap-Es diuretic and antihypertensive.

Histatapp TD antihistamine and decongestant (Upsher-Smith Laboratories, Inc.), see Dimetapp antihistamine and decongestant.

Hydergine vasodilator

Manufacturer: Sandoz Pharmaceuticals
Ingredient: ergoloid mesylates
Equivalent Products: Circanol, Riker Laboratories, Inc.; Deapril-ST, Mead

Johnson Co.; ergoloid mesylates, various manufacturers; Gerimal, Rugby Laboratories; Hydroloid-G, Major Pharmaceuticals

Dosage Forms: Sublingual tablets: 0.5 mg (white); 1 mg (white). Oral tablets: 0.5 mg (white); 1 mg (white). Capsules: 1 mg (off white). Liquid: 1 mg per ml

Use: To reduce symptoms associated with senility

Minor Side Effects: Blurred vision; dizziness; drowsiness; flushing; headache; irritation under the tongue (sublingual form only); light-headedness; loss of appetite; nasal congestion; nausea; stomach cramps; vomiting

Major Side Effects: None

Contraindications: This drug should not be taken by people who are allergic to it. Consult your doctor immediately if this drug has been prescribed for you and you have such an allergy.

Warnings: Although this drug may increase the flow of blood to the brain, objective improvement of symptoms of senility is difficult to document. Because it is difficult to determine the cause of symptoms associated with senility, careful diagnosis is advised before this drug is prescribed. ● This drug should be used cautiously by those people with migraine headaches, porphyria, liver disease, low blood pressure, and severe mental illness.

Comments: Effects of this therapy may not be apparent for three to four weeks. ● The sublingual form of this drug must be placed under the tongue and allowed to dissolve completely. Try not to swallow for as long as possible. Do not drink any liquids for ten minutes after placing the tablet under the tongue. ● The capsule and oral tablet forms of this drug must be swallowed whole. Do not crush or chew them. ● This medication may cause transient nausea and heartburn. Do not be alarmed. These side effects usually pass quickly.

hydralazine hydrochloride antihypertensive (various manufacturers), see Apresoline antihypertensive.

Hydrap-Es diuretic and antihypertensive (Lemmon Company), see Ser-Ap-Es diuretic and antihypertensive.

Hydro-Chlor diuretic and antihypertensive (North American Pharmacal), see hydrochlorothiazide diuretic and antihypertensive.

hydrochlorothiazide diuretic and antihypertensive

Manufacturer: various manufacturers

Ingredient: hydrochlorothiazide

Equivalent Products: Aquazide H, Western Research Laboratories, Inc.; Chlorzide, Foy Laboratories; Diaqua, W. E. Hauck, Inc.; Diu-Scrip, Scrip-Physician Supply Co.; Esidrix, CIBA Pharmaceutical Company; Hydro-Clor, North American Pharmacal; HydroDIURIL, Merck Sharp & Dohme; Hydromal, Mallard, Inc.; Hydro-T, Major Pharmaceuticals; Hydro-Z, Mayrand Pharmaceuticals, Inc.; Mictin, Econo-Med; Oretic, Abbott Laboratories; SK-Hydrochlorothiazide, Smith Kline & French Laboratories; Thiuretic, Parke-Davis; Zide, Reid-Provident Labs., Inc.

Dosage Form: Tablet: 25 mg; 50 mg; 100 mg (various colors)

Use: Treatment of high blood pressure; prevention of fluid accumulation

Minor Side Effects: Constipation; cramps; diarrhea; dizziness; drowsiness; headache; heartburn; itching; loss of appetite; nausea; restlessness; sun sensitivity; vomiting

Major Side Effects: Blood disorders; blurred vision; bruising; elevated blood sugar; elevated uric acid; fever; jaundice; muscle spasm; palpitations; skin rash; sore throat; tingling in fingers and toes; weakness

Contraindications: This drug should not be used by people who are allergic to it or to sulfa drugs, or by people with kidney disease or lack of urination. Consult your doctor immediately if you have any of these conditions.

Warnings: This drug should be used cautiously by people who have diabetes, liver disease, a history of allergy or asthma; or by those who are pregnant. Be sure your doctor knows if you have any of these conditions. • Nursing mothers who must take this drug should stop nursing. • This drug may affect the potency of, or your need for, other blood pressure drugs, antidiabetics, and some surgical muscle relaxants; dosage adjustment may be necessary. • This drug interacts with colestipol hydrochloride, digitalis, indomethacin, lithium, and steroids. If you are currently taking any drugs of these types, consult your doctor about their use. If you are unsure about the type or contents of your medications, ask your doctor or pharmacist. • This drug may affect thyroid and other laboratory tests; be sure your doctor knows that you are taking this drug if you are having any tests done. • This drug may cause gout or high blood levels of calcium. The drug may cause the onset of diabetes that has been latent. • This drug can cause potassium loss. Signs of such loss include dry mouth, thirst, weakness, muscle pain or cramps, nausea, and vomiting. Call your doctor if you experience any of these symptoms. To help prevent this problem you should have blood tests done periodically while taking this drug. To help avoid potassium loss, take this product with a glass of fresh or frozen orange juice, or eat a banana every day. The use of a salt substitute also helps prevent potassium loss. • While taking this product, limit your consumption of alcoholic beverages in order to prevent dizziness or light-headedness. • If you are taking digitalis in addition to this drug, watch carefully for symptoms of increased digitalis toxicity (e.g., nausea, blurred vision, palpitations) and notify your doctor immediately if they occur. • If you have high blood pressure, do not take any nonprescription item for weight control or cough, cold, or sinus problems without first checking with your doctor.

Comments: Try to plan your dosage schedule to avoid taking this drug at bedtime. • To avoid dizziness or light-headedness when you stand, contract and relax the muscles of your legs for a few moments before rising. Do this by pushing one foot against the floor while raising the other foot slightly, alternating feet so that you are "pumping" your legs in a pedaling motion. • This product causes frequent urination. • This drug must be taken as directed. Do not take extra doses or skip a dose without first consulting your doctor.

hydrochlorothiazide, reserpine, and hydralazine diuretic and antihypertensive (various manufacturers), see Ser-Ap-Es diuretic and antihypertensive.

hydrochlorothiazide with reserpine diuretic and antihypertensive (various manufacturers), see Hydropres diuretic and antihypertensive.

hydrocortisone acetate topical steroid

Manufacturer: various manufacturers
Ingredient: hydrocortisone acetate
Equivalent Products: Carmol HC, Syntex Laboratories, Inc.; Cortef Acetate, The Upjohn Company; Hydrocorton, Merck Sharp & Dohme
Dosage Forms: Cream; Lotion; Ointment
Use: For temporary relief of skin inflammation, irritation; itching, and rashes associated with such conditions as dermatitis, eczema, or poison ivy

Minor Side Effects: Burning sensation; dryness; irritation; itching; rash

Major Side Effects: Blisters; increased hair growth; pain; redness; secondary infection; skin wasting

Contraindications: This drug should not be used in the presence of fungal infections, diseases that impair circulation, or tuberculosis of the skin. People with a perforated eardrum should not use this product in the ear. It should not be used by those with an allergy to hydrocortisone. Consult your doctor immediately if you have any of the conditions listed and this drug has been prescribed for you. ● This drug should not be used in or near the eyes.

Warnings: This product is for external use only. ● Avoid contact with the eyes. Wash your hands after applying this product. ● Do not use this product for prolonged periods of time, and do not use it more frequently than directed on the label. If the condition does not improve after three days, discontinue use and consult your doctor or pharmacist. ● If irritation (pain, itching, swelling, or rash) occurs, discontinue use. Consult your doctor. ● Do not use on children under two years of age without consulting a physician. ● Pregnant women should use this product cautiously.

Comments: While this product relieves itching, this action may take a couple of days to achieve. Use this product as directed; meanwhile, apply rubbing alcohol or witch hazel diluted with an equal amount of water to the area to relieve itching. ● Do not bandage or wrap the skin during treatment with this drug unless directed to do so by your physician. ● If the affected area is extremely dry or is scaling, the skin may be moistened before applying the medication by soaking in water or by applying water with a clean cloth. The ointment form is preferred for use on dry skin. ● Until recently, hydrocortisone-containing products required a prescription for purchase. They are now sold without a prescription in strengths of up to 0.5%. ● There are several brands on the market. Consult your pharmacist.

Hydrocortisone steroid hormone

Manufacturer: various manufacturers

Ingredient: hydrocortisone

Equivalent Products: Cortef, The Upjohn Company; cortisol, various manufacturers; Hydrocortisone, various manufacturers; Hydrocortone, Merck, Sharp and Dohme.

Dosage Form: Tablets: 5 mg; 10 mg; 20 mg

Use: Treatment of endocrine or rheumatic disorders; asthma; blood diseases; certain cancers; eye disorders; gastrointestinal disturbances such as ulcerative colitis; respiratory diseases; inflammations such as arthritis, dermatitis, poison ivy

Minor Side Effects: Dizziness; headache; increased hair growth; increased susceptibility to infection; increased sweating; indigestion; insomnia; menstrual irregularities; muscle weakness; nervousness; reddening of the skin on the face; restlessness; thin skin; weight gain

Major Side Effects: Abdominal enlargement; blurred vision; bone loss; bruising; cataracts; convulsions; diabetes; euphoria; fluid retention; fracture; glaucoma; growth impairment in children; heart failure; high blood pressure; impaired healing of wounds; mood changes; mouth sores; muscle wasting; nightmares; peptic ulcer; potassium loss; salt retention; weakness

Contraindications: This drug should not be taken by people who are allergic to it or who have systemic fungal infections. Consult your doctor if this drug has been prescribed for you and you have either of these conditions.

Warnings: If you are using this drug for longer than a week, you may need to receive higher dosages if you are subjected to stress such as serious infection, injury, or surgery. ● This drug may mask signs of an infection or cause new infections to develop. ● This drug may cause glaucoma or cataracts, high blood pressure, high blood sugar, fluid retention, and potassium loss. ● This drug has not been proven safe for use during pregnancy. ● While you are taking this drug you should not be vaccinated or immunized. ● This drug should be used very cautiously by people who have had tuberculosis and those who have thyroid disease, liver disease, severe ulcerative colitis, diabetes, seizures, a history of ulcers, kidney disease, high blood pressure, a bone disease, or myasthenia gravis. Be sure your doctor knows if you fit any of these categories. ● If you have been taking this drug for more than a week, do not stop taking it suddenly. Never increase the dose or take the drug for a longer time than prescribed without consulting your doctor. ● Report mood swings or depression to your doctor. ● Growth of children may be affected by this drug. ● This drug interacts with aspirin, barbiturates, diuretics, rifampin, cyclophosphamide, estrogens, indomethacin, oral anticoagulants, antidiabetics, and phenytoin; if you are currently taking any drugs of these types, consult your doctor about their use. If you are unsure of the type or contents of your medications, ask your doctor or pharmacist. ● Blood pressure, body weight, and vision should be checked at regular intervals. Stomach x-rays are advised for persons with suspected or known peptic ulcers.

Comments: This drug is often taken on a decreasing-dosage schedule (four times a day for several days, then three times a day, etc.). ● Often, taking the entire daily dose at one time (about 8:00 A.M.) gives the best results. ● To help avoid potassium loss while using this drug, take your dose with a glass of fresh or frozen orange juice and eat a banana each day. The use of a salt substitute also helps prevent potassium loss. ● If you are using this drug chronically, you should wear or carry a notice that you are taking a steroid. ● To prevent stomach upset, take this drug with food or a snack. ● Take this drug exactly as directed. Do not take extra doses or skip a dose without first consulting your doctor. For long-term treatment, taking the drug every other day is preferred. Ask your doctor about alternate-day dosing.

hydrocortisone with iodochlorhydroxyquin steroid hormone and anti-infective (various manufacturers), see Vioform-Hydrocortisone steroid hormone and anti-infective.

Hydrocorton topical steroid (Merck, Sharp & Dohme), see hydrocortisone acetate topical steroid.

Hydrocortone steroid hormone (Merck, Sharp and Dohme), see hydrocortisone steroid hormone.

HydroDIURIL diuretic and antihypertensive (Merck Sharp & Dohme), see hydrochlorothiazide diuretic and antihypertensive.

Hydroloid-G vasodilator (Major Pharmaceuticals), see Hydergine vasodilator.

Hydromal diuretic and antihypertensive (Mallard, Inc.), see hydrochlorothiazide diuretic and antihypertensive.

Hydro Plus diuretic and antihypertensive (Reid-Provident Labs., Inc.), see Hydropres diuretic and antihypertensive.

Hydropres diuretic and antihypertensive

Manufacturer: Merck Sharp & Dohme
Ingredients: hydrochlorothiazide; reserpine
Equivalent Products: hydrochlorothiazide with reserpine, various manufacturers; Hydro Plus, Reid-Provident Labs., Inc.; Hydroserp, various manufacturers; Hydroserpine, various manufacturers; Hydrosine, Major Pharmaceuticals; Hydrotensin, Mayrand Pharmaceuticals, Inc.; Mallopress, Mallard, Inc.
Dosage Form: Tablet: hydrochlorothiazide, 25 mg; 50 mg; reserpine, 0.125 mg (both green)
Use: Treatment of high blood pressure
Minor Side Effects: Abdominal pain; colds; constipation; cramping; decrease in sexual desire; diarrhea; dizziness; drooling; dry mouth; flushing; headache; impotence; itching; light sensitivity; loss of appetite; muscle aches; nasal congestion; nausea; nosebleed; restlessness; slow pulse; tremor; vomiting; weight gain
Major Side Effects: Anemia; anxiety; blood disorders; blurred vision; bruising; chest pain; depression; difficult urination; drowsiness; fainting; fluid retention; glaucoma; hearing loss; heart failure; jaundice; muscle spasms; nervousness; nightmares; palpitations; rash; rise in blood sugar; sedation; shortness of breath; sore throat; tingling in the fingers and toes; ulcer; weakness
Contraindications: This drug should not be taken by persons allergic to either of its components. Consult your doctor immediately if this drug has been prescribed for you and you have such an allergy. This drug should not be taken by persons suffering from anuria (no urine), peptic ulcer, ulcerative colitis, or severe depression. This drug should not be taken by patients undergoing electroshock therapy. Consult your doctor immediately if this drug has been prescribed for you and you have any of these conditions.
Warnings: This drug should be used cautiously by pregnant women, and persons with kidney disease, liver disease, coronary artery disease, allergies, diabetes, epilepsy, gallstones, Parkinson's disease, gout, or asthma. Nursing mothers who must take this drug should stop nursing. Be sure your doctor knows if you fit into any of these categories. • Use of this drug could bring about the appearance of diabetes that has been latent. It could also cause low potassium and sodium levels, gout, high calcium levels, ulcers, colitis, gallstones, or asthma. • Persons taking this drug should have periodic blood and urine tests. • This drug could affect thyroid tests. If you are having such tests done, be sure your doctor knows you are taking this drug. • If you are scheduled for surgery, be sure your doctor knows you are taking this drug. • Persons taking this drug and digitalis should watch carefully for signs of increased toxicity (e.g., nausea, blurred vision, palpitations). • This drug should not be taken with amphetamine, colestipol hydrochloride, decongestants, levodopa, lithium carbonate, quinidine, monoamine oxidase inhibitors, or oral antidiabetics. This drug should be used cautiously in conjunction with digitalis, nonsteroidal anti-inflammatory drugs, curare, steroids, or other blood pressure drugs. If you are currently taking any drugs of these types, consult your doctor about their use. If you are unsure of the type or contents of your medications, ask your doctor or pharmacist. • This drug may cause drowsiness or depression; avoid tasks that require alertness. • To prevent oversedation, avoid the use of other sedative drugs. If you feel continually tired or depressed, consult your doctor. • While taking this product (as with many drugs that lower blood pressure), you should limit your consumption of alcoholic beverages in order to prevent dizziness or light-headedness.
Comments: A doctor probably should not prescribe this drug or other "fixed dose" products as the first choice in the treatment of high blood pressure. The patient should receive each of the ingredients individually, and if response is

adequate to the fixed doses contained in this drug, this product can then be substituted. The advantage of a combination product such as this drug is based on increased convenience to the patient. • Take this drug with food or milk. • This drug causes frequent urination. Expect this effect; it should not alarm you. • The effects of therapy with this drug may not be apparent for at least two weeks. • Mild side effects (e.g., nasal congestion) are most noticeable during the first two weeks of therapy and become less bothersome after this period. • This drug can cause potassium loss. Some of the symptoms of potassium loss include dry mouth, thirst, and muscle cramps. Call your doctor if you notice such symptoms. To help avoid potassium loss, take this drug with a glass of fresh or frozen orange juice. You may also eat a banana each day. The use of a salt substitute helps prevent potassium loss. • To avoid dizziness or light-headedness when you stand, contract and relax the muscles of your legs for a few moments before rising. Do this by pushing one foot against the floor while raising the other foot slightly, alternating feet so that you are "pumping" your legs in a pedaling motion. • This drug may make you more sensitive to sunlight. Be careful while in the sun to avoid burning. • Take this drug exactly as directed. Do not take extra doses or skip a dose without first consulting your doctor. • While taking this drug, do not take any nonprescription item for weight control or cough, cold, or sinus problems without first checking with your doctor. • Products equivalent to this drug are available and vary widely in cost. Ask your doctor to prescribe a generic preparation; then ask your pharmacist to fill it with the least expensive brand. • Reserpine causes cancer in rats. It has not been shown to cause cancer in people. • If you are allergic to a sulfa drug, you may likewise be allergic to this drug.

Hydroserp diuretic and antihypertensive (various manufacturers), see Hydropres diuretic and antihypertensive.

Hydroserpine diuretic and antihypertensive (various manufacturers), see Hydropres diuretic and antihypertensive.

Hydrosine diuretic and antihypertensive (Major Pharmaceuticals), see Hydropres diuretic and antihypertensive.

Hydro-T diuretic and antihypertensive (Major Pharmaceuticals), see hydrochlorothiazide diuretic and antihypertensive.

Hydrotensin diuretic and antihypertensive (Mayrand Pharmaceuticals, Inc.), see Hydropres diuretic and antihypertensive.

hydroxyzine hydrochloride sedative (various manufacturers), see Atarax sedative.

Hydro-Z diuretic and antihypertensive (Mayrand Pharmaceuticals, Inc.), see hydrochlorothiazide diuretic and antihypertensive.

Hygroton diuretic and antihypertensive

Manufacturer: USV Laboratories, Inc.
Ingredient: chlorthalidone
Equivalent Products: chlorthalidone, various manufacturers; Hylidone, Major Pharmaceuticals; Thalitone, Boehringer Ingelheim Ltd.
Dosage Form: Tablet: 25 mg (peach); 50 mg (aqua); 100 mg (white)

Use: Treatment of high blood pressure and removal of fluid from body tissues

Minor Side Effects: Constipation; cramps; diarrhea; dizziness; drowsiness; headache; heartburn; loss of appetite; nausea; restlessness; sun sensitivity; vomiting

Major Side Effects: Blood disorders; blurred vision; bruising; elevated blood sugar; elevated uric acid; fever; jaundice; mood changes; muscle spasm; rash; palpitations; sore throat; tingling in the fingers and toes; weakness; weak pulse

Contraindications: This drug should not be taken by persons suffering from anuria (inability to urinate). This drug should not be taken by people who are allergic to it or to sulfa drugs. Consult your doctor immediately if this drug has been prescribed for you and you have anuria or such an allergy.

Warnings: This drug should be used with caution by pregnant and nursing women, persons with kidney disease, liver disease, diabetes, gout, allergies, or asthma. Be sure your doctor knows if you have any of these conditions. ● This drug should be used with caution, since it may cause low blood levels of potassium, and also gout and diabetes that has been latent. ● Use of this drug may affect thyroid tests. ● Use of this drug requires the periodic taking of lab tests. ● This drug may add to the actions of other blood pressure drugs. This drug also interacts with digitalis, indomethacin, lithium, oral antidiabetics, steroids, and curare. Persons taking this drug and digitalis should watch carefully for signs of increased toxicity (e.g., nausea, blurred vision, palpitations), and notify their doctors immediately if symptoms occur. If you are currently taking any drugs of these types, consult your doctor about their use. If you are unsure of the type or contents of your medications, ask your doctor or pharmacist.

Comments: This drug causes frequent urination. Expect this effect; it should not alarm you. ● This drug can cause potassium loss. Signs of such loss include dry mouth, thirst, weakness, muscle pain or cramps, nausea, and vomiting. If you experience such symptoms, call your doctor. To help avoid potassium loss, take this drug with a glass of fresh or frozen orange juice. You may also eat a banana each day. The use of a salt substitute helps prevent potassium loss. ● Try not to take this drug at bedtime. This drug is best taken as a single dose in the morning, with food. ● This drug must be taken exactly as directed. Do not take extra doses or skip a dose without first consulting your doctor. ● While taking this drug, as with many drugs that lower blood pressure, you should limit your consumption of alcoholic beverages in order to prevent dizziness or light-headedness. ● To avoid dizziness or light-headedness when you stand, contract and relax the muscles of your legs for a few moments before rising. Do this by pushing one foot against the floor while raising the other foot slightly, alternating feet so that you are "pumping" your legs in a pedaling motion. ● If you are allergic to a sulfa drug, you may likewise be allergic to this drug. ● If you have high blood pressure, do not take any nonprescription item for weight control or cough, cold, or sinus problems without first checking with your doctor.

Hylidone diuretic and antihypertensive (Major Pharmaceuticals), see Hygroton diuretic and antihypertensive.

Hyosophen sedative and anticholinergic (Rugby Laboratories), see Donnatal sedative and anticholinergic.

Hy-Pam sedative (Premo Pharmaceutical Labs., Inc.), see Atarax sedative.

Hyserp diuretic and antihypertensive (Reid-Provident Labs., Inc.), see Ser-Ap-Es diuretic and antihypertensive.

Hysone steroid hormone and anti-infective (Mallard, Inc.), see Vioform-Hydrocortisone steroid hormone and anti-infective.

ibuprofen anti-inflammatory (Par Pharmaceuticals), see Motrin anti-inflammatory.

Ilosone antibiotic (Dista Products Co.), see erythromycin antibiotic.

Ilotycin antibiotic (Dista Products Co.), see erythromycin antibiotic.

imipramine hydrochloride antidepressant (various manufacturers), see Tofranil antidepressant.

Imodium antidiarrheal

Manufacturer: Janssen Pharmaceutical Inc.
Ingredient: loperamide hydrochloride
Dosage Forms: Capsule: 2 mg (two-tone green). Liquid (content per 5 ml teaspoon): 1 mg
Use: Treatment of severe diarrhea
Minor Side Effects: Dizziness; drowsiness; dry mouth; fatigue; loss of appetite; nausea; vomiting
Major Side Effects: Abdominal bloating or pain; constipation; fever; rash; sore throat; stomach pain
Contraindications: This drug should not be used by persons allergic to it. Consult your doctor immediately if this drug has been prescribed for you and you have such an allergy. This drug should not be used by people who must avoid the possibility of constipation. This drug is not recommended for diarrhea that results from infection of the intestinal lining by amebas, viruses, or bacteria. Consult your doctor immediately if this drug has been prescribed for you and you have this condition.
Warnings: This drug should be used with caution in people who have colitis, liver disease, or a history of drug dependency. • This drug should be used cautiously by pregnant women or nursing mothers. Consult your doctor immediately if this drug has been prescribed for you and you have any of these conditions. • This drug may cause drowsiness; avoid tasks that require alertness.
Comments: This drug is usually prescribed in conjunction with other drugs to treat severe diarrhea. It should be used for short periods only. If diarrhea continues after two days of taking this drug, consult your doctor. • This drug can be habit-forming if taken for longer than 10 days. • No more than eight capsules of this product should be taken in 24 hours. • Notify your doctor if abdominal bloating or pain or fever occurs. • Do not exceed prescribed dosage. • This drug may cause dry mouth. Chew gum or suck on ice chips or hard candy to relieve mouth dryness.

Inderal beta blocker

Manufacturer: Ayerst Laboratories
Ingredient: propranolol hydrochloride
Equivalent Product: propranolol, Rugby Laboratories
Dosage Form: Tablet: 10 mg (peach); 20 mg (blue); 40 mg (green); 60 mg (pink); 80 mg (yellow); 90 mg (lavender). Capsule, sustained release: 80 mg (light blue); 120 mg (two-tone blue); 160 mg (dark blue)

Use: Treatment of angina pectoris, certain heart arrhythmias, heart attacks, high blood pressure; prevention of migraine headaches

Minor Side Effects: Abdominal cramps; blurred vision; constipation; dry mouth; fatigue; gas; insomnia; light-headedness; loss of appetite; nausea; sweating; vomiting; weakness

Major Side Effects: Bruises; cold hands and feet; decreased sexual ability; depression; diarrhea; difficult breathing; difficult urination; dizziness; fever; hair loss; hallucinations; heart failure; nightmares; rash; ringing in the ears; shortness of breath; slow pulse; slurred speech; sore throat; tingling in fingers; visual disturbances

Contraindications: This drug should not be used by persons with bronchial asthma, severe hay fever, or certain types of heart problems. Be sure your doctor knows if you have any of these conditions. This drug should not be used with monoamine oxidase inhibitors, or during the two-week withdrawal period from such drugs. If you are currently taking any drugs of this type, consult your doctor about their use. If you are unsure of the type or contents of your medications, ask your doctor or pharmacist.

Warnings: This drug should be used with caution by persons with certain respiratory problems, diabetes, certain types of heart problems, liver and kidney diseases, hypoglycemia, or thyroid disease. Be sure your doctor knows if you have any of these conditions. ● This drug should be used cautiously by pregnant women. ● This drug should be used with care during anesthesia and by patients undergoing major surgery. If possible, this drug should be withdrawn 48 hours prior to surgery. ● This drug should be used cautiously when reserpine, cimetidine, theophylline, or aminophylline are taken. ● This drug is a potent medication, and it should not be stopped abruptly. Heart attacks have occurred when the medication was stopped suddenly.

Comments: Your doctor may want you to take your pulse every day while you take this medication. Consult your doctor. ● Be sure to take your medication doses at the same time each day. ● While taking this drug, do not take any nonprescription item for cough, cold, or sinus problems without first checking with your doctor. ● Notify your doctor if dizziness or diarrhea develops. ● This drug is of value in preventing further heart attacks among patients who have already suffered a heart attack. ● This drug may make you more sensitive to the cold. Dress warmly. ● This drug is available in sustained-release capsule form, which requires less frequent dosing. Consult your doctor about its use.

Inderide diuretic and antihypertensive

Manufacturer: Ayerst Laboratories
Ingredients: propranolol; hydrochlorothiazide
Dosage Form: Tablet: propranolol, 40 mg, 80 mg; hydrochlorothiazide, 25 mg (off-white)
Uses: Treatment of high blood pressure; removal of fluid from body tissues

Minor Side Effects: Abdominal cramps; blurred vision; constipation; drowsiness; fatigue; gas; headache; heartburn; insomnia; light-headedness; loss of appetite; muscle spasm; nasal congestion; nausea; restlessness; sweating; vomiting; weakness

Major Side Effects: Blood disorders; bruises; cold hands and feet; decreased sexual ability; depression; diarrhea; difficulty breathing; difficulty urinating; dizziness; dry mouth; elevated uric acid; fever; hair loss; hallucinations; heart failure; jaundice; nightmares; rash; ringing in the ears; slow pulse; sore throat; sun sensitivity; tingling in the fingers; visual disturbances

Contraindications: This drug should not be used by persons with bronchial asthma, severe hay fever, certain types of heart problems, or allergies to either of the components of this medication, or to sulfa drugs. Be sure your doctor

CONSUMER GUIDE®

knows if you have any of these conditions. This drug should not be used concurrently with monoamine oxidase inhibitors or during the two week withdrawal period from such drugs. If you are currently taking any drugs of this type, consult your physician. If you are unsure of the types or contents of your medications, ask your doctor or pharmacist.

Warnings: This drug should be used with caution by persons with certain types of heart problems, thyroid disease, certain respiratory disorders, severe kidney disease, severe liver disease, diabetes, gout, hypoglycemia, and those undergoing major surgery. Be sure your doctor knows if you have any of these conditions. • This drug should be used in pregnancy only if the benefits outweigh the risks. Discuss the risks and benefits with your doctor. • Nursing mothers who must take this drug should stop nursing. • This drug is a potent medication, and it should not be stopped abruptly. Heart attacks have occurred when the drug was stopped suddenly. • This drug may interact with reserpine, digitalis, cimetidine, theophylline, aminophylline, indomethacin, colestipol, lithium, and corticosteroids. If you are currently taking any drugs of these types, consult your doctor about their use. If you are unsure about the type or contents of your medications, ask your doctor or pharmacist. • This drug may affect thyroid and other laboratory tests; be sure your doctor knows that you are taking this drug if you are having any tests done. • Because this drug may add to the effect of other blood pressure drugs, the doses may need to be adjusted if taken concurrently. • If you are taking digitalis in addition to this drug, watch for symptoms of increased digitalis toxicity (e.g., nausea, blurred vision, palpitations) and notify your doctor immediately if they occur. • Because of the hydrochlorothiazide component, this drug may cause gout or increased blood levels of calcium. It may also cause the onset of diabetes that has been latent. • This drug can cause potassium loss. Some of the symptoms of potassium loss are thirst, dry mouth, and muscle cramps. Notify your doctor if you experience such symptoms. To help prevent potassium loss, take this drug with a glass of fresh or frozen orange juice, or eat a banana every day. The use of a salt substitute also helps prevent potassium loss.

Comments: This drug causes increased urination. Expect this effect. • A doctor probably should not prescribe this drug or other "fixed dose" products as the first choice in treatment of high blood pressure. The patient should be treated first with each of the component drugs individually. If the response is adequate to the doses contained in this product, then this fixed dose product can be substituted. Combination products offer the advantage of increased convenience to the patient. • To avoid dizziness or light-headedness when you stand, contract and relax the muscles of your legs for a few minutes before rising. Do this by pushing one foot against the floor while raising the other foot slightly, alternating feet so you are "pumping" your legs in a pedaling motion. • Your doctor may want you to take your pulse every day while you are on this medication. Consult your doctor. • Take this drug exactly as directed. Be sure to take your medication doses at the same time each day. Do not take extra doses or skip a dose without first consulting your doctor. • While you are taking Inderide do not take any nonprescription drug for weight control or for cough, cold, or sinus problems, without first checking with your doctor or pharmacist. • While taking this drug, limit your consumption of alcohol-containing beverages, in order to prevent dizziness and light-headedness. • Notify your doctor if dizziness or diarrhea develops. • This drug may make you more sensitive to the cold. Dress warmly.

Indocin anti-inflammatory

Manufacturer: Merck Sharp & Dohme
Ingredient: indomethacin

Dosage Forms: Capsule: 25 mg; 50 mg (both are blue/white). Sustained-release capsule: 75 mg (blue/clear)

Use: Reduction of pain, redness, and swelling due to arthritis

Minor Side Effects: Bloating; confusion; constipation; diarrhea; dizziness; drowsiness; gas; headache; heartburn; insomnia; loss of appetite; nausea; vomiting

Major Side Effects: Anemia; blood disorders; blood in stools, urine, or mouth; blurred vision; chest tightness; depression; difficult breathing; difficult urination; fatigue; fluid retention; high blood pressure; itching; jaundice; loss of hair; loss of hearing; numbness or tingling in fingers or toes; ringing in the ears; severe abdominal pain; skin rash; sore throat; ulcer; weight gain

Contraindications: This drug should not be used by people who are allergic to it or to aspirin or other nonsteroidal anti-inflammatory drugs. Consult your doctor immediately if this drug has been prescribed for you and you have such an allergy. This drug should not be used by persons with nasal polyps associated with swelling. If you have this condition and this drug has been prescribed for you, consult your doctor immediately.

Warnings: This drug should be used cautiously by elderly people; pregnant women; children under 14; people with a history of gastrointestinal disorders; and by people with mental illness, epilepsy, Parkinson's disease, infections, bleeding disorders, colitis, kidney or liver disease, high blood pressure, or heart failure. Be sure your doctor knows if you fit into any of these categories. • Nursing women who must use this drug should stop nursing. • The severity of the side effects caused by this drug depends upon the dosage taken. Use the least amount possible and watch carefully for side effects. • This drug may irritate the stomach or intestines. Call your doctor if you experience stomach pain or your stools are black and tarry. • If you notice changes in your vision, call your doctor. • If you have headaches while taking this drug, notify your doctor. • This drug may cause drowsiness; avoid tasks that require alertness. • Side effects are more likely to occur in the elderly. • This drug interacts with aspirin, probenecid, oral antidiabetics, lithium, anticoagulants, and furosemide. If you are currently taking any drugs of these types, talk to your doctor about their use. If you are not sure about the type or contents of your medications, talk to your doctor or pharmacist.

Comments: This drug is potent and is not intended for general aches and pains. • Regular checkups by the doctor, including blood tests, are required of persons taking this drug. • This drug must be taken with food or milk, immediately after meals, or with antacids. Never take this drug on an empty stomach or with aspirin or alcohol. • If you are taking an anticoagulant ("blood thinner"), remind your doctor. • This drug may cause discoloration of the urine or feces. If you notice a change in color, call your doctor. • It may take a month before you feel the full effect of this drug. • This drug should be taken regularly to control symptoms of arthritis. Do not take it only when you feel pain.

insulin antidiabetic

Manufacturer: various manufacturers

Ingredient: insulin

Equivalent Products: This drug is usually prescribed according to time of onset and duration of action, rather than by trade name.

Dosage Form: This drug is available only as an injectable. Various types of insulin provide different times of onset and duration of action. The types of insulin and their times of onset and duration are as follows:

	Onset (hr.)	Duration (hr.)
regular insulin	1/2	6
insulin zinc suspension, prompt	1/2	14
isophane insulin (NPH)	1	24
insulin zinc suspension	1	24
globin zinc insulin	2	24
protamine zinc insulin (PZI)	6	36
insulin zinc suspension, extended	6	36

Use: Treatment of diabetes mellitus

Minor Side Effect: Low blood sugar level

Major Side Effects: No major side effects when used as directed

Contraindications: There are no specific contraindications to the use of insulin, but before you begin therapy, your doctor must determine your specific needs and carefully work out your dosage regimen.

Warnings: This drug should be used only under the direction of a doctor, and a prescribed diet should be followed precisely. ● Do not substitute one type of this drug for another. Stick to your prescribed type. ● Roll insulin vial in hands to mix gently before withdrawing a dose in the syringe. ● Purchase disposable syringes if possible and remember to dispose of them properly. Once you have started using a particular brand of disposable insulin syringe and needle, do not switch brands without first talking with your doctor. A dosage error may occur. ● When using this drug, be on guard for signs of low blood sugar—fatigue, nervousness, nausea, rapid heartbeat, and a cold sweat. If signs of low blood sugar are evident, eat a piece of candy or drink a glass of orange juice and try to contact your doctor who will instruct you on what to do in such a situation. ● Also, be on the alert for signs of too much sugar. These signs include thirst, excess urination, and vision changes. Your urine test should show sugar in your urine if there is too much sugar in your blood. Call your doctor if you experience any of these symptoms. ● Allergy to insulin is unusual, but it may happen. Symptoms of such an allergy are similar to those of other allergies, including rash and asthma. ● If you become ill—if you catch a cold or the flu or become nauseated, for example—your insulin requirement may change. Consult your doctor. ● Injection sites for this drug should be rotated. It is important that this be done. Be sure to follow your doctor's instructions carefully. ● This drug interacts with guanethidine, monoamine oxidase inhibitors, propranolol, steroids, tetracycline, and thyroid hormone. If you are currently taking any drugs of these types, consult your doctor about their use. If you are unsure of the type or contents of your medications, ask your doctor or pharmacist. ● While taking this drug, do not take any nonprescription item for cough, cold, or sinus problems without first checking with your doctor.

Comments: This drug is stored in the refrigerator in the pharmacy, but once the bottle has been opened, most forms (except U-500 strength) may be kept at room temperature if the contents are used within a month. ● This drug comes in various strengths. Be sure to buy the right strength of the drug and the right syringes. ● Special injection kits are available for blind diabetics. Ask your doctor for help in obtaining them. ● Doses of this drug may be prepared in advance. Ask your pharmacist for advice. ● Most insulin products are composed of a mixture of both pork and beef insulins. However, products are available that contain all beef insulin or all pork insulin. Human insulin is also available. Never switch from one form to another unless your doctor tells you to do so. ● If you are diabetic, you should wear a medical I.D. alert bracelet or carry a medical I.D. alert card in your wallet.

Iodocort steroid hormone and anti-infective (Ulmer Pharmacal Co.), see Vioform-Hydrocortisone steroid hormone and anti-infective.

Ionamin anorectic

Manufacturer: Pennwalt Pharmaceutical Division
Ingredient: phentermine resin
Dosage Form: Capsule: 15 mg (yellow/gray); 30 mg (yellow)
Use: Short-term treatment of obesity
Minor Side Effects: Abdominal pain; blurred vision; constipation; diarrhea; dizziness; drowsiness; dry mouth; false sense of well-being; headache; impotence; increase or decrease in sexual desire; insomnia; loss of appetite; nausea; restlessness; sweating; unpleasant taste in the mouth; vomiting; weight loss
Major Side Effects: Chest pain; difficult or painful urination; euphoria; fever; hair loss; high blood pressure; involuntary muscle movements; menstrual irregularities; mood changes; overstimulation of nerves; painful breasts in men or women; palpitations; rapid heartbeat; rash; sore throat; tremors
Contraindications: This drug should not be taken by people who have heart disease (certain types), thyroid disease, glaucoma, or moderate to severe high blood pressure. People with a history of drug abuse, those allergic to this drug, people who are agitated, and those who are taking or have recently taken a monoamine oxidase inhibitor (ask your pharmacist if you are unsure) should not use this drug. Consult your doctor immediately if this drug has been prescribed for you and you fit any of these categories.
Warnings: This drug has the potential for abuse and must be used with caution. Tolerance to this drug may develop quickly; do not increase the dose without first consulting your doctor. If you feel this drug is no longer working for you, call your doctor. • This drug should be used cautiously by pregnant women and by people with mild high blood pressure, epilepsy, or diabetes. Be sure your doctor knows if you have any of these conditions. • This drug is not recommended for use by children under 12. • This drug interacts with acetazolamide, guanethidine, phenothiazines, sodium bicarbonate, and antidepressants; if you are currently taking any drugs of these types, consult your doctor about their use. If you are unsure of the type or contents of your medications, ask your doctor or pharmacist. • While taking this drug, do not take any nonprescription item for cough, cold, or sinus problems without first checking with your doctor. • This drug may mask symptoms of fatigue and impair the ability to perform tasks that require alertness. • Do not take this drug as a stimulant to keep awake.
Comments: The effects of this drug on appetite control wear off; do not take this drug for more than three weeks at a time. • To be effective, therapy with this drug must be accompanied by a low-calorie diet. • Avoid foods high in tyramine; ask your doctor for a list of these foods. • To avoid sleeplessness, do not take this drug later than 10:00 A.M. • Do not crush or break the capsule; it must be swallowed whole. • Fastin anorectic (Beecham Laboratories) is not an exact generic equivalent of this drug, but in the body they become identical substances.

Iso-Bid anti-anginal (Geriatric Pharmaceutical Corp.), see Isordil anti-anginal.

Isollyl analgesic and sedative (Rugby Laboratories), see Fiorinal analgesic and sedative.

Isollyl with Codeine analgesic and sedative (Rugby Laboratories), see Fiorinal with Codeine analgesic and sedative.

Isonate anti-anginal (Major Pharmaceuticals), see Isordil anti-anginal.

isoniazid antitubercular

Manufacturer: various manufacturers
Ingredient: isonicotinic acid hydrazide (INH)
Equivalent Products: isoniazid, various manufacturers; Laniazid, The Lannett Company, Inc.; Niconyl, Parke-Davis; Panazid, Panray Division; Teebaconin, Consolidated Midland Corp.
Dosage Form: Tablet: 50 mg; 100 mg; 300 mg (white)
Use: Treatment and prevention of tuberculosis
Minor Side Effects: Abdominal pain; dizziness; heartburn; nausea; vomiting
Major Side Effects: Blood disorders; breast enlargement in men and women; chills; darkening of the urine; fever; severe and sometimes fatal hepatitis; hyperglycemia; jaundice; liver damage; malaise; memory impairment; numbness and tingling of fingers and toes; rash; skin eruptions; vision changes; vitamin B_6 deficiency; weakness
Contraindications: This drug should not be taken by people who have had previous liver damage resulting from isoniazid therapy. This drug should not be taken by people who have had severe adverse reactions to it, such as drug fever, chills, arthritis. Make sure your doctor knows if you have had such reactions. This drug should not be taken by people who have acute liver disease from any cause. Be sure your doctor knows if you have this condition.
Warnings: Persons undergoing therapy with this drug should have their eyes examined before and during its use. • This drug should be used with caution by pregnant women and nursing mothers. • The use of this drug should be discontinued at the first sign of hypersensitivity to it. • This drug should be used cautiously by people with kidney disease, alcoholism, epilepsy, or chronic liver disease. Be sure your doctor is aware of your having this condition. • This drug should not be taken with aluminum-containing antacids or aminosalicylic acid (PAS). If it is taken with phenytoin, oral anticoagulants, disulfiram, or primidone, dosage adjustments will be needed. If you are currently taking any drugs of these types, consult your doctor about their use. If you are unsure about the type or contents of your medications, ask your doctor or pharmacist.
Comments: This drug is also referred to as INH. • This drug must be taken for long periods (months to years) to assure that the tuberculosis organism is completely eradicated. Do not discontinue therapy, except on the advice of your doctor. • Doses of this drug should not be skipped. This drug should be taken on an empty stomach, at least one hour before or two hours after a meal. • Consult your doctor if any of the major side effects listed are observed. • This drug has been reported to induce lung tumors in a number of strains of mice. • Your doctor may want you to take vitamin B_6 (pyridoxine) each day while taking this drug to help reduce the incidence of side effects. • Limit consumption of alcohol while taking this drug. • Notify your doctor if you develop fatigue, loss of appetite, nausea, or vomiting.

Isopro T.D. anticholinergic and phenothiazine (Rugby Laboratories), see Combid Spansule anticholinergic and phenothiazine.

Isoptin anti-anginal

Manufacturer: Knoll Pharmaceutical Company

Ingredient: verapamil hydrochloride
Equivalent Product: Calan, Searle Labs
Dosage Form: Tablet: 80 mg (yellow); 120 mg (white)
Use: Prevention and control of angina pectoris
Minor Side Effects: Abdominal pain; blurred vision; constipation; fatigue; headache; sleeplessness; loss of balance; muscle cramps; nausea; sweating; tremors
Major Side Effects: Changes in menstruation; confusion; depression; fainting; hair loss; itching; limping; shortness of breath; slow or irregular heartbeat; swelling of the hands and feet; unusual weakness
Contraindications: This drug should not be taken by people who are allergic to it or who have certain types of heart disease or extremely low blood pressure. Contact your doctor immediately if you have one of these conditions and this drug has been prescribed for you. Mothers who are breast-feeding should not take this drug. Do not take this drug until at least two days after stopping the drug disopyramide (Norpace).
Warnings: This drug should be used with caution in people who have cardiogenic shock, AV block, sick sinus syndrome, congestive heart failure, irregular heart rhythms, or liver or kidney disease. • This drug may interact with beta blockers, antihypertensive drugs, digitalis, diuretics, calcium supplements, and quinidine. If you are currently using any of these types of drugs, consult your doctor about their use. If you are unsure about the type or contents of your medication, ask your doctor or pharmacist.
Comments: This drug is not effective in treating an attack of angina already in progress. • It may take several weeks before any effect from the drug is noticed. • Contact your doctor if this drug causes severe or persistent dizziness, constipation, or nausea.

Isopto Carpine ophthalmic solution

Manufacturer: Alcon Laboratories, Inc.
Ingredient: pilocarpine hydrochloride
Equivalent Products: Adsorbocarpine, Alcon Laboratories, Inc.; Akarpine, Akorn; Almocarpine, Ayerst Laboratories; Pilocar, Coopervision Pharmaceutical, Inc.; pilocarpine hydrochloride, various manufacturers; Pilocel, Professional Pharmacal Co.; Pilomiotin, Coopervision Pharmaceutical, Inc.; Piloptic, Muro Pharmacal Labs., Inc.
Dosage Forms: Drops: 0.25%; 0.5%; 1%; 2%; 3%; 4%; 5%; 6%; 8%; 10%. Ocular therapeutic system (see Comments): 20 mcg; 40 mcg
Use: Treatment of glaucoma
Minor Side Effects: Blurred vision; browache; headache; loss of night vision; twitching of eyelids
Major Side Effects: Diarrhea; difficult urination; flushing; muscle tremors; nausea; nearsightedness; other changes in vision; palpitations; shortness of breath; stomach cramps; sweating
Contraindications: This drug should not be used by people who are allergic to pilocarpine. Consult your doctor immediately if this drug has been prescribed for you and you have such an allergy.
Warnings: This drug should be used cautiously by people who have heart damage, asthma, peptic ulcer, thyroid disease, spasms of the gastrointestinal tract, blockage of the urinary tract, seizures, and Parkinson's disease. Be sure your doctor knows if you have any of these conditions. • Be careful about the contamination of solutions used for the eyes. Wash your hands before using eyedrops. Do not touch dropper to your eye. Wash or wipe the dropper before replacing it in the bottle. Close the bottle tightly to keep out moisture.

Comments: To administer eyedrops, lie or sit down and tilt your head back. Carefully pull your lower eyelid down to form a pouch. Hold the dropper close to, but not touching, the eyelid, and place the prescribed number of drops into the pouch. Do not place the drops directly on the eyeball; you probably will blink and lose the medication. Close your eye and keep it shut for a few moments. • This drug may sting when first administered; this sensation usually goes away quickly. • Like other eyedrops, this drug may cause some clouding or blurring of vision. This side effect will go away quickly. • The ocular therapeutic system mentioned is an oval ring of plastic that contains pilocarpine. This ring is placed in the eye, and the drug is released gradually over a period of seven days. Use of these rings has made possible the control of glaucoma for some patients. If you are having trouble controlling glaucoma, ask your doctor about the possibility of using one of these devices.

Isordil anti-anginal

Manufacturer: Ives Laboratories, Inc.
Ingredient: isosorbide dinitrate
Equivalent Products: Dilitrate SR, Reed & Carnrick; Iso-Bid, Geriatric Pharmaceutical Corp.; Isonate, Major Pharmaceuticals; isosorbide dinitrate, various manufacturers; Isotrate Timecelles, W. E. Hauck, Inc.; Onset-10, Bock Pharmacal Co.; Sorate, Trimen Laboratories, Inc.; Sorbide T. D., Mayrand Pharmaceuticals, Inc.; Sorbitrate, Stuart Pharmaceuticals
Dosage Forms: Chewable tablet: 5 mg (orange); 10 mg (yellow). Sublingual tablet: 2.5 mg (yellow); 5 mg (pink); 10 mg (white). Sustained-action capsule: 40 mg (blue/clear with beads). Sustained-action tablet: 40 mg (green). Tablet: 5 mg (pink); 10 mg (white); 20 mg (green); 30 mg (blue); 40 mg (blue)
Use: Prevention (tablet and capsule) and relief (chewable and sublingual tablets) of chest pain (angina) due to heart disease
Minor Side Effects: Dizziness; flushing; headache; nausea; vomiting
Major Side Effects: Fainting spells; low blood pressure; palpitations; rash; restlessness; sweating; weakness
Contraindications: This drug should not be taken by people allergic to it or who are recovering from a heart attack. Consult your doctor if this drug has been prescribed for you and you have either of these conditions.
Warnings: This drug interacts with nitroglycerin; if you are currently using nitroglycerin, consult your doctor about its use. • Before using this drug to relieve chest pain, be certain pain arises from the heart and is not due to a muscle spasm or to indigestion. • If your chest pain is not relieved by use of this drug, if pain arises from a different location or differs in severity, consult your doctor immediately. • This drug should be used cautiously by those with glaucoma, severe anemia, thyroid disease, or frequent diarrhea.
Comments: Although the sublingual and chewable tablets are effective in relieving chest pain, there is some question about the effectiveness of the other forms in preventing pain. Carefully discuss the possible benefits of this drug with your doctor before purchasing it. • With continued use, you may develop a tolerance to this drug; many adverse side effects disappear after two to three weeks of drug use, but you may also become less responsive to the drug's beneficial effects. • The chewable tablets must be chewed to release the medication they contain. • The sustained-action forms must be swallowed whole. • Do not suddenly stop taking this medication without first consulting with your doctor. • To take a sublingual tablet properly, place the tablet under your tongue, close your mouth, and hold the saliva in your mouth and under your tongue as long as you can before swallowing it. If you have a bitter taste in your mouth after five minutes, the drug has not been completely absorbed. Wait five more minutes before drinking water. It may be necessary to take another

tablet in ten minutes if the pain still exists. If you still have pain after using three tablets in a 30-minute period, call your doctor or go to a hospital. • To avoid dizziness or light-headedness when you stand, contract and relax the muscles of your legs for a few moments before rising. Do this by pushing one foot against the floor while raising the other foot slightly, alternating feet so that you are "pumping" your legs in a pedaling motion. • Alcoholic beverages should be avoided or used with caution, as they may enhance the severity of this drug's side effects.

isosorbide dinitrate anti-anginal (various manufacturers), see Isordil anti-anginal.

Isotrate Timecelles anti-anginal (W. E. Hauck, Inc.), see Isordil anti-anginal.

Janimine antidepressant (Abbott Laboratories), see Tofranil antidepressant.

Kaochlor potassium chloride replacement (Adria Laboratories, Inc.), see potassium chloride replacement.

Kaon potassium chloride replacement (Adria Laboratories, Inc.), see potassium chloride replacement.

Kato potassium chloride replacement (Legere Laboratories), see potassium chloride replacement.

Kay Ciel potassium chloride replacement (Berlex Laboratories, Inc.), see potassium chloride replacement.

Keflex antibiotic

Manufacturer: Dista Products Co.
Ingredient: cephalexin
Dosage Forms: Capsule: 250 mg (white/dark green); 500 mg (light green/dark green). Drop (content per ml): 100 mg. Liquid (content per 5 ml teaspoon): 125 mg; 250 mg. Tablet: 1 g (green)
Use: Treatment of bacterial infections
Minor Side Effects: Abdominal pain; diarrhea; dizziness; fatigue; headache; heartburn; itching; loss of appetite; nausea; vomiting
Major Side Effects: Difficult breathing; fever; rash; rectal and vaginal itching; severe diarrhea; sore mouth; stomach cramps; superinfection; tingling in the hands or feet; unusual bruising or bleeding
Contraindications: This drug should not be used by people who are allergic to it or to other antibiotics similar to it. Consult your doctor immediately if this drug has been prescribed for you and you have such an allergy.
Warnings: This drug should be used cautiously by people who are allergic to penicillin or cephalosporin antibiotics or who have other allergies; by women who are pregnant or nursing; and by people with kidney disease. Be sure your doctor knows if you fit into any of these categories. • This drug should be used cautiously in newborn infants. • Prolonged use of this drug may allow organisms that are not susceptible to it to grow wildly. Do not use this drug unless your

doctor has specifically told you to do so. Be sure to follow directions carefully and report any unusual reactions to your doctor at once. •This drug should be used cautiously in conjunction with diuretics, probenecid, and aminoglycoside antibiotics. If you are not certain about what kind of medications you use, ask your doctor or pharmacist. • This drug may interfere with some blood tests. Be sure your doctor knows you are taking it. • Diabetics using Clinitest urine test may get a false high sugar reading. Change to Clinistix urine test or Tes-Tape urine test to avoid this problem.

Comments: It is generally believed that about 10 percent of all people who are allergic to penicillin will be allergic to an antibiotic like this as well. • This drug is frequently prescribed for infections that can be adequately treated with penicillin, which is less expensive. Ask your doctor if you could take penicillin instead of this drug. You may be able to save money. • This drug should be taken for at least ten full days. • Take this drug with food or milk if stomach upset occurs. • The liquid form of this drug should be refrigerated and any unused portion should be discarded after 14 days. Shake well before using.

Kenac steroid hormone (NMC Laboratories), see Kenalog steroid hormone.

Kenalog steroid hormone

Manufacturer: E. R. Squibb & Sons, Inc.
Ingredient: triamcinolone acetonide
Equivalent Products: Aristocort and Aristocort A, Lederle Laboratories; Flutex, Syosset Labs., Inc.; Kenac, NMC Laboratories; Triacet, Lemmon Company; triamcinolone acetonide, various manufacturers; Triderm, Del-Ray Laboratories, Inc.; Trymex, Savage Laboratories
Dosage Forms: Cream: 0.025%; 0.1%; 0.5%. Lotion: 0.025%; 0.1%. Ointment: 0.025%; 0.5%; 0.1%. Spray: 0.2 mg per two-second spray
Use: Relief of skin inflammation associated with conditions such as eczema, poison ivy, or other dermatoses
Minor Side Effects: Burning sensation; dryness; irritation of affected area; itching; rash
Major Side Effects: Blistering; increased hair growth; loss of skin color; secondary infection; skin wasting
Contraindications: This drug should not be used by people who are allergic to it. This drug should not be used in the ear if the eardrum is perforated or by people who have viral or fungal skin diseases, tuberculosis of the skin, or severe circulatory disorders. Consult your doctor immediately if this drug has been prescribed for you and you have any of these conditions.
Warnings: If irritation develops when using this drug, immediately discontinue its use and notify your doctor. • If extensive areas are treated or if an occlusive bandage is used, there will be increased systemic absorption of this drug, and suitable precautions should be taken, particularly in children and infants. • This drug is not for use in the eyes. • When the spray form of this drug is used about the face, the eyes should be covered and inhalation of the spray should be avoided. • This drug should be used cautiously by pregnant women.
Comments: The spray form of this drug produces a cooling sensation, which may be uncomfortable for some persons. • If the affected area is extremely dry or is scaling, the skin may be moistened before applying the product by soaking the affected area in water or by applying water with a clean cloth. The ointment form is probably the better product for dry skin. • Do not use the drug with an occlusive wrap of transparent plastic film unless directed to do so by your

doctor. If it is necessary for you to use this drug under a wrap, follow your doctor's instructions exactly; do not leave the wrap in place longer than specified.

Klavikordal anti-anginal (U.S. Ethicals), see Nitro-Bid anti-anginal.

Klor-Con potassium chloride replacement (Upsher-Smith Laboratories, Inc.), see potassium chloride replacement.

K-Lor potassium chloride replacement (Abbott Laboratories), see potassium chloride replacement.

Klor potassium chloride replacement (Upsher-Smith Laboratories, Inc.), see potassium chloride replacement.

Klorvess potassium chloride replacement (Sandoz Pharmaceuticals), see potassium chloride replacement.

Klotrix potassium chloride replacement (Mead Johnson Co.), see potassium chloride replacement.

K-Lyte/Cl potassium chloride replacement (Mead Johnson Co.), see potassium chloride replacement.

K-Lyte DS potassium replacement (Mead Johnson Co.), see K-Lyte potassium replacement.

K-Lyte potassium replacement

Manufacturer: Mead Johnson Co.
Ingredients: potassium bicarbonate; potassium citrate
Equivalent Product: Effer-K, Nomax Pharmaceutical, Inc.
Dosage Form: Effervescent tablet: 25 mEq potassium; 50 mEq potassium (fruit flavors)
Use: Prevention or treatment of potassium deficiency
Minor Side Effects: Abdominal discomfort; diarrhea; nausea; vomiting
Major Side Effects: Anxiety; confusion; difficult breathing; irregular heartbeat; numbness or tingling in the arms or legs; severe stomach pain; ulcer
Contraindications: This drug should not be taken by people with severe kidney disease, Addison's disease, high blood potassium, or by those who are allergic to it. Consult your doctor immediately if this drug has been prescribed for you and you have any of these conditions or such an allergy.
Warnings: Supplements of potassium should be administered with caution, since the amount of potassium deficiency may be difficult to determine accurately. • Potassium intoxication rarely occurs in patients with normal kidney function. • This drug should be taken cautiously by digitalized patients and such patients should be monitored by ECG for heart problems. • This drug should be used cautiously by people with stomach ulcers, intestinal blockage, or acute dehydration. • This drug interacts with spironolactone and triamterene. If you are currently taking any drugs of these types, consult your doctor about their use. If you are unsure of the type or contents of your medications, ask your doctor or pharmacist.

Comments: Carefully dissolve each dose completely in the stated amount of water. Do not take this tablet whole. • Potassium supplements usually have a low rate of patient compliance. People usually take it infrequently, or they stop taking it altogether. If a potassium product is prescribed for you, be sure to take the medication as directed and do not stop taking it without first consulting your doctor. • This drug should be taken with meals. • Consult your doctor about using salt substitutes instead of, or along with this drug. Another product, K-Lyte DS (Mead Johnson Co.), is identical to K-Lyte, except it is twice the strength.

Kolyum potassium chloride replacement (Pennwalt Pharmaceutical Division), see potassium chloride replacement.

Korostatin antifungal agent (Holland-Rantos Co., Inc.), see Mycostatin antifungal agent.

K-Tab potassium chloride replacement (Abbott Laboratories), see potassium chloride replacement.

Kwell pediculocide and scabicide

Manufacturer: Reed & Carnrick
Ingredient: lindane (gamma benzene hexachloride)
Equivalent Products: G-well, Goldline Laboratories; Kwildane, Major Pharmaceuticals; lindane, various manufacturers; Scabene, Stiefel Laboratories, Inc.
Dosage Forms: Cream; Lotion; Shampoo: 1.0%
Use: Elimination of crab lice, head lice and their nits, and scabies
Minor Side Effects: Rash; skin irritation if product is improperly used
Major Side Effects: See Warnings
Contraindications: This drug should not be used by people who are allergic to it. Consult your doctor immediately if this drug has been prescribed for you and you have such an allergy.
Warnings: Side effects to this drug are rare if the directions for use are followed. However, convulsions and even death can result if the drug is swallowed or overused. If swallowed, do not take mineral oil; call the poison control center, your doctor, or pharmacist immediately. • Do not use this drug with other skin products. • Special caution must be used in treating children, infants, and pregnant women with this drug. • If you get any of this product in your eyes, flush them immediately with water. • Do not use this product over a longer period or more often than recommended by your doctor. • Do not use this product on your face. • Be sure to rinse this product off completely, as is stated in the directions.
Comments: Complete directions for the use of this drug are supplied by the manufacturer. Ask your pharmacist for these directions if he does not supply them. • Lice are easily transmitted from one person to another. All family members should be carefully examined. Personal items (clothing, towels) need only be machine-washed on the "hot" temperature cycle and dried. No unusual cleaning measures are required. Combs, brushes, and other such washable items may be soaked in boiling water for one hour. • After using this product you must remove the dead nits (eggs). Use a fine-tooth comb to remove them from your hair, or mix a solution of equal parts of water and vinegar and apply it to the affected area. Rub the solution in well. After several minutes, shampoo with your regular shampoo and then brush your hair. This process should remove all nits. • A lice infestation can be treated just as effectively with a nonprescription

product as with this product. Consult your pharmacist. However, this product is effective for scabies. The nonprescription medication is not.

Kwildane pediculocide and scabicide (Major Pharmaceuticals), see Kwell pediculocide and scabicide.

LaBID bronchodilator (Norwich-Eaton Pharmaceuticals), see Theodur bronchodilator.

Laniazid antitubercular (The Lannett Company, Inc.), see isoniazid antitubercular.

Lanophyllin-GG expectorant and smooth muscle relaxant (The Lannett Company, Inc.), see Quibron expectorant and smooth muscle relaxant.

Lanorinal analgesic and sedative (The Lannett Company, Inc.), see Fiorinal analgesic and sedative.

Lanoxin heart drug

Manufacturer: Burroughs Wellcome Co.
Ingredient: digoxin
Equivalent Products: digoxin, various manufacturers; SK-Digoxin, Smith Kline & French Laboratories. (see Comments)
Dosage Forms: Elixir, pediatric (content per cc): 0.05 mg. Tablet: 0.125 mg (yellow); 0.25 mg (white); 0.5 mg (green). Capsules: 0.05 mg (red); 0.1 mg (yellow); 0.2 mg (green)
Use: To strengthen heartbeat and improve heart rhythm
Minor Side Effects: Apathy; diarrhea; drowsiness; headache; muscle weakness; weakness
Major Side Effects: Disorientation; enlarged breasts; hallucinations; loss of appetite; mental depression; nausea; palpitations; slow heart rate; visual disturbances (such as blurred or yellow vision); vomiting
Contraindications: People who have suffered heart stoppage, and people who are allergic to this drug should not take it; consult your doctor immediately if this drug has been prescribed for you and you have any of these conditions.
Warnings: This drug should be used cautiously by people who have kidney disease, thyroid disease, certain heart diseases, lung diseases, potassium depletion, or calcium accumulation. Be sure your doctor knows if you have any of these conditions. • This drug should be used cautiously in infants. • Some people develop toxic reactions to this drug. If you suffer any side effects that are prolonged or especially bothersome, contact your doctor. • The elderly may have more side effects from this drug than younger people, and they should have regular checkups while taking it. • This drug interacts with aminoglycosides, antacids, antibiotics, amphotericin B, cholestyramine, colestipol hydrochloride, diuretics, phenylbutazone, propantheline, propranolol, and spironolactone; if you are currently taking any drugs of these types, consult your doctor about their use. If you are unsure of the type or contents of your medications, ask your doctor or pharmacist. • This drug should never be used for weight loss. • The pharmacologic activity of the different brands of this drug varies widely due to how well the tablets or capsules dissolve in the stomach and bowels. Because of this variation it is important not to change brands of the drug without consulting your doctor.

Comments: Dosages of this drug must be carefully adjusted to the needs and responses of the individual patient. Your doctor may find it necessary to adjust your dosage of this drug frequently. • Your doctor may want you to take your pulse daily while you are using this drug. • Take this drug at the same time every day. Do not skip any doses and do not stop taking this medication. • While taking this drug, do not take any nonprescription item for cough, cold, or sinus problems without first checking with your doctor. • There are no products exactly equivalent to Lanoxin heart drug. You should not switch to another brand of digoxin unless your doctor is monitoring your condition closely. Because this product is priced inexpensively, you will probably save little, if any, money by switching to another brand. • Notify your doctor if you experience a loss of appetite, pain in the stomach, nausea, vomiting, diarrhea, unusual tiredness or weakness, blurred or yellow vision, or mental depression.

Lanvisone steroid hormone and anti-infective (The Lannett Company, Inc.), see Vioform-Hydrocortisone steroid hormone and anti-infective.

Larotid antibiotic (Beecham Laboratories), see amoxicillin antibiotic.

Lasix diuretic and antihypertensive

Manufacturer: Hoechst-Roussel Pharmaceuticals, Inc.
Ingredient: furosemide
Equivalent Products: furosemide, various manufacturers; SK-Furosemide, Smith Kline & French Laboratories
Dosage Forms: Liquid (content per ml): 10 mg. Tablet: 20 mg; 40 mg; 80 mg (all are white)
Use: Treatment of high blood pressure; removal of fluid from body tissues
Minor Side Effects: Blurred vision; constipation; cramping; diarrhea; dizziness; headache; itching; loss of appetite; muscle spasm; nausea; sore mouth; stomach upset; sun sensitivity; vomiting; weakness
Major Side Effects: Anemia; blood disorders; bruising; dry mouth; gout; jaundice; loss of appetite; low blood pressure; muscle cramps; palpitations; pancreatitis; rash; ringing in the ears; rise in blood sugar; sore throat; thirst; tingling in the fingers and toes
Contraindications: This drug should not be used by pregnant women or by women who may become pregnant. It should not be used by persons with anuria (inability to urinate). This drug should not be used by people who are allergic to it. Consult your doctor immediately if this drug has been prescribed for you and you fit any of these descriptions.
Warnings: Use of this drug may cause gout, diabetes, hearing loss, and loss of potassium, calcium, water, and salt. • Persons hypersensitive to sulfa drugs may also be hypersensitive to this drug. If this drug has been prescribed for you and you are allergic to sulfa drugs, consult your doctor immediately. • Persons taking this drug should have periodic blood and urine tests. • This drug should be used cautiously by persons with cirrhosis of the liver or other liver problems, or with kidney disease. This drug should be used cautiously by children. Nursing mothers who must take this drug should stop nursing. Be sure your doctor knows if you fit any of these descriptions. • This drug should be used with caution in conjunction with other high blood pressure drugs. • Use of this drug may activate the appearance of systemic lupus erythematosus. • Whenever adverse reactions to this drug are moderate to severe, this drug should be reduced or discontinued. Consult your doctor promptly if side effects occur. •

This drug interacts with aspirin, curare, indomethacin, digitalis, lithium carbonate, steroids, or cephaloridine. If you are currently taking any drugs of these types, consult your doctor about their use. If you are unsure of the type or contents of your medications, ask your doctor or pharmacist.

Comments: This drug causes frequent urination. Expect this effect; it should not alarm you. • This drug has potent activity. If another drug to decrease blood pressure is also prescribed, your doctor may decide to decrease the dose of one of the drugs to avoid an excessive drop in blood pressure. • This drug can cause potassium loss. Signs of such loss include dry mouth, thirst, muscle cramps, weakness, and nausea or vomiting. If you experience any of these side effects, notify your doctor. To help avoid such loss, take this drug with a glass of fresh or frozen orange juice. You may also eat a banana each day. The use of a salt substitute helps prevent potassium loss. • To avoid dizziness or light-headedness when you stand, contract and relax the muscles of your legs for a few moments before rising. Do this by pushing one foot against the floor while raising the other foot slightly, alternating feet so that you are "pumping" your legs in a pedaling motion. • Persons taking this product and digitalis should watch carefully for symptoms of increased digitalis toxicity (e.g., nausea, blurred vision, palpitations) and notify their doctors immediately if symptoms occur. • If you have high blood pressure, do not take any nonprescription item for weight control or cough, cold, or sinus problems without first checking with your doctor. • When taking this drug (or other drugs for high blood pressure), limit the use of alcohol to avoid dizziness or light-headedness. • Take this drug exactly as directed. Do not take extra doses or skip a dose without first consulting your doctor. • The liquid form of this drug should be stored in the refrigerator in a light-resistant container.

Ledercillin VK antibiotic (Lederle Laboratories), see penicillin potassium phenoxymethyl (penicillin VK) antibiotic.

Levothroid thyroid hormone (USV Laboratories), see Synthroid thyroid hormone.

levothyroxine sodium thyroid hormone (Lederle Laboratories), see Synthroid thyroid hormone.

Librax sedative and anticholinergic

Manufacturer: Roche Products, Inc.
Ingredients: chlordiazepoxide hydrochloride; clidinium bromide
Equivalent Products: Chlordinium, Lemmon Company; Clindex, Rugby Laboratories; Clinoxide, Geneva Generics, Inc.; Clipoxide, Henry Schein, Inc.; Lidox, Major Pharmaceuticals
Dosage Form: Capsule: chlordiazepoxide hydrochloride, 5 mg; clidinium bromide, 2.5 mg (green)
Use: In conjunction with other drugs, treatment of peptic ulcer or irritable bowel syndrome
Minor Side Effects: Blurred vision; change in sense of taste; confusion; constipation; depression; diarrhea; dizziness; drowsiness; dry mouth; fatigue; fluid retention; headache; increased sensitivity to light; insomnia; menstrual irregularities; nausea; reduced sweating; vomiting
Major Side Effects: Decreased sexual ability; difficult breathing; difficult urination; double vision; excitation; hallucinations; jaundice; palpitations; rash; sore throat; uncoordinated movements

Contraindications: This drug should not be taken by people who have glaucoma, enlarged prostate, or obstructed bladder or intestine. Consult your doctor immediately if this drug has been prescribed for you and you have any of these conditions.

Warnings: This drug should be used cautiously by people who have severe heart or lung disease, liver or kidney disease, porphyria, high blood pressure, myasthenia gravis, epilepsy, thyroid disease, or colitis; or by those who are pregnant or nursing. Be sure your doctor knows if you have any of these conditions. • This drug should not be used in conjunction with amantadine, haloperidol, other central nervous system depressants, phenothiazines, alcohol, or antacids; if you are currently taking any drugs of these types, consult your doctor about their use. If you are unsure of the type or contents of your medications, ask your doctor or pharmacist. • Call your doctor if you notice a rash, flushing, or pain in the eye. • This drug has a slight potential for abuse, but taken as directed, there is little danger. Do not increase or decrease the dose of this drug without first consulting your doctor. • Elderly patients generally should take the smallest effective dosage of this drug.

Comments: This drug is best taken one-half to one hour before meals. • This drug does not cure ulcers, but may help them improve. • Chew gum or suck on ice chips or a piece of hard candy to reduce mouth dryness. • This drug always produces certain side effects, which may include dry mouth, blurred vision, reduced sweating, drowsiness, difficult urination, constipation, increased sensitivity to light, and palpitations. Avoid tasks that require alertness. Avoid excessive work or exercise in hot weather. • To prevent oversedation, avoid taking alcohol or other drugs that have sedative properties. • If this drug makes it hard for you to urinate, try to do so just before you take each dose.

Libritabs sedative and hypnotic (Roche Products, Inc.), see Librium sedative and hypnotic.

Librium sedative and hypnotic

Manufacturer: Roche Products, Inc.

Ingredient: chlordiazepoxide hydrochloride

Equivalent Products: A-poxide, Abbott Laboratories; chlordiazepoxide hydrochloride, various manufacturers; Libritabs, Roche Products, Inc.; Lipoxide, Major Pharmaceuticals; Murcil, Reid-Provident Labs., Inc.; Reposans-10, Wesley Pharmacal Co.; Sereen, Foy Laboratories; SK-Lygen, Smith Kline & French Laboratories

Dosage Forms: Capsule: 5 mg (green/yellow); 10 mg (green/black); 25 mg (green/white). Tablet: 5 mg; 10 mg; 25 mg (green)

Use: Relief of anxiety; nervousness; tension; muscle spasms; withdrawal symptoms of alcohol addiction

Minor Side Effects: Confusion; constipation; depression; dizziness; drooling; drowsiness; dry mouth; fainting; fatigue; fluid retention; headache; heartburn; insomnia; loss of appetite; menstrual irregularities; nausea; sweating

Major Side Effects: Blood disorders; blurred vision; decrease or increase in sex drive; difficult breathing; difficult urination; double vision; excitation; fever; hallucinations; jaundice; low blood pressure; rash; slow heart rate; slurred speech; sore throat; stimulation; tremors; weakness

Contraindications: This drug should not be used by people who are allergic to it or by pregnant or nursing women. Consult your doctor immediately if this drug has been prescribed for you and you have any of these conditions.

Warnings: This drug should be used cautiously by people who have liver or kidney disease; those with acute, narrow-angle glaucoma; and those who are depressed. Be sure your doctor knows if you have any of these conditions. • Elderly people should use this drug cautiously and take the smallest effective dose. • This drug has the potential for abuse and must be used with caution. Tolerance may develop quickly; do not increase the dose of this drug without first consulting your doctor. • Taken alone, this drug is safe. Do not take it with other sedative drugs, central nervous system depressants, or alcohol, however, or serious adverse reactions may develop. • This drug should be used cautiously in conjunction with phenytoin, cimetidine, lithium, levodopa, isoniazid, rifampin, or disulfiram. • This drug may cause drowsiness; avoid tasks that require alertness. • Consult your doctor if you wish to discontinue use of this drug; do not stop taking the drug suddenly. If you have been using the drug for an extended period of time, it will be necessary to reduce the dosage gradually, following medical advice. • Unexpected excitement sometimes occurs in persons taking this drug. This effect is especially likely to occur in psychotics. If such an effect occurs, the drug should be stopped. • Persons taking this drug for a long period should have periodic blood counts and liver function tests.

Comments: It is important to try to remove the cause of the nervousness. Consult your doctor. • Chew gum or suck on ice chips or a piece of hard candy to reduce mouth dryness. • Take this medication with food or a full glass of water if stomach upset occurs. Do not take it with an antacid; it may retard absorption of the drug.

Lidex topical steroid hormone

Manufacturer: Syntex Laboratories, Inc.
Ingredient: fluocinonide
Dosage Forms: Cream; Gel; Ointment; Solution: 0.05%
Use: Relief of skin inflammation associated with conditions such as eczema or poison ivy
Minor Side Effects: Burning sensation; dryness; irritation of affected area; itching; rash
Major Side Effects: Blistering; increased hair growth; loss of skin color; secondary infection; skin wasting
Contraindications: This drug should not be taken by people who are allergic to it. This drug should not be used in the ear if the eardrum is perforated or by people who have viral or fungal skin disease, tuberculosis of the skin, or severe circulatory disorders. Consult your doctor immediately if this drug has been prescribed for you and you have any of these conditions.
Warnings: If irritation develops, consult your doctor. • If extensive areas are treated or if occlusive dressings are used, there will be increased systemic absorption of this drug and suitable precautions should be taken, especially in children and infants. • This drug should be used cautiously by pregnant women. • This drug should not be used in the eyes.
Comments: The gel form may produce a cooling sensation on the skin. • If the affected area is dry or is scaling, the skin may be moistened before applying the product by soaking in water or by applying water with a clean cloth. The ointment form is probably the better product for dry skin. • Do not use these products with an occlusive wrap of transparent plastic film unless directed to do so by your doctor. If it is necessary for you to use this drug under a wrap, follow your doctor's directions exactly. Do not leave the wrap in place for a longer time than specified. • Lidex-E topical steroid hormone is also manufactured by Syntex Laboratories, Inc. It contains fluocinonide in a cream form similar to

Lidex, but has more skin-softening ingredients. For all practical purposes Lidex and Lidex-E are the same.

Lidox sedative and anticholinergic (Major Pharmaceuticals), see Librax sedative and anticholinergic.

Limbitrol antidepressant

Manufacturer: Roche Products, Inc.
Ingredients: amitriptyline; chlordiazepoxide
Dosage Form: Tablet 10-25: chlordiazepoxide, 10 mg; amitriptyline, 25 mg (white). Tablet 5-12.5: chlordiazepoxide, 5 mg; amitriptyline, 12.5 mg (blue)
Use: Treatment of depression and anxiety
Minor Side Effects: Agitation; bloating; blurred vision; confusion; constipation; cramps; diarrhea; dizziness; drowsiness; dry mouth; fatigue; headache; heartburn; increased sensitivity to light; insomnia; loss of appetite; nasal congestion; nausea; numbness in fingers or toes; peculiar tastes; restlessness; stomach upset; sweating; vomiting; weakness
Major Side Effects: Bleeding; convulsions; difficult urination; enlarged or painful breasts (in both sexes); fainting; fever; fluid retention; hair loss; hallucinations; heart attack; high or low blood pressure; imbalance; impotence; jaundice; menstrual irregularities; mood changes; mouth sores; nervousness; nightmares; palpitations; psychosis; rash; ringing in the ears; sleep disorders; sore throat; stroke; tremors; uncoordination; weight loss or gain
Contraindications: This drug should not be taken by people who are allergic to it or by anyone who has recently had a heart attack. The drug should not be taken by people who are using monoamine oxidase inhibitors (ask your pharmacist if you are unsure). Consult your doctor immediately if this drug has been prescribed for you and you have any of these conditions.
Warnings: This drug should be used cautiously by the elderly and by people who have glaucoma (certain types), lung disease, high blood pressure, myasthenia gravis, enlarged prostate, intestinal blockage, heart disease (certain types), epilepsy, thyroid disease, liver or kidney disease, or who have ever had urinary retention problems. Pregnant or nursing women; people who are receiving electroshock therapy; or those who use drugs that lower blood pressure should also use this drug cautiously. Be sure your doctor knows if you have any of these conditions. • If you are about to undergo surgery, be sure your doctor knows you are taking this drug. • Close medical supervision is required when this drug is taken with guanethidine or Placidyl hypnotic. • This drug may cause changes in blood sugar levels. • This drug interacts with alcohol, amphetamine, anticholinergics, barbiturates, clonidine, epinephrine, phenylephrine, and depressants. If you are currently taking any drugs of these types, consult your doctor about their use. If you are unsure of the type or contents of your medications, ask your doctor or pharmacist. • This drug may cause drowsiness; avoid tasks that require alertness. • To prevent oversedation, avoid the use of alcohol or other drugs that have sedative properties. • Report any sudden mood changes to your doctor. • Do not stop taking this drug suddenly. If you have been using this drug for an extended period, it will be necessary to reduce the dosage gradually, following medical advice. • Unexpected excitement sometimes occurs in persons taking this drug. If this occurs, the drug should be stopped. • Persons taking this drug for long periods of time should have periodic blood and liver function tests.
Comments: While taking this drug, do not take any nonprescription item for cough, cold, or sinus problems without first checking with your doctor. Be sure your doctor is aware of every medication you use, and do not stop or start any

other drug without your doctor's approval. • The full effects of therapy with this drug may not be apparent for two weeks. • Chew gum or suck on ice chips or a piece of hard candy to reduce mouth dryness. • Avoid long exposure to the sun while taking this drug. • To decrease stomach upset caused by this drug, take it with food or milk. • To avoid dizziness or light-headedness when you stand, contract and relax the muscles of your legs for a few moments before rising. Do this by pushing one foot against the floor while raising the other foot slightly, alternating feet so that you are "pumping" your legs in a pedaling motion. • Many people receive as much benefit from taking a single dose of this drug at bedtime as from taking multiple doses throughout the day. Talk to your doctor about this. • Taken alone this drug is safe. When it is mixed with other sedatives, especially alcohol, it may not be.

Lipo Gantrisin antibacterial (Roche Products, Inc.), see Gantisin antibacterial.

Lipoxide sedative and hypnotic (Major Pharmaceuticals), see Librium sedative and hypnotic.

Lixaminol bronchodilator (Ferndale Laboratories, Inc.), see aminophylline bronchodilator.

Lofene anticholinergic and antispasmodic (The Lannett Company, Inc.), see Lomotil anticholinergic and antispasmodic.

Lomotil anticholinergic and antispasmodic

Manufacturer: Searle & Co.
Ingredients: diphenoxylate hydrochloride with atropine sulfate
Equivalent Products: Diphenatol, Rugby Laboratories; diphenoxylate hydrochloride with atropine sulfate, various manufacturers; Enoxa, Reid-Provident Labs., Inc.; Lofene, The Lannett Company, Inc.; Lonox, Geneva Generics, Inc.; Lo-Trol, Vangard Laboratories; Low-Quel, Halsey Drug Co., Inc.; Nor-Mil, Vortech; SK-Diphenoxylate, Smith Kline & French Laboratories
Dosage Forms: Liquid (content per 5 ml teaspoon); Tablet (white): atropine sulfate, 0.025 mg; diphenoxylate hydrochloride, 2.5 mg
Use: Treatment of diarrhea
Minor Side Effects: Blurred vision; constipation; dizziness; drowsiness; dry mouth; fever; flushing; headache; increased heart rate; itching; loss of appetite; nervousness; sedation; sweating; swollen gums
Major Side Effects: Abdominal pain; bloating; breathing difficulties; coma; depression; difficult urination; euphoria; fever; hives; numbness in fingers or toes; palpitations; rash; severe nausea; vomiting; weakness
Contraindications: This drug should not be taken by children under the age of two. This drug should not be taken by people who have jaundice or drug-induced diarrhea, or by those who are allergic to it. Consult your doctor immediately if this drug has been prescribed for you and you have any of these conditions.
Warnings: This drug should be used cautiously by children, pregnant or nursing women, women of childbearing age, and people who have liver or kidney disease, lung disease, glaucoma, high blood pressure, myasthenia gravis, gallstones, enlarged prostate, thyroid disease, certain types of heart disease, or ulcerative colitis. Be sure your doctor knows if you have any of

these conditions. ● This drug has the potential for abuse and must be used with caution. Tolerance to this drug may develop quickly; do not increase the dose of this drug without first checking with your doctor. ● This drug may add to the effect of alcohol and other drugs with sedative properties. Do not use them without first checking with your doctor. ● This drug interacts with amantadine, haloperidol, phenothiazines, and monoamine oxidase inhibitors; if you are currently taking any drugs of these types, consult your doctor about their use. If you are unsure of the type or contents of your medications, ask your doctor or pharmacist.

Comments: While taking this drug, drink at least eight to ten glasses of water a day. ● This drug may interfere with your ability to perform hazardous tasks such as driving. ● Unless your doctor prescribes otherwise, do not take this drug for more than five days. ● Check with your doctor if diarrhea does not subside within two or three days. ● If you take this drug with you when traveling to a foreign country, do not use it unless you absolutely have to. Make sure that the diarrhea is not just a temporary occurrence (two to three hours). ● Call your doctor if you notice a rash or if fever or heart palpitations occur.

Lonox anticholinergic and antispasmodic (Geneva Generics, Inc.), see Lomotil anticholinergic and antispasmodic.

Lopressor beta blocker

Manufacturer: GEIGY Pharmaceuticals
Ingredient: metoprolol tartrate
Dosage Form: Tablet: 50 mg (light red); 100 mg (light blue)
Use: Management of high blood pressure and prevention of irregular heartbeat after heart attack
Minor Side Effects: Abdominal cramps; constipation; diarrhea; drowsiness; dry eyes; dry mouth; gas; gastric pain; headache; heartburn; insomnia; loss of appetite; nasal congestion; nausea; slow heart rate
Major Side Effects: Bruising; cold extremities; confusion; depression; dizziness; fainting; fever; hallucinations; heart failure; itching; nightmares; numbness or tingling in the hands and feet; palpitations; rash; reversible loss of hair; ringing in the ears; shortness of breath; slurred speech; sore throat; tiredness; visual disturbances; weak pulse; wheezing
Contraindications: This drug should not be used by people with certain types of heart disease (such as bradycardia, overt cardiac failure, heart block, or cardiogenic shock). Consult your doctor about the use of this drug if you have any of these heart diseases.
Warnings: This drug should be used with caution by people with thyroid disease, impaired kidney or liver function, asthma, or diabetes. Be sure your doctor knows if you have any of these conditions. ● Diabetics should be aware that this drug may mask signs of hypoglycemia such as changes in pulse rate and blood pressure. ● Persons about to undergo surgery should use this drug with caution. ● Pregnant women, nursing mothers, and children should take this drug only when clearly needed. ● Extra care is needed if this drug is used with reserpine, phenytoin, terbutaline, aminophylline, theophylline, digitalis, phenobarbital, or cimetidine. If you are currently taking this drug, consult your doctor about its use. If you are unsure of the type or contents of your medications, ask your doctor or pharmacist. ● This drug is potent and should not be stopped abruptly (unless your doctor advises you to do so). Chest pain and even heart attacks have occurred when this drug has been stopped suddenly.
Comments: It is best to take this drug with food. ● While taking this drug, do not take any nonprescription item for cough, cold, or sinus problems without

first checking with your doctor. • Your doctor may want you to take your pulse every day while you are taking this drug. Check with your doctor about this possibility. • Be sure to take the doses of this drug at the same time each day. • The action of this drug is similar to that of Inderal beta blocker (Ayerst Laboratories), except that Inderal is usually taken four times a day; Lopressor is usually taken twice a day. • Notify your doctor if dizziness, diarrhea, rash, or difficulty breathing develops.

Lopurin gout drug (Boots Pharmaceuticals, Inc.), see Zyloprim gout drug.

lorazepam sedative and hypnotic (Quantum Pharmics), see Ativan sedative and hypnotic.

Lotrimin antifungal agent

Manufacturer: Schering Corp.
Ingredient: clotrimazole
Equivalent Product: Mycelex, Miles Pharmaceuticals
Dosage Forms: Cream (content per gram); Solution; Lotion (content per ml): 1%
Use: Treatment of superficial fungal infections of the skin
Minor Side Effects: Redness; stinging sensation
Major Side Effects: Blistering; irritation; peeling of skin; swelling
Contraindications: This drug should not be used by people who are allergic to it. Consult your doctor immediately if this drug has been prescribed for you and you have such an allergy.
Warnings: This drug should be used with caution by pregnant women. • Do not use this drug in or near the eyes. • If irritation occurs, stop using this product and call your doctor.
Comments: This drug should be gently rubbed into the affected area and the surrounding skin. • Do not use a dressing over this drug unless instructed to do so by your physician. • Improvement in your condition may not be seen for one week after beginning treatment with this drug. Nevertheless, be sure to complete a full course of therapy. If the condition has not improved after four weeks, consult your doctor. • This drug is also available in vaginal cream and vaginal tablet forms to treat certain fungal infections of the vagina. Mycelex-G (Miles Pharmaceuticals) and Gyne-Lotrimin (Schering Corp.) antifungal agents are trademarked products of this type. • If you have a fungal infection of the vagina, wear cotton panties rather than those made of nylon or other nonporous materials. • Careful attention to personal hygiene may help prevent subsequent fungal infections of the vagina. • Apply this product after cleansing the area, unless your doctor has directed otherwise.

Lo-Trol anticholinergic and antispasmodic (Vangard Laboratories), see Lomotil anticholinergic and antispasmodic.

Low-Quel anticholinergic and antispasmodic (Halsey Drug Co., Inc.), see Lomotil anticholinergic and antispasmodic.

Ludiomil antidepressant

Manufacturer: CIBA Pharmaceutical Company
Ingredient: maprotiline hydrochloride

Dosage Form: Tablet: 25 mg; 50 mg (dark orange); 75 mg (white)

Use: Treatment of depression in persons with manic-depressive illness and of anxiety associated with depression

Minor side effects: Abdominal cramps; bitter taste in mouth; black tongue; bloating; blurred vision; constipation; diarrhea; dizziness; drowsiness; drooling; dry mouth; false sense of well-being; headache; increased appetite; increased or decreased sexual urge; increased salivation; irregular heartbeat; loss of memory; nasal congestion; nausea; nervousness; nightmares; pupil dilation; restlessness; sensitivity to sunlight; shaking; stomach distress; sweating; trouble in sleeping; vomiting; weight loss or gain

Major Side Effects: Anxiety; breast enlargement in men or women; confusion; convulsions; dark-colored urine; difficulty swallowing; disturbed concentration; eye pain; fever; frequent or difficult urination; hair loss; hallucinations; impotence; itching; menstrual irregularities; palpitations; panic; ringing in the ears; severe mental disorders; severe weakness; skin rash; sore throat; sores on the skin or mouth; swelling of the testicles; tingling in the hands or feet; yellowing of the skin or eyes

Contraindications: This drug should not be taken by anyone who is allergic to it. This drug should not be taken by anyone who has seizure disorders, who has recently had a heart attack, or who is taking or recently has taken monoamine oxidase inhibitors. Consult your doctor immediately if this drug has been prescribed for you and you have any of these conditions. Children under the age of 18 should not take this drug.

Warnings: This drug should be used with caution by persons with certain types of heart disease, high blood pressure, thyroid problems, glaucoma, urinary tract problems, stomach or intestinal problems, an enlarged prostate gland, schizophrenia, liver or kidney disease, or with a history of suicidal tendencies, alcoholism, or electroshock treatments. This drug should be used cautiously by those about to undergo surgery. Be sure your doctor knows if you have any of these conditions. • This drug should be used cautiously by pregnant or nursing women. • This drug may cause changes in blood sugar levels. • This drug interacts with anticholinergic or sympathomimetic drugs, amphetamines, oral contraceptives, epinephrine, phenylephrine, anti-Parkinson drugs, methylphenidate, barbiturates, phenothiazines, oral anticoagulants, beta blockers, anti-arrhythmics, thyroid drugs, blood pressure medications, and some painkillers and sedatives. If you are using any drugs of these types, consult your doctor about their use. If you are unsure about the type or contents of your medications, ask your doctor or pharmacist. • Avoid drinking alcohol while taking this drug. • If this drug causes drowsiness or dizziness, avoid tasks requiring alertness. • Report any mood changes to your doctor.

Comments: It may take one to two weeks before the therapeutic effect of this drug is evident. • If this drug causes stomach upset, take it with food. • This drug increases your sensitivity to sunlight; wear protective clothing and sunglasses and use an effective sunscreen. • Sucking on ice chips may relieve a dry mouth. • If you take this drug for a prolonged period of time, you will need to see your doctor regularly for blood cell counts, and liver function tests. • Do not stop taking this drug suddenly and do not increase the dosage without your doctor's approval. • To minimize dizziness and light-headedness, rise slowly from a sitting or lying position.

Luminal Ovoids sedative and hypnotic (Winthrop Laboratories), see phenobarbital sedative and hypnotic.

Macrodantin antibacterial

Manufacturer: Norwich-Eaton Pharmaceuticals
Ingredient: nitrofurantoin (macrocrystals)
Equivalent Product: nitrofurantoin, various manufacturers (see Comments)
Dosage Form: Capsule: 25 mg (white); 50 mg (yellow/white); 100 mg (yellow)
Use: Treatment of bacterial urinary tract infections such as pyelonephritis, pyelitis, or cystitis
Minor Side Effects: Abdominal cramps; change in urine color; diarrhea; dizziness; drowsiness; headache; loss of appetite; nausea; vomiting
Major Side Effects: Anemia; chest pain; chills; difficult breathing; fever; hair loss; hepatitis; irritation of the mouth; low blood pressure; muscle aches; numbness and tingling in face; rash; rectal and vaginal itching; superinfection; symptoms of lung infection; weakness; yellowing of eyes and skin
Contraindications: This drug should not be used by persons with severe kidney disease or little or no urine production. Be sure your doctor knows if you have such a condition. This drug should not be used by pregnant women at term or in infants under one month of age. This drug should not be used by people who are allergic to it. Consult your doctor immediately if this drug has been prescribed for you and you have such an allergy.
Warnings: This drug should be taken cautiously; it has been associated with lung problems. If such problems occur, your doctor will discontinue this drug and appropriate measures will be taken. Report to your doctor any symptoms such as chest pain, shortness of breath, or cough. ● This drug should be used with caution by blacks and by ethnic groups of Mediterranean and Near Eastern origin, since cases of hemolytic anemia have been known to be brought about in a percentage of such persons while using this drug. If you experience fever, pallor, weakness, or jaundice, stop taking this drug and consult your doctor. The problem usually ceases when the drug is withdrawn. ● This drug should be used with caution by pregnant women, women of childbearing age, and nursing mothers. ● This drug should be used cautiously by people with kidney disease, anemia, diabetes, vitamin-B imbalance, electrolyte imbalance, and certain other debilitating diseases. Be sure your doctor knows if you have any of these conditions. ● This drug may interact with naldixic acid, probenecid, magnesium trisilicate, and sulfinpyrazone. If you are currently taking any drugs of these types, consult your doctor. If you are unsure about the type or contents of your medications, ask your doctor or pharmacist. ● This drug may cause nerve damage and liver disease. ● This drug may interfere with certain blood and urine laboratory tests.
Comments: This drug is similar to the generic product nitrofurantoin. However, this drug is much better tolerated (causes less nausea and stomach distress) than other nitrofurantoin products. Not all nitrofurantoin preparations are generic equivalents; consult your pharmacist about the use of generics. ● If you have a urinary tract infection, you should drink at least nine or ten glasses of water each day. ● To reduce nausea and vomiting, take this drug with a meal or glass of milk. ● This drug may cause false results with urine sugar tests. ● This drug may color your urine and stain your undergarments. Do not be alarmed. ● This drug should be taken for as long as prescribed; continue taking it for the prescribed period even if symptoms have disappeared within that time.

Malatal sedative and anticholinergic (Mallard, Inc.), see Donnatal sedative and anticholinergic.

Mallergan expectorant (Mallard, Inc.), see Phenergan, Phenergan with Codeine expectorants.

Mallergan VC with Codeine expectorant (Mallard, Inc.), see Phenergan VC, Phenergan VC with Codeine expectorants.

Mallopress diuretic and antihypertensive (Mallard, Inc.), see Hydropres diuretic and antihypertensive.

Marnal analgesic and sedative (Vortech Pharmaceutical, Ltd.), see Fiorinal analgesic and sedative.

Materna vitamin-mineral supplement

Manufacturer: Lederle Laboratories
Ingredients: Calcium; iron; vitamins A, D, E, B_1, B_2, B_3, B_6, B_{12}, and C; copper; folic acid; iodine; magnesium; zinc
Equivalent Product: Momatal, Major Pharmaceuticals
Dosage Form: Tablet: Calcium, 250 mg; iron, 60 mg; vitamin A, 8000 I.U.; vitamin D, 400 I.U.; vitamin E, 30 I.U.; vitamin B_1, 3 mg; vitamin B_2, 3.4 mg; vitamin B_3, 20 mg; vitamin B_6, 4 mg; vitamin B_{12}, 12 mcg; vitamin C, 100 mg; copper, 2 mg; folic acid, 1 mg; iodine, 0.3 mg; magnesium, 25 mg; zinc, 25 mg
Use: A vitamin and mineral dietary supplement for use during pregnancy and nursing
Minor Side Effects: Constipation; diarrhea; nausea; stomach upset
Major Side Effects: None
Contraindications: This drug should not be used by persons allergic to any of its ingredients. Consult your doctor if you have any such allergies.
Warnings: Because this drug may mask signs of pernicious anemia, it should be used only under a doctor's supervision. • Due to the high content of iron, keep this (and all medications) out of the reach of children.
Comments: Take this drug with food or milk if it upsets your stomach. • You may wish to continue taking this product for a few weeks after delivery, especially if you are nursing your baby. • The iron in this product may cause your stools to become darker in color. This is normal. Do not be alarmed. • Iron may also cause constipation, diarrhea, nausea, or stomach pain. Taking your dose with food or milk may help minimize these effects. These symptoms usually disappear or become less severe as therapy continues. If they persist, ask your doctor or pharmacist to recommend another product. • There are many similar types of prenatal vitamin-mineral supplements on the market. These products vary slightly in ingredients and amounts. Discuss the various products with your doctor or pharmacist.

M-cillin B 400 antibiotic (Misemer Pharmaceuticals, Inc.), see penicillin G potassium antibiotic.

meclizine hydrochloride antinauseant (various manufacturers), see Antivert antinauseant.

Meclomen anti-inflammatory

Manufacturer: Parke-Davis
Ingredient: meclofenamate sodium
Dosage Form: Capsule: 50 mg (orange and peach); 100 mg (orange and beige)

Use: Treatment of symptoms of arthritis and relief of mild to moderate pain

Minor Side Effects: Bloating; confusion; constipation; diarrhea; dizziness; drowsiness; gas; headache; heartburn; insomnia; loss of appetite; nausea; vomiting

Major Side Effects: Anemia; blood disorders; blood in stools, urine, or mouth; blurred vision; chest tightness; depression; difficult breathing; difficult urination; fatigue; fluid retention; high blood pressure; itching; jaundice; loss of hair; loss of hearing; numbness or tingling in fingers or toes; ringing in the ears; severe abdominal pain; skin rash; sore throat; ulcer; weight gain

Contraindications: This drug should not be used by people who are allergic to it or to aspirin or other nonsteroidal anti-inflammatory drugs. Consult your doctor immediately if this drug has been prescribed for you and you have such an allergy. This drug should not be used by children under the age of 14.

Warnings: This drug should be used cautiously by elderly people; pregnant women; people with a history of gastrointestinal disorders; and by people with mental illness, epilepsy, Parkinson's disease, infections, bleeding disorders, colitis, kidney or liver disease, high blood pressure, or heart failure. Be sure your doctor knows if you fit into any of these categories. • Nursing women who must use this drug should stop nursing. • The severity of the side effects caused by this drug depends upon the dosage taken. Use the least amount possible and watch carefully for side effects. • This drug may irritate the stomach or intestines. Call your doctor if you experience stomach pain or your stools are black and tarry. • If you notice changes in your vision, call your doctor. • If you have headaches while taking this drug, notify your doctor. • This drug may cause drowsiness; avoid tasks that require alertness. • Side effects are more likely to occur in the elderly. • This drug interacts with aspirin, probenecid, lithium, oral antidiabetics, anticoagulants, anticonvulsants, sulfa drugs, beta blockers, and diuretics. If you are currently taking any drugs of these types, talk to your doctor about their use. If you are not sure about the type or contents of your medications, talk to your doctor or pharmacist.

Comments: Regular checkups by the doctor, including blood tests, are required of persons taking this drug. • This drug must be taken with food or milk, immediately after meals, or with antacids, but not sodium bicarbonate. Never take this drug on an empty stomach or with aspirin or alcohol. • If you are taking an anticoagulant ("blood thinner"), remind your doctor. • This drug may cause discoloration of the urine or feces. If you notice a change in color, call your doctor. • It may take a month before you feel the full effect of this drug.

Medrol steroid hormone

Manufacturer: The Upjohn Company

Ingredient: methylprednisolone

Equivalent Product: methylprednisolone, various manufacturers

Dosage Form: Tablet: 2 mg (pink); 4 mg (white); 8 mg (peach); 16 mg (white); 24 mg (yellow); 32 mg (peach)

Use: Treatment of endocrine or rheumatic disorders; asthma; blood diseases; certain cancers; eye disorders; gastrointestinal disturbances such as ulcerative colitis; respiratory diseases; inflammations such as arthritis, dermatitis, poison ivy

Minor Side Effects: Dizziness; false sense of well-being; headache; increased appetite; increased susceptibility to infection; increased sweating; indigestion; menstrual irregularities; muscle weakness; reddening of the skin on the face; restlessness; thin skin

Major Side Effects: Abdominal enlargement; bone loss; bruising; cataracts; convulsions; diabetes; fluid retention; glaucoma; growth impairment in children; heart failure; high blood pressure; impaired healing of wounds; mood changes; muscle wasting; peptic ulcer; potassium loss; salt retention; weakness

Contraindications: This drug should not be taken by people who are allergic to it or who have systemic fungal infections. Consult your doctor if this drug has been prescribed for you and you have either of these conditions.

Warnings: If you are using this drug for longer than a week, you may need to receive higher dosages if you are subjected to stress such as serious infection, injury, or surgery. • This drug may mask signs of an infection or cause new infections to develop. • This drug may cause glaucoma or cataracts, high blood pressure, high blood sugar, fluid retention, and potassium loss. • This drug has not been proven safe for use during pregnancy. • While you are taking this drug you should not be vaccinated or immunized. • This drug should be used very cautiously by people who have had tuberculosis and those who have thyroid disease, liver disease, severe ulcerative colitis, a history of ulcers, kidney disease, high blood pressure, a bone disease, or myasthenia gravis. Be sure your doctor knows if you fit any of these categories. • If you have been taking this drug for more than a week, do not stop taking it suddenly. Never increase the dose or take the drug for a longer time than prescribed without consulting your doctor. • Report mood swings or depression to your doctor. • Growth of children may be affected by this drug. • This drug interacts with aspirin, barbiturates, diuretics, estrogens, indomethacin, oral anticoagulants, antidiabetics, and phenytoin; if you are currently taking any drugs of these types, consult your doctor about their use. If you are unsure of the type or contents of your medications, ask your doctor or pharmacist. • Blood pressure, body weight, and vision should be checked at regular intervals. Stomach X rays are advised for persons with suspected or known peptic ulcers.

Comments: This drug is often taken on a decreasing-dosage schedule (four times a day for several days, then three times a day, etc.). • Often, taking the entire dose at one time (about 8:00 A.M.) gives the best results. Ask your doctor. • To help avoid potassium loss while using this drug, take your dose with a glass of fresh or frozen orange juice or eat a banana each day. The use of a salt substitute also helps prevent potassium loss. • If you are using this drug chronically, you should wear or carry a notice that you are taking a steroid. • To prevent stomach upset, take this drug with food or a snack. • It is best to limit alcohol consumption while taking this drug. Alcohol may aggravate stomach problems. • Take this drug exactly as directed. Do not take extra doses or skip a dose without first consulting your doctor.

Mellaril phenothiazine

Manufacturer: Sandoz Pharmaceuticals
Ingredient: thioridazine hydrochloride
Dosage Forms: Liquid concentrate (content per ml): thioridazine hydrochloride, 30 mg; alcohol, 3%. Liquid concentrate (content per ml): thioridazine hydrochloride, 100 mg; alcohol, 4.2%. Tablet: 10 mg (chartreuse); 15 mg (pink); 25 mg (tan); 50 mg (white); 100 mg (green); 150 mg (yellow); 200 mg (pink). Mellaril-S: Suspension (content per 5 ml teaspoon): 25 mg; 100 mg
Use: Relief of certain types of psychoses and depressions; control of agitation, aggressiveness, and hyperactivity in children
Minor Side Effects: Blurred vision; constipation; decreased sweating; dizziness; drooling; drowsiness; dry mouth; fatigue; headache; impotence; insomnia; jitteriness; loss of appetite; menstrual irregularities; milk production; nasal congestion; nausea; photosensitivity; restlessness; tremors; weakness

Major Side Effects: Arthritis; asthma; blood disorders; breast enlargement (in men and women); convulsions; difficult breathing; eye changes; fever; fluid retention; heart attack; involuntary movements of the mouth, face, neck, and tongue; liver damage; low blood pressure; rash; skin darkening; sore throat

Contraindications: This drug should not be taken by persons with severe heart disease, central nervous system depression, or bone marrow disease, or by those who are allergic to it. Be sure your doctor knows if you have such a condition or such an allergy.

Warnings: This drug should be taken with extreme caution, since it may cause convulsions, blood disorders, or eye disease. This drug should be used with caution by pregnant women. • Since this drug may cause drowsiness, tasks requiring mental alertness should be avoided. • This drug may cause discoloration of the urine; this is harmless. • To prevent oversedation, avoid the use of alcohol or other drugs with sedative properties. • This drug is not recommended for use by children under two years of age. • This drug should be used cautiously by people who have high or low blood pressure, glaucoma, liver or kidney disease, brain damage, ulcers, Parkinson's disease, or an enlarged prostate. • This drug may interact with anticholinergics, antihypertensive drugs, barbiturates, lithium, oral antidiabetics, oral anticoagulants, and oral contraceptives. If you are currently taking any drugs of this type, consult your doctor about their use. If you are unsure of the type or contents of your medications, ask your doctor or pharmacist.

Comments: The effects of this drug may not be apparent for at least two weeks. • This drug has persistent action; never take it more frequently than your doctor prescribes. A serious overdose may result. • While taking this drug, do not take any nonprescription item for cough, cold, or sinus problems without first checking with your doctor. • This drug may cause dryness of the mouth. To reduce this feeling, chew gum or suck on ice chips or a piece of hard candy. • To avoid dizziness or light-headedness when you stand, contract and relax the muscles of your legs for a few moments before rising. Do this by pushing one foot against the floor while raising the other foot slightly, alternating feet so that you are "pumping" your legs in a pedaling motion. • Because this drug decreases sweating, avoid excessive work or exercise in hot weather. • The liquid concentrate form of this drug should be added to 60 ml (1/4 cup) or more of water, milk, juice, coffee, tea, or carbonated beverages, or to pulpy foods (applesauce, etc.) just prior to administration. • If you get a sore throat or notice that your vision is darkening or that your tongue is moving involuntarily, call your doctor. • This drug may cause tumors in rats. This effect has not been shown to occur in humans. • Antacids may prevent the absorption of this drug. Don't take them at the same time as you take this drug.

meprobamate sedative and hypnotic

Manufacturer: various manufacturers

Ingredient: meprobamate

Equivalent Products: Equanil, Wyeth Laboratories; Meprospan, Wallace Laboratories; Miltown, Wallace Laboratories; Neuramate, Halsey Drug Co., Inc.; Neurate-400, Trimen Laboratories, Inc.; Sedabamate, Mallard, Inc.; SK-Bamate, Smith Kline & French Laboratories; Tranmep, Reid-Provident Labs., Inc.

Dosage Forms: Capsule: 400 mg. Sustained-release capsule: 200 mg; 400 mg. Tablet: 200 mg; 400 mg; 600 mg (variety of colors)

Use: Relief of anxiety or tension; sleeping aid

Minor Side Effects: Blurred vision; diarrhea; dizziness; dry mouth; headache; nausea; sedation; vomiting; weakness

Major Side Effects: Bruising; clumsiness; confusion; convulsions; difficult breathing; euphoria; fainting; fever; fluid retention; kidney damage; low blood pressure; nightmares; numbness or tingling; palpitations; rash; slurred speech; sore throat; stimulation; weakness

Contraindications: This drug should not be used by people allergic to it or by those who have porphyria. Consult your doctor immediately if this drug has been prescribed for you and you have either condition.

Warnings: This drug should be used cautiously by people with epilepsy or liver or kidney diseases; pregnant or nursing women; children under age six; and the elderly. Be sure your doctor knows if you fit into any of these categories. • This drug adds to the effect of other sedative drugs. If you are currently taking any other sedatives, consult your doctor about their use. If you are unsure of the type or contents of your medications, ask your doctor or pharmacist. • This drug may cause drowsiness; avoid tasks that require alertness. • To prevent oversedation, avoid the use of alcohol. • This drug has the potential for abuse and must be used with caution. Tolerance may develop quickly; do not increase the dose of this drug without first consulting your doctor. • Call your doctor if you get a rash, sore throat, or fever while taking this drug. • If you have been taking this drug for two to three months, do not stop taking it abruptly. Talk to your doctor about tapering off slowly.

Comments: The sustained-release form of this drug must be swallowed whole.

Meprogesic Q analgesic (Quantum Pharmics), see Equagesic analgesic.

Meprospan sedative and hypnotic (Wallace Laboratories), see meprobamate sedative and hypnotic.

methotrexate antimetabolite

Manufacturer: Lederle Laboratories
Ingredient: methotrexate
Dosage Form: Tablet: 2.5 mg (yellow)
Use: Treatment of certain types of cancer; severe psoriasis
Minor Side Effects: Abdominal distress; fatigue; loss of appetite; nasal congestion; nausea; vomiting
Major Side Effects: Abnormal tissue changes; abortion; acne; anemia; back pain; birth defects; bleeding; blood disorders; blurred vision; convulsions; dental problems; depigmentation; diabetes; diarrhea; drowsiness; fever; headache; infection; infertility; itching; kidney failure; liver damage; loss of hair; lung damage; menstrual dysfunction; mouth sores; paralysis; rash; sunlight sensitivity; ulcer

Contraindications: This drug should not be taken by people with severe kidney, liver, or blood disease; or by women who are pregnant. Be sure your doctor knows if you have any of these conditions.

Warnings: This drug should be used very cautiously by people who have infections, gout, peptic ulcer, kidney disease, ulcerative colitis, or debility. Be sure your doctor knows if you have any of these conditions. • This drug should be used with caution by children and the elderly. • Since this drug is excreted principally by the kidneys, its use in the presence of impaired kidney function may result in an accumulation of toxic amounts of the drug or even additional kidney damage. Therefore, your kidney status should be carefully determined prior to and during the use of this drug. • Various lab tests should be performed prior to therapy with this drug, at appropriate periods during therapy, and after stoppage of the therapy. • This drug has been reported to damage the liver, impair the blood-making process, and suppress the immune system. • This drug interacts with salicylates, sulfonamides, phenylbutazone, phenytoin, tetracycline, chloramphenicol, probenecid, oral antidiabetics, oral anticoagulants, diuretics, folic acid, and para-aminobenzoic acid (PABA). If you are currently taking any drugs of these types, consult your doctor about their use. If you are unsure of the type or contents of your medications, ask your doctor or pharmacist. • This drug should never be taken for psoriasis unless other treatments have been tried and have failed. • This drug has caused birth defects and fetal death. • If you develop diarrhea or sores in the mouth, call your doctor.

Comments: This drug is extremely toxic. For the cancer patient, this drug's benefits may outweigh its risks. However, its use for treating psoriasis must be carefully considered. • While taking this drug, do not begin taking any over-the-counter vitamin product without your doctor's knowledge. • Pharmacists are advised by the manufacturer that a maximum of seven days' therapy be dispensed at any one time. This is to help prevent overdosage. • Never increase the dose of this drug without the permission of your doctor. • Do not drink alcohol while taking this drug; alcohol may increase the risk of liver damage.

methyclothiazide diuretic and antihypertensive (various manufacturers), see Enduron diuretic and antihypertensive.

methylphenidate hydrochloride central nervous system stimulant (various manufacturers), see Ritalin central nervous system stimulant.

methylprednisolone steroid hormone (various manufacturers), see Medrol steroid hormone.

Meticorten steroid hormone (Schering Corp.), see prednisone steroid hormone.

Metoclopromide gastrointestinal stimulant (various manufacturers), see Reglan gastrointestinal stimulant.

metolazone diuretic and antihypertensive (various manufacturers), see Zaroxolyn diuretic and antihypertensive.

metronidazole antimicrobial and antiparasitic (various manufacturers), see Flagyl antimicrobial and antiparasitic.

Metryl antimicrobial and antiparasitic (Lemmon Company), see Flagyl antimicrobial and antiparasitic.

Micrainin analgesic (Wallace Laboratories), see Equagesic analgesic.

Micro-K potassium chloride replacement (A. H. Robins Company), see potassium chloride replacement.

Mictin diuretic and antihypertensive (Econo-Med), see hydrochlorothiazide diuretic and antihypertensive.

Midatap antihistamine and decongestant (Vangard Laboratories), see Dimetapp antihistamine and decongestant.

Miltown sedative and hypnotic (Wallace Laboratories), see meprobamate sedative and hypnotic.

Minipress antihypertensive

Manufacturer: Pfizer Laboratories Division
Ingredient: prazosin hydrochloride
Dosage Form: Capsule: 1 mg (white); 2 mg (pink/white); 5 mg (blue/white)
Use: Treatment of high blood pressure
Minor Side Effects: Abdominal pain; constipation; diarrhea; dizziness; drowsiness; dry mouth; frequent urination; headache; impotence; itching; loss of appetite; nasal congestion; nausea; nervousness; sweating; tiredness; vivid dreams; vomiting; weakness
Major Side Effects: Blurred vision; chest pain; constant erection; depression; difficult urination; fainting; fast pulse; fluid retention; hallucinations; loss of hair; nosebleed; palpitations; rash; ringing in the ears; shortness of breath; tingling in the fingers and toes
Contraindications: This drug should not be taken by people who are allergic to it. Consult your doctor if this drug has been prescribed for you and you have such an allergy.
Warnings: This drug should be used with caution in conjunction with other antihypertensive drugs and with beta-blocker drugs such as propranolol. If you are currently taking either of these drug types, consult your doctor about their use. If you are unsure of the type or contents of your medications, ask your doctor or pharmacist. • This drug should be used very cautiously by pregnant women and children. • Because initial therapy with this drug may cause dizziness and fainting, your doctor will probably start you on a low dose and gradually increase your dosage.
Comments: The effects of this drug may not be apparent for at least two weeks. • Mild side effects (e.g., nasal congestion) are most noticeable during the first two weeks of therapy and become less bothersome after this period. Do not drive or operate machinery for four hours after taking the first dose of this drug. • Do not discontinue this medication unless your doctor directs you to do so. • Take this drug exactly as directed. Do not take extra doses or skip a dose without consulting your doctor first. • While taking this drug, do not take any nonprescription item for weight control or cough, cold, or sinus problems without first checking with your doctor. • While taking this drug, you should limit your consumption of alcoholic beverages in order to prevent dizziness or light-headedness. • To avoid dizziness or light-headedness when you stand, contract and relax the muscles of your legs for a few moments before rising. Do this by pushing one foot against the floor while raising the other foot slightly, alternating feet so that you are "pumping" your legs in a pedaling motion. • If you are taking this drug and begin therapy with another antihypertensive drug, your doctor will probably reduce the dosage of Minipress to 1 or 2 mg three times a day, then recalculate your correct dose over the next couple of weeks.

Minocin antibiotic

Manufacturer: Lederle Laboratories

Ingredient: minocycline hydrochloride

Dosage Forms: Capsule: 50 mg (orange); 100 mg (purple/orange). Syrup (content per 5 ml teaspoon): 50 mg. Tablet: 50 mg; 100 mg (both orange)

Use: Treatment of a wide variety of bacterial infections

Minor Side Effects: Diarrhea; dizziness; drowsiness; increased sensitivity to light; loss of appetite; nausea; upset stomach; vomiting

Major Side Effects: Anemia; difficult breathing; irritation of the mouth; itching; rash; rectal and vaginal itching; sore throat; superinfection

Contraindications: Anyone who has demonstrated an allergy to any of the tetracyclines should not take this drug. Consult your doctor immediately if this drug has been prescribed for you and you have such a history.

Warnings: This drug should be used cautiously by people who have liver and kidney diseases; children under age eight; and women who are nursing or pregnant. Be sure your doctor knows if you fit any of these descriptions. • This drug may impair your ability to perform tasks that require alertness, such as driving and operating machinery. • This drug can cause permanent discoloration of the teeth when taken by children under eight. When taken during the last half of pregnancy, it can cause permanent discoloration of the fetus's teeth. • Call the doctor if you develop a fever, headache, sore throat, or nausea while taking this drug. • This drug interacts with penicillin, lithium, oral antidiabetics, steroids, and anticoagulants. If you are currently taking any drugs of these types, consult your doctor about their use. If you are unsure of the type or contents of your medications, ask your doctor or pharmacist. • Prolonged use of this drug may allow organisms that are not susceptible to it to grow wildly. Do not use this drug unless your doctor has specifically told you to do so. Be sure to follow the directions carefully, and report any unusual reactions to your doctor at once. • Complete blood cell counts and liver and kidney function tests should be done if you take this drug for a prolonged period. • Do not take this drug within two hours of the time you take an antacid or within three hours of taking an iron preparation. • This drug may affect tests for syphilis. Make sure your doctor knows you are taking this drug if you are scheduled for this test.

Comments: Try to take this drug on an empty stomach (one hour before or two hours after a meal) with at least eight ounces of water. If you find the drug upsets your stomach, you may try taking it with food. • While taking this drug, avoid prolonged exposure to sunlight. • This drug is taken once or twice a day. Never increase the dosage unless your doctor tells you to do so. • When used to treat strep throat, this drug should be taken for at least ten days even if symptoms have disappeared. Make sure that your prescription is marked with the drug's expiration date. Do not use this drug after the expiration date has passed.

Mity-Quin steroid hormone and anti-infective (Reid-Provident Labs., Inc.), see Vioform-Hydrocortisone steroid hormone and anti-infective.

Momatal vitamin-mineral supplement (Major Pharmaceuticals), see Materna vitamin-mineral supplement.

Monistat 7 antifungal agent

Manufacturer: Ortho Pharmaceutical Corporation

Ingredient: miconazole nitrate
Dosage Forms: Vaginal cream: 2%. Vaginal suppository: 100 mg
Use: Treatment of fungal infections of the vagina
Minor Side Effects: Burning; irritation; itching
Major Side Effects: Headache; hives; pelvic cramps; skin rash
Contraindications: This drug should not be used by people who are allergic to it. Consult your doctor immediately if this drug has been prescribed for you and you have such an allergy.
Warnings: This drug should be used with caution by pregnant women in the first three months of their pregnancy. Be sure your doctor knows if you are pregnant. • Notify your doctor immediately if sensitization, burning, itching, or irritation occurs during use of this drug.
Comments: Usually, one seven-day course of this drug is sufficient, but it may be repeated for another seven days. • This drug is effective in the treatment of fungal infections in pregnant and nonpregnant women, as well as in women taking oral contraceptives. However, because small amounts of the drug may be absorbed through the vaginal wall, this drug generally should not be used during the first three months of pregnancy. • This drug should be used until the prescribed amount is gone. Be sure to complete a full course of therapy. • Avoid sexual intercourse, or ask your partner to use a condom until treatment is complete to avoid reinfection. • Wear cotton panties rather than those made of nylon or other nonporous materials while treating fungal infections. • Careful attention to personal hygiene may help prevent subsequent fungal infections of the vagina. • Apply this product after cleansing the area unless otherwise directed by your doctor. • Unless otherwise instructed by your doctor, do not douche during treatment with this drug, or for two to three weeks thereafter.

Motrin anti-inflammatory

Manufacturer: The Upjohn Company
Ingredient: ibuprofen
Equivalent Products: Advil, Whitehall Labs.; ibuprofen, Par Pharmaceuticals; Nuprin, Bristol-Myers; Rufen, Boots Pharmaceuticals, Inc.
Dosage Form: Tablet: 300 mg (white); 400 mg (orange); 600 mg (peach); 800 mg (apricot)
Use: Reduction of pain and swelling due to arthritis; relief of menstrual pain, dental pain, postoperative pain, and musculoskeletal pain
Minor Side Effects: Bloating; constipation; cramps; diarrhea; dizziness; drowsiness; dry mouth; gas; headache; heartburn; indigestion; insomnia; itching; loss of appetite; nausea; nervousness; peculiar taste in mouth; stomach pain; vomiting
Major Side Effects: Anemia; bleeding; breast enlargement (in men and women); blood in stools; chest tightness; convulsions; depression; fever; fluid retention; hair loss; hallucinations; high blood pressure; jaundice; menstrual irregularities; palpitations; rash; ringing in the ears; shortness of breath; sore throat; ulcer; urination difficulty; visual disturbances
Contraindications: This drug should not be taken by people who are allergic to it or to aspirin or similar drugs. Consult your doctor immediately if this drug has been prescribed for you and you have such an allergy.
Warnings: This drug should be used with extreme caution by patients with a history of ulcers or gastrointestinal disease. Peptic ulcers and gastrointestinal bleeding, sometimes severe, have been reported in persons taking this drug. Make sure your doctor knows if you have or have had either condition. • This drug should be used with caution by persons with anemia, heart disease,

bleeding diseases, high blood pressure, liver disease, or kidney disease. Be sure your doctor knows if you have any of these conditions. • Should any eye problems arise while taking this drug, notify your doctor immediately. • This drug should not be used by pregnant women or nursing mothers. It should be used cautiously by children. • Use of this drug has been reported to bring about fluid retention, skin rash, and weight gain. If you notice any of these symptoms, you should immediately consult your doctor. • This drug should be used with caution if you are also taking anticoagulants, since this drug has been found to prolong bleeding time, even in normal subjects. • This drug interacts with anticoagulants, oral antidiabetics, barbiturates, diuretics, steroids, phenytoin, and aspirin. If you are currently taking any drugs of these types, consult your doctor about their use. If you are unsure of the type or contents of your medications, ask your doctor or pharmacist. • This drug has been reported to cause ulcers. Notify your doctor if you experience frequent indigestion or notice blood in your stools.

Comments: In numerous tests, this drug has been shown to be as effective as aspirin in the treatment of arthritis, but aspirin is still the drug of choice for the disease. • Do not take aspirin or alcohol while taking this drug without first consulting your doctor. • You should note improvement in your condition soon after you start using this drug; however, full benefit may not be obtained for one to two weeks. It is important not to stop taking this drug even though symptoms have diminished or disappeared. • This drug is not a substitute for rest, physical therapy, or other measures recommended by your doctor to treat your condition. • Notify your doctor if skin rash, itching, swelling of the hands or feet, or persistent headache occurs. • Take this drug with food or milk to decrease stomach upset. • Advil and Nuprin contain 200 mg of ibuprofen. These products are available without a prescription. Consult your doctor or pharmacist about their use.

Murcil sedative and hypnotic (Reid-Provident Labs., Inc.), see Librium sedative and hypnotic.

Mycelex antifungal agent (Miles Pharmaceuticals), see Lotrimin antifungal agent.

Mycelex-G antifungal agent (Miles Pharmaceuticals), see Gyne-Lotrimin antifungal agent.

Mycogen topical steroid hormone and anti-infective (Goldline Laboratories), see Mycolog topical steroid hormone and anti-infective.

Mycolog topical steroid hormone and anti-infective

Manufacturer: E. R. Squibb & Sons, Inc.
Ingredients: gramicidin; neomycin sulfate; nystatin; triamcinolone acetonide
Equivalent Products: Mycogen, Goldline Laboratories; Myco Triacet, various manufacturers; Mykacet, NMC Laboratories; Mytrex, Savage Laboratories; N.G.T., Geneva Generics, Inc.; triamcinolone, neomycin, gramicidin, and nystatin, various manufacturers; Tri-Statin, Rugby Laboratories
Dosage Forms: Cream; Ointment (content per gram): gramicidin, 0.25 mg; neomycin sulfate equivalent to 2.5 mg neomycin base; nystatin, 100,000 units; triamcinolone acetonide, 0.1%

Use: Relief of skin inflammations associated with conditions such as dermatitis, eczema, or poison ivy

Minor Side Effects: Burning sensation; dryness; irritation; itching

Major Side Effects: Allergy; blistering; increased hair growth; loss of hearing; loss of skin color; rash; secondary infection; skin wasting

Contraindications: This drug should not be used for viral diseases of the skin, for most fungal lesions of the skin, or in circumstances when circulation is markedly impaired. This drug should not be used in the eyes or in the external ear canals of patients with perforated eardrums. Be sure your doctor knows if you have any of these conditions. This drug should not be used by people who are allergic to any of its ingredients. Consult your doctor immediately if this drug has been prescribed for you and you have such an allergy.

Warnings: Prolonged use of large amounts of this drug should be avoided in the treatment of skin infections following extensive burns and other conditions where absorption of neomycin is possible. Prolonged use of this drug may result in secondary infection. • If extensive areas are treated or if an occlusive bandage is used, the possibility exists of increased absorption of this drug into the bloodstream. • If irritation develops, discontinue use of this drug and notify your doctor immediately. • This drug should not be used extensively, in large amounts, or for prolonged periods on pregnant women.

Comments: If the affected area is extremely dry or is scaling, the skin may be moistened before applying the medication by soaking in water or by applying water with a clean cloth and then drying thoroughly. The ointment form is probably better for dry skin. • Apply a thin layer of this product to the affected area and rub in gently. • Do not use this product with an occlusive wrap of transparent plastic film unless instructed to do so by your doctor. If it is necessary for you to use this drug under a wrap, follow your doctor's directions exactly. Do not leave the wrap in place for a longer time than specified.

Mycostatin antifungal agent

Manufacturer: E. R. Squibb & Sons, Inc.

Ingredient: nystatin

Equivalent Products: Korostatin, Holland-Rantos Company, Inc.; Nilstat, Lederle Laboratories; nystatin, various manufacturers

Dosage Forms: Cream; Ointment; Powder (per gram): 100,000 units. Oral suspension (per ml): 100,000 units. Oral tablet: 500,000 units. Vaginal tablet: 100,000 units

Use: Treatment of fungal infections

Minor Side Effects: Oral forms: diarrhea; nausea; vomiting. Topical and vaginal forms: itching

Major Side Effect: Rash

Contraindications: This drug should not be used by people who are allergic to it. Contact your doctor immediately if this drug has been prescribed for you and you have such an allergy.

Warnings: If you suffer allergic reactions (e.g., rash) from taking this drug, consult your doctor; use of the drug will probably be discontinued.

Comments: If you are using the powder form of this drug to treat a foot infection, sprinkle the powder liberally into your shoes and socks. • Moist lesions or sores are best treated with the powder form of this drug. • If you are using the oral suspension form of this drug to treat an infection in the mouth, rinse the drug around in your mouth as long as possible before swallowing. The oral suspension must be shaken well before use. It need not be refrigerated. • If you are using this drug to treat a vaginal infection, avoid sexual intercourse or ask your partner to wear a condom until treatment is completed; these measures will help prevent reinfection. • The vaginal tablets are supplied with an applicator that should be used to insert the tablets high into the vagina. • Unless instructed otherwise by your doctor, do not douche two to three weeks after you use vaginal tablets or during the treatment period. • Use the vaginal tablets continuously, including during a menstrual period, until your doctor tells you to stop. Be sure to complete a full course of therapy. • Wear cotton panties rather than those made of nylon or other nonporous materials while fungal infections of the vagina are being treated. • You may wish to wear a sanitary napkin while using the vaginal tablets to prevent soiling of your underwear. • If you are using the topical cream or ointment form of this drug, apply it after cleaning the area unless otherwise specified by your doctor. • Careful attention to personal hygiene may help prevent subsequent fungal infections of the vagina.

Myco Triacet topical steroid hormone and anti-infective (Premo Pharmaceutical Labs., Inc.), see Mycolog topical steroid hormone and anti-infective.

Mykacet topical steroid hormone and anti-infective (NMC Laboratories), see Mycolog topical steroid hormone and anti-infective.

Myobid vasodilator and smooth muscle relaxant (Laser, Inc.), see Pavabid Plateau Caps vasodilator and smooth muscle relaxant.

Mytrex topical steroid hormone and anti-infective (Savage Laboratories), see Mycolog topical steroid hormone and anti-infective.

Naldecon adrenergic and antihistamine

Manufacturer: Bristol Labs
Ingredients: chlorpheniramine maleate; phenylephrine hydrochloride; phenylpropanolamine hydrochloride; phenyltoloxamine citrate
Equivalent Products: Amaril "D" Spantab, Vortech Pharmaceutical, Ltd.; Decongestabs, various manufacturers; Naldelate, various manufacturers; Nalgest, Major Pharmaceuticals; Sinocon, Vangard Laboratories; Tri-Phen-Chlor, Rugby Laboratories; Tudecon, Reid-Provident Labs., Inc.
Dosage Forms: Pediatric drops (content per ml); Pediatric syrup (content per 5 ml teaspoon): chlorpheniramine maleate, 0.5 mg; phenylephrine hydrochloride, 1.25 mg; phenylpropanolamine hydrochloride, 5.0 mg; phenyltoloxamine citrate, 2.0 mg. Sustained-action tablet: chlorpheniramine maleate, 5 mg; phenylephrine hydrochloride, 10 mg; phenylpropanolamine hydrochloride, 40 mg; phenyltoloxamine citrate, 15 mg (white with red specks). Syrup (content per 5 ml teaspoon): chlorpheniramine maleate, 2.5 mg; phenylephrine hydrochloride, 5.0 mg; phenylpropanolamine hydrochloride, 20 mg; phenyltoloxamine citrate, 7.5 mg
Use: Relief of symptoms of hay fever and other allergies, sinusitis, and upper respiratory tract infections
Minor Side Effects: Blurred vision; confusion; constipation; diarrhea; dizziness; drowsiness; dry mouth; headache; heartburn; insomnia; loss of appetite; nasal congestion; nausea; reduced sweating; restlessness; sensitivity to sunlight; vomiting; weakness
Major Side Effects: Chest pain; difficult breathing; difficult urination; hallucinations; high blood pressure; low blood pressure; palpitations; rash; severe abdominal pain; sore throat; unusual bleeding or bruising

Contraindications: This drug should not be taken by people who are allergic to any of its components; nor by people who have severe high blood pressure, severe heart disease, glaucoma (certain types), urinary retention, ulcers, or asthma. Consult your doctor immediately if this drug has been prescribed for you and you have such an allergy or any of these conditions. • This drug should not be used in conjunction with guanethidine or monoamine oxidase inhibitors; if you are currently taking any drugs of these types, consult your doctor about their use. If you are unsure of the type or contents of your medications, ask your doctor or pharmacist.

Warnings: This drug should be used cautiously by children; pregnant or nursing women; and people who have high blood pressure, heart disease, diabetes, urinary tract or intestinal blockage, epilepsy, thyroid disease, glaucoma, vessel disease, or enlarged prostate. Be sure your doctor knows if you have any of these conditions. • This drug interacts with beta blockers and certain drugs used to treat high blood pressure. If you are unsure about the nature of the drugs you take, ask your doctor or pharmacist. • This drug may cause drowsiness; avoid tasks that require alertness. • To prevent oversedation, avoid the use of alcohol or other drugs that have sedative properties.

Comments: Because this drug reduces sweating, avoid excessive work or exercise in hot weather. • The tablet form of this drug has sustained action; never increase your dose or take it more frequently than your doctor prescribes. A serious overdose could result. • The tablet form of this drug must be swallowed whole. • Chew gum or suck on ice chips or a piece of hard candy to reduce mouth dryness. • While taking this drug, do not take any nonprescription item for cough, cold, or sinus problems without first checking with your doctor.

Naldelate adrenergic and antihistamine (various manufacturers), see Naldecon adrenergic and antihistamine.

Nalfon anti-inflammatory

Manufacturer: Dista Products Co.
Ingredient: fenoprofen calcium
Dosage Forms: Capsule: 200 mg (white/ocher); 300 mg (yellow). Tablet: 600 mg (yellow)
Use: Relief of pain and swelling due to arthritis; relief of menstrual pain, dental pain, postoperative pain, and musculoskeletal pain
Minor Side Effects: Abdominal pain; bloating; confusion; constipation; cramps; diarrhea; dizziness; drowsiness; dry mouth; flatulence; headache; heartburn; insomnia; itching; loss of appetite; nausea; nervousness; peculiar taste in mouth; rapid heart rate; sweating; vomiting; weakness
Major Side Effects: Anemia; blood in stools; bruising; chest tightness; difficult breathing; difficult urination; fluid retention; hair loss; hearing loss; jaundice; kidney disease; menstrual irregularities; nightmares; palpitations; rash; ringing in the ears; seizures; tremors; ulcer; visual disturbances
Contraindications: This drug should not be taken by persons with kidney disease, or by those who are allergic to this drug or to aspirin or other drugs like it. Consult your doctor immediately if this drug has been prescribed for you and you have such an allergy or kidney disease.
Warnings: This drug should be taken with caution by patients with a history of upper gastrointestinal tract disease. Gastrointestinal bleeding, sometimes severe, has been reported in persons receiving this drug. Be sure your doctor knows if you have had such a problem. • This drug should be used cautiously by persons with peptic ulcer, anemia, heart disease, high blood pressure,

bleeding diseases, liver disease, or kidney disease. Be sure your doctor knows if you have any of these conditions. • This drug should be used with caution by pregnant women, nursing mothers, and children. • Since this drug may cause drowsiness, tasks requiring alertness should be avoided while taking this drug. • Patients with impaired hearing who take this drug for a long time should have periodic tests of auditory function. • Use of this drug may prolong bleeding times, so persons taking anticoagulants in addition to this drug should use this drug with extreme caution. • It is desirable to have periodic eye tests while receiving this drug. • This drug interacts with aspirin, diuretics, anticoagulants, oral antidiabetics, phenobarbital, phenytoin, and sulfonamides. If you are currently taking any drugs of these types, consult your doctor about their use. If you are unsure of the type or contents of your medications, ask your doctor or pharmacist.

Comments: In numerous tests, this drug has been shown to be as effective as aspirin in the treatment of arthritis, but aspirin is still the drug of choice for the disease. Because of the high cost of this drug, consult your doctor about prescribing proper doses of aspirin instead. • Do not take aspirin or alcohol while taking this drug without first consulting your doctor. • You should note improvement in your condition soon after you start using this drug; however, full benefit may not be obtained for one to two weeks. It is important not to stop taking this drug even though symptoms have diminished or disappeared. • This drug is not a substitute for rest, physical therapy, or other measures recommended by your doctor to treat your condition. • This drug is best taken on an empty stomach, but it may be taken with food or milk to reduce stomach upset. • Notify your doctor if skin rash, itching, black tarry stools, swelling of the hands or feet, or persistent headache occurs.

Nalgest adrenergic and antihistamine (Major Pharmaceuticals), see Naldecon adrenergic and antihistamine.

Naprosyn anti-inflammatory

Manufacturer: Syntex Laboratories, Inc.
Ingredient: naproxen
Dosage Form: Tablet: 250 mg (yellow); 375 mg (peach); 500 mg (yellow)
Use: Relief of pain and swelling due to rheumatoid arthritis; relief of mild to moderate pain; relief of menstrual pain
Minor Side Effects: Abdominal pain; bloating; bruising; constipation; diarrhea; dizziness; drowsiness; dry mouth; headache; heartburn; insomnia; itching; loss of appetite; nausea; nervousness; peculiar taste in mouth; sore mouth; sweating; vomiting; weakness
Major Side Effects: Blood in stools; chest tightness; depression; difficult breathing; difficult urination; enlarged breasts in men or women; fluid retention; hair loss; hallucinations; hearing loss; jaundice; kidney disease; menstrual irregularities; palpitations; rash; ringing in the ears; sore throat; tingling in hands or feet; ulcers; visual disturbances
Contraindications: This drug should not be taken by people who are allergic to it or to aspirin or similar drugs. Consult your doctor immediately if this drug has been prescribed for you and you have such an allergy.
Warnings: This drug should be used with caution by pregnant women, nursing mothers, and children. This drug should be used with caution by persons with anemia, ulcers, bleeding disorders, high blood pressure, liver disease, heart disease, or kidney disease. Be sure your doctor knows if you have any of these conditions. • This drug should be taken under close supervision by patients prone to upper gastrointestinal tract disease. Gastrointestinal

bleeding, sometimes severe, has been reported in patients receiving this drug. • It is recommended that persons taking this drug for a long time have eye tests performed periodically. • This drug may cause drowsiness, dizziness, or depression; avoid activities that require alertness. • This drug may prolong bleeding times, so persons also taking anticoagulants should use this drug with extreme caution. • This drug interacts with anticoagulants, diuretics, aspirin, oral antidiabetics, phenytoin, and sulfonamides. If you are currently taking any drugs of these types, consult your doctor about their use. If you are unsure of the type or contents of your medications, ask your doctor or pharmacist.

Comments: In numerous tests, this drug has been shown to be as effective as aspirin in the treatment of arthritis, but aspirin is still the drug of choice for the disease. Because of the high cost of this drug, consult your doctor about prescribing proper doses of aspirin instead. • You should note improvement in your condition soon after you start using this drug; however, full benefit may not be obtained for one to two weeks. It is important not to stop taking this drug even though symptoms have diminished or disappeared. • This drug is not a substitute for rest, physical therapy, or other measures recommended by your doctor to treat your condition. • Do not take aspirin or alcohol while taking this drug without first consulting your doctor. • This drug is best taken on an empty stomach, but it may be taken with food or milk to reduce stomach upset. • Syntex Laboratories, Inc. also produces a related drug (naproxen sodium) as Anaprox. This drug is converted in the body to naproxen. The two drugs should not be taken together. • Notify your doctor if skin rash, itching, black tarry stools, swelling of the hands or feet, or persistent headache occurs.

Nembutal Sodium sedative and hypnotic (Abbott Laboratories), see Butisol Sodium sedative and hypnotic.

Neomycin Sulfate-Polymyxin B Sulfate-Gramicidin Solution (Rugby Laboratories), see Neosporin antibiotic ophthalmic solution and ointment.

Neoquess sedative and anticholinergic (O'Neal, Jones & Feldman), see Donnatal sedative and anticholinergic.

Neosporin antibiotic
ophthalmic solution and ointment

Manufacturer: Burroughs Wellcome Co.

Ingredients: gramicidin (solution only); neomycin sulfate; polymyxin B sulfate; alcohol; thimerosal (solution only); bacitracin (ointment only)

Equivalent Products: AK-Sporin Ophthalmic Ointment, Akorn, Inc.; Neomycin Sulfate-Polymyxin B Sulfate-Gramicidin Solution, Rugby Laboratories

Dosage Forms: Solution (content per ml): gramicidin, 0.025 mg; neomycin sulfate, 2.5 mg; polymyxin B sulfate, 10,000 units; alcohol, 0.5%; thimerosal, 0.001%. Ointment (content per gram): bacitracin, 400 units; neomycin sulfate, 5 mg; polymyxin B sulfate, 10,000 units

Use: Short-term treatment of superficial bacterial infections of the eye

Minor Side Effects: Burning; stinging; blurred vision

Major Side Effects: None

Contraindications: This drug should not be taken by people with known sensitivity to any of its ingredients. Make sure your doctor knows if you have such sensitivity if this drug is prescribed for you.

Warnings: Prolonged use of this drug may result in secondary infection. •
Tests should be performed during treatment to be sure the drug is working. •
This drug should be used cautiously by people who have an injured cornea,
kidney disease, inner ear disease, myasthenia gravis, or Parkinson's disease.
Comments: Minor side effects will go away quickly. • If symptoms do not
improve within a few days, contact your doctor. Continue using this drug for the
full period prescribed even if symptoms have subsided. • Be careful about the
contamination of solutions used for the eyes. Wash your hands before administering eyedrops. Do not touch the dropper to your eye. Do not wash or wipe the
dropper before replacing it in the bottle. Close the bottle tightly to keep out
moisture. • See the chapter, Administering Medication Correctly, for instructions on using eyedrops.

**Neotep antihistamine and adrenergic (Reid-Provident Labs., Inc.),
see Ornade Spansule antihistamine and adrenergic.**

**Neuramate sedative and hypnotic (Halsey Drug Co., Inc.), see mep-
robamate sedative and hypnotic.**

**Neurate-400 sedative and hypnotic (Trimen Laboratories, Inc.), see
meprobamate sedative and hypnotic.**

**N-G-C anti-anginal (Kay Pharmacal Co., Inc.), see Nitro-Bid anti-
anginal.**

**N.G.T. topical steroid hormone and anti-infective (Geneva Generics,
Inc.), see Mycolog topical steroid hormone and anti-infective.**

Niconyl antitubercular (Parke-Davis), see isoniazid antitubercular.

Nicorette smoking deterrent

Manufacturer: Merrell Dow Pharmaceuticals, Inc.
Ingredient: nicotine resin complex
Dosage Form: Chewing gum (content per piece): 2 mg (beige)
Use: An aid to stop smoking
Minor Side Effects: Constipation; diarrhea; dizziness; dry mouth; gas pains;
headache; hiccoughs; hoarseness; insomnia; light-headedness; mouth sores;
sneezing; sore throat
Major Side Effects: Cold sweats; difficulty breathing; euphoria; faintness;
flushing; heart palpitations; visual disturbances
Contraindications: Nonsmokers; people who have recently suffered a
heart attack; people with certain heart diseases, such as chest pain or severe
arrhythmias; and pregnant and nursing women. Consult your doctor if this drug
has been prescribed for you and you have any of these conditions.
Warnings: This drug must be used with caution by persons with certain types
of heart disease, thyroid disease, diabetes, hypertension, or peptic ulcer
disease. If you fit any of these categories, discuss the use of this drug with your
doctor. • Nursing mothers should stop nursing while taking this drug. • Dental
problems may be exacerbated while using this drug. • Nicorette contains
nicotine, as do cigarettes. Therefore concurrent use can lead to overdose. •
Because nicotine is known to be addictive, this drug is not recommended to be
used for longer than six months. After three months of therapy, your doctor may

want to gradually reduce the amount of Nicorette that you chew. • This drug interacts with caffeine, theophylline, imipramine, pentazocine, furosemide, propranolol, glutethimide, and propoxyphene. If you are taking any of these medicines, consult with your doctor or pharmacist about their use. If you are unsure of the types or contents of your medicines, ask your doctor or pharmacist.

Comments: Nicotine is similar in action to caffeine. Try to limit your consumption of coffee, tea, cola, chocolate, and other caffeine-containing products while taking this drug. • Patient information sheets are available for Nicorette. If one is not dispensed with your prescription, ask your pharmacist for one. Read the information carefully before taking this drug. • To be most effective, this drug is to be used in conjunction with a smoking cessation program by persons who have a desire to stop smoking. • The gum should be chewed slowly. Chewing the gum too quickly can cause symptoms similar to oversmoking (nausea, hiccoughs, and throat irritation). • Take this drug as directed by your doctor. Do not use more than recommended. • Remember to keep this gum out of the reach of children; it is medicine, not candy.

nicotine resin complex smoking deterrent (Merrell Dow Pharmaceuticals, Inc.), see Nicorette smoking deterrent.

Nilstat antifungal agent (Lederle Laboratories), see Mycostatin antifungal agent.

Niong anti-anginal (U.S. Ethicals), see Nitro-Bid anti-anginal.

Nitro-Bid anti-anginal

Manufacturer: Marion Laboratories, Inc.
Ingredient: nitroglycerin
Equivalent Products: Klavikordal, U.S. Ethicals; Niong, U.S. Ethicals; N-G-C, Kay Pharmacal Co., Inc.; Nitrocap T.D., Vortech Pharmaceutical, Ltd.; nitroglycerin, various manufacturers; Nitroglyn, Key Pharmaceuticals; Nitrol, William H. Rorer, Inc.; Nitrolin, Henry Schein, Inc.; Nitro-Long, Major Pharmaceuticals; Nitronet, U.S. Ethicals; Nitrong, Wharton Laboratories, Inc.; Nitrospan, USV Laboratories; Nitrostat SR, Parke-Davis; Trates Granucaps, Reid-Provident Labs., Inc.
Dosage Forms: Time-release capsule: 2.5 mg (purple/clear with white beads); 6.5 mg (blue/yellow with white beads); 9 mg (yellow/green with white beads). Ointment: 2%
Use: Prevention of chest pain (angina) due to heart disease; possibly effective for management of attacks of angina
Minor Side Effects: Dizziness; flushing of the face; headache; nausea; vomiting; weakness
Major Side Effects: Fainting; palpitations; rash; sweating
Contraindications: This drug should not be taken by people who have a head injury, low blood pressure, severe anemia, or glaucoma; those who have recently suffered a heart attack; and those who are allergic to this drug. Consult your doctor immediately if this drug has been prescribed for you and you have any of these conditions.
Warnings: If you develop blurred vision or dry mouth, contact your doctor. • This drug is not effective against an attack of angina that is already in progress. • This drug may not continue to relieve chest pain after one to three months because tolerance to nitroglycerin develops quickly. If this drug begins to seem

less effective, consult your doctor. • The capsule form of this drug must be swallowed; do not crush or break the capsules. • This drug should be used cautiously in conjunction with antihypertensive drugs.

Comments: Side effects generally disappear after two to three weeks of continued therapy. • Headache is a common side effect. It occurs after taking a dose and lasts a short time. However, the headaches should be less noticeable with continued treatment. • If they persist, contact your doctor. • The ointment form should be applied using the special applicators. Measure the prescribed dose onto the applicator and spread it in a thin, even layer over the skin. Do not rub ointment into the skin. Use an occlusive wrapping only if instructed to do so by your physician. • To avoid dizziness or light-headedness when you stand, contract and relax the muscles of your legs for a few moments before rising. Do this by pushing one foot against the floor while raising the other foot slightly, alternating feet so that you are "pumping" your legs in a pedaling motion. • Do not drink alcohol unless your doctor has told you that you may.

Nitrocap T.D. anti-anginal (Vortech Pharmaceuticals, Ltd.), see Nitro-Bid anti-anginal.

Nitrodisc anti-anginal (Searle & Co.), see Transderm Nitro anti-anginal.

Nitro-Dur anti-anginal (Key Pharmaceuticals, Inc.), see Transderm Nitro anti-anginal.

nitrofurantoin antibacterial (various manufacturers), see Macrodantin antibacterial.

nitroglycerin anti-anginal (Eli Lilly & Co.), see Nitrostat anti-anginal.

nitroglycerin anti-anginal (various manufacturers), see Nitro-Bid and Nitrostat anti-anginals.

Nitroglyn anti-anginal (Key Pharmaceuticals), see Nitro-Bid anti-anginal.

Nitrol anti-anginal (William H. Rorer, Inc.), see Nitro-Bid anti-anginal.

Nitrolin anti-anginal (Henry Schein, Inc.), see Nitro-Bid anti-anginal.

Nitro-Long anti-anginal (Major Pharmaceuticals), see Nitro-Bid anti-anginal.

Nitronet anti-anginal (U.S. Ethicals), see Nitro-Bid anti-anginal.

Nitrong anti-anginal (Wharton Laboratories, Inc.), see Nitro-Bid anti-anginal.

Nitrospan anti-anginal (USV Laboratories), see Nitro-Bid anti-anginal.

Nitrostat anti-anginal

Manufacturer: Parke-Davis
Ingredient: nitroglycerin
Equivalent Product: nitroglycerin, Eli Lilly & Co.
Dosage Form: Sublingual tablet: 0.15 mg; 0.3 mg; 0.4 mg; 0.6 mg (all are white)
Use: Relief of chest pain (angina) due to heart disease
Minor Side Effects: Dizziness; flushing of the face; headache; nausea; vomiting
Major Side Effects: Fainting; palpitations; sweating
Contraindications: This drug should not be used by people who are allergic to it; those who have low blood pressure, glaucoma, or severe anemia; or those who have suffered a head injury or recent heart attack. Consult your doctor immediately if this drug has been prescribed for you and you have any of these conditions.
Warnings: Do not swallow this drug. The tablets must be placed under the tongue. Do not drink water or swallow for five minutes after taking this drug. • If you use too much of this product, you are likely to get a severe headache. • This drug should be used cautiously by pregnant women. Be sure your doctor knows if you are pregnant. • If you develop blurred vision or dry mouth, contact your doctor. • This drug interacts with alcohol and other vasodilators. Consult your doctor about their use. If you are unsure of the type or contents of your medications, ask your doctor or pharmacist. • If you require more tablets than usual to relieve chest pain, contact your doctor. You may have developed a tolerance to the drug, or the drug may not be working effectively because of interference with other medication. • If this drug does not relieve pain, or if pain arises from a different location or differs in severity, call your doctor immediately. • Before using this drug to relieve pain, be certain the pain arises from the heart and is not due to a muscle spasm or indigestion.
Comments: Frequently chest pain will be relieved in two to five minutes simply by sitting down. • When you take this drug, sit down, lower your head, and breathe deeply. • Side effects caused by this drug are most bothersome the first two weeks after starting therapy. • This drug must be stored in a tightly capped glass container. Screw cap on tightly after each use. Store the bottle in a cool, dry place. Never store the tablets in a metal box, plastic vial, or in the refrigerator or the bathroom medicine cabinet, as the drug may lose potency. The tablet should cause a slight stinging sensation when placed under the tongue. If this does not occur, it indicates loss of potency and a new bottle of pills is necessary.

Nitrostat SR anti-anginal (Parke-Davis), see Nitro-Bid anti-anginal.

Norgesic, Norgesic Forte analgesics

Manufacturer: Riker Laboratories, Inc.
Ingredients: aspirin; caffeine; orphenadrine citrate
Dosage Form: Norgesic: Tablet: aspirin, 385 mg; caffeine, 30 mg; orphenadrine citrate, 25 mg. Norgesic Forte: Tablet: aspirin, 770 mg; caffeine, 60 mg; orphenadrine citrate, 50 mg (both trilayered green/white/yellow)
Use: Relief of mild to moderate pain in muscles or joints
Minor Side Effects: Blurred vision; confusion; constipation; diarrhea; dilation of pupils; dizziness; drowsiness; dry mouth; headache; indigestion; insomnia; nausea; nervousness; slight blood loss; vomiting; weakness

Major Side Effects: Abdominal pain; blood in the stools; chest tightness; difficult breathing; hearing loss; palpitations; rapid heartbeat; rash; ringing in the ears; urinary hesitancy or retention

Contraindications: This drug should not be used by patients with glaucoma, intestinal obstruction, difficulty in swallowing, enlarged prostate, obstructions of the bladder, or myasthenia gravis. Be sure your doctor knows if you have any of these conditions. This drug should not be taken by persons allergic to any of its ingredients. Contact your doctor immediately if this drug has been prescribed for you and you have such an allergy.

Warnings: This drug may cause drowsiness; avoid engaging in potentially hazardous activities, such as operating machinery or driving a motor vehicle. • To prevent oversedation, avoid the use of alcohol or other drugs that have sedative properties. • This drug should be used cautiously by pregnant women, nursing mothers, and by women of childbearing age. It is not recommended for use by children under 12 years of age. This drug should be used with caution by persons with peptic ulcers, anemia, gout, liver disease, kidney disease, or coagulation problems. Be sure your doctor knows if you fit into any of these categories. • If this drug is prescribed for a long period, periodic monitoring of blood, urine, and liver function is recommended. • This drug interacts with central nervous system depressants, propoxyphene (for example, Darvon analgesic), anticoagulants, methotrexate, 6-mercaptopurine, phenytoin, oral antidiabetics, and gout medications (probenecid, sulfinpyrazone). If you are currently taking any drugs of these types, ask your doctor about their use. If you are unsure about the type or contents of your medications, ask your doctor or pharmacist. • Avoid the use of aspirin and aspirin containing products while taking this drug.

Comments: This drug is not a substitute for rest, physical therapy, or other measures recommended by your doctor to treat your condition. • This drug may be taken with food or milk to lessen stomach upset. • If you hear buzzing or ringing, if your ears feel strange, or if your stomach hurts, your dosage may need adjustment. Call your doctor. • Chew gum or suck on ice chips or a piece of hard candy to reduce mouth dryness.

Normatane antihistamine and decongestant (Vortech Pharmaceutical, Ltd.), see Dimetapp antihistamine and decongestant

Nor-Mil anticholinergic and antispasmodic (Vortech Pharmaceutical, Ltd.), see Lomotil anticholinergic and antispasmodic.

Norpace anti-arrhythmic

Manufacturer: Searle & Co.
Ingredient: disopyramide phosphate
Dosage Form: Capsule: 100 mg (white/orange); 150 mg (brown/orange). Controlled-release capsules: 100 mg (light green/white); 150 mg (light green/brown).
Use: Treatment of some heart arrhythmias
Minor Side Effects: Abdominal pain; aches and pains; blurred vision; constipation; diarrhea; dizziness; dry mouth; dry nose, eyes, throat; fatigue; gas; headache; impotence; increased sensitivity to sunlight; loss of appetite; muscle pain; muscle weakness; nausea; nervousness; pain; rash; vomiting
Major Side Effects: Chest pain; difficult urination; edema and weight gain; fainting; fever; heart failure; jaundice; low blood pressure; low blood sugar; numbness or tingling sensation; palpitations; psychosis; severe mental disorders; shortness of breath; sore throat

CONSUMER GUIDE®

Contraindications: This drug should not be taken by persons who have certain types of severe heart disease. This drug should not be taken by people who are allergic to it. Consult your doctor immediately if this drug has been prescribed for you and you have such an allergy or condition.

Warnings: This drug should be used with caution, since its use may cause low blood pressure and heart failure. • This drug should be used cautiously in conjunction with certain other agents such as quinidine or procainamide, beta blockers, and alcohol. If you are currently taking any drugs of these types, consult your doctor about their use. If you are unsure of the type or contents of your medications, ask your doctor or pharmacist. • Patients receiving more than one anti-arrhythmic drug must be carefully monitored. • This drug should be used with caution by persons with glaucoma, myasthenia gravis, enlarged prostate, low blood sugar (hypoglycemia), malnutrition, urinary retention, low blood potassium (hypokalemia), liver and kidney disease; by those who are pregnant; and by nursing mothers. Be sure your doctor knows if any of these conditions relates to you. • This drug should be used with caution by children.

Comments: This drug is similar in action to procainamide and to quinidine sulfate. • While taking this drug, do not take any nonprescription item for cough, cold, or sinus problems without first checking with your doctor. • This drug must be taken exactly as directed. Do not take extra doses or skip a dose. • Chew gum or suck on ice chips to reduce mouth dryness. • To minimize dizziness, rise from a lying or sitting position slowly.

Nor-Tet antibiotic (Vortech Pharmaceutical, Ltd.), see tetracycline hydrochloride antibiotic.

Nuprin anti-inflammatory (Bristol-Myers), see Motrin anti-inflammatory.

nystatin antifungal agent (various manufacturers), see Mycostatin antifungal agent.

Obe-Nix anorectic (Holloway, Inc.), see Fastin anorectic.

Obephen anorectic (Mallard, Inc.), see Fastin anorectic.

Obermine anorectic (Forest Pharmaceuticals), see Fastin anorectic.

Obestin-30 anorectic (Ferndale Laboratories, Inc.), see Fastin anorectic.

Omnipen antibiotic (Wyeth Laboratories), see ampicillin antibiotic.

Onset-10 anti-anginal (Bock Pharmacal Company), see Isordil anti-anginal.

Ophthacet ophthalmic solution and ointment (Vortech Pharmaceuticals, Ltd.), see Sodium Sulamyd ophthalmic solution and ointment.

Orahist antihistamine and adrenergic (Vangard Laboratories), see Ornade Spansule antihistamine and adrenergic.

oral contraceptives

"Oral contraceptives" is a descriptive term.

Examples: Brevicon, Syntex (F.P.) Inc.; Demulen, Searle & Co.; Enovid, Searle & Co.; Loestrin, Parke-Davis; Lo/Ovral, Wyeth Laboratories; Micronor, Wyeth Laboratories; Modicon, Ortho Pharmaceutical Corporation; Nordette (Wyeth Laboratories); Norinyl, Syntex (F.P.) Inc.; Norlestrin, Parke-Davis; Nor-Q.D., Syntex Laboratories, Inc.; Ortho-Novum, Ortho Pharmaceutical Corporation; Ovcon, Mead Johnson Pharmaceutical Division; Ovral, Wyeth Laboratories; Ovrette, Wyeth Laboratories; Ovulen, Searle & Co.; Tri-Norinyl, Syntex Laboratories, Inc.; Triphasil, Wyeth Laboratories

Dosage Form: Tablets in packages. Some contain 20 or 21 tablets; others 28. When 28 are present, 7 are blank or contain iron (see Comments).

Use: Birth control

Minor Side Effects: Abdominal cramps; acne; backache; bloating; change in appetite; change in sexual desire; diarrhea; dizziness; fatigue; headache; hearing changes; itching; nasal congestion; nausea; nervousness; vaginal irritation; vomiting

Major Side Effects: Anemia; arthritis; birth defects; blood clots; breakthrough bleeding (spotting); cancer; cervical damage; changes in menstrual flow; colitis; depression; elevated blood sugar; enlarged or tender breasts; eye damage; fluid retention; gallbladder disease; heart attack; high blood pressure; increase or decrease in hair growth; internal bleeding; jaundice; kidney damage; liver damage; lung damage; migraine; numbness or tingling; pain during or cessation of menstruation; pancreatic changes; rash; reduced ability to conceive after drug is stopped; skin color changes; stroke; tumor growth; weight changes; yeast infection

Contraindications: This type of drug should not be used by people with breast cancer or certain types of heart disease, liver disease, blood disease, vaginal bleeding, blood clots, clotting disorders, strokes or mir strokes, heart attack, or chest pain. This type of drug should not be taken by people who smoke cigarettes or those who are nursing. Be sure your doctor knows if you have or have had any of these conditions. It should not be used by people who may have breast cancer or who have had liver tumors as a result of using drugs like this. Women who have certain other cancers or abnormal vaginal bleeding and those who may be pregnant should not take this drug.

Warnings: This type of drug has been known or suspected to cause cancer. If you have a family history of cancer, you should inform your doctor of it before taking oral contraceptives. ● This type of drug should be used cautiously by women over age 30. ● Oral contraceptives are known to cause an increased risk of heart attacks, stroke, liver disease, gallbladder disease, fluid retention, depression, clotting disorders, blood diseases, eye disease, cancer, birth defects, diabetes, high blood pressure, headache, bleeding disorders, and poor production of breast milk. ● Caution should be observed while taking oral contraceptives if you have uterine tumors, mental depression, epilepsy, migraine, asthma, kidney disease, jaundice, or vitamin deficiency. Be sure your doctor knows if you have any of these conditions. ● Oral contraceptives interact with oral anticoagulants, barbiturates, phenylbutazone, isoniazid, carbamazepine, primidone, chloramphenicol, phenytoin, ampicillin, tetracycline, rifampin, and steroids. Contact your doctor immediately if you are currently taking any drugs of these types. If you are unsure of the type or contents of your medications, ask your doctor or pharmacist. ● Some women who have used oral contraceptives have had trouble becoming pregnant after they stopped using the drug. Most of these women had had scanty or irregular menstrual periods before they started taking oral contraceptives. ● You should have a complete physical, including a Pap smear, before you start taking oral contraceptives and every year that you are taking them. • Oral contraceptives affect a wide variety of lab tests. Be sure your doctor knows you are taking oral contraceptives if you are being tested or examined for any reason. • Little is known about the long-term effects of the use of this type of drug on pituitary, ovarian, adrenal, liver or uterine function or on the immune system. • Use of this drug may make it difficult to tell when menopause occurs.

Comments: Oral contraceptives currently are considered the most effective reversible method of birth control. The table below shows various methods of birth control and their effectiveness.

Birth Control Method	Effectiveness*
Oral contraceptives	up to 3
Intrauterine device (IUD)	up to 6
Diaphragm (with cream or gel)	up to 20
Vaginal sponge	up to 20
Aerosol foam	up to 29
Condom	up to 36
Gel or cream	up to 36
Rhythm	up to 47
No contraception	up to 80

*Pregnancies per 100 woman years

Take an oral contraceptive at the same time every day to get into the habit of taking the pills. If you skip one day, take a tablet for the day you missed as soon as you think of it and another tablet at the regular time. • Missing a day increases your chances of pregnancy; use other methods of contraception for the rest of the cycle and continue taking the tablets. • If you do not start to menstruate on schedule at the end of the pill cycle, begin the next cycle of pills at the prescribed time, anyway. Many women taking oral contraceptives have irregular menstruation. Do not be alarmed, but consult your doctor. • Stop taking oral contraceptive tablets at least three months before you wish to become pregnant. Use another type of contraceptive during this three-month period. • Some oral contraceptive packets contain 28 tablets rather than the usual 20 or 21 tablets. The 28-tablet packets contain seven placebos (sugar pills) or iron tablets. The placebos help you remember to take a tablet each day even while you are menstruating, and the iron tablets help replace the iron that is lost in menstruation. • Nausea is common, especially during the first two or three months, but may be prevented by taking the tablets at bedtime. If nausea persists for more than three months, consult your doctor. • Although many brands of oral contraceptives are available, most differ in only minor ways, and you may have to try several brands before you find the product that is ideal for you. • Your pharmacist will give you a booklet explaining birth control pills with every prescription. Read this booklet carefully. It contains exact directions on how to use medication correctly. • If you use oral contraceptives, you must not smoke cigarettes. You should visit your doctor for a checkup at least twice a year while you are taking oral contraceptives. • Women over 30 have an increased risk of adverse effects from use of oral contraceptives. • Spotting or breakthrough bleeding may occur during the first months of use of this drug. Call your physician if it continues past the second month. • Use a supplemental method of birth control the first three weeks that you start taking oral contraceptives.

Oramide oral antidiabetic (Major Pharmaceuticals), see Orinase oral antidiabetic.

Oraminic Spancaps antihistamine and adrenergic (Vortech Pharmaceutical, Ltd.), see Ornade Spansule antihistamine and adrenergic.

Orasone steroid hormone (Rowell Laboratories, Inc.), see prednisone steroid hormone.

Oretic diuretic and antihypertensive (Abbott Laboratories), see hydrochlorothiazide diuretic and antihypertensive.

Orinase oral antidiabetic

Manufacturer: The Upjohn Company
Ingredient: tolbutamide
Equivalent Products: Oramide, Major Pharmaceuticals; SK-Tolbutamide, Smith Kline & French Laboratories; tolbutamide, various manufacturers
Dosage Form: Tablet: 250 mg; 500 mg (both white)
Use: Treatment of diabetes mellitus
Minor Side Effects: Cramps; diarrhea; dizziness; fatigue; headache; heartburn; loss of appetite; nausea; stomach upset; sun sensitivity; vomiting; weakness
Major Side Effects: Blood disorders; bruising; difficult breathing; jaundice; low blood sugar; muscle cramps; rash; ringing in the ears; seizures; sore throat; tingling in hands and feet
Contraindications: This drug should not be used to treat juvenile (insulin-dependent) or unstable diabetes. Diabetics subject to acidosis, ketosis, or with a history of repeated diabetic comas should not use this drug. This drug should not be used by people with severe renal impairment. In the presence of fever, severe trauma, or infections, insulin should be used instead, at least during the acute stage of the problem. If you fit into any of these categories, be sure your doctor knows before you begin taking this drug.
Warnings: Tolbutamide may not be safe for use during pregnancy. If you are or might become pregnant, be sure to tell your doctor before taking this drug. • Be sure you recognize the symptoms of low blood sugar and know what to do if you begin to experience these symptoms. You will have to be especially careful during the transition from insulin to tolbutamide. • People with thyroid disease or kidney or liver damage and those who are malnourished must use this drug cautiously. Be sure your doctor knows if you fit into any of these categories. • Thiazide diuretics (commonly used to treat high blood pressure) and beta-blocking drugs may interfere with control of your diabetes. If you are taking any drugs of either type, talk to your physician before you take this drug. If you are not sure of the type of your medications, ask your doctor or pharmacist. • Do not drink alcohol and do not take any other drugs unless directed to do so by your doctor while you are taking this drug. Be especially careful with nonprescription cold remedies. • This drug interacts with anabolic steroids, anticoagulants, anticonvulsants, aspirin, chloramphenicol, guanethidine, propranolol, monoamine oxidase inhibitors, phenylbutazone, steroids, tetracycline, thiazide diuretics, and thyroid hormones; if you are currently taking any drugs of these types, consult your doctor about their use. If you are unsure of the type or contents of your medications, ask your doctor or pharmacist.
Comments: Take this drug at the same time everyday. • Recent evidence indicates that not all generic forms of tolbutamide are equivalent. Ask your pharmacist for a product that is bioequivalent. • Avoid long exposure to sunlight while taking this drug. • This drug is not an oral form of insulin. • Studies have shown that a good diet and exercise program may be just as effective as oral

antidiabetic drugs. However, these drugs allow diabetics more leeway in their lifestyles. Persons taking this drug should carefully watch their diet and exercise program and avoid infection. • Persons taking this drug should visit the doctor at least once a week for the first six weeks of therapy. They should check their urine for sugar and ketones at least three times a day, and they should know how to recognize the first signs of low blood sugar. Signs of low blood sugar include chills; cold sweat; cool, pale skin; drowsiness; headache; nausea; nervousness; rapid pulse; tremors; weakness. If these symptoms develop, eat or drink something containing sugar and call your doctor. • It may be advised that you carry a medical alert card or wear a medical alert bracelet indicating you are on this medication.

Ornade Spansule antihistamine and adrenergic

Manufacturer: Smith Kline & French Laboratories
Ingredients: chlorpheniramine maleate; phenylpropanolamine hydrochloride
Equivalent Products: Condrin-LA, Mallard, Inc.; Deconade, H. L. Moore; Drize, B. F. Ascher & Co., Inc.; Neotep, Reid-Provident Labs., Inc.; Orahist, Vangard Laboratories; Oraminic Spancaps, Vortech Pharmaceutical, Ltd.; Resaid T. D., Geneva Generics, Inc.; Rhinolar-EX 12, McGregor Pharmaceuticals; Tuss-genade, Goldline Laboratories
Dosage Form: Capsule: chlorpheniramine maleate, 12 mg; phenylpropanolamine hydrochloride, 75 mg (blue/clear with red and white beads)
Use: Symptomatic relief of upper respiratory tract congestion
Minor Side Effects: Acne; blurred vision; confusion; constipation; diarrhea; dizziness; drowsiness; dry mouth; headache; heartburn; insomnia; irritability; loss of appetite; nasal congestion; nausea; restlessness; sun sensitivity; sweating; vomiting; weakness
Major Side Effects: Bruising; chest pain; convulsions; difficult urination; high blood pressure; loss of coordination; low blood pressure; mood changes; palpitations; rash; severe abdominal pain; sore throat
Contraindications: This drug should not be taken by people who are allergic to any of its components. The drug should not be taken by people who are using monoamine oxidase inhibitors (ask your pharmacist if you are unsure); or by those who have asthma, heart disease, severe high blood pressure, obstructed bladder, obstructed intestine, or ulcer (certain types). Consult your doctor immediately if this drug has been prescribed for you and you have any of these conditions. This drug should not be given to children under six years of age.
Warnings: This drug should be used cautiously by people who have glaucoma, heart or blood vessel disease, thyroid disease, diabetes, epilepsy, myasthenia gravis, hiatal hernia, or enlarged prostate; and by women who are pregnant or nursing. Be sure your doctor knows if you have any of these conditions. • This drug may cause drowsiness; avoid tasks that require alertness. • To prevent oversedation, avoid the use of alcohol or other drugs that have sedative properties.
Comments: Chew gum or suck on ice chips or a piece of hard candy to reduce mouth dryness. • This drug has sustained action; never increase your dose or take it more frequently than your doctor prescribes. A serious overdose could result. • While taking this drug, do not take any nonprescription item for weight control or cough, cold, or sinus problems without first checking with your doctor. • This drug may be taken with food or milk to lessen stomach upset.

Ortega Otic M otic solution (Ortega Pharmaceutical Co.), see Cortisporin otic solution/suspension.

Otobione otic suspension (Schering Corp.), see Cortisporin otic solution/suspension.

oxycodone hydrochloride, oxycodone terephthalate, and aspirin analgesic (various manufacturers), see Percodan analgesic.

Palbar sedative and anticholinergic (W. E. Hauck, Inc.), see Donnatal sedative and anticholinergic.

Panadol with Codeine analgesic (Winthrop Laboratories), see acetaminophen with codeine analgesic.

Panasol steroid hormone (Seatrace Co.), see prednisone steroid hormone.

Panazid antitubercular (Panray Division), see isoniazid antitubercular.

Panmycin antibiotic (The Upjohn Company), see tetracycline hydrochloride antibiotic.

Panwarfin anticoagulant (Abbott Laboratories) see Coumadin anticoagulant.

Papacon vasodilator and smooth muscle relaxant (Consolidated Midland Corp.), see Pavabid Plateau Caps vasodilator and smooth muscle relaxant.

papaverine hydrochloride vasodilator and smooth muscle relaxant (various manufacturers), see Pavabid Plateau Caps vasodilator and smooth muscle relaxant.

Parafon Forte analgesic

Manufacturer: McNeil Laboratories
Ingredients: acetaminophen; chlorzoxazone
Equivalent Products: Chlorofon-F, Rugby Laboratories; Chlorzone Forte, Henry Schein, Inc.; chlorzoxazone w/APAP, various manufacturers; Polyflex, Holloway, Inc.; Zoxaphen, Mallard, Inc.
Dosage Form: Tablet: acetaminophen, 300 mg; chlorzoxazone, 250 mg (green)
Use: Relief of pain from strained muscles
Minor Side Effects: Change in urine color; constipation; diarrhea; dizziness; drowsiness; fatigue; headache; heartburn; light-headedness; nausea; nervousness; overstimulation; stomach cramps; vomiting
Major Side Effects: Black stools; bleeding; fever; jaundice; rash; sore throat; ulcer; weakness
Contraindications: This drug should not be taken by people allergic to either of its components. Consult your doctor immediately if this drug has been prescribed for you and you have such an allergy.
Warnings: This drug should be used cautiously by people who have heart, lung, kidney, or liver disease; significant allergies; certain blood disorders; and

by those who are pregnant. Be sure your doctor knows if you fit into any of these categories. • This drug may cause allergic reactions. Contact your doctor if you develop a rash. • This drug may cause drowsiness; avoid tasks that require alertness. • To prevent oversedation, avoid the use of alcohol or other drugs that have sedative properties. • Avoid the use of other medicines containing acetaminophen. Ask your pharmacist or physician to help you choose a cough or cold product.

Comments: This drug may color the urine orange or reddish purple. This side effect is usually not serious and persists only as long as the drug is taken. • This drug is not a substitute for rest, physical therapy, or other measures recommended by your doctor.

Pavabid Plateau Caps vasodilator and smooth muscle relaxant

Manufacturer: Marion Laboratories, Inc.

Ingredient: papaverine hydrochloride

Equivalent Products: Cerespan, USV (P.R.) Development Corp.; Delapav, Dunhall Pharmaceuticals, Inc.; Dilart, Trimen Laboratories, Inc.; Myobid, Laser, Inc.; Papacon, Consolidated Midland Corp.; papaverine hydrochloride, various manufacturers; Pavacap Unicelles, Reid-Provident Labs., Inc.; Pavacen Cen-ules, The Central Pharmacal, Inc.; Pavadur, Century Pharmaceuticals, Inc.; Pavadyl, Bock Pharmacal Company; Pavagen, Rugby Laboratories; Pava-Par, Parmed Pharmaceuticals, Inc.; Pava-RX, Blaine Co., Inc.; Pavased, Mallard, Inc.; Pavasule T.D., Misemer Pharmaceuticals, Inc.; Pavatine, Major Pharma-ceuticals, Inc.; Pavatym, Everett Laboratories, Inc.; Paverine Spancaps, Vor-tech Pharmaceutical, Ltd.; Paverolan Lanacaps, The Lannett Company, Inc.; Vasocap-150, Keene Pharmaceuticals, Inc.; Vasospan, Ulmer Pharmacal Co.

Dosage Form: Time-release capsule: 150 mg (black/clear)

Use: To promote blood flow to the heart muscle and brain

Minor Side Effects: Abdominal distress; blurred vision; constipation; diar-rhea; dizziness; drowsiness; fatigue; flushing; headache; loss of appetite; nausea; sweating

Major Side Effects: Blood disorders; depression; difficult breathing; jaun-dice; palpitations; rash

Contraindications: This drug should not be taken by people who are allergic to it. Consult your doctor immediately if you have any of these conditions.

Warnings: This drug should be used cautiously by people who have glau-coma, heart block, certain types of heart disease, high or low blood pressure, Parkinson's disease, or liver disease. Be sure your doctor knows if you have any of these conditions.

Comments: This drug and many of its equivalents are also available as tablets which do not provide sustained action. • This drug increases the flow of blood to the brain and heart muscle, but this activity has not been shown to alleviate chest pain or the aftereffects of a stroke. In addition, the AMA Drug Evaluations (1985) states that no objective study has proven this drug effective in peripheral blood vessel disease. Discuss the merits of this drug with your doctor before starting therapy. • This drug may cause drowsiness; avoid tasks that require alertness. • To prevent oversedation, avoid the use of alcohol or other drugs that have sedative properties. • While taking this drug, do not take any nonprescription item for cough, cold, or sinus problems without first check-ing with your doctor. • This product may cause dizziness; avoid sudden changes in posture. Use caution when driving, climbing stairs, etc. Alcohol may intensify this side effect. • Notify your doctor if you experience any symptoms of flushing, sweating, headache, tiredness, or pronounced gastrointestinal distress, or if jaundice or skin rash appears. ● The sustained-release forms of this product must be swallowed whole. Do not crush or chew the drug.

Pavacap Unicelles vasodilator and smooth muscle relaxant (Reid-Provident Labs., Inc.), see Pavabid Plateau Caps vasodilator and smooth muscle relaxant.

Pavacen Cenules vasodilator and smooth muscle relaxant (Central Pharmaceuticals, Inc.), see Pavabid Plateau Caps vasodilator and smooth muscle relaxant.

Pavadur vasodilator and smooth muscle relaxant (Century Pharmaceuticals, Inc.), see Pavabid Plateau Caps vasodilator and smooth muscle relaxant.

Pavadyl vasodilator and smooth muscle relaxant (Bock Pharmacal Company), see Pavabid Plateau Caps vasodilator and smooth muscle relaxant.

Pavagen vasodilator and smooth muscle relaxant (Rugby Laboratories), see Pavabid Plateau Caps vasodilator and smooth muscle relaxant.

Pava-Par vasodilator and smooth muscle relaxant (Parmed Pharmaceuticals, Inc.), see Pavabid Plateau Caps vasodilator and smooth muscle relaxant.

Pava-RX vasodilator and smooth muscle relaxant (Blaine Co., Inc.), see Pavabid Plateau Caps vasodilator and smooth muscle relaxant.

Pavased vasodilator and smooth muscle relaxant (Mallard, Inc.), see Pavabid Plateau Caps vasodilator and smooth muscle relaxant.

Pavasule T.D. vasodilator and smooth muscle relaxant (Misemer Pharmaceuticals, Inc.), see Pavabid Plateau Caps vasodilator and smooth muscle relaxant.

Pavatine vasodilator and smooth muscle relaxant (Major Pharmaceuticals, Inc.), see Pavabid Plateau Caps vasodilator and smooth muscle relaxant.

Pavatym vasodilator and smooth muscle relaxant (Everett Laboratories, Inc.), see Pavabid Plateau Caps vasodilator and smooth muscle relaxant.

Paverine Spancaps vasodilator and smooth muscle relaxant (Vortech Pharmaceuticals, Ltd.), see Pavabid Plateau Caps vasodilator and smooth muscle relaxant.

Paverolan Lanacaps vasodilator and smooth muscle relaxant (The

Lannett Company, Inc.), see Pavabid Plateau Caps vasodilator and smooth muscle relaxant.

PBR/12 sedative and hypnotic (Scott-Alison Pharmaceuticals, Inc.), see phenobarbital sedative and hypnotic.

Pediamycin antibiotic (Ross Laboratories), see erythromycin antibiotic.

Pedi-Cort V steroid hormone and anti-infective (Pedinol Pharmacal, Inc.), see Vioform-Hydrocortisone steroid hormone and anti-infective.

Penapar VK antibiotic (Parke-Davis), see penicillin potassium phenoxymethyl (penicillin VK) antibiotic.

penicillin G potassium antibiotic

Manufacturer: various manufacturers
Ingredient: penicillin G potassium
Equivalent Products: M-cillin B 400, Misemer Pharmaceuticals, Inc.; Pentids, E. R. Squibb & Sons, Inc.; Pfizerpen G, Pfipharmecs Division; SK-Penicillin G, Smith Kline & French Laboratories.
Dosage Forms: Liquid; Tablet (various dosages and various colors)
Use: Treatment of a wide variety of bacterial infections
Minor Side Effects: Diarrhea; heartburn; nausea; vomiting
Major Side Effects: Bloating; chills; cough; difficult breathing; fever; irritation of the mouth; muscle aches; rash; rectal and vaginal itching; severe diarrhea; sore throat; superinfection
Contraindications: This drug should not be taken by people who are allergic to any penicillin drug. Consult your doctor immediately if this drug has been prescribed for you and you have such an allergy.
Warnings: This drug should be used cautiously by people who have kidney disease, asthma, or other significant allergies. Be sure your doctor knows if you have any type of allergy. • This drug interacts with aspirin, probenecid, phenylbutazone, indomethacin, sulfinpyrazone, chloramphenicol, erythromycin, and tetracycline; if you are currently taking any drugs of these types, consult your doctor about their use. If you are unsure of the type or contents of your medications, ask your doctor or pharmacist. • This drug is readily destroyed by acids in the stomach; do not take this medication with orange juice or other beverages with high acid contents. It is best taken with water or milk. • Severe allergic reactions to this drug (indicated by breathing difficulties or a drop in blood pressure) have been reported, but are rare when the drug is taken orally. • Diabetics using Clinitest urine test may get a false high sugar reading while taking this drug. Change to Clinistix, Diastix, or Tes-Tape urine test to avoid this problem. • Prolonged use of this drug may allow organisms that are not susceptible to it to grow wildly. Do not use this drug unless your doctor has specifically told you to do so. Be sure to follow the directions carefully and report any unusual reactions to your doctor at once. • Complete blood cell counts and liver and kidney function tests should be done if you take this drug for a prolonged period.
Comments: This drug is similar in nature and action to amoxicillin and ampicillin. • This drug should be taken for the full prescribed period, even if

symptoms disappear within that time. ● The liquid form of this drug should be stored in the refrigerator. Any unused portion should be discarded after 14 days. Shake well before using. ● Take this drug on an empty stomach (one hour before or two hours after a meal). ● It is best to take this drug at evenly spaced times throughout the day and night. Your pharmacist or physician will help you set up a dosing schedule.

penicillin potassium phenoxymethyl (penicillin VK) antibiotic

Manufacturer: various manufacturers

Ingredient: penicillin potassium phenoxymethyl

Equivalent Products: Beepen VK, Beecham Laboratories; Betapen-VK, Bristol Labs; Deltapen-VK, Trimen Laboratories, Inc.; Ledercillin VK, Lederle Laboratories; Penapar VK, Parke-Davis; Pen-Vee K, Wyeth Laboratories; Pfizerpen VK, Pfipharmecs Division; Repen-VK, Reid-Provident Labs., Inc.; Robicillin VK, A. H. Robins Company; SK-Penicillin VK, Smith Kline & French Laboratories; Suspen, Circle Pharmaceuticals, Inc.; Uticillin VK, The Upjohn Company; V-Cillin K, Eli Lilly & Co.; Veetids, E. R. Squibb & Sons, Inc.

Dosage Forms: Liquid; Tablet (various dosages and various colors)

Use: Treatment of a wide variety of bacterial infections

Minor Side Effects: Diarrhea; heartburn; nausea; vomiting

Major Side Effects: Bloating; chills; cough; difficult breathing; fever; irritation of the mouth; muscle aches; rash; rectal and vaginal itching; severe diarrhea; sore throat; superinfection

Contraindications: This drug should not be used by people allergic to any penicillin drug. Consult your doctor immediately if this drug has been prescribed for you and you have such an allergy.

Warnings: This drug should be used cautiously by people who have kidney disease or asthma or other significant allergies. Be sure your doctor knows if you have either of these conditions. ● Contact your doctor if you develop a fever, rash, or sore throat. ● This drug interacts with chloramphenicol, probenecid, aspirin, phenylbutazone, indomethacin, sulfinpyrazone, erythromycin, and tetracycline; if you are currently taking any drugs of these types, consult your doctor about their use. If you are unsure of the type or contents of your medications, ask your doctor or pharmacist. ● Severe allergic reactions to this drug (indicated by breathing difficulties or a drop in blood pressure) have been reported, but are rare when the drug is taken orally. ● Diabetics using Clinitest urine test may get a false high sugar reading while taking this drug. Change to Clinistix, Diastix, or Tes-Tape urine test to avoid this problem. ● Prolonged use of this drug may allow organisms that are not susceptible to it to grow wildly. Do not use this drug unless your doctor has specifically told you to do so. Be sure to follow directions carefully and report any unusual reactions to your doctor at once. ● This drug may affect the potency of oral contraceptives. Consult your doctor about using supplementary contraceptive measures while you are taking this drug.

Comments: "Penicillin V" is another name for this drug. ● This drug has approximately the same antibacterial activity as the less expensive product penicillin G. However, this drug is more stable in the stomach and is worth the extra cost. ● This drug is similar in nature and action to amoxicillin and ampicillin. ● This drug should be taken for the full prescribed course, even if symptoms disappear within that time. ● The liquid form of this drug should be stored in the refrigerator. Any unused portion should be discarded after 14 days. Shake well before use. ● Take this drug on an empty stomach (one hour before or two hours after a meal). ● It is best to take this drug at evenly spaced times throughout the day and night. Your pharmacist or physician will help you set up a dosing schedule.

Pentids antibiotic (E. R. Squibb & Sons, Inc.), see penicillin G potassium antibiotic.

Pen-Vee K antibiotic (Wyeth Laboratories), see penicillin potassium phenoxymethyl (penicillin VK) antibiotic.

Percodan analgesic

Manufacturer: DuPont Laboratories, Inc.
Ingredients: aspirin; oxycodone hydrochloride; oxycodone terephthalate
Equivalent Products: Codoxy, Halsey Drug Co., Inc.; oxycodone hydrochloride, oxycodone terephthalate, and aspirin, various manufacturers
Dosage Form: Tablet: aspirin, 325 mg; oxycodone hydrochloride, 4.50 mg; oxycodone terephthalate, 0.38 mg (yellow)
Use: Relief of moderate to moderately severe pain
Minor Side Effects: Constipation; dizziness; drowsiness; dry mouth; euphoria; flushing; itching; light-headedness; loss of appetite; nausea; sedation; sweating; vomiting
Major Side Effects: Bloody stools; chest tightness; difficult breathing; difficult urination; jaundice; kidney disease; low blood sugar; odd movements; palpitations; rapid or slow heartbeat; rash; ringing in the ears; tremors; ulcer
Contraindications: This drug should not be taken by people who are allergic to any of its components. Consult your doctor immediately if this drug has been prescribed for you and you have such an allergy.
Warnings: This drug should be used cautiously by pregnant women, the elderly, children, and debilitated persons. It should be used cautiously by persons with anemia, brain disease, colitis, lung disease, gallbladder disease, bleeding disorders, peptic ulcer, abdominal disease, head injuries, liver disease, kidney disease, thyroid disease, or prostate disease. Be sure your doctor knows if you fit into any of these categories. ● This drug should not be taken with alcohol, methotrexate, 6-mercaptopurine, oral antidiabetics, phenytoin, oral anticoagulants, aspirin, or gout medications (probenecid, sulfinpyrazone). If you are unsure of the type or contents of your medications, ask your doctor or pharmacist. ● This drug has the potential for abuse and must be used with caution. Tolerance may develop quickly; do not increase the dose of this drug without first consulting your doctor. ● Products containing narcotics (e.g., oxycodone) are usually not used for more than seven to ten days. ● This drug may cause drowsiness; avoid tasks requiring alertness, such as driving a car or operating machinery. ● To prevent oversedation, avoid the use of alcohol or other drugs that have sedative properties.
Comments: Take this drug with food or milk to lessen stomach upset. ● Side effects caused by this drug may be somewhat relieved by lying down. ● If your ears feel strange, if you hear buzzing or ringing, or if your stomach hurts, your dosage may need adjustment. Call your doctor. ● There is a half-strength form of this drug available. It is called Percodan-Demi and is also made by DuPont Laboratories, Inc. (Only the oxycodone components are half strength.)

Periactin antihistamine

Manufacturer: Merck Sharp & Dohme
Ingredient: cyproheptadine hydrochloride
Equivalent Product: cyproheptadine hydrochloride, various manufacturers
Dosage Forms: Syrup (content per 5 ml teaspoon): 2 mg. Tablet: 4 mg (white)

Use: Relief of hay fever symptoms; itching; rash

Minor Side Effects: Blurred vision; change in appetite; confusion; constipation; diarrhea; dizziness; drowsiness; dry mouth; headache; heartburn; insomnia; nasal congestion; nausea; nervousness; reduced sweating; restlessness; sensitivity to sunlight; vomiting; weakness

Major Side Effects: Bruising; chest tightness; convulsions; difficult urination; hallucinations; loss of coordination; low blood pressure; menstrual irregularities; nightmares; rash; ringing in the ears; severe abdominal pain; sore throat

Contraindications: This drug should not be taken by people who have asthma, glaucoma (certain types), ulcer (certain types), enlarged prostate, obstructed bladder, or obstructed intestine. It should not be taken by infants, nursing mothers, those who are allergic to it, or those who are taking monoamine oxidase inhibitors. Consult your doctor immediately if you have any of these conditions or fit into any of these categories.

Warnings: This drug should be used cautiously by pregnant women. Be sure your doctor knows if you are pregnant. ● Children under 12 who take this drug may become excited or restless. ● This drug may add to the effects of alcohol, other sedatives, and central nervous system depressants. Avoid using drugs of these types while taking this product. If you are unsure of the type or contents of your medications, ask your doctor or pharmacist. ● This drug may cause drowsiness; avoid tasks that require alertness. ● This drug may cause the following conditions to worsen: asthma, glaucoma, thyroid disease, heart disease, high blood pressure. Consult your doctor if you have any of these conditions and this drug has been prescribed for you.

Comments: Chew gum or suck on ice chips or a piece of hard candy to reduce mouth dryness. ● While taking this drug, do not take any nonprescription item for cough, cold, or sinus problems without first checking with your doctor. ● The elderly are more likely to suffer side effects, especially sedation, dizziness, and low blood pressure, from this drug than are other people. ● This drug may be taken with food or milk if stomach irritation occurs. ● This drug has been used to stimulate appetite in persons with anorexia nervosa. It has also been used to treat cluster headaches.

Persantine anti-anginal

Manufacturer: Boehringer Ingelheim Ltd.

Ingredient: dipyridamole

Equivalent Products: Cordilate, Foy Laboratories; dipyridamole, various manufacturers; Pyridamole, Major Pharmaceuticals

Dosage Form: Tablet: 25 mg; 50 mg; 75 mg (all orange)

Use: Prevention of chronic chest pain (angina) due to heart disease

Minor Side Effects: Cramps; dizziness; fainting; fatigue; flushing; headache; nausea; weakness

Major Side Effect: Rash; worsening of chest pain (mainly at start of therapy)

Contraindications: No known

Warnings: This drug should be used cautiously by patients with low blood pressure. This drug may cause allergic-type reactions, particularly in persons with aspirin hypersensitivity. Be sure your doctor knows if you have low blood pressure or such sensitivity.

Comments: The effectiveness of this drug for prevention of chronic angina is controversial. This drug is more frequently prescribed to prevent blood clot formation, although use of the drug for this purpose is not approved by the FDA. ● This drug should be taken on an empty stomach (one hour before or two hours after a meal) and taken only in the prescribed amount. ● The effects of this drug may not be apparent for at least two months. ● This drug will not stop chest pain from angina that has already begun. It is used only to prevent such pain from occurring. • To avoid dizziness or light-headedness when you stand, contract and relax the muscles of your legs for a few moments before rising. Do this by pushing one foot against the floor while raising the other foot slightly, alternating feet so that you are "pumping" your legs. • Not all generic forms of this drug are identical. Consult your doctor or pharmacist about the use of a generic product.

Pfizer-E antibiotic (Pfipharmecs Division), see erythromycin antibiotic.

Pfizerpen A antibiotic (Pfipharmecs Division), see ampicillin antibiotic.

Pfizerpen G antibiotic (Pfipharmecs Division), see penicillin G potassium antibiotic.

Pfizerpen VK antibiotic (Pfipharmecs Division), see penicillin potassium phenoxymethyl (penicillin VK) antibiotic.

Phen-Amin antihistamine (Scrip-Physician Supply Co.), see Benadryl antihistamine.

Phenaphen with Codeine analgesic (A. H. Robins Company), see acetaminophen with codeine analgesic.

Phenazodine analgesic (The Lannett Company, Inc.), see Pyridium analgesic.

phenazopyridine hydrochloride analgesic (various manufacturers), see Pyridium analgesic.

Phenergan, Phenergan with Codeine expectorants

Manufacturer: Wyeth Laboratories
Ingredients: potassium guaiacolsulfonate; promethazine hydrochloride; codeine phosphate; sodium citrate; citric acid; alcohol
Equivalent Products: Phenergan: Mallergan, Mallard, Inc.; promethazine hydrochloride expectorant plain, various manufacturers; Prothazine, Vortech Pharmaceutical, Ltd. Phenergan with Codeine: promethazine hydrochloride with codeine, various manufacturers; Prothazine with Codeine, Vortech Pharmaceutical, Ltd.
Dosage Form: Phenergan: Liquid (content per 5 ml teaspoon): potassium guaiacolsulfonate, 44 mg; promethazine hydrochloride, 5 mg; sodium citrate, 197 mg; citric acid, 60 mg; alcohol, 7%. Phenergan with Codeine: Liquid (content per 5 ml teaspoon): codeine phosphate, 10 mg; potassium guaiacolsulfonate, 44 mg; promethazine hydrochloride, 5 mg; sodium citrate, 197 mg; citric acid, 60 mg; alcohol, 7%
Use: Cough suppressant
Minor Side Effects: Blurred vision; confusion; constipation; diarrhea; dizziness; drowsiness; dry mouth, nose, and throat; headache; heartburn; insomnia; loss of appetite; nasal congestion; nausea; nervousness; rash; restlessness; sweating; trembling; vomiting; weakness

Major Side Effects: Convulsions; difficult breathing; difficult urination; disturbed coordination; excitation; jaundice; low blood pressure; muscle spasms; nightmares; palpitations; rash from exposure to sunlight; severe abdominal pain; sore throat

Contraindications: This drug should not be taken by nursing mothers, newborns, people who are allergic to any of its components, and those taking monoamine oxidase inhibitors (consult your pharmacist if you are unsure). Consult your doctor immediately if this drug has been prescribed for you and you fit into any of these categories.

Warnings: This drug interacts with amphetamine, anticholinergics, levodopa, antacids, and trihexyphenidyl; if you are currently taking any drugs of these types, consult your doctor about their use. If you are unsure of the type or contents of your medications, ask your doctor or pharmacist. • This drug may cause drowsiness; avoid tasks that require alertness. • To prevent oversedation, avoid the use of alcohol or other drugs that have sedative properties. • The codeine-containing form of this product has the potential for abuse and must be used with caution. It usually should not be taken for more than ten days. Tolerance may develop quickly; do not increase the dosage without consulting your doctor. An overdose usually sedates an adult, but may cause excitation leading to convulsions and death in a child. • This drug should be used cautiously by people who have glaucoma (certain types), asthma, high blood pressure, brain disease, colitis, gallbladder disease, liver disease, ulcers, blood vessel or heart disease, kidney disease, thyroid disease, bowel or bladder obstruction, prostate trouble, or diabetes. Be sure your doctor knows if you have any of these conditions if this drug has been prescribed for you.

Comments: If you need an expectorant, you need more moisture in your environment. Drink nine to ten glasses of water daily. The use of a vaporizer or humidifier may also be beneficial. Consult your doctor. • Chew gum or suck on ice chips or a piece of hard candy to reduce mouth dryness. • While taking this drug, do not take any nonprescription item for cough, cold, or sinus problems without first checking with your doctor. • This drug may make you more sensitive to the sun. Avoid prolonged sun exposure and use a sunscreen lotion.

Phenergan VC, Phenergan VC with Codeine expectorants

Manufacturer: Wyeth Laboratories

Ingredients: phenylephrine hydrochloride; potassium guaiacolsulfonate; promethazine hydrochloride; codeine phosphate; sodium citrate; citric acid; alcohol

Equivalent Products: Phenergan VC: promethazine hydrochloride VC expectorant plain, various manufacturers. Phenergan VC with Codeine: Mallergan VC with Codeine, Mallard, Inc.; promethazine hydrochloride VC with codeine, various manufacturers; Prometh VC with Codeine, Barre Drug Co., Inc.

Dosage Form: Phenergan VC: Liquid (content per 5 ml teaspoon): phenylephrine hydrochloride, 5 mg; potassium guaiacolsulfonate, 44 mg; promethazine hydrochloride, 5 mg; sodium citrate, 197 mg; citric acid, 60 mg; alcohol, 7%. Phenergan VC with Codeine: Liquid (content per 5 ml teaspoon): codeine phosphate, 10 mg; phenylephrine hydrochloride, 5 mg; potassium guaiacolsulfonate, 44 mg; promethazine hydrochloride, 5 mg; sodium citrate, 197 mg; citric acid, 60 mg; alcohol, 7%

Use: Relief of coughing, congestion, and other symptoms of the common cold

Minor Side Effects: Blurred vision; confusion; constipation; diarrhea; dizziness; drowsiness; dry mouth, nose, and throat; headache; heartburn; insomnia; loss of appetite; nasal congestion; nausea; nervousness; rash; restlessness; sweating; trembling; vomiting; weakness

Major Side Effects: Convulsions; difficult breathing; difficult urination; disturbed coordination; excitation; jaundice; low blood pressure; muscle spasms; nightmares; palpitations; rash from exposure to sunlight; severe abdominal pain; sore throat

Contraindications: This drug should not be taken by nursing mothers, newborns, people who are allergic to any of its components, and those taking monoamine oxidase inhibitors. Consult your doctor immediately if this drug has been prescribed for you and you fit into any of these categories.

Warnings: This drug interacts with amphetamine, anticholinergics, levodopa, guanethidine, antacids, and trihexyphenidyl; if you are currently taking any drugs of these types, consult your doctor about their use. If you are unsure of the type or contents of your medications, ask your doctor or pharmacist. ● This drug may cause drowsiness; avoid tasks that require alertness. ● To prevent oversedation, avoid the use of alcohol or other drugs that have sedative properties. ● The codeine-containing form of this product has the potential for abuse and must be used with caution. It usually should not be taken for more than ten days. Tolerance may develop quickly; do not increase the dosage without consulting your doctor. An overdose usually sedates an adult, but may cause excitation leading to convulsions and death in a child. ● This drug should be used cautiously by people who have glaucoma (certain types), asthma, high blood pressure, brain disease, colitis, gallbladder disease, liver disease, ulcers, blood vessel or heart disease, kidney disease, thyroid disease, bowel or bladder obstruction, prostate trouble, or diabetes. Be sure your doctor knows if you have any of these conditions.

Comments: If you need an expectorant, you need more moisture in your environment. Drink nine to ten glasses of water daily. The use of a vaporizer or humidifier may also be beneficial. Consult your doctor. ● Chew gum or suck on ice chips or a piece of hard candy to reduce mouth dryness. ● While taking this drug, do not take any nonprescription item for cough, cold, or sinus problems without first checking with your doctor. ● This drug may make you more sensitive to the sun. Avoid prolonged sun exposure and use a sunscreen lotion.

phenobarbital sedative and hypnotic

Manufacturer: various manufacturers
Ingredient: phenobarbital
Equivalent Products: Barbita, Vortech Pharmaceutical, Ltd.; Luminal Ovoids, Winthrop Laboratories; PBR/12, Scott-Alison Pharmaceuticals, Inc.; Sedadrops, Merrell Dow Pharmaceuticals, Inc.; SK-Phenobarbital, Smith Kline & French Laboratories; Solfoton, Wm. P. Poythress & Co., Inc.
Dosage Forms: Capsule; Drops; Liquid; Tablet; Time-release capsules (various dosages and various colors)
Use: Control of convulsions; relief of anxiety or tension; sleeping aid
Minor Side Effects: Diarrhea; dizziness; drowsiness; headache; muscle pain; nausea; stomach upset; vomiting
Major Side Effects: Breathing difficulty or other allergic reactions; bruising; chest tightness; confusion; depression; excitation; loss of coordination; low blood pressure; skin rash; slow heart rate; slurred speech
Contraindications: This drug should not be used by people who are allergic to it; those who have porphyria or respiratory disease; and those with a history of drug abuse. Consult your doctor immediately if this drug has been prescribed for you and you fit any of these categories.
Warnings: This drug should be used cautiously by people who have liver or kidney disease, or certain lung diseases; women who are pregnant or nursing;

and children. Be sure your doctor knows if you have any of these conditions. •
This drug interacts with alcohol, central nervous system depressants, griseofulvin, oral contraceptives, cyclophosphamide, digitalis, rifampin, chloramphenicol, theophylline, aminophylline, oral anticoagulants, phenytoin, steroids,
sulfonamides, tetracycline, and antidepressants; if you are currently taking any
drugs of these types, consult your doctor about their use. If you are unsure of
the type or contents of your medications, ask your doctor or pharmacist. • This
drug may cause drowsiness; avoid tasks that require alertness. • To prevent
oversedation, avoid the use of alcohol or other drugs that have sedative
properties. • This drug has the potential for abuse and must be used with
caution. Tolerance may develop quickly; do not increase the dose without first
consulting your doctor. • Do not stop taking this drug without first consulting
your physician. If you have been taking the drug for a long time, the dose should
be reduced gradually.

Comments: Phenobarbital is an effective sedative and hypnotic, and it is
relatively inexpensive. • Notify your doctor if any of the following occur while
taking this drug: fever, mouth sores, sore throat, unusual bleeding or bruising. •
The time-release capsules must be swallowed whole. Do not crush or chew
them.

**phentermine hydrochloride anorectic (various manufacturers), see
Fastin anorectic.**

**Phentrol No. 2 anorectic (Vortech Pharmaceutical, Ltd.), see Fastin
anorectic.**

**phenytoin sodium anticonvulsant (various manufacturers), see
Dilantin anticonvulsant.**

**Phyllocontin bronchodilator (Purdue Frederick Company), see ami-
nophylline bronchodilator.**

**Pilocar ophthalmic solution (Coopervision Pharmaceutical, Inc.),
see Isopto Carpine ophthalmic solution.**

**pilocarpine hydrochloride ophthalmic solution (various manufac-
turers), see Isopto Carpine ophthalmic solution.**

**Pilocel ophthalmic solution (Professional Pharmacal Co.), see Isop-
to Carpine ophthalmic solution.**

**Pilomiotin ophthalmic solution (Coopervision Pharmaceutical,
Inc.), see Isopto Carpine ophthalmic solution.**

**Piloptic ophthalmic solution (Muro Pharmacal Labs., Inc.), see
Isopto Carpine ophthalmic solution.**

Polycillin antibiotic (Bristol Labs), see ampicillin antibiotic.

Polyflex analgesic (Holloway, Inc.), see Parafon Forte analgesic.

Polymox antibiotic (Bristol Labs), see amoxicillin antibiotic.

Poly Tabs-F vitamin and fluoride supplement (Major Pharmaceuticals), see Poly-Vi-Flor vitamin and fluoride supplement.

Poly-Vi-Flor vitamin and fluoride supplement

Manufacturer: Mead Johnson Nutritional Division
Ingredients: vitamins A, D, E, C; folic acid; thiamine; riboflavin; niacin; vitamins B_6, B_{12}; fluoride
Equivalent Products: Florvite, Everett Laboratories, Inc.; Poly Tabs-F, Major Pharmaceuticals; Polyvite with Fluoride Drops, Geneva Generics, Inc.; Vi-Daylin, Ross Laboratories
Dosage Forms: Chewable tablet: vitamin A, 2500 I.U.; vitamin D, 400 I.U.; vitamin E, 15 I.U.; vitamin C, 60 mg; folic acid, 0.3 mg; thiamine, 1 mg; riboflavin, 1.2 mg; niacin, 13.5 mg; vitamin B_6, 1 mg; vitamin B_{12}, 4.5 mcg; fluoride, 1.0 mg. Drops (content per ml): vitamin A, 1500 I.U.; vitamin D, 400 I.U.; vitamin E, 5 I.U.; vitamin C, 35 mg; thiamine, 0.5 mg; riboflavin, 0.6 mg; niacin, 8 mg; vitamin B_6, 0.4 mg; vitamin B_{12}, 2 mcg; fluoride, 0.5 mg
Use: Protection against tooth decay and vitamin deficiencies in children
Minor Side Effect: Rash (rare)
Major Side Effects: Blood in stools; breathing difficulty; cramps; discoloration of teeth; excitation; fainting; mouth sores; tremors
Contraindications: This product should not be used when fluoride content of drinking water is 0.7 parts per million or more. The drops form should not be used by infants from birth to two years of age in areas where the drinking water contains 0.3 parts per million or more of fluoride. This product should not be used in the presence of frank dental fluorosis.
Warnings: The recommended dose should not be exceeded or other fluoride-containing drugs given concurrently, since prolonged, excessive fluoride intake may cause dental fluorosis in children. • This drug should be used cautiously by those people with heart disease, kidney disease, bone disease, or thyroid disease. • Keep this product out of the reach of children.
Comments: This product should never be referred to as candy or "candy-flavored vitamins." Your child may take you literally and swallow too many. • If you are unsure of the fluoride content of your drinking water, ask your doctor, or call your County Health Department. • Mead Johnson Nutritional Division also manufactures a similar product, Tri-Vi-Flor vitamin and fluoride supplement, which contains only vitamins A, C, and D, and sodium fluoride. • The chewable tablets and drops discussed here are very similar to each other, but they do not contain exactly the same kinds and amounts of vitamins. • The drops are best suited for infants, and the chewable tablets for young children and adults.

Polyvite with Fluoride Drops vitamin and fluoride supplement (Geneva Generics, Inc.), see Poly-Vi-Flor vitamin and fluoride supplement.

Potachlor potassium chloride replacement (Bay Pharmaceuticals, Inc.), see potassium chloride replacement.

Potage potassium chloride replacement (Lemmon Company), see potassium chloride replacement.

Potasalan potassium chloride replacement (The Lannett Company, Inc.), see potassium chloride replacement.

Potassine potassium chloride replacement (Recsei Laboratories), see potassium chloride replacement.

potassium chloride replacement

Manufacturer: various manufacturers

Ingredient: potassium chloride

Equivalent Products: Cena-K, Century Pharmaceuticals, Inc.; Kaochlor, Adria Laboratories, Inc.; Kaon, Adria Laboratories, Inc.; Kato, Legere Laboratories; Kay Ciel, Berlex Laboratories, Inc.; K-Lor, Abbott Laboratories; Klor, Upsher-Smith Laboratories, Inc.; Klor-Con, Upsher-Smith Laboratories, Inc.; Klorvess, Sandoz Pharmaceuticals; Klotrix, Mead Johnson Co.; K-Lyte/Cl, Mead Johnson Co.; Kolyum, Pennwalt Pharmaceutical Division; K-Tab, Abbott Laboratories; Micro-K, A. H. Robins Company; Potachlor, Bay Pharmaceuticals, Inc.; Potage, Lemmon Company; Potasalan, The Lannett Company, Inc.; Potassine, Recsei Laboratories; Rum-K, Fleming & Co.; SK-Potassium Chloride, Smith Kline & French Laboratories; Slow-K, CIBA Pharmaceutical Co.

Dosage Forms: Effervescent tablet; Liquid; Powder; Slow-release tablet; Controlled-release capsule (various dosages and various colors)

Use: Prevention or treatment of potassium deficiency, especially that caused by diuretics

Minor Side Effects: Diarrhea; nausea; stomach pains; vomiting

Major Side Effects: Breathing difficulty; confusion; numbness or tingling in arms or legs; palpitations; ulcer

Contraindications: This drug should not be used by people who have severe kidney disease, high blood levels of potassium, or Addison's disease. This drug should not be used by those allergic to it. Consult your doctor immediately if you have any of these conditions.

Warnings: This drug should be used cautiously by people who have heart disease (certain types), intestinal blockage, peptic ulcer, and acute dehydration. Be sure your doctor knows if you have such a condition. ● This drug interacts with amiloride, spironolactone, and triamterene; if you are currently taking any drugs of these types, consult your doctor about their use. If you are unsure of the type or contents of your medications, ask your doctor or pharmacist. ● Follow your doctor's dosage instructions exactly and do not stop taking this medication without first consulting your doctor. ● Supplements of potassium should be administered with caution, since the amount of potassium deficiency may be difficult to determine accurately. ● Potassium intoxication rarely occurs in patients with normal kidney function. ● This drug should be taken cautiously by digitalized patients and such patients should be monitored by ECG for heart problems.

Comments: This drug should be taken with food. ● The liquid and powder forms of this drug may be added to one-half or one full glass of cold water, then swallowed. The effervescent tablet form of this drug must be completely dissolved in a full glass of water before being swallowed. Do not crush or chew the slow-release tablets; this form of the drug must be swallowed whole. ● Ask your doctor about using a salt substitute instead of potassium chloride. ● Potassium supplements usually have a low rate of patient compliance. People usually take them infrequently, or they stop taking them altogether. If a potassium product is prescribed for you, be sure to take the medication exactly as directed and do not stop taking it without first consulting your doctor.

Prednicen-M steroid hormone (Central Pharmaceuticals, Inc.), see prednisone steroid hormone.

prednisone steroid hormone

Manufacturer: various manufacturers

Ingredient: prednisone

Equivalent Products: Cortan, Halsey Drug Co., Inc.; Deltasone, The Upjohn Company; Meticorten, Schering Corp.; Orasone, Rowell Laboratories, Inc.; Panasol, Seatrace Co.; Prednicen-M, The Central Pharmacal Co.; SK-Prednisone, Smith Kline & French Laboratories

Dosage Form: Tablet: 1 mg; 2.5 mg; 5 mg; 10 mg; 20 mg; 50 mg (various colors). Oral Solution; Syrup (content per 5 ml teaspoon): 5 mg.

Use: Treatment of endocrine or rheumatic disorders; asthma; blood diseases; certain cancers; eye disorders; gastrointestinal disturbances such as ulcerative colitis; respiratory diseases; inflammations such as arthritis, dermatitis, poison ivy

Minor Side Effects: Dizziness; headache; increased hair growth; increased susceptibility to infection; increased sweating; indigestion; insomnia; menstrual irregularities; muscle weakness; nervousness; reddening of the skin on the face; restlessness; thin skin; weight gain

Major Side Effects: Abdominal enlargement; blurred vision; bone loss; bruising; cataracts; convulsions; diabetes; euphoria; fluid retention; fracture; glaucoma; growth impairment in children; heart failure; high blood pressure; impaired healing of wounds; mood changes; mouth sores; muscle wasting; nightmares; peptic ulcer; potassium loss; salt retention; weakness

Contraindications: This drug should not be taken by people who are allergic to it or who have systemic fungal infections. Consult your doctor if this drug has been prescribed for you and you have either of these conditions.

Warnings: If you are using this drug for longer than a week, you may need to receive higher dosages if you are subjected to stress such as serious infection, injury, or surgery. • This drug may mask signs of an infection or cause new infections to develop. • This drug may cause glaucoma or cataracts, high blood pressure, high blood sugar, fluid retention, and potassium loss. • This drug has not been proven safe for use during pregnancy. • While you are taking this drug you should not be vaccinated or immunized. • This drug should be used very cautiously by people who have had tuberculosis and those who have thyroid disease, liver disease, severe ulcerative colitis, diabetes, seizures, a history of ulcers, kidney disease, high blood pressure, a bone disease, or myasthenia gravis. Be sure your doctor knows if you fit any of these categories. • If you have been taking this drug for more than a week, do not stop taking it suddenly. Never increase the dose or take the drug for a longer time than prescribed without consulting your doctor. • Report mood swings or depression to your doctor. • Growth of children may be affected by this drug. • This drug interacts with aspirin, barbiturates, diuretics, rifampin, cyclophosphamide, estrogens, indomethacin, oral anticoagulants, antidiabetics, and phenytoin; if you are currently taking any drugs of these types, consult your doctor about their use. If you are unsure of the type or contents of your medications, ask your doctor or pharmacist. • Blood pressure, body weight, and vision should be checked at regular intervals. Stomach x-rays are advised for persons with suspected or known peptic ulcers.

Comments: This drug is often taken on a decreasing-dosage schedule (four times a day for several days, then three times a day, etc.). • Often, taking the entire daily dose at one time (about 8:00 A.M.) gives the best results. • To help avoid potassium loss while using this drug, take your dose with a glass of fresh or frozen orange juice and eat a banana each day. The use of a salt substitute also helps prevent potassium loss. • If you are using this drug chronically, you should wear or carry a notice that you are taking a steroid. • To prevent stomach upset, take this drug with food or a snack. • Take this drug exactly as directed. Do not take extra doses or skip a dose without first consulting your doctor. For long-term treatment, taking the drug every other day is preferred. Ask your doctor about alternate-day dosing.

Preludin anorectic

Manufacturer: Boehringer Ingelheim Ltd.

Ingredient: phenmetrazine hydrochloride

Dosage Forms: Prolonged-action tablet: 50 mg (white); 75 mg (pink). Tablet: 25 mg (white)

Use: Short-term treatment of obesity

Minor Side Effects: Blurred vision; constipation; diarrhea; dizziness; dry mouth; euphoria; fatigue; headache; insomnia; irritability; nausea; nervousness; restlessness; stomach pain; sweating; tremor; unpleasant taste in the mouth; vomiting

Major Side Effects: Changes in sexual desire; chest pain; difficult urination; enlarged breasts in men and women; high blood pressure; impotence; menstrual irregularities; mood changes; palpitations; rapid heart rate; rash; sore throat

Contraindications: This drug should not be taken by people who have heart disease (certain types), thyroid disease, glaucoma, or moderate to severe high blood pressure. People with a history of drug abuse, those allergic to this drug, people who are agitated, and those who are taking or have recently taken a monoamine oxidase inhibitor (ask your pharmacist if you are unsure) should not use this drug. Consult your doctor immediately if this drug has been prescribed for you and you fit any of these categories.

Warnings: This drug should be used with caution by pregnant women, nursing mothers, and children under 12 years of age. This drug should be used cautiously by people with diabetes, heart disease, or mild high blood pressure. Be sure your doctor knows if you fit into any of these categories. • This drug has the potential for abuse and must be used with caution. Tolerance may develop within a few weeks. Do not increase the dose of this drug without first consulting your doctor. If the drug seems to stop working for you, notify your doctor; probably the drug will be discontinued, but do not stop taking the drug suddenly without consulting your doctor. • This drug interacts with central nervous system depressants, antidiabetic drugs, monoamine oxidase inhibitors, guanethidine, and other adrenergics. Consult your doctor immediately about their use if you are taking any of these drugs. If you are unsure about the type or contents of your medications, ask your doctor or pharmacist. • Avoid foods rich in tyramine; ask your doctor for a list of these foods. • This drug may mask symptoms of extreme fatigue and decrease your ability to perform potentially dangerous or hazardous tasks, such as driving or operating machinery. Use appropriate caution.

Comments: The prolonged-action tablet form of this drug, called Endurets, must not be chewed or crushed, but swallowed whole. • Weight loss is greatest during the first three weeks of taking this drug. • To be effective, therapy with this drug must be accompanied by a low-calorie diet. • The effects of this drug on appetite control wear off; do not take this drug for more than three weeks at a time. One way to get full benefit from this drug is to take it for three weeks, stop for three weeks, then resume taking the drug again. Consult your doctor about this regimen. • While taking this drug, do not take any nonprescription item for weight control or cough, cold, or sinus problems without first checking with your doctor. • Do not take an Enduret later than 3:00 P.M. to avoid sleeplessness. • Never take this drug more frequently than your doctor prescribes. A serious overdose may result. • Dry mouth can be relieved by sucking on ice chips or hard sugarless candy.

Premarin estrogen hormone

Manufacturer: Ayerst Laboratories

Ingredient: conjugated estrogens

Equivalent Products: conjugated estrogens, various manufacturers; Estrocon, Savage Laboratories; Progens, Major Pharmaceuticals

Dosage Form: Tablet: 0.3 mg (green); 0.625 mg (maroon); 0.9 mg (white); 1.25 mg (yellow); 2.5 mg (purple)

Use: Estrogen replacement therapy; symptoms due to menopause; prostatic cancer in men; uterine bleeding; and some cases of breast cancer

Minor Side Effects: Bleeding; bloating; change in sexual desire; cramps; depression; diarrhea; dizziness; headache; increased sensitivity to sunlight; loss of appetite; nausea; swelling of ankles and feet; vomiting

Major Side Effects: Allergic rash; cervical damage; change in menstrual patterns; chest pain; cystitis; diabetes; difficult breathing; eye damage; fibroid growth; fluid retention; fungal infections; gallbladder disease; high blood pressure; jaundice; loss of coordination; migraine; pain in calves; severe headache; skin color changes; slurred speech; vision changes; weight gain or loss

Contraindications: This drug should not be used by pregnant women; or by people who have blood clotting disorders or a history of such disorders due to estrogen use, certain cancers, or vaginal bleeding. In most cases this drug should not be used by people who have breast cancer. Consult your doctor immediately if this drug has been prescribed for you and you have any of these conditions.

Warnings: Studies have shown that prolonged use of estrogens increases the risk of endometrial cancer. Your pharmacist has a brochure that describes the benefits and risks involved with estrogen therapy. He is required by law to give you a copy each time he fills a prescription for this drug. Read this material carefully. • This drug should be used cautiously by people who have asthma, diabetes, epilepsy, gallbladder disease, heart disease, high blood levels of calcium, high blood pressure, kidney disease, liver disease, migraine, porphyria, uterine fibroid tumors, a history of depression, and by nursing women. Be sure your doctor knows if you have any of these conditions. • This drug may retard bone growth, and therefore should be used cautiously by young patients who have not yet completed puberty. • This drug interacts with oral anticoagulants, barbiturates, rifampin, ampicillin, anticonvulsants, and steroids; if you are currently taking any drugs of these types, consult your doctor about their use. If you are unsure of the type of your medications, ask your doctor or pharmacist. • Notify your doctor immediately if you experience any of the following symptoms: abnormal vaginal bleeding, breast lumps, pains in the calves or chest, sudden shortness of breath, coughing of blood, severe headache, dizziness, faintness, changes in vision or skin color. • This drug may affect a number of laboratory tests; remind your doctor that you are taking it if you are scheduled for any tests. • You should have a complete physical examination at least once a year while you are on this medication.

Comments: This drug is usually taken for 21 days followed by a 7-day rest. • Compliance is mandatory with this drug. Take it exactly as prescribed.

Principen antibiotic (E. R. Squibb & Sons, Inc.), see ampicillin antibiotic.

procainamide hydrochloride anti-arrhythmic (various manufacturers), see Pronestyl anti-arrhythmic.

Procan anti-arrhythmic (Parke-Davis), see Pronestyl anti-arrhythmic.

Procardia anti-anginal

Manufacturer: Pfizer Laboratories Division
Ingredient: nifedipine
Dosage Form: Capsule: 10 mg (orange)
Use: Treatment of various types of angina
Minor Side Effects: Bloating; blurred vision; cough; dizziness; flushing; gas; giddiness; headache; heartburn; heat sensation; muscle cramps; nasal congestion; nausea; nervousness; sleep disturbances; sweating; tremors; weakness
Major Side Effects: Chills; confusion; difficult breathing; fainting; fever; impotence; low blood pressure; mood changes; rapid and pounding heart rate; sore throat; swelling of ankles, feet or lower legs
Contraindications: This drug should not be used by people who are allergic to it. Consult your doctor immediately if this drug has been prescribed for you and you are allergic to it.
Warnings: This drug should be used cautiously by people who have low blood pressure or heart disease and by pregnant women or nursing mothers. Be sure your doctor knows if you have any of these conditions. ● This drug may interact with beta blockers, digoxin, phenytoin, quinidine, warfarin, and digitalis. If you are taking antihypertensive medication, the dose may have to be adjusted. If you are currently taking any of these drug types, consult your doctor about their use. ● If you are unsure of the type or ingredients of your medication, ask your doctor or pharmacist. ● This drug may make you dizzy; avoid any activity that requires alertness.
Comments: Your doctor will want to see you regularly while you are taking this drug to check your response to the drug and to conduct liver function tests. ● Compliance is necessary to prevent chest pain. Do not take this drug just to treat attacks. ● Swallow the capsule whole without breaking or chewing it unless otherwise instructed by your physician. ● Do not suddenly stop taking this drug, unless you consult with your doctor first. Your dosage may have to be decreased gradually. ● Protect this drug from light and moisture.

Prochlor-Iso anticholinergic and phenothiazine (Henry Schein, Inc.), see Combid Spansule anticholinergic and phenothiazine.

prochlorperazine phenothiazine (various manufacturers), see Compazine phenothiazine.

Progens estrogen hormone (Major Pharmaceuticals), see Premarin estrogen hormone.

Pro-Iso anticholinergic and phenothiazine (Geneva Generics, Inc.), see Combid Spansule anticholinergic and phenothiazine.

Promapar phenothiazine (Parke-Davis), see Thorazine phenothiazine.

promethazine hydrochloride expectorant plain (various manufacturers), see Phenergan, Phenergan with Codeine expectorants.

promethazine hydrochloride VC expectorant plain (various manufacturers), see Phenergan VC, Phenergan VC with Codeine expectorants.

promethazine hydrochloride VC with codeine expectorant (various manufacturers), see Phenergan VC, Phenergan VC with Codeine expectorants.

promethazine hydrochloride with codeine expectorant (various manufacturers), see Phenergan, Phenergan with Codeine expectorants.

Prometh VC with Codeine expectorant (Barre Drug Co., Inc.), see Phenergan VC, Phenergan VC with Codeine expectorants.

Promine anti-arrhythmic (Major Pharmaceuticals), see Pronestyl anti-arrhythmic.

Pronestyl anti-arrhythmic

Manufacturer: E. R. Squibb & Sons, Inc.
Ingredient: procainamide hydrochloride
Equivalent Products: procainamide hydrochloride, various manufacturers; Procan, Parke-Davis; Promine, Major Pharmaceuticals
Dosage Forms: Capsule: 250 mg (yellow); 375 mg (orange/white); 500 mg (yellow/orange). Tablet: 250 mg (yellow); 375 mg (deep orange); 500 mg (red). Sustained-release tablet: 250 mg (green); 500 mg (greenish-yellow); 750 mg (orange); 1000 mg (red)
Use: Treatment of some heart arrhythmias
Minor Side Effects: Bitter taste in the mouth; diarrhea; dizziness; dry mouth; headache; itching; loss of appetite; nausea; stomach upset; vomiting
Major Side Effects: Bruising; chest pains; chills; confusion; depression; fatigue; fever; giddiness; hallucinations; low blood pressure; pain in the joints; palpitations; psychosis; rash; sore throat; weakness
Contraindications: This drug should not be taken by people who are allergic to it or to some local anesthetics. The drug should not be taken by people who have myasthenia gravis or certain types of heart disease. Consult your doctor immediately if this drug has been prescribed for you and you fit into any of these categories.
Warnings: People who have liver or kidney disease or certain types of heart disease should use this drug with caution. Be sure your doctor knows if you have any of these conditions. ● Notify your doctor if you experience soreness around the mouth, throat, or gums, unexplained fever, a head cold or respiratory infection, or joint pain or stiffness.
Comments: While taking this drug, do not take any nonprescription item for cough, cold, or sinus problems without first checking with your doctor. ● Follow your doctor's dosage instructions carefully; it is especially important that this drug be taken on time. It should be taken at evenly spaced intervals around the clock. Do not take extra doses and do not skip a dose without first consulting your doctor. ● It is best to take this drug on an empty stomach (one hour before or two hours after meals). However, if this drug causes you stomach upset, it may be taken with food or milk. ● This drug may cause a sensation of mouth dryness. Chew gum or suck on ice chips or a piece of hard candy to reduce this feeling. ● Do not break or crush the capsules or tablets; they must be swallowed whole. ● Sustained-release tablets require less frequent dosing than the regular tablets. Sustained-release tablets should not be used for initial therapy, but can be substituted once the dosage is stabilized. Consult your doctor about the use of this dosage form. ● Do not be alarmed if you notice an empty tablet in

your bowel movements. This is the core of the tablet, which is made of wax. Since it is not digestable, it is excreted from the body. ● Your doctor may want to check your blood levels of this drug periodically. Blood levels indicate how effective the dosage is.

propoxyphene hydrochloride compound analgesic (various manufacturers), see Darvon Compound-65 analgesic.

propranolol and hydrochlorothiazide diuretic and antihypertensive (Ayerst Laboratories), see Inderide diuretic and antihypertensive.

Propranolol beta blocker (Rugby Laboratories), see Inderal beta blocker.

Protension analgesic and sedative (Blaine Co., Inc.), see Fiorinal analgesic and sedative.

Prothazine expectorant (Vortech Pharmaceutical, Ltd.), see Phenergan, Phenergan with Codeine expectorants.

Prothazine with Codeine expectorant (Vortech Pharmaceutical, Ltd.), see Phenergan, Phenergan with Codeine expectorants.

Protostat antimicrobial and antiparasitic (Ortho Pharmaceutical Corp.), see Flagyl antimicrobial and antiparasitic.

Proventil anti-asthmatic (Schering Corp.), see Ventolin bronchodilator

Provera progesterone hormone

Manufacturer: The Upjohn Company
Ingredient: medroxyprogesterone acetate
Equivalent Products: Amen, Carnrick Laboratories, Inc.; Curretab, Reid-Provident Labs., Inc.
Dosage Form: Tablet: 2.5 mg (peach); 10 mg (white)
Use: Treatment of abnormal menstrual bleeding, difficult menstruation, or lack of menstruation
Minor Side Effects: Acne; dizziness; hair growth; headache; nausea; vomiting
Major Side Effects: Breast tenderness; birth defects (if used during pregnancy); cervical damage; change in menstrual patterns; depression; fainting; fluid retention; hair loss; itching; jaundice; rash; spotting or breakthrough or unusual vaginal bleeding; weight gain or loss
Contraindications: This drug should not be taken by people who may have cancer of the breast or genitals, clotting disorders or a history of clotting disorders, stroke, a history of stroke, vaginal bleeding of unknown cause, liver disease; or by those who are pregnant, especially in the first trimester. The drug should not be used by anyone with a history of missed abortion (retention of a dead fetus in the uterus for a number of weeks). This drug should not be used if you are allergic to it. Consult your doctor immediately if this drug has been prescribed for you and you have any of these conditions, such a history or such an allergy. This drug should not be used as a test to determine pregnancy.

Warnings: This drug should be used cautiously by nursing women; and by people who have porphyria, gallbladder disease, epilepsy, migraines, asthma, heart or kidney disease, depression, or diabetes. Be sure your doctor knows if you have any of these conditions. • Watch for early signs of clotting disorders, loss of vision, or headache and report any such signs to your doctor immediately. Notify your doctor if any unusual vaginal bleeding occurs. • If you take this drug and later discover that you are pregnant while using this medication, consult your doctor immediately. • This drug should not be used in conjunction with oral anticoagulants, barbiturates, or steroids; if you are currently taking any drugs of these types, consult your doctor about their use. If you are unsure about the type or contents of your medications, ask your doctor or pharmacist. • Before you begin to take this drug, you should have a complete physical examination, including a Pap smear. • Very little is known about the long-term effects of using this drug. Consider your decision to use it carefully. • This drug may mask the signs of menopause. • This drug may affect the results of many laboratory tests and other medical examinations. Be sure your doctor knows you are taking this drug if you are being tested for any medical condition.

Comments: Progesterone-type drugs have been included in birth control pills. It is thought that most of the adverse effects of the pill are due to the estrogen component rather than the progesterone, but this has not been proven. For a more complete listing of the adverse effects associated with these hormones, see the profile on oral contraceptives. • Your pharmacist has a brochure that describes this drug. He is required by law to give you a copy each time he fills a prescription for it. Read this material carefully.

pseudoephedrine with azatadine antihistamine and decongestant (Schering Corp.), see Trinalin antihistamine and decongestant.

Purebrom TD antihistamine and decongestant (Purepac Pharmaceutical Co.), see Dimetapp antihistamine and decongestant.

Pyridamole anti-anginal (Major Pharmaceuticals), see Persantine anti-anginal.

Pyridiate analgesic (various manufacturers), see Pyridium analgesic.

Pyridium analgesic

Manufacturer: Parke-Davis
Ingredient: phenazopyridine hydrochloride
Equivalent Products: Phenazodine, The Lannett Company, Inc.; phenazopyridine hydrochloride, various manufacturers; Pyridiate, various manufacturers
Dosage Form: Tablet: 100 mg; 200 mg (both dark maroon)
Use: Symptomatic relief of the burning and pain of urinary tract disorders
Minor Side Effects: Change in urine color; dizziness; headache; indigestion; nausea; stomach cramps; vomiting
Major Side Effects: Anemia; jaundice
Contraindications: This drug should not be taken by people who are allergic to phenazopyridine hydrochloride or by those who have severe kidney disease. Consult your doctor immediately if this drug has been prescribed for you and you fit into either category.

Warnings: This drug will cause your urine to become orange-red in color. Do not be alarmed by this side effect. The urine will return to its normal color soon after the drug has been discontinued. • This drug should not be used for pain other than that associated with the urinary tract. • Diabetics may get a false reading for sugar or ketones while using this drug. • This drug may interfere with certain urine and blood laboratory tests.

Comments: Take this drug with at least a full glass of water. Drink at least eight to ten glasses of water daily. • Parke-Davis also sells Pyridium Plus tablets; each tablet contains phenazopyridine hydrochloride, 150 mg; hyoscyamine hydrobromide, 0.3 mg; and butabarbital, 15 mg. Due to the antispasmodic and sedative ingredients, it may be more effective than Pyridium for some persons.

Pyridium Plus analgesic (Parke-Davis), see Pyridium analgesic.

Quibron expectorant and smooth muscle relaxant

Manufacturer: Mead Johnson Co.
Ingredients: guaifenesin; theophylline
Equivalent Products: Bronchial, Geneva Drugs Ltd.; Glyceryl-T, Rugby Laboratories; Lanophyllin-GG, The Lannett Company, Inc.; Slo-Phyllin GG, William H. Rorer, Inc.; Theocolate, Bay Pharmaceuticals, Inc.; Theolate, various manufacturers
Dosage Forms: Capsule: guaifenesin, 90 mg; theophylline, 150 mg (yellow). Liquid (content per 15 ml or three teaspoons): guaifenesin, 90 mg; theophylline, 150 mg. Quibron-300: Capsule: guaifenesin, 180 mg; theophylline, 300 mg
Use: Prevention and treatment of asthmatic attacks or related conditions
Minor Side Effects: Diarrhea; headache; heartburn; increased urination; insomnia; irritability; loss of appetite; nausea; restlessness; vomiting
Major Side Effects: Convulsions; low blood pressure; muscle twitching; palpitations; rapid breathing; ulcer
Contraindications: This drug should not be taken by people who are allergic to either of its components or to any related drugs (such as caffeine). Consult your doctor immediately if this drug has been prescribed for you and you have such an allergy.
Warnings: Excessive doses of this drug are toxic, so follow your doctor's dosage instructions exactly. • This drug should be used cautiously by people over age 55 (particularly males); and by people who have heart disease, thyroid disease, emphysema, high blood pressure, liver or kidney disease, alcoholism, or a history of peptic ulcer; and by those who are pregnant or nursing. Be sure your doctor knows if you have any of these conditions. • This drug interacts with cimetidine, barbiturates, lithium carbonate, propranolol, furosemide, reserpine, chlordiazepoxide, some antibiotics, and other xanthines; if you are currently taking any drugs of these types, consult your doctor about their use. If you are unsure of the type or contents of your medications, ask your doctor or pharmacist. • This drug may affect the results of urine tests; remind your doctor that you are taking it if you are scheduled for any such tests.
Comments: While taking this drug, drink at least eight glasses of water daily. Take your dose with food or milk. • While taking this drug, do not use any nonprescription item for asthma without first checking with your doctor. • Avoid drinking coffee, tea, cola drinks, cocoa, or other beverages that contain caffeine. • Smoking may affect this drug's action. Be sure your doctor knows that you smoke if you are taking this drug. Do not suddenly stop smoking without informing your doctor. • Call your doctor if you have severe stomach pain, vomiting, or restlessness, because this drug may aggravate an ulcer. • This

drug should not be taken more frequently than once every six hours or within 12 hours of any similar product given rectally. Be sure to take your dose at exactly the right time.

Quibron-T/SR bronchodilator (Mead-Johnson Co.), see Theo-dur bronchodilator.

Quinidex Extentabs anti-arrhythmic (A. H. Robins Company), see quinidine sulfate anti-arrhythmic.

quinidine sulfate anti-arrhythmic

Manufacturer: various manufacturers

Ingredient: quinidine sulfate

Equivalent Products: Cin-Quin, Rowell Laboratories. Inc.; Quinidex Extentabs, A. H. Robins Company; Quinora, Key Pharmaceuticals. Inc.; SK-Quinidine Sulfate, Smith Kline & French Laboratories (see Comments)

Dosage Forms: Capsule: 200 mg; 300 mg. Tablet: 100 mg; 200 mg; 300 mg. Sustained-release tablet: 300 mg; (various colors)

Use: Treatment of certain types of heart arrhythmias

Minor Side Effects: Abdominal pain; bitter taste in mouth; confusion; cramping; diarrhea; flushing; loss of appetite; nausea; restlessness; vomiting

Major Side Effects: Anemia; bleeding; blurred vision; bruising; difficult breathing; dizziness; fainting; fever; headache; light-headedness; palpitations; ringing in the ears; sore throat

Contraindications: This drug should not be used by people who are allergic to it, or by those who have had a blood disease caused by previous quinidine therapy. Consult your doctor immediately if this drug has been prescribed for you and you fit into any of these categories.

Warnings: This drug should be used cautiously by people who are also taking digitalis; and by those who have liver or kidney disease. low blood pressure, low blood levels of potassium, myasthenia gravis. thyroid disease. certain types of heart disease; and by pregnant women. Be sure your doctor knows if you have any of these conditions. • The amount of potassium in your blood affects the activity of quinidine. Your doctor will want to check your blood potassium levels occasionally while you take quinidine. • This drug interacts with acetazolamide, anticholinergics, antacids, anticonvulsants. diuretics. oral anticoagulants, sodium bicarbonate, and potassium. If you are currently taking any drugs of these types, consult your doctor about their use. If you are unsure of the type or contents of your medications, ask your doctor or pharmacist. • If you develop ringing or thumping in your ears, light-headedness. or blurred vision, contact your doctor immediately; these may be symptoms of toxicity of this drug.

Comments: Although many quinidine sulfate products are on the market. they are not all bioequivalent; that is, they may not all be absorbed into the bloodstream at the same rate or have the same overall pharmacologic activity. Don't change brands of this drug without consulting your doctor or pharmacist to make sure you are receiving an identically functioning product. • If you are being treated for a heart arrhythmia, do not take any nonprescription item for cough, cold, or sinus problems without first checking with your doctor. • Take with food or milk to help avoid stomach upset. • Take this drug exactly as directed. Do not take extra doses or skip a dose without first consulting your doctor. • The sustained-release tablet form of this drug must be swallowed whole. Do not crush or chew.

Quinora anti-arrhythmic (Key Pharmaceuticals, Inc.), see quinidine sulfate anti-arrhythmic.

Racet steroid hormone and anti-infective (Lemmon Company), see Vioform-Hydrocortisone steroid hormone and anti-infective.

Rectacort steroid-hormone-containing anorectal product (Century Pharmaceuticals, Inc.), see Anusol-HC steroid-hormone-containing anorectal product.

Reglan gastrointestinal stimulant

Manufacturer: A.H. Robins Company
Ingredient: metoclopramide
Equivalent Products: metoclopramide, Geneva Generics; Goldline Laboratories; Rugby Laboratories
Dosage Forms: Tablet: 10 mg (pink); syrup (content per 5 ml teaspoon): 5 mg
Use: To relieve the symptoms associated with diabetic gastric stasis or gastric reflux, and to prevent nausea and vomiting
Minor Side Effects: Diarrhea; dizziness; drowsiness; fatigue; headache; insomnia; nausea; restlessness
Major Side Effects: Anxiety; depression; involuntary movements of the face, mouth, jaw, and tongue; uncoordinated movements
Contraindications: This drug should not be used by persons with pheochromocytoma or epilepsy; or in the presence of gastrointestinal bleeding, obstruction, or perforation. Reglan should not be prescribed for persons who are sensitive or intolerant to it. Consult your doctor if this drug has been prescribed for you and you have any of these conditions.
Warnings: This drug should be used cautiously by children and nursing mothers. • This drug should be used in pregnant females only when clearly needed and when the benefits outweigh the risks. Talk to your doctor about the use of this medication if you are pregnant. • Diabetics who require insulin should use this drug cautiously, as the dosage or timing of the insulin may need adjustment. Discuss this with your doctor. • This drug may cause motor restlessness, uncoordinated movements, or fine tremors of the tongue. Contact your doctor immediately if you notice any of these symptoms. • Because this drug may cause drowsiness, avoid tasks that require alertness for a few hours after taking each dose. • This drug interacts with narcotic analgesics, anticholinergics, alcohol, sedatives, hypnotics, and tranquilizers. If you are currently taking any drugs of these types, consult your doctor about their use. If you are unsure about the types or contents of your medications, ask your doctor or pharmacist. • Use of this drug should be monitored closely in persons with previously detected breast cancer. An increase in breast cancer has been found in laboratory rats who were given large doses of this drug for a prolonged period. These findings have not been duplicated in humans.
Comments: This medication is usually taken 30 minutes before each meal. For maximum benefit, take this drug exactly as prescribed. Do not take extra doses or skip doses without first consulting with your doctor. • The syrup form of this drug is sugar-free. • Because this drug causes stimulation of the gastrointestinal tract, talk to your doctor about the effect this may have on any other medications you are taking. For some drugs, the timing of doses may need to be adjusted.

Relaxadon sedative and anticholinergic (Geneva Generics, Inc.), see Donnatal sedative and anticholinergic.

Repen-VK antibiotic (Reid-Provident Labs., Inc.), see penicillin potassium phenoxymethyl (penicillin VK) antibiotic.

Reposans-10 sedative and hypnotic (Wesley Pharmacal Co.), see Librium sedative and hypnotic.

Resaid T.D. antihistamine and adrenergic (Geneva Generics, Inc.), see Ornade Spansule antihistamine and adrenergic.

reserpine antihypertensive

Manufacturer: various manufacturers
Ingredient: reserpine
Equivalent Products: Sandril, Eli Lilly & Co.; Serpalan, The Lannett Company, Inc.; Serpanray, Panray Division; Serpasil, CIBA Pharmaceutical Company; Serpate, The Vale Chemical Co., Inc.; SK-Reserpine, Smith Kline & French Laboratories; Zepine, Foy Laboratories
Dosage Forms: Liquid; Tablet; Capsule (various dosages and colors)
Use: Treatment of high blood pressure
Minor Side Effects: Acid stomach; constipation; decrease in sexual desire; diarrhea; dizziness; dry mouth; headache; impotence; itching; loss of appetite; muscle aches; nasal congestion; nausea; nosebleeds; tremors; vomiting; weight gain
Major Side Effects: Anxiety; black stools; bruising; chest pain; deafness; depression; difficult urination; drowsiness; enlarged breasts in men and women; fainting; fluid retention; glaucoma; irregular heartbeat; nervousness; nightmares; palpitations; rash; shortness of breath; slow pulse; weakness
Contraindications: This drug should not be taken by people who are allergic to it; or by those who have active peptic ulcer, ulcerative colitis, mental depression, or who are receiving electroshock therapy. Consult your doctor immediately if this drug has been prescribed for you and you have any of these conditions.
Warnings: This is a powerful drug that may persist in the body for several months after the medication is discontinued. If you feel continually tired or depressed, consult your doctor. • This drug should be used cautiously by pregnant women and by people who are taking monoamine oxidase inhibitors (ask your pharmacist if you are unsure), or who have Parkinson's disease, kidney disease, or a history of ulcer, gallstones, or colitis. Be sure your doctor knows if you have any of these conditions. • Nursing women who must take this drug should stop nursing. • This drug interacts with amphetamine, decongestants, levodopa, and monoamine oxidase inhibitors; if you are currently taking any drugs of these types, consult your doctor about their use. If you are unsure of the type or contents of your medications, ask your doctor or pharmacist. • This drug must be used cautiously with digitalis and quinidine; be sure your doctor knows if you are taking either of these drugs. Watch for symptoms of increased toxicity (e.g., nausea, blurred vision, palpitations) and notify your doctor if they occur. • While taking this drug, do not take any nonprescription item for weight control or cough, cold, or sinus problems without first checking with your doctor. • This drug may cause drowsiness; avoid tasks that require

alertness. • To prevent oversedation, avoid the use of alcohol or other drugs that have sedative properties. • Reserpine may cause cancer in rats. It has not been shown to cause cancer in people.

Comments: The effects of therapy with this drug may not be apparent for at least two weeks. • Take your dose with food or milk. • Mild side effects (e.g., nasal congestion) are most noticeable during the first two weeks of drug therapy and become less bothersome after this period. • Take this drug exactly as directed. Do not skip a dose or take extra doses without consulting your doctor first. • To avoid dizziness or light-headedness when you stand, contract and relax the muscles of your legs for a few moments before rising. Do this by pushing one foot against the floor while raising the other foot slightly, alternating feet so that you are "pumping" your legs in a pedaling motion. • Dry mouth may be relieved by chewing gum or by sucking on ice chips or hard candy.

Respbid bronchodilator (Boehringer-Ingelheim), see Theo-dur bronchodilator.

Restoril sedative and hypnotic

Manufacturer: Sandoz Pharmaceuticals
Ingredient: temazepam
Dosage Form: Capsule: 15 mg (maroon/pink); 30 mg (maroon/blue)
Use: Relief of insomnia
Minor Side Effects: Diarrhea; dizziness; drowsiness; lethargy; loss of appetite; relaxed feeling
Major Side Effects: Confusion; euphoria; hallucinations; palpitations; tremors; weakness
Contraindications: This drug should not be used by persons allergic to it or by pregnant women. Consult your doctor immediately if this drug has been prescribed for you and you have such a condition.
Warnings: This drug should be used with caution by depressed people; nursing mothers; persons under the age of 18; and people with liver or kidney diseases, narrow-angle glaucoma, or psychosis. Be sure your doctor knows if you belong in one of these groups. • Because this drug has the potential for abuse, it must be used with caution, especially by those with a history of drug dependence. Tolerance may develop quickly; do not increase the dose or take this drug more often than prescribed without first consulting your physician. • This drug is safe when taken alone; when it is combined with other sedative drugs or alcohol, serious adverse reactions may develop. Avoid the use of alcohol, other sedatives, or central nervous system depressants. If you are currently taking any drugs of these types, consult your doctor about their use. If you are unsure of the type or contents of your medications, ask your doctor or pharmacist. • This drug causes drowsiness; avoid tasks that require alertness.
Comments: After you stop taking this drug, your sleep may be disturbed for a few nights. • Take this drug one-half to one hour before bedtime unless otherwise prescribed.

Retet antibiotic (Reid-Provident Labs., Inc.), see tetracycline hydro-chloride antibiotic.

Retin-A acne preparation

Manufacturer: Ortho Pharmaceutical Corporation

Ingredient: tretinoin (retinoic acid; vitamin A acid)
Dosage Forms: Cream: 0.1%; 0.05%. Gel: 0.025%; 0.01%. Liquid: 0.05%
Use: Topical application in treatment of acne vulgaris
Minor Side Effects: Localized rash; stinging
Major Side Effects: Blistering or crusting of the skin; heightened susceptibility to sunlight; peeling; temporary change in skin color
Contraindications: This drug should not be used by people who are allergic to it. Consult your doctor immediately if this drug has been prescribed for you and you have such an allergy.
Warnings: This drug should not be used in conjunction with other acne preparations, particularly peeling agents containing sulfur, resorcinol, benzoyl peroxide, or salicylic acid. ● While using this drug, exposure to sunlight (or sunlamps), wind, and/or cold should be minimized or totally avoided to prevent skin irritation. If you are sunburned, wait for the sunburn to heal before using this product. ● This drug should be used with extreme caution by persons suffering from eczema. ● Medicated or abrasive soaps and cosmetics that have a strong drying effect, along with locally applied products containing high amounts of alcohol, spices, or lime, should be used with caution because of a possible negative interaction with the drug. ● Applying this product more often than recommended will not hasten improvement of the condition and is likely to cause further irritation.
Comments: This drug should be kept away from the eyes, the mouth, the angles of the nose, and the mucous membranes. ● A temporary feeling of warmth or a slight stinging may be noted following application of this drug. This effect is normal and not dangerous. ● The liquid form of this drug may be applied with a fingertip, gauze pad, or cotton swab. If gauze or cotton is used, do not oversaturate so that the liquid runs onto areas that are not intended for treatment. ● During the early weeks of using this drug, there may be an apparent increase in skin lesions. This is usually not a reason to discontinue its use. However, your doctor may wish to modify the concentration of the drug. Therapeutic effects may be noted within two to three weeks, although more than six weeks may be required before definite benefits are seen.

Rezide diuretic and antihypertensive (Edwards Pharmacal, Co.), see Ser-Ap-Es diuretic and antihypertensive.

Rhinolar-EX 12 antihistamine and adrenergic (McGregor Pharmaceuticals), see Ornade Spansule antihistamine and adrenergic.

Ritalin central nervous system stimulant

Manufacturer: CIBA Pharmaceutical Company
Ingredient: methylphenidate hydrochloride
Equivalent Product: methylphenidate hydrochloride, various manufacturers
Dosage Forms: Tablet: 5 mg (yellow); 10 mg (green); 20 mg (yellow). Sustained-release tablet: 20 mg (white)
Use: Treatment of hyperactivity in children; treatment of narcolepsy; relief of mild depression
Minor Side Effects: Abdominal pain; dizziness; drowsiness; dry mouth; headache; insomnia; loss of appetite; nausea; nervousness; vomiting; weakness
Major Side Effects: Bruising; chest pain; fever; hair loss; heart irregularities; high or low blood pressure; hives; joint pain; mood changes; palpitations;

psychosis; rash; seizures; sore throat; uncoordinated movements. In children: abdominal pain; impairment of growth; weight loss

Contraindications: This drug should not be taken by persons with marked anxiety, tension, or agitation, since it may aggravate these symptoms. This drug should not be taken by people who are allergic to it. Consult your doctor immediately if this drug has been prescribed for you and you have any of these conditions or such an allergy. This drug should not be taken by people with glaucoma. Be sure your doctor knows if you have this condition.

Warnings: This drug is not recommended for use by children under six years of age, since suppression of growth has been reported with long-term use. The long-term effects of this drug on children have not been well established. • This drug should be used cautiously by persons with severe depression, epilepsy, high blood pressure, or eye disease. Be sure your doctor knows if you have any of these conditions. • This drug should not be used for the prevention or treatment of normal fatigue. • This drug should be used with caution by women of childbearing age and pregnant women. • This drug should be used cautiously by people with a history of drug dependence or alcoholism. Do not increase the dose of this drug without consulting your doctor. Chronic abuse of this drug can lead to tolerance and psychological dependence. • Do not stop taking this drug without consulting your doctor. • Periodic blood tests are recommended for patients on long-term therapy with this drug. • This drug interacts with acetazolamide, guanethidine, monoamine oxidase inhibitors, sodium bicarbonate, antidepressants, anticoagulants, anticonvulsants, and phenylbutazone. If you are currently taking any drugs of these types, consult your doctor about their use. If you are unsure of the type or contents of your medications, ask your doctor or pharmacist.

Comments: This drug should not be taken later than 6:00 P.M. to avoid sleeplessness. • While taking this drug, do not take any nonprescription item for cough, cold, or sinus problems without first checking with your doctor. • Avoid foods rich in tyramine; ask your doctor for a list of such foods. • This drug may mask symptoms of fatigue and pose serious danger; never take this drug as a stimulant to keep awake. • If your child's teacher tells you your child is hyperkinetic (hyperactive), take the child to a physician for a thorough diagnosis. If the hyperkinetic child needs to take a dose of this drug at noontime, make arrangements with the school nurse.

Robicillin VK antibiotic (A. H. Robins Company), see penicillin potassium phenoxymethyl (penicillin VK) antibiotic.

Robimycin antibiotic (A. H. Robins Company), see erythromycin antibiotic.

Robitet antibiotic (A. H. Robins Company), see tetracycline hydrochloride antibiotic.

Rofed-C expectorant (Three P Products Corp.), see Actifed-C expectorant.

Rotapp antihistamine and decongestant (Three P Products Corp.), see Dimetapp antihistamine and decongestant.

RP-Mycin antibiotic (Reid-Provident Labs., Inc.), see erythromycin antibiotic.

Rufen anti-inflammatory (Boots Pharmaceuticals, Inc.), see Motrin anti-inflammatory.

Rum-K potassium chloride replacement (Fleming & Co.), see potassium chloride replacement.

Sandril antihypertensive (Eli Lilly & Co.), see reserpine antihypertensive.

Satric antimicrobial and antiparasitic (Savage Laboratories), see Flagyl antimicrobial and antiparasitic.

Scabene pediculocide and scabicide (Stiefel Laboratories, Inc.), see Kwell pediculocide and scabicide.

Sedabamate sedative and hypnotic (Mallard, Inc.), see meprobamate sedative and hypnotic.

Sedadrops sedative and hypnotic (Merrell Dow Pharmaceuticals, Inc.), see phenobarbital sedative and hypnotic.

Seds sedative and anticholinergic (Pasadena Research Laboratories, Inc.), see Donnatal sedative and anticholinergic.

Septra and Septra DS antibacterials (Burroughs Wellcome Co.), see Bactrim and Bactrim DS antibacterials.

Ser-A-Gen diuretic and antihypertensive (Goldline Laboratories), see Ser-Ap-Es diuretic and antihypertensive.

Seralazide diuretic and antihypertensive (The Lannett Company, Inc.), see Ser-Ap-Es diuretic and antihypertensive.

Ser-Ap-Es diuretic and antihypertensive

Manufacturer: CIBA Pharmaceutical Company
Ingredients: hydralazine hydrochloride; hydrochlorothiazide; reserpine
Equivalent Products: Cam-ap-es, Camall Company; Cherapas, Kay Pharmacal Co., Inc.; H-H-R, Geneva Generics, Inc.; Hydrap-Es, Lemmon Company; hydrochlorothiazide, reserpine, and hydralazine, various manufacturers; Hyserp, Reid-Provident Labs., Inc.; Rezide, Edwards Pharmacal, Co.; Ser-A-Gen, Goldline Laboratories; Seralazide, The Lannett Company, Inc.; Serpazide, Major Pharmaceuticals; Tri-Hydroserpine, Rugby Laboratories; Unipres, Reid-Provident Labs., Inc.
Dosage Form: Tablet: hydralazine hydrochloride, 25 mg; hydrochlorothiazide, 15 mg; reserpine, 0.1 mg (salmon pink)
Use: Treatment of high blood pressure
Minor Side Effects: Abdominal pains; constipation; decrease in sexual desire; diarrhea; dizziness; dry mouth; flushing; headache; impotence; itching;

loss of appetite; nasal congestion; nausea; nosebleed; slow pulse; sun sensitivity; tremors; vomiting; weight gain

Major Side Effects: Anemia; anxiety; blood disorders; blurred vision; breast enlargement (in men and women); bruising; chest pain; deafness; depression; difficult urination; drowsiness; fainting; fast heart rate; fever; fluid retention; glaucoma; gout; irregular heart rate; jaundice; joint tenderness; liver damage; low or high blood pressure; mood changes; muscle spasms; nervousness; nightmares; palpitations; rash; rise in blood sugar; sedation; shortness of breath; sore throat; tingling in fingers and toes; ulcers; weakness

Contraindications: This drug should not be taken by people who are allergic to any of its components or to sulfa drugs. The drug should not be taken by those who have active peptic ulcer, ulcerative colitis, certain types of heart disease, anuria (inability to urinate), mental depression or suicidal tendencies; and by people receiving electroshock therapy. Consult your doctor immediately if this drug has been prescribed for you and you have any of these conditions.

Warnings: This drug should be used cautiously by pregnant women and by people who are taking monoamine oxidase inhibitors (ask your pharmacist if you are unsure), or who have asthma or allergies, kidney or liver disease, diabetes, epilepsy, stroke, angina, Parkinson's disease, blood disease, or a history of ulcers, gallstones, colitis, or heart disease. Be sure your doctor knows if you have any of these conditions. • Nursing women who must take this drug should stop nursing. • Remind your doctor that you are taking this drug if you are scheduled for surgery. • This drug interacts with amphetamine, decongestants, digitalis, levodopa, lithium carbonate, monoamine oxidase inhibitors, nonsteroidal anti-inflammatory drugs, oral antidiabetics, and steroids; if you are currently taking any drugs of these types, consult your doctor about their use. If you are unsure of the type or contents of your medications, ask your doctor or pharmacist. • This drug may affect the potency of, or your need for, other blood pressure drugs and antidiabetics; dosage adjustment may be necessary. • This drug must be used cautiously with digitalis and quinidine; be sure your doctor knows if you are taking either of these drugs. Watch for symptoms of increased toxicity (e.g., nausea, blurred vision, palpitations) and notify your doctor immediately if they occur. • Notify your doctor if this drug makes you feel unusually depressed. • While taking this drug, do not take any nonprescription item for weight control or cough, cold, or sinus problems without first checking with your doctor. • This drug may cause drowsiness, dizziness, or light-headedness; avoid tasks that require alertness. • To prevent oversedation, avoid the use of alcohol or other drugs that have sedative properties. • This drug can cause potassium loss. Watch for signs of such loss (dry mouth, thirst, and muscle cramps), and notify your doctor if they occur. To help avoid potassium loss while using this product, take your dose with a glass of fresh or frozen orange juice and eat a banana each day. The use of a salt substitute also helps prevent potassium loss. • This drug may influence the results of thyroid function tests; if you are scheduled to have such a test, remind your doctor that you are taking this drug. • This drug may cause gout, high blood levels of calcium, lupus erythematosus, nerve damage, blood diseases, or the onset of diabetes that has been latent. Contact your doctor if any unexplained symptoms of generalized tiredness, weakness, fever, aching joints, or chest pain (angina) occur. • Periodic blood tests are advisable while you are on this drug. • One of the components of this product, reserpine, causes cancer in rats. It has not been shown to cause cancer in people.

Comments: This product combines three antihypertensive ingredients in a single tablet. A doctor probably should not prescribe this or other "fixed dose" combination products as the first choice in the treatment of high blood pressure. The patient should receive each of the ingredients individually. If response is adequate to the fixed doses contained in this product, it may then be substituted. The advantage of a combination product such as this one is based on increased convenience to the patient. • The effects of therapy with this drug may not be apparent for at least two weeks. • Mild side effects (e.g., nasal congestion or headache) are most noticeable during the first two weeks of drug therapy and become less bothersome after this period. • This drug causes frequent urination. Expect this effect; it should not alarm you. • If you experience numbness or tingling in your fingers or toes while using this drug, your doctor may recommend that you take vitamin B_6 (pyridoxine) to relieve the symptoms. • To avoid dizziness or light-headedness when you stand, contract and relax the muscles of your legs for a few moments before rising. Do this by pushing one foot against the floor while raising the other foot slightly, alternating feet so that you are "pumping" your legs in a pedaling motion. • Take this drug exactly as directed. Do not skip a dose or take extra doses without first consulting your doctor. • This drug may be taken with food or milk to lessen stomach upset.

Serax sedative and hypnotic

Manufacturer: Wyeth Laboratories
Ingredient: oxazepam
Dosage Forms: Capsule: 10 mg (pink/white); 15 mg (red/white); 30 mg (maroon/white). Tablet: 15 mg (yellow)
Use: Relief of anxiety, nervousness, tension; relief of muscle spasms; withdrawal from alcohol addiction
Minor Side Effects: Confusion; constipation; depression; diarrhea; dizziness; drooling; drowsiness; dry mouth; fatigue; headache; heartburn; nausea; sweating
Major Side Effects: Blurred vision; decreased or increased sexual drive; difficult breathing; euphoria; excitement; fainting; fever; fluid retention; hallucinations; jaundice; menstrual irregularities; palpitations; rash; slurred speech; sore throat; tremors; uncoordinated movements
Contraindications: This drug should not be used by persons allergic to it or with acute narrow-angle glaucoma. Consult your doctor immediately if this drug has been prescribed for you and you have such a condition. This drug should not be used to treat psychotics.
Warnings: This drug should be used cautiously by pregnant women; people with a history of drug abuse; by people with lung disease, epilepsy, porphyria, liver or kidney disease, or myasthenia gravis; and by people for whom a drop in blood pressure may lead to heart problems. Be sure your doctor knows if you fit into any of these categories. • Do not stop taking this drug suddenly without consulting your doctor. If you have been taking this drug for a long period, your dosage should be reduced gradually according to your doctor's directions. • This drug may cause drowsiness; avoid tasks that require alertness. • To prevent oversedation, avoid the use of alcohol or other drugs with sedative properties. • This drug is not recommended for children under six years of age and should be used with caution in children between six and twelve years of age. • Persons taking this drug should have periodic liver function and blood count tests. • This drug should not be taken with other sedatives, alcohol, or central nervous system depressants. This drug should be used cautiously in conjunction with cimetidine or phenytoin. If you are currently taking any drugs of these types, consult your doctor about their use. If you are unsure of the type or contents of your medications, ask your doctor or pharmacist. • This drug has the potential for abuse and must be used with caution. Tolerance may develop quickly; do not increase the dose of this drug without first consulting your doctor.

Comments: This drug currently is used by many people to relieve nervousness. It is effective for this purpose, but it is important to try to remove the cause of the anxiety as well. ● This drug may cause dryness of the mouth. To reduce this feeling, chew gum or suck on ice chips or a piece of hard candy. ● To lessen stomach upset, take this drug with food or a full glass of water.

Sereen sedative and hypnotic (Foy Laboratories), see Librium sedative and hypnotic.

Serpalan antihypertensive (The Lannett Company, Inc.), see reserpine antihypertensive.

Serpanray antihypertensive (Panray Division), see reserpine antihypertensive.

Serpasil antihypertensive (CIBA Pharmaceutical Company), see reserpine antihypertensive.

Serpate antihypertensive (The Vale Chemical Co., Inc.), see reserpine antihypertensive.

Serpazide diuretic and antihypertensive (Major Pharmaceuticals), see Ser-Ap-Es diuretic and antihypertensive.

Sinemet antiparkinson drug

Manufacturer: Merck Sharp & Dohme
Ingredients: carbidopa; levodopa
Dosage Forms: Sinemet-10/100: Tablet: carbidopa, 10 mg; levodopa, 100 mg (dark blue). Sinemet-25/100: Tablet: carbidopa, 25 mg; levodopa, 100 mg (yellow). Sinemet-25/250: Tablet: carbidopa, 25 mg; levodopa, 250 mg (light blue)
Use: Treatment of symptoms of Parkinson's disease
Minor Side Effects: Abdominal pain; agitation; anxiety; bitter taste in the mouth; confusion; constipation; diarrhea; discoloration or darkening of the urine; dizziness; dry mouth; excessive salivation; faintness; fatigue; fluid retention; flushing; headache; hiccups; hot flashes; increased sexual interest; insomnia; loss of appetite; low blood pressure; nausea; offensive body odor; sweating; vision changes; vomiting; weakness
Major Side Effects: Aggressive behavior; anemia; blood clots; blood disorders; burning of the tongue; convulsions; delusions; depression; difficult swallowing; difficult urination; double vision; euphoria; gastrointestinal bleeding; grinding of teeth; hallucinations; high blood pressure; involuntary movements; irregular heartbeats; jaw stiffness; loss of balance; loss of hair; mental changes; nightmares; numbness; palpitations; persistent erection; skin rash; suicidal tendencies; tremors; ulcer; weight gain or loss
Contraindications: Monoamine oxidase inhibitors and this drug should not be taken together. You must stop taking such drugs at least two weeks prior to starting therapy with this drug. Be sure your doctor knows about all the medications you take. This drug should not be taken by people with narrow-angle glaucoma or hypersensitivity to either of the drug's ingredients. This drug should not be taken by people with certain cancers or skin diseases. Consult your doctor immediately if you fit into any of these categories.

Warnings: This drug should be used with caution by people with heart, lung, kidney, liver, or glandular diseases, epilepsy, diabetes, low blood pressure, asthma, or ulcers. Be sure your doctor knows if you have any of these conditions. • Pregnant women, nursing mothers, and children should use this drug with caution. • Consult your doctor if you experience a drastic mood change. • Periodic evaluations of liver, blood, heart, and kidney functions are recommended during extended therapy with this drug. • This drug should be taken with caution by people who are taking drugs to treat high blood pressure. When this drug is started, dosage adjustment of the antihypertensive drug may be required. • This drug interacts with hypoglycemics, monoamine oxidase inhibitors, antipsychotics, phenytoin, papaverine, adrenergics, and antidepressants. If you are currently taking any drugs of these types, consult your doctor about their use. If you are unsure about the type or contents of your medications, ask your doctor or pharmacist. • When this drug is administered to patients currently taking levodopa (L-dopa), the levodopa must be discontinued at least eight hours before. • This drug may cause dizziness or drowsiness; avoid tasks that require alertness.

Comments: Persons taking levodopa products are told to avoid taking vitamin B_6 (pyridoxine) products and to avoid eating foods rich in this vitamin. This precaution is not necessary with Sinemet antiparkinson drug. This drug causes beneficial effects in Parkinson's disease similar to levodopa. Because of its ingredient, carbidopa, lower doses of levodopa contained in the tablet give better results than if the levodopa were taken alone. • If dizziness or light-headedness occurs when you stand up, contract and relax the muscles of your legs for a few moments before rising. Do this by pushing one foot against the floor while raising the other foot slightly, alternating feet so that you are "pumping" your legs in a pedaling motion. • Take with food or milk to lessen stomach upset. • It may take several weeks before the full effect of this drug is evident. Compliance with therapy will ensure maximum effectiveness.

Sinequan antidepressant and antianxiety

Manufacturer: Roerig
Ingredient: doxepin hydrochloride
Equivalent Product: Adapin, Pennwalt Pharmaceutical Division
Dosage Forms: Capsule: 10 mg (red/pink); 25 mg (blue/pink); 50 mg (light pink/pink); 75 mg (light brown); 100 mg (blue/light pink); 150 mg (blue). Oral concentrate liquid (content per ml): 10 mg
Use: Relief of depression and anxiety
Minor Side Effects: Agitation; anxiety; blurred vision; confusion; constipation; cramps; diarrhea; dizziness; drowsiness; dry mouth; fatigue; flushing; headache; increased sensitivity to light; indigestion; insomnia; loss of appetite; nausea; peculiar tastes; restlessness; stomach upset; sweating; vomiting; weakness
Major Side Effects: Chills; convulsions; difficult urination; enlarged or painful breasts in men and women; fluid retention; hair loss; hallucinations; high or low blood pressure; impotence; jaundice; mood changes; nervousness; nightmares; numbness in fingers or toes; palpitations; psychosis; rash; ringing in the ears; mental disorders; sleep disorders; sore throat; tendency to bleed or bruise; testicular swelling; tremors; uncoordinated movements or balance problems; weight loss or gain
Contraindications: This drug should not be used by people who are allergic to it. Consult your doctor immediately if this drug has been prescribed for you and you have such an allergy. This drug should not be used by persons with glaucoma or with a tendency to urinary retention, particularly by older patients. Be sure your doctor knows if you have such conditions.

Warnings: The dosage of this drug should be carefully adjusted in elderly patients; those with other illnesses; or those taking other medications. • This drug should be used cautiously by pregnant women, nursing mothers, and children under 12. • This drug interacts with alcohol and other sedatives, monoamine oxidase inhibitors, amphetamines, epinephrine, methylphenidate, and phenylephrine. If you are currently taking any drugs of these types, consult your doctor about their use. If you are unsure of the type or contents of your medications, ask your doctor or pharmacist. • This drug may cause drowsiness; avoid tasks requiring alertness. • To prevent oversedation avoid the use of alcohol or other drugs with sedative properties. • Report any sudden mood swings to your doctor as well as eye pain, sore throat, fever, or unusual bruising or bleeding.

Comments: The effects of this drug may not be apparent for at least two weeks. • Minor side effects such as dizziness, light-headedness, and blurred vision tend to disappear as therapy is continued. If they persist and become a problem, consult your physician. • While taking this drug, do not take any nonprescription item for cough, cold, or sinus problems without first checking with your doctor. Do not stop or start any other drug without notifying your doctor or pharmacist. • This drug may cause dryness of the mouth. To reduce this feeling, chew gum or suck on ice chips or a piece of hard candy. • Take with food or milk to lessen stomach upset. • Products equivalent to this drug are available and vary widely in cost. Ask your doctor to prescribe a generic preparation; then ask your pharmacist to fill it with the least expensive brand. • Avoid long exposure to the sun while taking this drug. • Immediately before you take the oral concentrate form, it should be diluted in about a half-glassful of water, juice (not grape), or milk. Do not mix your dose until just before you take it. Do not use carbonated beverages to dilute this drug. • To avoid dizziness or light-headedness when you stand, contract and relax the muscles of your legs for a few moments before rising. Do this by pushing one foot against the floor while raising the other foot slightly, alternating feet so that you are "pumping" your legs in a pedaling motion.

Sinocon adrenergic and antihistamine (Vangard Laboratories), see Naldecon adrenergic and antihistamine.

SK-Amitriptyline antidepressant (Smith Kline & French Laboratories), see Elavil antidepressant.

SK-Ampicillin antibiotic (Smith Kline & French Laboratories), see ampicillin antibiotic.

SK-APAP with Codeine analgesic (Smith Kline & French Laboratories), see acetaminophen with codeine analgesic.

SK-Bamate sedative and hypnotic (Smith Kline & French Laboratories), see meprobamate sedative and hypnotic.

SK-Chlorothiazide diuretic and antihypertensive (Smith Kline & French Laboratories), see Diuril diuretic and antihypertensive.

SK-Digoxin heart drug (Smith Kline & French Laboratories), see Lanoxin heart drug.

SK-Diphenhydramine antihistamine (Smith Kline & French Laboratories), see Benadryl antihistamine.

SK-Diphenoxylate anticholinergic and antispasmodic (Smith Kline & French Laboratories), see Lomotil anticholinergic and antispasmodic.

SK-Erythromycin antibiotic (Smith Kline & French Laboratories), see erythromycin antibiotic.

SK-Furosemide diuretic and antihypertensive (Smith Kline & French Laboratories), see Lasix diuretic and antihypertensive.

SK-Hydrochlorothiazide diuretic and antihypertensive (Smith Kline & French Laboratories), see hydrochlorothiazide diuretic and antihypertensive.

SK-Lygen sedative and hypnotic (Smith Kline & French Laboratories), see Librium sedative and hypnotic.

SK-Penicillin G antibiotic (Smith Kline & French Laboratories), see penicillin G potassium antibiotic.

SK-Penicillin VK antibiotic (Smith Kline & French Laboratories), see penicillin potassium phenoxymethyl (penicillin VK) antibiotic.

SK-Phenobarbital sedative and hypnotic (Smith Kline & French Laboratories), see phenobarbital sedative and hypnotic.

SK-Potassium Chloride potassium chloride replacement (Smith Kline & French Laboratories), see potassium chloride replacement.

SK-Pramine antidepressant (Smith, Kline & French Laboratories), see Tofranil antidepressant.

SK-Prednisone steroid hormone (Smith Kline & French Laboratories), see prednisone steroid hormone.

SK-Quinidine Sulfate anti-arrhythmic (Smith Kline & French Laboratories), see quinidine sulfate anti-arrhythmic.

SK-Reserpine antihypertensive (Smith Kline & French Laboratories), see reserpine antihypertensive.

SK-65 Compound analgesic (Smith Kline & French Laboratories), see Darvon Compound-65 analgesic.

SK-Soxazole antibacterial (Smith Kline & French Laboratories), see Gantrisin antibacterial.

SK-Tetracycline antibiotic (Smith Kline & French Laboratories), see tetracycline hydrochloride antibiotic.

SK-Tolbutamide oral antidiabetic (Smith Kline & French Laboratories), see Orinase oral antidiabetic.

Slo-Phyllin bronchodilator

Manufacturer: William H. Rorer, Inc.

Ingredient: theophylline, anhydrous

Equivalent Products: Aquaphyllin, Ferndale Labs., Inc.; Elixophyllin SR, Berlex Labs., Inc.; Theoclear, Central Pharmaceuticals; Theophylline, Generix Drug Corp.; Theostat, Laser, Inc.

Dosage Forms: Syrup (content per 15 ml or three teaspoons): 80 mg. Tablet: 100 mg; 200 mg (white). Time-release capsule: 60 mg (white); 125 mg (brown); 250 mg (purple)

Use: Symptomatic relief of bronchial asthma, bronchospasm, emphysema, and other lung diseases

Minor Side Effects: Dizziness; flushing; gastrointestinal disturbances (diarrhea, nausea, stomach pain, vomiting); headache; heartburn; increased urination; insomnia; irritability; loss of appetite; low blood pressure; nervousness; paleness

Major Side Effects: Black, tarry stools; confusion; convulsions; difficult breathing; high blood sugar; muscle twitches; palpitations; rash; ulcer; weakness

Contraindications: This drug should not be taken by people who are allergic to it. Consult your doctor immediately if you have such an allergy.

Warnings: This drug should be used cautiously by newborns and the elderly; by people who have peptic ulcer, liver disease, chronic obstructive lung disease, heart disease, kidney disease, low or high blood pressure, or thyroid disease; or by those who are pregnant. Be sure your doctor knows if you have any of these conditions. • This drug should be used with caution in conjunction with furosemide, reserpine, chlordiazepoxide, cimetidine, oral anticoagulants, phenobarbital, certain antibiotics, disulfiram, ephedrine, lithium carbonate, propranolol, or certain xanthines; if you are currently taking any drugs of these types, consult your doctor about their use. If you are unsure of the type or contents of your medications, ask your doctor or pharmacist. • This drug may interfere with certain blood and urine laboratory tests. Remind your doctor you are taking this drug before undergoing tests. • Before receiving an influenza vaccine, tell your doctor you are taking this drug.

Comments: While taking this drug, do not use any nonprescription item for asthma without first checking with your doctor. • Avoid drinking alcohol, coffee, tea, cola drinks, cocoa, or other beverages that contain caffeine. • Call your doctor if you have severe stomach pain, vomiting, or restlessness, because this drug may aggravate an ulcer. • While taking this drug, drink at least eight glasses of water daily. • Be sure to take your dose at exactly the right time. Take this drug with food or milk. • If taking this drug causes you minor gastrointestinal distress, use a nonprescription antacid product for relief. • The time-release capsule must be swallowed whole. Do not chew or crush. If you are unable to swallow the capsule, you may mix its contents with jelly or applesauce and swallow the mixture without chewing. • Your doctor may want to check your blood levels of this drug—to ensure its effectiveness. • Cigarette smoking may affect this drug's action. Be sure your doctor knows you smoke. Also, do not suddenly stop smoking without informing your doctor. • Do not switch brands without checking with your doctor or pharmacist, as your dosage may need to be adjusted. There are many other products that are similar to Slo-Phyllin, but are not true "generic" substitutes. Consult with your doctor or pharmacist about the use of a less expensive product.

Slo-Phyllin GG expectorant and smooth muscle relaxant (William H. Rorer, Inc.), see Quibron expectorant and smooth muscle relaxant.

Slow-K potassium chloride replacement (CIBA Pharmaceutical Company), see potassium chloride replacement.

SMZ-TMP and SMZ-TMP DS antibacterials (Biocraft Laboratories, Inc.), see Bactrim and Bactrim DS antibacterials.

Sodium Sulamyd ophthalmic solution and ointment

Manufacturer: Schering Corp.
Ingredient: sodium sulfacetamide
Equivalent Products: Ak-Sulf, Akorn, Inc.; Bleph-10 Liquifilm, Allergan Pharmaceuticals, Inc.; Cetamide, Alcon Laboratories, Inc.; Opthacet, Vortech Pharmaceutical, Ltd.; sodium sulfacetamide, various manufacturers; Sulf-10, Coopervision Pharmaceutical, Inc.; Sulten-10, Muro Pharmacal Labs, Inc.
Dosage Forms: Drop: 10%; 30%. Ointment: 10%
Use: Treatment of conjunctivitis; corneal ulcers; and certain other eye infections caused by microorganisms
Minor Side Effects: Local irritation; transient stinging or burning (usually associated only with 30% drops)
Major Side Effects: Chills; difficult swallowing; fever; itching, headache
Contraindications: This drug should not be used by people who are allergic to it or to any other sulfa drug. Consult your doctor immediately if this drug has been prescribed for you and you have such an allergy.
Warnings: This drug should not be used in conjunction with products containing silver. • The use of the ointment form of this product may retard the healing of the cornea of the eye. • Certain organisms that are not susceptible to this drug, such as fungi, may grow rapidly during its use. • If any pus is produced during the use of this product, the pus may impair the product's effectiveness. • If irritation occurs, stop using this drug, and call your doctor.
Comments: Use this drug for the entire period prescribed, even if symptoms disappear within that time. • Be careful about the contamination of eyedrops. Wash your hands before administering eyedrops. Do not touch the dropper to the eye. Do not wash or wipe the dropper before replacing it in the bottle. Close the bottle tightly to keep out moisture. • If this drug gets darker in color, discard it. • Like other eye products, this drug may cause some clouding or blurring of vision. This symptom will go away quickly. • See the chapter, Administering Medication Correctly, for instructions on using eyedrops.

sodium sulfacetamide ophthalmic solution and ointment (various manufacturers), see Sodium Sulamyd ophthalmic solution and ointment.

sodium warfarin anticoagulant (various manufacturers), see Coumadin anticoagulant.

Solfoton sedative and hypnotic (Wm. P. Poythress & Co., Inc.), see phenobarbital sedative and hypnotic.

Somophyllin bronchodilator (Fisons Corporation Pharmaceutical Division), see aminophylline bronchodilator.

Somophyllin-DF bronchodilator (Fisons Corporation Pharmaceutical Division), see aminophylline bronchodilator.

Sorate anti-anginal (Trimen Laboratories, Inc.), see Isordil anti-anginal.

Sorbide T.D. anti-anginal (Mayrand Pharmaceuticals, Inc.), see Isordil anti-anginal.

Sorbitrate anti-anginal (Stuart Pharmaceuticals), see Isordil anti-anginal.

Spaslin sedative and anticholinergic (Blaine Co., Inc.), see Donnatal sedative and anticholinergic.

Spasmolin sedative and anticholinergic (various manufacturers), see Donnatal sedative and anticholinergic.

Spasmophen sedative and anticholinergic (The Lannett Company, Inc.), see Donnatal sedative and anticholinergic.

Spasquid sedative and anticholinergic (Geneva Generics, Inc.), see Donnatal sedative and anticholinergic.

Spironazide diuretic and antihypertensive (Henry Schein, Inc.), see Aldactazide diuretic and antihypertensive.

spironolactone diuretic and antihypertensive (various manufacturers), see Aldactone diuretic and antihypertensive.

spironolactone with hydrochlorothiazide diuretic and antihypertensive (various manufacturers), see Aldactazide diuretic and antihypertensive.

Spirozide diuretic and antihypertensive (Rugby Laboratories), see Aldactazide diuretic and antihypertensive.

S-P-T thyroid hormone (Fleming & Co.), see thyroid hormone.

S/T Decongest antihistamine and decongestant (Scot-Tussin Pharmacal Co., Inc.), see Dimetapp antihistamine and decongestant.

Stelazine phenothiazine

Manufacturer: Smith Kline & French Laboratories
Ingredient: trifluoperazine hydrochloride
Dosage Forms: Liquid concentrate (content per ml): 10 mg. Tablet: 1 mg; 2 mg; 5 mg; 10 mg (all blue)
Use: Management of certain psychotic disorders; relief of excessive anxiety or tension

Minor Side Effects: Blurred vision; change in urine color; constipation; decreased sweating; diarrhea; dizziness; drooling; drowsiness; dry mouth; fatigue; headache; impotence; insomnia; jitteriness; loss of appetite; menstrual irregularities; milk production; nausea; photosensitivity; restlessness; tremors; weakness

Major Side Effects: Arthritis; blood disorders; breast enlargement; convulsions; difficult breathing or swallowing; difficult urination; eye changes; fluid retention; heart attack; involuntary movements of the mouth, face, neck, and tongue; liver damage; low blood pressure; muscle spasm; rash; skin darkening

Contraindications: This drug should not be taken by persons who have drug-induced depression, or have blood disease, severe high or low blood pressure, bone-marrow depression, or liver damage. This drug should not be used by children under the age of two. Consult your doctor immediately if this drug has been prescribed for you and you fit into any of these categories.

Warnings: This drug should be used with caution by patients who are allergic to a phenothiazine. Consult your doctor immediately if this drug has been prescribed for you and you have exhibited such an allergy. • This drug may cause drowsiness; avoid tasks that require alertness. • To prevent oversedation, avoid the use of alcohol or other drugs with sedative properties. • This drug should be used cautiously by pregnant women and by people with heart or blood vessel disease, diabetes, epilepsy, brain damage, kidney disease, Parkinson's disease, peptic ulcer, breast cancer, or enlarged prostate. Be sure your doctor knows if you fit into either category. • Use of this drug may cause blood diseases, jaundice, liver damage, or motor restlessness. Notify your doctor immediately if you notice visual disturbances. • This drug interacts with other depressant drugs, antacids, alcohol, or anticholinergics. If you are currently taking any drugs of these types, consult your doctor about their use. If you are unsure of the type or contents of your medications, ask your doctor or pharmacist. • If you take this drug for a prolonged time, it may be desirable for you to stop taking it for awhile in order to see if you still need it. However, do not stop taking this drug without talking to your doctor first. You may have to reduce your dosage gradually. • This drug may interfere with certain laboratory tests. Remind your doctor you are taking this drug before undergoing any tests.

Comments: The effects of therapy with this drug may not be apparent for at least two weeks. • This drug has sustained action; never take it more frequently than your doctor prescribes. A serious overdose may result. • While taking this drug, do not take any nonprescription item for cough, cold, or sinus problems without first checking with your doctor. • This drug may cause dryness of mouth. To reduce this feeling, chew gum or suck on ice chips or a piece of hard candy. • The liquid concentrate form of this drug should be added to 60 ml (1/4 cup) or more of water, milk, juice, coffee, tea, or carbonated beverages, or to pulpy foods (applesauce, etc.) just prior to administration. • To avoid dizziness or light-headedness when you stand, contract and relax the muscles of your legs for a few moments before rising. Do this by pushing one foot against the floor while raising the other foot slightly, alternating feet so that you are "pumping" your legs in a pedaling motion. • This drug may cause tumors in rats. This effect has not been shown to occur in humans. • If you notice fine tremors of your tongue, call your doctor. • Some of the side effects of this drug can be prevented by taking an antiparkinson drug. Discuss this with your doctor. • Antacids may prevent the absorption of this drug. Don't take them at the same time as you take this drug. • This drug may make you more sensitive to sunlight. Avoid prolonged exposure to the sun or use a protective sunscreen lotion.

Stuartnatal 1+1 vitamin-mineral supplement

Manufacturer: Stuart Pharmaceuticals

Ingredients: calcium; iron; vitamins A, D, E, B_1, B_2, B_3, B_6, B_{12}, C; folic acid; iodine; magnesium

Dosage Form: Tablet: calcium, 200 mg; iron, 65 mg; vitamin A, 8000 I.U.; vitamin D, 400 I.U.; vitamin E, 30 I.U.; vitamin B_1, 2.55 mg; vitamin B_2, 3 mg; vitamin B_3, 20 mg; vitamin B_6, 10 mg; vitamin B_{12}, 12 mcg; vitamin C, 90 mg; folic acid, 1.0 mg; iodine, 150 mcg; magnesium, 100 mg (yellow)

Use: Vitamin-mineral supplement for use during pregnancy and nursing

Minor Side Effects: Constipation; diarrhea; nausea; stomach upset; vomiting

Major Side Effects: None

Contraindications: This drug should not be used by anyone who is allergic to its ingredients. Contact your doctor if you have such an allergy.

Warnings: Because this product may mask symptoms of pernicious anemia, it should be used only under a doctor's supervision.

Comments: If this drug upsets your stomach, take it with food or milk. • You may wish to continue taking this product for a few weeks after delivery, especially if you are nursing your baby. • While not all prenatal vitamin-mineral formulations are identical to this product, some are similar. Ask your doctor if you can use a cheaper version, then discuss various products with your pharmacist. • Because of its iron content, this product may cause constipation, diarrhea, nausea, or stomach pain. These symptoms usually disappear or become less severe after two to three days. Taking your dose with food or milk may help minimize these side effects. If they persist, ask your pharmacist to recommend another product. • Black stools are a normal consequence of iron therapy. Do not be alarmed.

Sulfa-Gyn vaginal anti-infective (Mayrand Pharmaceuticals, Inc.), see Sultrin vaginal anti-infective.

sulfamethoxazole antibacterial (various manufacturers), see Gantanol antibacterial.

Sulfatrim and Sulfatrim DS antibacterials (various manufacturers), see Bactrim and Bactrim DS antibacterials.

sulfisoxazole antibacterial (various manufacturers), see Gantrisin antibacterial.

Sulfizin antibacterial (Reid-Provident Labs., Inc.) see Gantrisin antibacterial.

Sulf-10 ophthalmic solution and ointment (Coopervision Pharmaceutical, Inc.), see Sodium Sulamyd ophthalmic solution and ointment.

Sulten-10 ophthalmic solution and ointment (Muro Pharmacal Labs, Inc.), see Sodium Sulamyd ophthalmic solution and ointment.

Sultrin vaginal anti-infective

Manufacturer: Ortho Pharmaceutical Corporation
Ingredients: sulfabenzamide; sulfacetamide; sulfathiazole; urea

Equivalent Products: Sulfa-Gyn, Mayrand Pharmaceuticals, Inc.; Triple Sulfa, various manufacturers (see Comments); Trysul, Savage Laboratories

Dosage Forms: Vaginal cream: sulfabenzamide, 3.7%; sulfacetamide, 2.86%; sulfathiazole, 3.42%. Vaginal tablet: sulfabenzamide, 184.0 mg; sulfacetamide, 143.75 mg; sulfathiazole, 172.5 mg; compounded with urea, lactose, guar gum, starch, and magnesium stearate

Use: Treatment of vaginal infections

Minor Side Effects: Mild vaginal itching and irritation

Major Side Effects: None

Contraindications: This drug should not be used by people allergic to sulfa drugs. Consult your doctor immediately if this drug has been prescribed for you and you have such an allergy. This drug should not be used by people with kidney disease. Be sure your doctor knows if you have such a condition.

Warnings: This drug should be used until the prescribed amount of medication is gone. • Call your doctor if you develop burning or itching. • Refrain from sexual intercourse, or ask your partner to use a condom, until treatment is finished to avoid reinfection.

Comments: Several manufacturers produce Triple Sulfa vaginal cream, which contains the same ingredients as this drug, but at different strengths. • Wear cotton panties rather than those made of nylon or other nonporous materials while treating vaginal infections.

Sumox antibiotic (Reid-Provident Labs., Inc.), see amoxicillin antibiotic.

Sumycin antibiotic (E. R. Squibb & Sons, Inc.), see tetracycline hydrochloride antibiotic.

Supen antibiotic (Reid-Provident Labs., Inc.), see ampicillin antibiotic.

Susano sedative and anticholinergic (Halsey Drug Co., Inc.), see Donnatal sedative and anticholinergic.

Suspen antibiotic (Circle Pharmaceuticals, Inc.), see penicillin potassium phenoxymethyl (penicillin VK) antibiotic.

Sustaire bronchodilator (Roerig Pharmaceutical), see Theo-dur bronchodilator.

Synalar steroid hormone

Manufacturer: Syntex Laboratories, Inc.

Ingredient: fluocinolone acetonide

Equivalent Products: fluocinolone acetonide, various manufacturers; Fluonid, Herbert Laboratories; Flurosyn, Rugby Laboratories; Synemol, Syntex Laboratories, Inc.

Dosage Forms: Cream: 0.025%; 0.01%. Ointment: 0.025%. Topical solution: 0.01%

Use: Relief of skin inflammation associated with such conditions as dermatitis, eczema, or poison ivy

Minor Side Effects: Blistering, burning sensation; dryness; increased hair growth; irritation; itching; rash

Major Side Effects: Loss of skin color; secondary infection; skin wasting

Contraindications: This drug should not be used by people who are allergic to it. Consult your doctor immediately if this drug has been prescribed for you and you have such an allergy. This drug should not be used by infants less than two years old. This drug should not be used in the presence of infection, severe circulatory system disease, or in the ear if the eardrum is perforated.

Warnings: If irritation develops when using this drug, immediately discontinue its use and notify your doctor. • If extensive areas are treated or if an occlusive bandage is used, there will be increased systemic absorption of this drug, and suitable precautions should be taken, particularly in children and infants. • This drug should be used with caution by pregnant women. • This drug is not meant for use in the eyes.

Comments: If the affected area is extremely dry or is scaling, the skin may be moistened before applying the medication by soaking in water or by applying water with a clean cloth. The ointment form is probably better for dry skin. The solution form is best for hairy areas. • A mild, temporary stinging may be apparent after the medicine is applied. • Do not use this drug with an occlusive wrap unless directed to do so by your doctor. If it is necessary for you to use this drug under a wrap, follow your doctor's instructions exactly; do not leave the wrap in place longer than specified. • Use this drug only as prescribed. Do not use more often or for a longer period than your doctor ordered.

Synalgos analgesic (Ives Laboratories, Inc.), see Synalgos-DC analgesic.

Synalgos-DC analgesic

Manufacturer: Ives Laboratories, Inc.

Ingredients: aspirin; caffeine; dihydrocodeine bitartrate; promethazine hydrochloride

Dosage Form: Capsule: aspirin, 356.4 mg; caffeine, 30 mg; dihydrocodeine bitartrate, 16 mg; promethazine hydrochloride, 6.25 mg (blue/gray)

Use: Relief of moderate to severe pain

Minor Side Effects: Blurred vision; constipation; dizziness; drowsiness; dry mouth; headache; indigestion; insomnia; itching; light-headedness; loss of appetite; nausea; nervousness; restlessness; sedation; sunlight sensitivity; sweating; vomiting

Major Side Effects: Bruising; chest tightness; difficult breathing; difficult urination; fall in blood pressure; fever; jaundice; loss of coordination; palpitations; ringing in the ears; skin rash; sore throat; ulcer

Contraindications: This drug should not be used by people who are allergic to any of its components. Consult your doctor immediately if this drug has been prescribed for you and you have such an allergy.

Warnings: This drug should be used with extreme caution in the presence of peptic ulcer, blood coagulation problems, gallbladder disease, glaucoma, brain disease, anemia, high blood pressure, certain types of heart disease, kidney disease, liver disease, prostate disease, or thyroid disease. Be sure your doctor knows if you have any of these problems. • The drug should be used with caution by pregnant women, the elderly, and children. • This drug may cause drowsiness; avoid tasks requiring alertness, such as driving a motor vehicle or operating machinery. • To prevent oversedation, avoid the use of alcohol and other drugs that have sedative effects. • This drug can produce drug dependence of the codeine type and, therefore, has the potential for abuse. Products containing narcotics (e.g., dihydrocodeine bitartrate) are usually not taken for more than seven to ten days. Tolerance may develop quickly; do not increase the dose of the drug without first consulting your doctor. • This drug should not be taken with alcohol, ammonium chloride, methotrexate, 6-mercaptopurine, phenytoin, antacids, oral anticoagulants, oral antidiabetics, probenecid, steroids, sulfinpyrazone, or central nervous system depressants. If you are currently taking any drugs of these types, consult your doctor about their use. If you are unsure of the type or contents of your medications, ask your doctor or pharmacist.

Comments: While taking this drug, do not take any nonprescription item for cough, cold, or sinus problems without first checking with your doctor. • Although no product exactly equivalent to this drug is available, similar products are, and buying them may save you money. Consult your doctor. • Take this product with food or milk to lessen stomach upset. • Nausea may occur after the first few doses of this drug. It is usually relieved by lying down for awhile. • Avoid sudden changes in position to alleviate dizziness, lightheadedness, or fainting. • If your ears feel strange, if you hear buzzing or ringing, or if your stomach hurts, your dosage may need adjustment. Consult your doctor. • Another product from Ives Laboratories, Inc., Synalgos analgesic, is identical to Synalgos-DC analgesic, except that it does not contain dihydrocodeine bitartrate.

Synemol steroid hormone (Syntex Laboratories, Inc.), see Synalar steroid hormone.

Synthroid thyroid hormone

Manufacturer: Flint Laboratories
Ingredient: levothyroxine sodium
Equivalent Products: Levothroid, USV Laboratories; levothyroxine sodium, Lederle Laboratories; Synthrox, Vortech Pharmaceutical, Ltd.; Syroxine, Major Pharmaceuticals
Dosage Form: Tablet: 0.025 mg (orange); 0.05 mg (white); 0.1 mg (yellow); 0.15 mg (blue); 0.2 mg (pink); 0.3 mg (green)
Use: Thyroid replacement therapy
Minor Side Effects: Diarrhea; headache; irritability; vomiting
Major Side Effects: In overdose: Chest pain; diarrhea; fever; heat intolerance; insomnia; leg cramps; menstrual irregularities; nervousness; palpitations; shortness of breath; sweating; trembling; weight loss
Contraindications: Although there are no absolute contraindications to this drug, special care should be taken if it is used by persons who have recently had a heart attack and those with defective adrenal glands or overactive thyroid glands.
Warnings: This drug should be used cautiously by people who have heart disease, high blood pressure, kidney disease, or diabetes. Be sure your doctor knows if you have any of these conditions. • This drug interacts with cholestyramine, digitalis, oral anticoagulants, oral antidiabetics, oral contraceptives, epinephrine, and phenytoin; if you are currently taking any drugs of these types, consult your doctor about their use. If you are unsure of the type or contents of your medications, ask your doctor or pharmacist. • While taking this drug, do not take any nonprescription item for cough, cold, or sinus problems without first checking with your doctor. • If you are taking digitalis in addition to this drug, watch carefully for symptoms of increased toxicity (e.g., nausea, blurred vision, palpitations) and notify your doctor immediately if they occur. • Be sure to follow your doctor's dosage instructions exactly. Most side effects from this drug can be controlled by dosage adjustment; consult your doctor if you

experience side effects. • This drug should not be used to treat obesity. Using this drug in conjunction with appetite suppressants is particularly dangerous.

Comments: For most patients, generic thyroid hormone tablets (see the profile on thyroid hormone) will work as well as this drug and are less expensive. Check with your doctor. • Do not stop taking this drug without first consulting your physician.

Synthrox thyroid hormone (Vortech Pharmaceutical, Ltd.), see Synthroid thyroid hormone.

Syroxine thyroid hormone (Major Pharmaceuticals), see Synthroid thyroid hormone.

Tagamet antisecretory

Manufacturer: Smith Kline & French Laboratories
Ingredient: cimetidine
Dosage Forms: Tablet: 200 mg; 300 mg (pale green); 400 mg (pale green). Liquid (content per 5 ml teaspoon): 300 mg; alcohol, 2.8%
Use: Treatment of duodenal and gastric ulcer; long-term treatment of excessive gastric acid secretion; prevention of recurrent ulcers
Minor Side Effects: Diarrhea; dizziness; headache; muscle pain
Major Side Effects: Easy bruising; confusion; fever; hair loss; increased breast size; impotence; jaundice; palpitations; rash; sore throat; weakness
Contraindications: This drug should not be taken by anyone who is allergic to it. Consult your doctor if this drug has been prescribed for you and you have such an allergy.
Warnings: This drug should be used with caution by the elderly, women of childbearing age, by pregnant women, and by nursing mothers. Because the use of this drug in children has been limited, this drug is not recommended for use by children under 16 years of age unless your doctor feels the benefits outweigh any potential risks. • This drug should be used with caution by people with liver disease, kidney disease, or organic brain syndrome. Be sure your doctor knows if you have such a condition. • This drug may affect the functioning of theophylline, aminophylline, phenytoin, beta blockers, anticoagulants, and certain tranquilizers. If you are currently taking any drugs of these types, consult your doctor about their use. If you are unsure about the type or contents of your medications, ask your doctor or pharmacist.
Comments: Although this drug is classed as a histamine blocker, its major action on histamine in the body is in the stomach and intestine. • This drug should not be crushed or chewed because cimetidine has a bitter taste and an unpleasant odor. • Antacid therapy may be continued while taking this drug, but the two drugs should not be taken at the same time. For maximum benefit stagger the doses of antacid and Tagamet. • This drug is usually taken throughout the day. It should be taken with, or immediately following, a meal. • When used as a preventive, the medication may be taken as a single dose at bedtime. • Take this drug for the prescribed period, even if you feel better. • This drug may cause changes in blood cells; therefore, periodic blood tests may be requested by your doctor.

Tagatap antihistamine and decongestant (Tutag Pharmaceuticals, Inc.), see Dimetapp antihistamine and decongestant.

Talacen Caplets analgesic (Winthrop Laboratories), see Talwin Nx analgesic.

Talwin Compound analgesic (Winthrop Laboratories), see Talwin Nx analgesic.

Talwin Nx analgesic

Manufacturer: Winthrop Laboratories
Ingredients: pentazocine hydrochloride, naloxone hydrochloride
Dosage Form: Tablet: pentazocine hydrochloride, 50 mg; naloxone hydrochloride, 0.5 mg (yellow)
Use: Relief of moderate to severe pain
Minor Side Effects: Change in sense of taste; constipation; diarrhea; dizziness; drowsiness; dry mouth; flushing; headache; indigestion; insomnia; light-headedness; loss of appetite; nausea; vomiting
Major Side Effects: Blurred vision; chest tightness; difficult breathing; difficult urination; disorientation; euphoria; hallucinations; loss of hearing; mood changes; nightmares; ringing in the ears; tingling in the hands and feet
Contraindications: This drug should not be used by people who are allergic to it. Consult your doctor immediately if this drug has been prescribed for you and you have such an allergy.
Warnings: This drug should be used with caution by pregnant and nursing women; people who have been taking narcotics; and by people with head injuries, enlarged prostate, peptic ulcer, severe respiratory problems, severe bronchial asthma, liver and kidney diseases, epilepsy; those about to undergo gallbladder surgery; and those who have suffered a heart attack. This drug is not recommended for use by children under 12. Be sure your doctor knows if you fit into any of these categories. • This drug has the potential for abuse. Tolerance may develop quickly; do not increase the dose of this drug without first consulting your doctor. • Do not stop taking this drug suddenly without consulting your doctor. • This drug has, on rare occasions, produced hallucinations (usually visual), disorientation, and confusion in some patients. These side effects have cleared spontaneously in a few hours. • Use of this drug may cause drowsiness; avoid tasks that require alertness. • To prevent oversedation, avoid the use of alcohol or other drugs that have sedative properties. • This drug interacts with alcohol, narcotics, phenothiazines, antidepressants, monoamine oxidase inhibitors, and an antihistamine called Pyribenzamine (CIBA). If you are currently taking any drugs of these types, consult your doctor about their use. If you are unsure of the type or contents of your medications, ask your doctor or pharmacist.
Comments: Winthrop Laboratories also markets Talwin Compound Caplets, which contain pentazocine hydrochloride, 12.5 mg; and aspirin, 325 mg and Talacen Caplets, which contain pentazocine hydrochloride, 25 mg and acetaminophen, 650 mg.

Tandearil anti-inflammatory (GEIGY Pharmaceuticals), see Butazolidin anti-inflammatory.

Teebaconin antitubercular (Consolidated Midland Corp.), see isoniazid antitubercular.

Tegamide antinauseant (G&W Laboratories, Inc.), see Tigan antinauseant.

Tegretol anticonvulsant

Manufacturer: GEIGY Pharmaceuticals

Ingredient: carbamazepine
Dosage Forms: Tablet: 200 mg (white). Chewable tablet: 100 mg (red/pink)
Use: Treatment of seizure disorders; relief of neuralgia pain
Minor Side Effects: Agitation; blurred vision; confusion; constipation; diarrhea; dizziness; drowsiness; dry mouth; eye discomfort; fainting; headache; loss of appetite; muscle or joint pain; nausea; restlessness; sensitivity to sunlight; sweating; vomiting; weakness
Major Side Effects: Abdominal pain; bruising; chills; darkened urine; depression; difficult breathing; difficult urination; fever; hair loss; hallucinations; impotence; jaundice; loss of balance; mouth sores; nightmares; numbness or tingling; pale stools; rapid and pounding heart rate; ringing in the ears; sore throat; skin rash; swelling of hands or feet; twitching
Contraindications: This drug should not be used by people who are allergic to it or to tricyclic antidepressants. This drug should not be taken by anyone who has bone marrow depression or who has taken a monoamine oxidase inhibitor within the past two weeks. Consult your doctor immediately if this drug has been prescribed for you and you have such an allergy or condition.
Warnings: This drug should be used cautiously in people who have glaucoma, blood disorders, kidney or liver disease, or heart disease. Be sure your doctor knows if you have any of these conditions. • This drug interacts with oral anticoagulants, digitalis, erythromycin, tetracycline, troleandomycin, oral contraceptives, painkillers, tranquilizers, and other anticonvulsants. If you are currently taking any drugs of these types, consult your doctor about their use. If you are unsure of the type or ingredients of your medication, ask your doctor or pharmacist.
Comments: It is important that all doses of this medication are taken on time. • If this drug causes stomach upset, take it with food. • If this drug increases your sensitivity to sunlight, limit your exposure to the sun, wear protective clothing and sunglasses, and use an effective sunscreen. • Sucking on ice chips or hard candy may relieve a dry mouth. • This drug may cause dizziness or drowsiness; avoid tasks that require alertness. • While taking this drug, your doctor will want to see you regularly for blood cell counts, liver and kidney function tests, and eye examinations. • Notify your doctor if you develop a sore throat, mouth sores, fever, chills, unusual bruising, pale stools, dark urine, or edema (swelling) while taking this medication. • Do not stop taking this drug suddenly and do not increase the dosage without your doctor's approval.

Tenormin beta blocker

Manufacturer: Stuart Pharmaceuticals
Ingredient: atenolol
Dosage Form: Tablet: 50 mg; 100 mg (white)
Use: Treatment of high blood pressure
Minor Side Effects: Abdominal pain; bloating; blurred vision; constipation; drowsiness; dry eyes, mouth, or skin; gas or heartburn; headache; insomnia; loss of appetite; nasal congestion; nausea; slowed heart rate; sweating; vivid dreams; vomiting
Major Side Effects: Bleeding or bruising; confusion; decreased sexual ability; depression; diarrhea; difficult urination; dizziness; earache; fever; hair loss; hallucinations; mouth sores; night cough; nightmares; numbness and tingling in the fingers and toes; rash; ringing in the ears; shortness of breath; swelling in the hands or feet
Contraindications: This drug should not be used by people who are allergic to atenolol or any other beta blocker. This drug may interact with monoamine oxidase inhibitors. Consult your doctor if you are taking any drugs of this type. If

CONSUMER GUIDE®

you are unsure about the type or contents of your medications, ask your doctor or pharmacist.

Warnings: This drug should be used with caution by persons with certain respiratory problems, diabetes, certain heart problems, liver and kidney diseases, hypoglycemia, or thyroid disease. Be sure your doctor knows if you have any of these conditions. • This drug should be used cautiously by pregnant women and by women of childbearing age. • This drug should be used with care during anesthesia and by patients undergoing major surgery. If possible, this drug should be withdrawn 48 hours prior to surgery. • This drug should be used cautiously when reserpine is taken. • This drug is a potent medication; do not stop taking it abruptly, unless your doctor directs you to do so.

Comments: Your doctor may want you to take your pulse every day while you take this medication. Consult your doctor. • Be sure to take your medication doses at the same time each day. • While taking this drug, do not take any nonprescription items for cough, cold, or sinus problems without first checking with your doctor or pharmacist. • Notify your doctor if dizziness, diarrhea, depression, sore throat, or unusual bruising develops.

Tenstan analgesic and sedative (Halsom Laboratories), see Fiorinal analgesic and sedative.

Tenuate anorectic

Manufacturer: Lakeside Pharmaceuticals
Ingredient: diethylpropion hydrochloride
Equivalent Products: Depletite, Reid-Provident Labs., Inc.; diethylpropion hydrochloride, various manufacturers; Tepanil, Riker Laboratories, Inc.
Dosage Forms: Sustained-release tablet: 75 mg (white). Tablet: 25 mg (white)
Use: Short-term treatment of obesity
Minor Side Effects: Anxiety; blurred vision; constipation; diarrhea; dizziness; drowsiness; dry mouth; headache; insomnia; irritability; muscle pain; nausea; nervousness; rapid pulse; restlessness; sweating; unpleasant taste in the mouth; vomiting
Major Side Effects: Blood disorders; bruising; chest pain; depression; difficult breathing; difficult and frequent urination; enlarged breasts; euphoria; high blood pressure; impotence; increase or decrease in sexual desire; involuntary movements; menstrual upset; overstimulation of the nerves; palpitations; rash; stomach pain; tremors
Contraindications: This drug should not be taken by people who have heart disease (certain types), severe high blood pressure, thyroid disease, or glaucoma. People who have demonstrated a potential for drug abuse, those who are allergic to the drug, those who are in an agitated state, and those who are taking or recently have taken a monoamine oxidase inhibitor (ask your pharmacist if you are unsure) should not use this drug. Consult your doctor immediately if this drug has been prescribed for you and you fit into any of these categories.
Warnings: This drug should be used cautiously by people who have high blood pressure, heart disease, diabetes, or epilepsy; or by those who are pregnant. Be sure your doctor knows if you have any of these conditions. • This drug is not recommended for use by children under age 12. • This drug interacts with acetazolamide, guanethidine, phenothiazines, sodium bicarbonate, and antidepressants; if you are currently taking any drugs of these types, consult your doctor about their use. If you are unsure about the type or contents of your medications, ask your doctor or pharmacist. • While taking this drug, do not take any nonprescription item for cough, cold, or sinus problems without

first checking with your doctor. • This drug may mask symptoms of extreme fatigue and decrease your ability to perform potentially dangerous or hazardous tasks, such as driving or operating machinery. • This drug has the potential for abuse and must be used with caution. Tolerance may develop quickly; do not increase the dose of this drug or take it more frequently than prescribed without first consulting your doctor. A serious overdose could result, especially with the sustained-action form of the drug. Do not stop taking this drug without consulting your doctor. • Avoid foods rich in tyramine; ask your doctor for a list of such foods.

Comments: To be effective, therapy with this drug must be accompanied by a low-calorie diet. • Weight loss is greatest during the first three weeks of drug therapy. • This drug's effects on appetite control wear off; do not take the drug for longer than the prescribed period. • To avoid sleeplessness, do not take the sustained-release form of this drug later than 3:00 P.M. The sustained-release form must be swallowed whole; do not crush or chew it.

Tepanil anorectic (Riker Laboratories, Inc.), see Tenuate anorectic.

Tetra-C- antibiotic (Boots Pharmaceuticals, Inc.), see tetracycline hydrochloride antibiotic.

Tetracap antibiotic (Circle Pharmaceuticals, Inc.), see tetracycline hydrochloride antibiotic.

tetracycline hydrochloride antibiotic

Manufacturer: various manufacturers
Ingredient: tetracycline hydrochloride
Equivalent Products: Achromycin V, Lederle Laboratories; Cycline-250, Scrip-Physician Supply Co.; Cyclopar, Parke-Davis; Deltamycin, Trimen Laboratories, Inc.; Nor-Tet, Vortech Pharmaceutical, Ltd.; Panmycin, The Upjohn Company; Retet, Reid-Provident Labs., Inc.; Robitet, A. H. Robins Company; SK-Tetracycline, Smith Kline & French Laboratories; Sumycin, E. R. Squibb & Sons, Inc.; Tetra-C, Century Pharmaceuticals, Inc.; Tetracap, Circle Pharmaceuticals, Inc.; Tetracyn, Pfipharmecs Division; Tetralan-250 and Tetralan-500, The Lannett Company, Inc.; Tetram, Dunhall Pharmaceuticals, Inc.
Dosage Forms: Capsule; Liquid; Tablet (various strengths and colors)
Use: Treatment of acne and a wide variety of bacterial infections
Minor Side Effects: Diarrhea; dizziness; increased sensitivity to light; loss of appetite; nausea; stomach cramps and upset; vomiting
Major Side Effects: Anemia; black tongue; difficult breathing; mouth irritation; rash; rectal and vaginal itching; sore throat; superinfection
Contraindications: This drug should not be taken by people who are allergic to any tetracycline drug. Consult your doctor immediately if this drug has been prescribed for you and you have such an allergy.
Warnings: This drug may cause permanent discoloration of the teeth if used during tooth development; therefore, it should be used cautiously by pregnant or nursing women and infants and children under nine years of age. This drug should be used cautiously by people who have liver or kidney disease, or diabetes. Be sure your doctor knows if you have any of these conditions. • This drug interacts with antacids, barbiturates, carbamazepine, lithium, diuretics, digoxin, oral contraceptives, penicillin, and phenytoin; if you are currently taking any drugs of these types, consult your doctor about their use. If you are unsure of the type or contents of your medications, ask your doctor or pharma-

cist. • Milk and other dairy products interfere with the body's absorption of this drug, so separate taking this drug and any dairy product by at least two hours. Do not take this drug at the same time as any iron preparation; their use should be separated by at least two hours. • This drug may cause you to be especially sensitive to the sun, so avoid exposure to sunlight as much as possible. • This drug may affect syphilis tests; if you are being treated for this disease, make sure that your doctor knows you are taking this drug. • If you are taking an anticoagulant in addition to this drug, remind your doctor. • Prolonged use of this drug may allow organisms that are not susceptible to it to grow wildly. Do not use this drug unless your doctor has specifically told you to do so. Be sure to follow the directions carefully and report any unusual reactions to your doctor at once. • Complete blood cell counts and liver and kidney function tests should be done if you take this drug for a prolonged period.

Comments: Ideally, you should take this drug on an empty stomach (one hour before or two hours after a meal). If this drug causes stomach upset, you may take it with food. Take it with at least eight ounces of water. • When used to treat strep throat, this drug should be taken for at least ten full days, even if symptoms disappear within that time. • This drug is most effective when taken at evenly spaced intervals throughout the day and night. Ask your pharmacist or physician for help in planning a medication schedule. • The liquid form of this drug must be shaken before use. • Any unused medication should be discarded.

Tetracyn antibiotic (Pfipharmecs Division), see tetracycline hydrochloride antibiotic.

Tetralan-250 and Tetralan-500 antibiotics (The Lannett Company, Inc.), see tetracycline hydrochloride antibiotic.

Tetram antibiotic (Dunhall Pharmaceuticals, Inc.), see tetracycline hydrochloride antibiotic.

T-Gen antinauseant (Goldline Laboratories), see Tigan antinauseant.

Thalitone diuretic and antihypertensive (USV Laboratories), see Hygroton diuretic and antihypertensive.

Theoclear bronchodilator (Central Pharmaceuticals, Inc.), see Slo-Phyllin bronchodilator.

Theocolate expectorant and smooth muscle relaxant (Bay Pharmaceuticals, Inc.), see Quibron expectorant and smooth muscle relaxant.

Theo-Dur bronchodilator

Manufacturer: Key Pharmaceuticals, Inc.
Ingredient: theophylline, anhydrous
Equivalent Products: Constant-T, Geigy Pharmaceuticals; Duraphyl, McNeil Laboratories; LaBID, Norwich-Eaton Pharmaceuticals; Quibron-T/SR, Mead-Johnson Co.; Respbid, Boehringer-Ingelheim; Sustaire, Roerig Pharmaceutical; theophylline SR, various manufacturers; Theo-Time, Major Phar-

maceuticals; Uniphyl, Purdue Frederick Company (See Comments)

Dosage Form: Sustained-action tablet: 100 mg; 200 mg; 300 mg (all white)

Use: Symptomatic relief of bronchial asthma, bronchospasm, emphysema, and other lung diseases

Minor Side Effects: Dizziness; flushing; gastrointestinal disturbances (diarrhea, stomach pain, nausea, vomiting); headache; heartburn; increased urination; insomnia; irritability; loss of appetite; low blood pressure; nervousness; paleness

Major Side Effects: Confusion; convulsions; difficult breathing; high blood sugar; muscle twitches; palpitations; rash; ulcer; weakness

Contraindications: This drug should not be taken by people who are allergic to it. Consult your doctor immediately if you have such an allergy.

Warnings: This drug should be used cautiously by newborns and the elderly; by people who have peptic ulcer, liver disease, chronic obstructive lung disease, heart disease, kidney disease, low or high blood pressure, or thyroid disease; or by those who are pregnant. Be sure your doctor knows if you have any of these conditions. ● This drug should be used with caution in conjunction with furosemide, reserpine, chlordiazepoxide, cimetidine, disulfiram, oral anticoagulants, phenobarbital, certain antibiotics, ephedrine, lithium carbonate, propranolol, or other xanthines; if you are currently taking any drugs of these types, consult your doctor about their use. If you are unsure of the type or contents of your medications, ask your doctor or pharmacist.

Comments: While taking this drug, do not use any nonprescription item for asthma without first checking with your doctor. ● Avoid drinking alcohol, coffee, tea, cola drinks, cocoa, or other beverages that contain caffeine. ● Call your doctor if you have severe stomach pain, vomiting, or restlessness, because this drug may aggravate an ulcer. ● While taking this drug, drink at least eight glasses of water daily. ● Be sure to take your dose at exactly the right time. Take this drug with food or milk. ● If taking this drug causes you minor gastrointestinal distress, use a nonprescription antacid product for relief. ● Cigarette smoking may affect this drug's action. Be sure your doctor knows you smoke. Also, do not suddenly stop smoking without informing your doctor. ● While the other products listed are similar to Theo-Dur, you should not use them as "generic" substitutes. They may cause a different effect on your body. Do not change brands, unless directed to do so by your doctor. ● This is a sustained-release tablet. It must be swallowed whole. Do not crush or chew the tablet.

Theolate expectorant and smooth muscle relaxant (various manufacturers), see Quibron expectorant and smooth muscle relaxant.

Theophylline bronchodilator (Generix Drug Corp.), see Slo-Phyllin bronchodilator.

theophylline SR bronchodilator (various manufacturers), see Theo-Dur bronchodilator.

Theostat bronchodilator (Laser, Inc.), see Slo-Phyllin bronchodilator.

Theo-Time bronchodilator (Major Pharmaceuticals), see Theo-Dur bronchodilator.

Thiuretic diuretic and antihypertensive (Parke-Davis), see hydrochlorothiazide diuretic and antihypertensive.

Thorazine phenothiazine

Manufacturer: Smith Kline & French Laboratories
Ingredient: chlorpromazine hydrochloride
Equivalent Products: chlorpromazine hydrochloride, various manufacturers; Promapar, Parke-Davis; Thor-Prom, Major Pharmaceuticals
Dosage Forms: Concentrate (content per ml): 30 mg; 100 mg. Suppository: 25 mg; 100 mg. Syrup (content per 5 ml teaspoon): 10 mg. Tablet: 10 mg; 25 mg; 50 mg; 100 mg; 200 mg (all brown). Time-release capsule: 30 mg; 75 mg; 150 mg; 200 mg; 300 mg (all brown/clear with brown and white beads)
Use: Management of certain psychotic disorders; treatment of intractable hiccups; nausea; vomiting
Minor Side Effects: Blurred vision; constipation; decreased sweating; diarrhea; discoloration of the urine; dizziness; drooling; drowsiness; dry mouth; fainting; fatigue; jitteriness; low blood pressure; menstrual irregularities; nasal congestion; restlessness; sun sensitivity; tremors; vomiting; weight gain
Major Side Effects: Blood disorders; breast enlargement; bruising; convulsions; darkened skin; difficulty with swallowing or breathing; fever; heart attack; impotence; involuntary movements of the face, mouth, jaw, and tongue; jaundice; low or high blood sugar; palpitations; psychosis; rash; sleep disorders; sore throat; uncoordinated movements; visual disturbances
Contraindications: This drug should not be taken by people who have blood diseases, drug-induced depression, severe high or low blood pressure, or bone marrow disease. Consult your doctor immediately if this drug has been prescribed for you and you have any of these conditions.
Warnings: This drug should be used cautiously by pregnant or nursing women; people who have had an allergic reaction to a phenothiazine in the past; and persons with heart, liver, or lung disease; glaucoma; diabetes; epilepsy; brain disease; peptic ulcer; Parkinson's disease; breast cancer; enlarged prostate; or blockage in the urinary or digestive tracts. Be sure your doctor knows if you fit any of these categories. ● This drug may cause motor restlessness, uncoordinated movements, or muscle spasms. Contact your doctor immediately if you notice any such symptoms. ● This drug may cause drowsiness; avoid tasks that require alertness. ● To prevent oversedation, avoid the use of alcohol or other drugs that have sedative properties. ● This drug interacts with antacids, anticholinergics, central nervous system depressants, and guanethidine; if you are currently taking any drugs of these types, consult your doctor about their use. If you are unsure of the type or contents of your medications, ask your doctor or pharmacist. ● If you take this drug for a prolonged time, it may be desirable for you to stop taking it for awhile in order to see if you still need it. However, do not stop taking it without talking to your doctor first. You may have to reduce your dosage gradually. ● This drug interferes with certain laboratory tests; remind your doctor you are taking this drug before undergoing any tests.
Comments: The effects of this drug may not be apparent for at least two weeks. ● Chew gum or suck on ice chips or a piece of hard candy to reduce mouth dryness. ● To avoid dizziness or light-headedness when you stand, contract and relax the muscles of your legs for a few moments before rising. Do this by pushing one foot against the floor while raising the other foot slightly, alternating feet so that you are "pumping" your legs in a pedaling motion. ● The liquid concentrate form of this drug should be added to 60 ml (1/4 cup) or more of water, milk, juice, coffee, tea, or a carbonated beverage, or to pulpy foods immediately prior to administration. ● This drug has persistent action; never take it more frequently than your doctor prescribes. A serious overdose may result. ● While taking this drug, do not take any nonprescription item for cough, cold, or sinus problems without first checking with your doctor. ● This drug may

make you extra sensitive to sunlight; avoid prolonged exposure to sunlight or sunlamps while taking this drug. • If you notice fine tremors of your tongue, call your doctor. • Some of the side effects caused by this drug can be prevented by taking an antiparkinson drug. Discuss this with your doctor. • Antacids may prevent the absorption of this drug. Don't take them at the same time you are taking this drug. • This drug may cause tumors in rats. This effect has not been shown to occur in humans. • Take extra precautions if you are taking this medicine during hot weather. It may increase your risk of heat stroke. Avoid strenuous activity in hot weather. • This drug may cause discoloration of urine to pink/brown. Do not be alarmed.

Thor-Prom phenothiazine (Major Pharmaceuticals), see Thorazine phenothiazine.

Thyar thyroid hormone (USV [P. R.] Development Corp.), see thyroid hormone.

thyroid hormone

Manufacturer: various manufacturers
Ingredient: thyroid
Equivalent Products: Amour Thyroid, USV [P.R.] Development Corp.; S-P-T, Fleming & Co.; Thyrar, USV [P.R.] Development Corp.; Thyro-Teric, Mallard, Inc.
Dosage Forms: Capsule; Enteric-coated tablet; Tablet (various dosages and various colors)
Use: Thyroid replacement therapy
Minor Side Effects: Diarrhea; headache; irritability; vomiting
Major Side Effects: In overdose: Chest pain; fever; heat intolerance; insomnia; leg cramps; menstrual irregularities; nervousness; palpitations; shortness of breath; sweating; trembling; weight loss
Contraindications: This drug should not be used to treat obesity, especially in conjunction with amphetamine-type diet pills. This drug should not be used by people who have an overactive thyroid gland or by those whose adrenal gland is malfunctioning. In most cases this drug should not be used by people with heart disease. However, if the thyroid condition was a contributing or causative factor in the heart condition, this drug can be tried cautiously. Consult your doctor immediately if this drug has been prescribed for you and you fit into any of these categories.
Warnings: This drug should be used cautiously by people who have cardiovascular disease, high blood pressure, kidney disease, or diabetes. Be sure your doctor knows if you have any of these conditions. • This drug interacts with cholestyramine, epinephrine, digitalis, phenytoin, oral contraceptives, oral anticoagulants, and antidiabetics; if you are currently taking any drugs of these types, consult your doctor about their use. If you are unsure of the type or contents of your medications, ask your doctor or pharmacist. • While taking this drug, do not take any nonprescription item for cough, cold, or sinus problems without first checking with your doctor. • If you are taking digitalis in addition to this drug, watch carefully for symptoms of increased toxicity (e.g., nausea, blurred vision, palpitations) and notify your doctor immediately if they occur.
Comments: Compliance with prescribed therapy is essential with this drug. Be sure to follow your doctor's dosage instructions exactly. Get into the habit of taking the drug at the same time each day. • Most side effects from this drug can be controlled by dosage adjustment; consult your doctor if you experience side

effects. • Do not stop taking this drug without consulting your physician. • Although many thyroid products are on the market, they are not all bioequivalent; that is, they may not all be absorbed into the bloodstream at the same rate or have the same overall pharmacologic activity. Don't change brands of this drug without consulting your doctor or pharmacist to make sure you are receiving an identically functioning product.

Thyro-Teric thyroid hormone (Mallard, Inc.), see thyroid hormone.

Tigan antinauseant

Manufacturer: Beecham Laboratories
Ingredient: trimethobenzamide hydrochloride
Equivalent Products: Tegamid, G&W Laboratories, Inc.; T-Gen, Goldline Laboratories; trimethobenzamide, various manufacturers
Dosage Forms: Capsule: 100 mg (blue/white); 250 mg (blue). Pediatric suppository: 100 mg. Suppository: 200 mg
Use: Control of nausea and vomiting
Minor Side Effects: Diarrhea; dizziness; drowsiness; headache; muscle cramps
Major Side Effects: Back pain; blood disorders; blurred vision; coma; convulsions; depression; disorientation; jaundice; mouth sores; rash; tremors; unusual hand or face movements; vomiting
Contraindications: This drug should not be taken by people who are allergic to it. Consult your doctor immediately if this drug has been prescribed for you and you have such an allergy. The suppository form of this drug should not be given to newborn infants.
Warnings: This drug should be used with extreme caution by children for the treatment of vomiting. This drug is not recommended for treatment of uncomplicated vomiting in children and its use should be limited to prolonged vomiting of known cause. • Since this drug may cause drowsiness, patients should not operate motor vehicles or dangerous machinery until their individual responses to the drug have been determined. • To avoid excessive sedation, avoid taking alcohol and other depressive drugs while taking this drug. If you are unsure of the type of your medications, ask your doctor or pharmacist. • This drug should be used cautiously by pregnant women and nursing mothers. • This drug should be used with caution by patients with acute fever, encephalitis, viral infection, intestinal infection, gastroenteritis, dehydration, and electrolyte imbalance (especially by children and the elderly or debilitated). Be sure your doctor knows if you have any of these conditions. • This drug may render diagnosis more difficult in such conditions as appendicitis and obscure signs of toxicity due to overdose of other drugs. • This drug should be discontinued at the first sign of sensitivity to it.

Timoptic ophthalmic solution

Manufacturer: Merck Sharp & Dohme
Ingredient: timolol maleate
Dosage Form: Drop (content per ml): 0.25%; 0.5%
Use: Treatment of some types of chronic glaucoma and ocular hypertension
Minor Side Effects: Mild eye irritation
Major Side Effects: Major side effects are rare when this product is used correctly. However, rare occurrences of anxiety, bronchospasm, confusion, depression, dizziness, drowsiness, generalized rash, indigestion, loss of appe-

tite, nausea, weakness, and slight reduction of the resting heart rate have been observed in some users of this drug.

Contraindications: This drug should not be used by people who are allergic to it. Consult your doctor immediately if this drug has been prescribed for you and you have such an allergy.

Warnings: This drug should be used with caution by people with bronchial asthma, myasthenia gravis, heart disease, or narrow-angle glaucoma. Be sure your doctor knows if you have any of these conditions. • This drug is not recommended for use by children. • This drug should be used cautiously by pregnant women. If you are pregnant, be sure your doctor knows about your condition before you take this drug. • People taking beta blockers should use this drug with caution. If you are presently taking any drugs of this type, consult your doctor about their use. If you are unsure of the type of your medications, ask your doctor or pharmacist.

Comments: This product is also available in a white plastic ophthalmic dispenser with a controlled-drop tip, called an Ocumeter. Your pharmacist can give you details. • Be careful about the contamination of drops used for the eyes. Wash your hands before administering eyedrops. Do not touch the dropper to the eye. Do not wash or wipe the dropper before replacing it in the bottle. Close the bottle tightly to keep out moisture. • This product may sting at first, but this is normal and usually goes away after continued use. Like other eyedrops, this product may cause some clouding or blurring of vision. This symptom will go away quickly. • Unlike other drugs used to treat glaucoma, this agent needs to be administered only twice a day. • See the chapter, Administering Medication Correctly, for instructions on using eyedrops.

Tipramine antidepressant (Major Pharmaceuticals), see Tofranil antidepressant.

Tofranil antidepressant

Manufacturer: GEIGY Pharmaceuticals
Ingredient: imipramine hydrochloride
Equivalent Products: imipramine hydrochloride, various manufacturers; Janimine, Abbott Laboratories; SK-Pramine, Smith Kline & French Laboratories; Tipramine, Major Pharmaceuticals
Dosage Form: Tablet: 10 mg; 25 mg; 50 mg (all coral)
Use: Control of bed-wetting; relief of depression
Minor Side Effects: Agitation; anxiety; black tongue; blurred vision; confusion; constipation; cramps; diarrhea; dizziness; drowsiness; dry mouth; fatigue; flushing; headache; heartburn; increased sensitivity to light; insomnia; loss of appetite; nausea; peculiar tastes; restlessness; stomach upset; sweating; urine color change; vomiting; weakness
Major Side Effects: Bleeding; convulsions; difficult urination; enlarged or painful breasts (in both sexes); fainting; fever; fluid retention; hair loss; hallucinations; heart attack; high or low blood pressure; imbalance; impotence; jaundice; mood changes; mouth sores; nervousness; psychosis; nightmares; numbness in fingers or toes; palpitations; rash; ringing in the ears; sleep disorders; sore throat; stroke; testicular swelling; tremors; uncoordinated movements; weight loss or gain
Contraindications: This drug should not be taken by people who are allergic to it or by anyone who has recently had a heart attack. The drug should not be taken by people who are using monoamine oxidase inhibitors (ask your pharmacist if you are unsure). Consult your doctor immediately if this drug has been prescribed for you and you have any of these conditions.

Warnings: This drug should be used cautiously by the elderly and by people who have glaucoma, high blood pressure, enlarged prostate, porphyria, intestinal blockage, heart disease, epilepsy, thyroid disease, liver or kidney disease, or who have ever had urinary retention problems. Pregnant or nursing women; people who receive electroshock therapy; or those who use drugs that lower blood pressure should also use this drug cautiously. Be sure your doctor knows if you have any of these conditions. • This drug must be used cautiously by children; its safety has not been established for children under six years of age, or for long-term use by children over six years of age. • Notify your doctor if you experience abrupt changes in mood or if you have a sore throat with fever. • If you are going to have any type of surgery, be sure your doctor knows that you are taking this drug; the drug should be discontinued before surgery. (Consult your doctor before stopping the drug.) • This drug interacts with alcohol, amphetamine, barbiturates, central nervous system depressants, clonidine, anticholinergics, epinephrine, guanethidine, methylphenidate hydrochloride, monoamine oxidase inhibitors, oral anticoagulants, and phenylephrine; if you are currently taking any drugs of these types, consult your doctor about their use. If you are unsure of the type or contents of your medications, ask your doctor or pharmacist. • Do not stop taking this drug suddenly without consulting your doctor. It may be necessary to reduce your dosage gradually.

Comments: The effects of therapy with this drug may not be apparent for at least two weeks. • If this drug is being used to control bed-wetting, it should be taken one hour before bedtime. • Chew gum or suck on ice chips or a piece of hard candy to reduce mouth dryness. • Many people receive as much benefit from taking a single dose of this drug at bedtime as from taking multiple doses throughout the day. Talk to your doctor about this dosage plan. • Tofranil antidepressant is also available in capsules that contain larger doses of the drug than the tablets. The capsule form, called Tofranil-PM, should not be used by children because the greater potency increases the risk of overdose. • While taking this drug, do not take any nonprescription item for cough, cold, or sinus problems without first checking with your doctor. • This drug may cause drowsiness; avoid tasks that require alertness. • To prevent oversedation, avoid the use of alcohol or other drugs that have sedative properties. • This drug may cause you to be especially sensitive to the sun, so avoid exposure to sunlight as much as possible. • To avoid dizziness or light-headedness when you stand, contract and relax the muscles of your legs for a few moments before rising. Do this by pushing one foot against the floor while raising the other foot slightly, alternating feet so that you are "pumping" your legs in a pedaling motion. • This drug may be taken with food to lessen stomach upset.

Tofranil-PM antidepressant (GEIGY Pharmaceuticals), see Tofranil antidepressant.

tolbutamide oral antidiabetic (various manufacturers), see Orinase oral antidiabetic.

Tolectin anti-inflammatory

Manufacturer: McNeil Laboratories
Ingredient: tolmetin sodium
Dosage Forms: Capsule: 400 mg (orange). Tablet: 200 mg (white)
Use: Relief of pain and swelling due to arthritis
Minor Side Effects: Bloating; blurred vision; constipation; diarrhea; dizziness; drowsiness; flatulence; headache; heartburn; insomnia; itching; nausea; nervousness; stomach upset; vomiting; weakness

Major Side Effects: Blood in stools; chest pain; depression; difficult breathing; difficult urination; fluid retention; high blood pressure; rash; ringing in the ears; sore throat; ulcers; visual disturbances; weight gain

Contraindications: This drug should not be taken by people who are allergic to it or to aspirin or similar drugs. Consult your doctor immediately if this drug has been prescribed for you and you have such an allergy.

Warnings: This drug should be used with extreme caution by patients with upper gastrointestinal tract disease, peptic ulcer, heart disease, high blood pressure, kidney disease, or bleeding diseases. Be sure your doctor knows if you have any of these conditions. • Persons taking this drug should have regular eye examinations. • Use of this drug by pregnant women, nursing mothers, and children under two years of age is not recommended. • Persons using this drug should have periodic urine tests performed. • This drug should be used cautiously in conjunction with aspirin, diuretics, oral anticoagulants, oral antidiabetics, phenytoin, and probenecid. If you are currently taking any drugs of these types, consult your doctor. If you are unsure of the type or contents of your medications, ask your doctor or pharmacist.

Comments: In numerous tests, this drug has been shown to be as effective as aspirin in the treatment of arthritis, but aspirin is still the drug of choice for the disease. • If you are allergic to aspirin, you may not be able to use this drug. • Do not take aspirin or alcohol while taking this drug without first consulting your doctor. • This drug may cause drowsiness; avoid tasks that require alertness, such as driving and operating machinery. • You should note improvement of your condition soon after you start using this drug; however, full benefit may not be obtained for one to two weeks. It is important not to stop taking this drug even though symptoms have diminished or disappeared. • This drug is not a substitute for rest, physical therapy, or other measures recommended by your doctor to treat your condition. • If this drug upsets your stomach, take it with food or an antacid other than sodium bicarbonate. • Notify your doctor if skin rash, itching, black tarry stools, swelling of the hands or feet, or persistent headache occurs.

Tolinase oral antidiabetic

Manufacturer: The Upjohn Company
Ingredient: tolazamide
Dosage Form: Tablet: 100 mg; 250 mg; 500 mg (all white)
Use: Treatment of diabetes mellitus
Minor Side Effects: Cramps; diarrhea; dizziness; fatigue; gas; headache; heartburn; loss of appetite; nausea; rash; stomach upset; sun sensitivity; vomiting; weakness
Major Side Effects: Blood disorders; bruising; convulsions; difficult breathing; jaundice; low blood sugar; ringing in the ears; sore throat; tingling in the hands or feet; visual disturbances
Contraindications: This drug should not be taken by diabetic patients who have infections, severe trauma, or who are undergoing surgery; who have ketosis, acidosis, or coma or a history of repeated bouts of ketoacidosis or coma. This drug is not indicated for persons with insulin-dependent or "brittle" diabetes. This drug is not to be taken by people with liver disease, kidney disease, endocrine disease, or uremia. Be sure your doctor knows if you have any of these conditions. This drug should not be taken by pregnant women and probably not by women of childbearing age. Be sure your doctor knows if you are pregnant or might become so.
Warnings: Be sure you receive full instructions on how to take this drug and how to control your diabetes. Know how to prevent low blood sugar, recognize its symptoms, and what to do if such a complication occurs. You cannot neglect

your dietary restrictions or disregard instructions about weight, exercise, hygiene, and avoidance of infection. Be sure you know how and when to test your urine. You must be particularly careful during the transition from insulin to this oral antidiabetic. • This drug should be taken with caution when thiazide-type diuretics are also being taken, since such combinations can aggravate diabetes mellitus. • This drug should be used cautiously by persons with malnutrition, debility, advanced age, alcoholism, and adrenal and pituitary gland problems. Be sure your doctor knows if you have any of these conditions. • This drug interacts with alcohol, anabolic steroids, anticoagulants, aspirin, chloramphenicol, guanethidine, monoamine oxidase inhibitors, phenylbutazone, probenecid, propranolol, steroids, sulfonamides, tetracycline, thiazide diuretics, or thyroid hormone. If you are currently taking any drugs of these types, consult your doctor about their use. If you are unsure of the type or contents of your medications, ask your doctor or pharmacist.

Comments: Studies have shown that a good diet and exercise program may be just as effective as oral antidiabetic drugs. However, these drugs allow diabetics a bit more leeway in their lifestyles. Nonetheless, persons taking this drug should carefully watch their diet and exercise program. • Oral antidiabetic drugs are not effective in treating diabetes in children under age 12. • Take the dose of this drug at the same time each day. • Ask your doctor how to recognize the first signs of low blood sugar and how and when to test for glucose and ketones in the urine. • Signs of low blood sugar include cold sweat; chills; drowsiness; cool, pale skin; headache; nausea; rapid pulse; tremors; and weakness. If these signs develop, eat or drink something containing sugar and call your doctor immediately. • During the first six weeks of therapy with this drug, visit your doctor at least once a week. • You will have to be switched to insulin therapy if complications (e.g., ketoacidosis, severe trauma, severe infection, diarrhea, nausea, or vomiting) or the need for major surgery develop. • Do not use alcohol while taking this drug. Avoid any other drugs unless your doctor tells you to take them. Be especially careful of nonprescription cold remedies. • You may sunburn easily while taking this product. Avoid prolonged exposure to the sun and wear a protective sunscreen. • It is advised that you carry a medical alert card or wear a medical alert bracelet indicating that you take this drug.

Totacillin antibiotic (Beecham Laboratories), see ampicillin antibiotic.

Tranmep sedative and hypnotic (Reid-Provident Labs., Inc.), see meprobamate sedative and hypnotic.

Tranquigesic analgesic (Goldline Laboratories), see Equagesic analgesic.

Transderm-Nitro anti-anginal

Manufacturer: CIBA Pharmaceutical Company
Ingredient: nitroglycerin
Dosage Form: Transdermal system: various strengths
Equivalent Products: Nitrodisc, Searle & Co.; Nitro-Dur, Key Pharmaceuticals, Inc.
Use: Prevention of angina attacks
Minor Side Effects: Dizziness; flushing of face; headache; lightheadedness; nausea, skin irritation

Major Side Effects: Blurred vision; fainting; skin rash; vomiting; weakness

Contraindications: This product should not be used by people who are allergic to nitrates or who have anemia, certain types of glaucoma, or head injuries. Consult your doctor if this drug has been prescribed for you and you have any of these conditions.

Warnings: This drug should be used with caution by people who have had a recent heart attack or those with severe heart failure. Be sure your doctor knows if you fit into either category. • If you develop blurred vision or a rash, contact your doctor.

Comments: Side effects generally disappear after two to three weeks of continued therapy. • To avoid dizziness or light-headedness, avoid abrupt changes in position. When you stand, contract and relax the muscles of your legs for a few moments before rising. Do this by pushing one foot against the floor while raising the other foot slightly, alternating feet so that you are "pumping" your legs in a pedaling motion. • Do not drink alcohol unless your doctor has told you that you may. • This drug is supplied as a transdermal patch. Each patch is designed to continually release nitroglycerin over a 24-hour period. It may be necessary to clip hair prior to using these patches; hair may interfere with patch adhesion. • Do not apply patch to lower parts of arms or legs. Application sites should be changed slightly with each use to avoid skin irritation. Avoid placing patch on irritated or damaged skin. • One can shower or bathe while the patch is in place. If it loosens, a new patch should be used. • It is recommended that you apply a new patch 30 minutes before removing the old one. This will ensure constant protection. • Store the patches in a cool, dry place. Do not refrigerate. • Patient Instructions for application of these patches are available. Ask your pharmacist for them if they are not provided with your prescription. For maximum benefit, read and follow the instructions carefully.

Tranxene sedative and hypnotic

Manufacturer: Abbott Laboratories

Ingredient: clorazepate dipotassium

Dosage Forms: Tablet: 3.75 mg (blue); 7.5 mg (peach); 15 mg (lavender). Capsule: 3.75 mg (gray/white); 7.5 mg (gray/maroon); 15 mg (gray). Sustained-action tablet: 11.25 mg (blue); 22.5 mg (tan)

Use: Relief of anxiety, nervousness, tension; withdrawal from alcohol addiction

Minor Side Effects: Confusion; constipation; diarrhea; dizziness; drooling; drowsiness; dry mouth; fatigue; headache; heartburn; insomnia; irritability; loss of appetite; nausea; nervousness; sweating; vomiting

Major Side Effects: Blurred vision; depression; difficult breathing; difficult swallowing; difficult urination; double vision; fever; hallucinations; jaundice; low blood pressure; menstrual irregularities; palpitations; rash; slow heartbeat; slurred speech; sore throat; tremors

Contraindications: This drug should not be taken by people who are allergic to it or who have acute narrow-angle glaucoma. Consult your doctor immediately if this drug has been prescribed for you and you have such an allergy or condition.

Warnings: This drug is not recommended for use by people who are severely depressed; those who have severe mental illnesses; or people under the age of nine. This drug should be used cautiously by people with a history of drug dependence; pregnant women; nursing mothers; the elderly or debilitated; and people with impaired liver or kidney function, lung disease, epilepsy, porphyria, or myasthenia gravis. Be sure your doctor knows if you fit into any of these categories. • This drug may cause drowsiness; avoid tasks that require alertness, such as driving a car or operating machinery. • This drug should not be taken with alcohol or other central nervous system depressants. This drug should be used cautiously in conjunction with cimetidine, phenytoin, or oral anticoagulants. Taken alone, this drug is safe; when it is combined with alcohol or other sedative drugs, serious adverse reactions may develop. If you are currently taking any drugs of this type, consult your doctor about their use. If you are unsure about the type or contents of your medications, ask your doctor or pharmacist. • This drug has the potential for abuse and must be used with caution. Tolerance may develop quickly; do not increase the dose without first consulting your doctor. • Do not stop taking this drug suddenly without first consulting your doctor. If you have been taking this drug regularly, your dosage will have to be reduced gradually according to your doctor's directions. • If you take this drug for long periods, you may need to have periodic blood counts and liver function tests.

Comments: This drug currently is used by many people to relieve nervousness. It is effective for this purpose, but it is important to try to remove the cause of the anxiety as well. • This drug may cause dryness of the mouth. To reduce this feeling, chew gum or suck on ice chips or a piece of hard candy. • Do not stop taking this drug suddenly. • Never take the sustained-action tablets more frequently than your doctor prescribes. A serious overdose may result. • Take this medication with food or a full glass of water to lessen stomach upset. Do not take it with an antacid; it may retard absorption of the drug.

Trates Granucaps anti-anginal (Reid-Provident Labs., Inc.), see Nitro-Bid anti-anginal.

trazodone antidepressant (various manufacturers), see Desyrel antidepressant.

Tremin antiparkinson drug (Schering Corp.), see Artane anti-parkinson drug.

Triacet steroid hormone (Lemmon Company), see Aristocort and Kenalog steroid hormones.

Triacin C expectorant (various manufacturers), see Actifed-C expectorant.

triamcinolone acetonide steroid hormone (various manufacturers), see Aristocort and Kenalog steroid hormones.

triamcinolone, neomycin, gramicidin, and nystatin topical steroid hormone and anti-infective (various manufacturers), see Mycolog topical steroid hormone and anti-infective.

Triamterene with hydrochlorothiazide diuretic and anti-hypertensive (various manufacturers), see Dyazide diuretic and antihypertensive.

Triavil phenothiazine and antidepressant

Manufacturer: Merck Sharp & Dohme

Ingredients: amitriptyline hydrochloride; perphenazine
Equivalent Product: Etrafon, Schering Corp.
Dosage Forms: Tablet 2-10: amitriptyline hydrochloride, 10 mg; perphenazine, 2 mg (blue). Tablet 2-25: amitriptyline hydrochloride, 25 mg; perphenazine, 2 mg (orange). Tablet 4-10: amitriptyline hydrochloride, 10 mg; perphenazine, 4 mg (salmon). Tablet 4-25: amitriptyline hydrochloride, 25 mg; perphenazine, 4 mg (yellow). Tablet 4-50: amitriptyline hydrochloride, 50 mg; perphenazine, 4 mg (orange)
Use: Relief of anxiety or depression
Minor Side Effects: Blurred vision; change in urine color; confusion; constipation; decreased sweating; diarrhea; dizziness; drooling; drowsiness; dry mouth; excitement; fatigue; headache; heartburn; increased salivation; jitteriness; loss of appetite; menstrual irregularities; nasal congestion; nausea; peculiar taste in mouth; restlessness; skin darkening; sun sensitivity; vomiting; weakness
Major Side Effects: Aching or numbness in arms or legs; chest pain; convulsions; difficult urination; enlarged or painful breasts in men or women; eye pain; fainting; fluid retention; hair loss; high or low blood pressure; high or low blood sugar; imbalance; impotence; insomnia; involuntary movements of the face, mouth, jaw, and tongue; jaundice; mouth sores; muscle stiffness; nervousness; nightmares; palpitations; rash; ringing in the ears; sore throat; stroke; swelling of the testicles; tremors; weight gain or loss
Contraindications: This drug should not be taken by persons with drug-induced depression, recent heart attack, or blood disease. This drug should not be taken by people who are allergic to either of its components or by those taking monoamine oxidase inhibitors. Consult your doctor immediately if this drug has been prescribed for you and you have any of these conditions or such an allergy.
Warnings: This drug should be used with caution by persons with thyroid disease, certain types of glaucoma, impaired liver function, certain types of heart disease, epilepsy, difficult urination, intestinal blockage, high or low blood pressure, diabetes, brain disease, Parkinson's disease, peptic ulcer, enlarged prostate, breast cancer, or asthma and other respiratory disorders. Be sure your doctor knows if you have any of these conditions. • This drug may cause drowsiness; avoid tasks requiring alertness, such as driving a motor vehicle or operating machinery. • To prevent oversedation, avoid the use of alcohol or other drugs with sedative properties. • This drug is not recommended for use by pregnant women or by children. • Use of this drug may cause mood changes and a rise in body temperature. Call your doctor if you experience either. • This drug should be used with caution by persons undergoing elective surgery and electroshock therapy. • This drug has been shown to result in both elevation and lowering of blood sugar levels. This drug should not be administered in large amounts. • This drug should not be taken with alcohol, amphetamine, barbiturates, epinephrine, guanethidine, monoamine oxidase inhibitors, oral anticoagulants, phenylephrine, antacids, ethchlorvynol, anticholinergics, central nervous system depressants, or clonidine. If you are currently taking any drugs of these types, consult your doctor about their use. If you are unsure of the type or contents of your medications, ask your doctor or pharmacist. • Take this drug exactly as directed; an overdose could be fatal. • This drug may interfere with certain laboratory tests. Remind your doctor you are taking this drug before undergoing any tests.
Comments: The effects of this drug may not be apparent for at least two weeks. • While taking this drug, avoid using alcohol, and do not start or stop taking any other drug, including nonprescription items, without consulting your doctor. • This drug may cause dryness of the mouth. To reduce this feeling, chew gum or suck on ice chips or a piece of hard candy. • This drug may make

you more sensitive to sunlight. Avoid prolonged exposure to the sun and wear a protective sunscreen lotion. • To avoid dizziness or light-headedness when you stand, contract and relax the muscles of your legs for a few moments before rising. Do this by pushing one foot against the floor while raising the other foot slightly, alternating feet so that you are "pumping" your legs in a pedaling motion. • This drug may cause tumors in rats. This effect has not been shown to occur in humans. • If you notice fine tremors of your tongue, call your doctor. • Antacids may prevent the absorption of this drug. Don't take them at the same time as you take this drug. • If this drug causes stomach upset, you may take it with food or milk

triazolam sedative and hypnotic (various manufacturers) see Halcion sedative and hypnotic.

Triderm steroid hormone (Del-Ray Laboratories, Inc.), see Kenalog steroid hormone.

Trifed-C expectorant (Geneva Generics, Inc.), see Actifed-C expectorant.

Trihexane antiparkinson drug (Rugby Laboratories), see Artane antiparkinson drug.

Trihexidyl antiparkinson drug (Henry Schein, Inc.), see Artane antiparkinson drug.

Trihexy antiparkinson drug (Geneva Generics, Inc.), see Artane antiparkinson drug.

trihexyphenidyl hydrochloride antiparkinson drug (various manufacturers), see Artane antiparkinson drug.

Tri-Hydroserpine diuretic and antihypertensive (Rugby Laboratories), see Ser-Ap-Es diuretic and antihypertensive.

trimethobenzamide antinauseant (various manufacturers), see Tigan antinauseant.

Trimox antibiotic (E. R. Squibb & Sons, Inc.), see amoxicillin antibiotic.

Trinalin antihistamine and decongestant

Manufacturer: Schering Corp.
Ingredients: pseudoephedrine sulfate; azatadine maleate
Dosage Form: Sustained-release tablet: pseudoephedrine sulfate, 120 mg, azatadine maleate, 1 mg
Use: For the relief of nasal and upper respiratory congestion
Minor Side Effects: Anxiety; blurred vision; constipation; diarrhea; dizziness; drowsiness; dry mouth; headache; insomnia; irritability; nausea; rash; reduced sweating; sedation; stomach upset; weakness
Major Side Effects: Abdominal cramps; chest pain; confusion; difficulty

breathing; difficulty urinating; headache; high blood pressure; loss of coordination; low blood pressure; palpitations; sore throat; unusual bleeding or
bruising

Contraindications: This drug should not be used to treat asthma or symptoms of lower respiratory infections. This drug should not be taken by persons
allergic to it or to other antihistamines. If you are allergic to antihistamines,
check with your doctor or pharmacist before taking this drug. This drug should
not be used by persons with narrow-angle glaucoma, urinary retention, hyperthyroidism, severe hypertension, severe heart disease, or by persons concurrently taking monoamine oxidase inhibitors (ask your pharmacist if you are
unsure). Consult your doctor immediately if this drug has been prescribed for
you and you have any of these conditions. This drug should not be taken by
children under 12 years of age. This drug should be used during pregnancy only
if the benefits outweigh the risks. Discuss this with your doctor. Use of this drug
by nursing mothers is not recommended.

Warnings: This drug should be used cautiously by persons with peptic ulcer,
blood vessel disease, high blood pressure, diabetes, or by persons taking
digitalis or oral anticoagulants. If you are unsure of the medicines you are
taking, consult your doctor or pharmacist. ● Because this drug causes drowsiness, avoid tasks that require alertness. Persons over 60 years of age may be
more likely to experience dizziness, sedation and low blood pressure. Therefore, this drug must be used cautiously. To prevent oversedation, avoid the use
of alcohol and other drugs having sedative properties.

Comments: Because this is a sustained-release product, the tablets must be
swallowed whole; do not crush or chew them. ● Never increase your dose or
take it more frequently than prescribed, as a serious overdose could result. ● To
relieve dry mouth, chew gum or suck on ice chips or hard candy. ● While taking
this drug, do not take any nonprescription medicine for cough, cold, or sinus
problems without first checking with your doctor or pharmacist.

**Tri-Phen antihistamine and decongestant (Bay Pharmaceuticals,
Inc.), see Dimetapp antihistamine and decongestant.**

**Tri-Phen-Chlor adrenergic and antihistamine (Rugby Laboratories),
see Naldecon adrenergic and antihistamine.**

**Triple Sulfa vaginal anti-infective (various manufacturers), see Sul-
trin vaginal anti-infective.**

**Tri-Statin topical steroid hormone and anti-infective (Rugby Labo-
ratories), see Mycolog topical steroid hormone and anti-infective.**

**Truphylline bronchodilator (G & W Laboratories, Inc.), see amino-
phylline bronchodilator.**

**Trymex steroid hormone (Savage Laboratories), see Kenalog ste-
roid hormone.**

**Trysul vaginal anti-infective (Savage Laboratories), see Sultrin va-
ginal anti-infective.**

**Tudecon adrenergic and antihistamine (Reid-Provident Labs., Inc.),
see Naldecon adrenergic and antihistamine.**

Tuss-genade antihistamine and adrenergic (Goldline Laboratories), see Ornade Spansule antihistamine and adrenergic.

Tylenol with Codeine analgesic (McNeil Laboratories), see acetaminophen with codeine analgesic.

Ultracef antibiotic (Bristol Laboratories), see Duricef antibiotic.

Unifast Unicelles anorectic (Reid-Provident Labs., Inc.), see Fastin anorectic.

Uniphyl bronchodilator (Purdue Frederick), see Theo-dur bronchodilator.

Unipres diuretic and antihypertensive (Reid-Provident Labs., Inc.), see Ser-Ap-Es diuretic and antihypertensive.

Urobak antibacterial (Shionogi USA), see Gantanol antibacterial.

Uticillin VK antibiotic (The Upjohn Company), see penicillin potassium phenoxymethyl (penicillin VK) antibiotic.

Utimox antibiotic (Parke-Davis), see amoxicillin antibiotic.

Valisone steroid hormone

Manufacturer: Schering Corp.

Ingredient: betamethasone valerate

Equivalent Products: betamethasone valerate, various manufacturers; Betatrex, Savage Laboratories; Beta-Val, Lemmon Company

Dosage Forms: Aerosol spray: 0.15%. Cream: 0.01%; 0.1%. Lotion: 0,1%. Ointment: 0.1%

Use: Relief of skin inflammation associated with conditions such as dermatitis, eczema, or poison ivy

Minor Side Effects: Acne; burning sensation; dryness; irritation of the affected area; itching; rash

Major Side Effects: Blistering; increased hair growth; loss of skin color; secondary infection; skin wasting

Contraindications: This drug should not be used by people who are allergic to it. This drug should not be used by those with severe circulatory system disorders or infections of the skin. This drug should not be used in the ear if the eardrum is perforated. Consult your doctor immediately if this drug has been prescribed for you and you have any of these conditions.

Warnings: If irritation develops when using this drug, immediately discontinue its use and notify your doctor. • This drug should be used with caution during pregnancy. • These products are not for use in the eyes or other mucous membranes. • Systemic absorption of this drug will be increased if extensive areas of the body are treated, particularly if occlusive bandages are used. Therefore, suitable precautions should be taken under this circumstance and under long-term use, particularly in children and infants. • This drug should not be used in the presence of infection.

Comments: Use this drug exactly as prescribed. Do not use it more often or for a longer period than your doctor prescribed. • When the spray is used about the face, cover the eyes and do not inhale the spray. • The spray produces a cooling sensation which may be uncomfortable for some people. • The spray form is packed under pressure. Do not puncture the container or store near heat or open flame. • When using the spray form, avoid freezing of the tissue by not spraying for more than three seconds and by spraying at a distance of not less than six inches. • If the affected area is extremely dry or is scaling, the skin may be moistened before applying the medication by soaking in water or by applying water with a clean cloth. The ointment form is probably better for dry skin. • A mild, temporary stinging sensation may occur after this medication is applied. If this persists, contact your physician. • Do not use this product with an occlusive wrap unless your doctor directs you to do so. If it is necessary for you to use this drug under a wrap, follow your doctor's instructions exactly; do not leave the wrap in place longer than specified. • If the condition being treated worsens while using this drug, notify your doctor.

Valium sedative and hypnotic

Manufacturer: Roche Products, Inc.
Ingredient: diazepam
Equivalent Product: diazepam, Mylan Laboratories; Parke-Davis; Zenith Laboratories, Inc.
Dosage Form: Tablet: 2 mg (white); 5 mg (yellow); 10 mg (blue). Capsules, sustained-release: 15 mg (yellow/blue)
Use: Relief of anxiety, nervousness, tension; relief of muscle spasms; withdrawal from alcohol addiction
Minor Side Effects: Confusion; constipation; depression; diarrhea; dizziness; drowsiness; dry mouth; excess saliva; fatigue; headache; heartburn; loss of appetite; nausea; sweating; vomiting; weakness
Major Side Effects: Blurred vision; difficult breathing; difficult urination; double vision; excitement; fever; hallucinations; jaundice; low blood pressure; menstrual irregularities; palpitations; rash; slurred speech; sore throat; stimulation; tremors; uncoordinated movements
Contraindications: This drug should not be given to children under six months of age. This drug should not be taken by persons with certain types of glaucoma. This drug should not be taken by people who are allergic to it. Consult your doctor immediately if you have glaucoma or such an allergy.
Warnings: This drug is not recommended for use by people with severe mental illness. This drug should be used cautiously by people with epilepsy, respiratory problems, myasthenia gravis, porphyria, a history of drug abuse, or impaired liver or kidney function; pregnant women; and the elderly or debilitated. Be sure your doctor knows if you fit into any of these categories. • This drug may cause drowsiness; avoid tasks that require alertness. • This drug should not be taken simultaneously with alcohol or other central nervous system depressants. Taken alone, this drug is safe; when it is combined with alcohol or other sedative drugs, serious adverse reactions may develop. • This drug should be used cautiously in conjunction with cimetidine, oral anticoagulants, and phenytoin. • Do not stop taking this drug without informing your doctor. If you have been taking the drug regularly and wish to discontinue the drug's use, you must decrease the dose gradually, following your doctor's instructions. • This drug has the potential for abuse and must be used with caution. Tolerance may develop quickly; do not increase the dose without first consulting your doctor. • Persons taking this drug should have periodic blood counts and liver function tests.
Comments: This drug currently is used by many people to relieve nervousness. It is effective for this purpose, but it is important to try to remove the cause of the anxiety as well. • This drug may cause dryness of the mouth. To reduce this feeling, chew gum or suck on ice chips or a piece of hard candy. • To lessen

CONSUMER GUIDE®

stomach upset, take with food or a full glass of water. • The sustained-release form must be swallowed whole. Do not crush or chew the capsule.

Vanatal sedative and anticholinergic (Vangard Laboratories), see Donnatal sedative and anticholinergic.

Vanceril anti-asthmatic

Manufacturer: Schering Corp.
Ingredient: beclomethasone dipropionate
Equivalent Product: Beclovent, Glaxo, Inc.
Dosage Form: Pressurized inhaler for oral use (content per one actuation from mouthpiece): 42 mcg
Use: Symptomatic treatment of chronic asthma
Minor Side Effects: Bronchospasm; coughing; dry mouth; hoarseness; rash
Major Side Effects: Difficult breathing; nosebleeds; sore throat or infections of the mouth or throat
Contraindications: This drug is a steroid. It should not be used in the primary treatment of severe asthma attacks where intensive measures are required. This drug should not be used by people who are allergic to it or by those who have reacted adversely to other steroids.
Warnings: If you have been taking oral steroids to control your asthma, conversion to therapy with this inhaled drug will have to be accomplished slowly. You will have to exercise special caution if you develop an infection, need to have surgery, or experience other trauma. Talk with your doctor about this transition, and make sure you understand what is necessary to do. You should carry a card with you that explains how your asthma is being treated in case an emergency arises and you are unable to explain it yourself. • Pregnant women, nursing mothers, women of childbearing age, and children under the age of six should use this drug with caution. Consult your doctor immediately if this drug has been prescribed for you and you fit into any of these categories. • This drug is not for rapid relief of bronchospasm. If you have a bronchospasm and your dilator drugs do not help, call your doctor. • The dosage of this drug should be monitored very carefully. Taking more of this drug than is recommended will probably not give you more relief over the long term. • This drug may have to be discontinued if localized infections occur.
Comments: Take this drug exactly as prescribed. Do not use more often than prescribed. Full benefit from this drug may be apparent only after two to four weeks. • Shake the canister well before use. • Your pharmacist should dispense patient instructions with this drug to explain administration technique. • If you use a bronchodilator with this drug, use the bronchodilator first, wait a few minutes, then use this drug. This use has been shown to be the most effective with the least potential for toxicity. • The contents of one canister of this drug should provide at least 200 oral inhalations. • This drug is sealed in the canister under pressure. Do not puncture the canister. Do not store the canister near heat or an open flame. • Rinsing the mouth after inhalation of this drug is advised to reduce irritation and dryness of mouth and throat.

Vasocap-150 vasodilator and smooth muscle relaxant (Keene Pharmaceuticals, Inc.), see Pavabid Plateau Caps vasodilator and smooth muscle relaxant.

Vasospan vasodilator and smooth muscle relaxant (Ulmer Pharmacal Co.), see Pavabid Plateau Caps vasodilator and smooth muscle relaxant.

V-Cillin K antibiotic (Eli Lilly & Co.), see penicillin potassium phen-oxymethyl (penicillin VK) antibiotic.

Veetids antibiotic (E. R. Squibb & Sons, Inc.), see penicillin po-tassium phenoxymethyl (penicillin VK) antibiotic.

Veltap antihistamine and decongestant (The Lannett Company, Inc.), see Dimetapp antihistamine and decongestant.

Ventolin bronchodilator

Manufacturer: Glaxo, Inc.
Ingredient: albuterol
Equivalent Product: Proventil, Schering Corp.
Dosage Forms: Tablet: 2 mg (white); 4 mg (white); Inhaler
Use: Treatment of bronchial asthma, bronchitis, and emphysema
Minor Side Effects: Dizziness; dry mouth and throat; headache; increased blood pressure; nausea; nervousness; restlessness; stomach upset; unusual taste in mouth
Major Side Effects: Chest pain; flushing; irritability; mental confusion; muscle cramps; palpitations; trembling; vomiting; weakness
Contraindications: This drug should not be used by people who are allergic to it.
Warnings: This drug should be used with caution by people with diabetes, high blood pressure, or thyroid disease; and by pregnant or nursing women. Be sure your doctor knows if you belong in one of these groups. • This drug has been shown to interact with amphetamines, monoamine oxidase inhibitors, antidepressants, beta blockers, and epinephrine. If you are currently using any of these types of medicines, consult your doctor. If you are unsure of the type or contents of your medications, ask your doctor or pharmacist.
Comments: Take this drug as prescribed. Do not take it more often than prescribed without first consulting your doctor. Excessive use of the inhaler may lead to loss of effectiveness or adverse effects. • If two inhalations per dose are prescribed, wait at least one minute between inhalations for maximum effec-tiveness. • If your symptoms do not improve or if they get worse while using this drug, contact your doctor. • To help relieve dry mouth, chew gum, or suck on ice chips or hard candy. • If stomach upset occurs, take the tablets with food or milk. • Make sure you know how to use the inhaler form properly. Ask your pharmacist for the instructional sheet on use of the inhaler. Keep spray away from eyes. Store away from heat or open flame. Do not puncture, break, or burn the container.

Vibramycin antibiotic

Manufacturer: Pfizer Laboratories Division
Ingredient: doxycycline hyclate
Equivalent Products: Doxy-Caps, Barr and Edwards Co.; Doxychel, Rachelle Laboratories, Inc.; doxycycline hyclate, various manufacturers; Doxy-Lemmon, Lemmon Company; Doxy-Tabs, Barr Laboratories; Vibra-Tabs, Pfizer Laboratories Division
Dosage Forms: Capsule: 50 mg (blue/white); 100 mg (blue). Suspension (content per 5 ml teaspoon): 25 mg. Syrup (content per 5 ml teaspoon): 50 mg. Tablet: 100 mg (orange)

Use: Treatment of a wide variety of bacterial infections

Minor Side Effects: Diarrhea; discoloration of the nails; increased sensitivity to light; loss of appetite; nausea; stomach upset; vomiting

Major Side Effects: Anemia; blood disorders, difficult breathing; difficult swallowing; mouth irritation; rash; sore throat; rectal and vaginal itching; stomach cramps; superinfection

Contraindications: This drug should not be taken by people who are allergic to any tetracycline drug. Consult your doctor immediately if this drug has been prescribed for you and you have such an allergy.

Warnings: This drug may cause permanent discoloration of the teeth if used during tooth development; therefore, it should be used cautiously by pregnant or nursing women and infants and children under nine years of age. This drug should also be used cautiously by those with diabetes or kidney or liver disease.
• Prolonged use of this drug may allow organisms that are not susceptible to it to grow wildly. Do not use this drug unless your doctor has specifically told you to do so. Be sure to follow directions carefully and report any unusual reactions to your doctor at once. • Complete blood cell counts and liver and kidney function tests should be done if you take this drug for a prolonged period. • This drug interacts with penicillin, barbiturates, carbamazepine, diuretics, lithium, oral contraceptives, and phenytoin; if you are currently taking any of these drugs, consult your doctor about their use. If you are unsure of the type or contents of your medications, ask your doctor or pharmacist. • Milk and other dairy products interfere with the body's absorption of this drug, so separate taking this drug and any dairy product by at least two hours. Do not take this drug at the same time as any iron preparation; their use should be separated by at least two hours. Do not take this drug within three hours of taking an antacid.
• This drug may cause you to be especially sensitive to the sun, so avoid exposure to sunlight as much as possible. • This drug may affect syphilis tests; if you are being treated for this disease, make sure that your doctor knows you are taking this drug. • If you are taking an anticoagulant in addition to this drug, remind your doctor.

Comments: Take this drug on an empty stomach (one hour before or two hours after a meal). Take it with at least eight ounces of water. If the drug upsets your stomach, you may take your dose with food. • The syrup form of this drug should be shaken well before use. • Any unused medication should be discarded. • When used to treat strep throat, this drug should be taken for at least ten full days, even if symptoms disappear within that time.

Vibra Tabs antibiotic (Pfizer Laboratories Division), see Vibramycin antibiotic.

Viodo HC steroid hormone and anti-infective (NMC Laboratories), see Vioform-Hydrocortisone steroid hormone and anti-infective.

Vioform-Hydrocortisone
steroid hormone and anti-infective

Manufacturer: CIBA Pharmaceutical Company

Ingredients: hydrocortisone; iodochlorhydroxyquin

Equivalent Products: AP Creme, T.E. Edwards Co.; Caquin, Forest Pharmaceuticals; Corque, Geneva Generics, Inc.; Cortin, C & M Pharmacal, Inc.; HC-Form, Rescei Laboratories; hydrocortisone with iodochlorhydroxyquin, various manufacturers; Hysone, Mallard, Inc.; Iodocort, Ulmer Pharmacal Co.; Lanvisone, The Lannett Company, Inc.; Mity-Quin, Reid-Provident Labs., Inc.;

Pedi-Cort V, Pedinol Pharmacal, Inc.; Racet, Lemmon Company; Viodo HC, NMC Laboratories; Vioquin-HC, Scott-Alison Pharmaceuticals, Inc.; Viotag, Tutag Pharmaceuticals, Inc.

Dosage Forms: Cream; Jelly; Lotion; Ointment: hydrocortisone, 1%; 0.5%; iodochlorhydroxyquin, 3%

Use: Symptomatic relief of skin inflammation associated with such conditions as dermatitis, eczema

Minor Side Effects: Dryness; irritation; rash

Major Side Effects: Blistering; burning; increased hair growth; loss of skin color; redness; secondary infection; skin wasting; swelling

Contraindications: This drug should not be used by people who are allergic to any of its components or to related compounds. The drug should not be used in the eye or to treat tuberculosis of the skin or viral or fungal skin disease. Consult your doctor immediately if this drug has been prescribed for you and you have any of these conditions.

Warnings: This drug should be used cautiously by pregnant women. ● Notify your doctor if irritation develops. ● Prolonged or excessive use may result in secondary infection. ● If it is necessary for you to use this drug under a wrap, follow your doctor's instructions exactly; do not leave the wrap in place longer than specified. Do not use a wrap unless directed to do so by your doctor. ● This product may affect the results of thyroid function tests; if you are scheduled to have such a test, be sure your doctor knows that you are using this drug.

Comments: Apply this product as thinly as possible to the skin. ● The cream form of this drug is better than the ointment for use on the scalp or other hairy areas of the body. ● The ointment form of the drug is preferable for people with dry skin. ● If the affected area is extremely dry or is scaling, the skin may be moistened before applying the medication by soaking in water or by applying water with a clean cloth. ● Continue using this medication for as long as prescribed even if symptoms have disappeared.

Vioquin-HC steroid hormone and anti-infective (Scott-Alison Pharmaceuticals, Inc.), see Vioform-Hydrocortisone steroid hormone and anti-infective.

Viotag steroid hormone and anti-infective (Tutag Pharmaceuticals, Inc.), see Vioform-Hydrocortisone steroid hormone and anti-infective.

Vistaril sedative (Pfizer Laboratories Division), see Atarax sedative.

Westapp antihistamine and decongestant (Western Pharmacal Co.), see Dimetapp antihistamine and decongestant.

Wigraine migraine remedy (Organon Pharmaceuticals), see Cafergot migraine remedy.

Wilpowr anorectic (Foy Laboratories), see Fastin anorectic.

Wyamycin antibiotic (Wyeth Laboratories), see erythromycin antibiotic.

Wymox antibiotic (Wyeth Laboratories), see amoxicillin antibiotic.

Xanax antianxiety

Manufacturer: The Upjohn Company
Ingredient: alprazolam
Dosage Form: Tablet: 0.25 mg (white); 0.5 mg (peach); 1 mg (lavender)
Use: Relief of anxiety disorders and anxiety associated with depression
Minor Side Effects: Blurred vision; constipation; diarrhea; dizziness; drowsiness; dry mouth; fatigue; headache; irritability; nervousness; stomach pains; weakness
Major Side Effects: Clumsiness; depression; difficulty breathing; difficulty urinating; hallucinations; mental confusion; nervousness; rapid heartbeat; shakiness; skin rash; slurred speech; sore throat; trouble sleeping; uncoordinated movements
Contraindications: This drug should not be used by persons allergic to it or those with acute narrow-angle glaucoma. Consult your doctor immediately if this drug has been prescription for you and you have such a condition. This drug should not be used in the treatment of psychotic patients.
Warnings: This drug should be used cautiously by pregnant or nursing women, elderly people, children, or people with a history of kidney or liver disease. Be sure your doctor knows if you fit into any of these categories. • To prevent oversedation, avoid the use of alcohol or other drugs with sedative properties. • This drug may cause drowsiness; avoid tasks that require alertness. • Do not stop taking this drug suddenly without first consulting your doctor. If you have been taking this drug for a long period of time, your dosage should gradually be reduced, according to your physician's directions. • This drug should be used cautiously with psychotropic medications, pain medications, anticonvulsants, antihistamines, alcohol, or other central nervous system depressants. If you are currently taking any drugs of these types, consult your doctor about their use. If you are unsure of the type or content of your medications, ask your doctor or pharmacist. • This drug has the potential for abuse and must be used with caution. • Tolerance may develop; do not increase the dose of this medication without first consulting your doctor.
Comments: This drug is currently used by many people to relieve anxiety. Although it is effective for this purpose, it is important to try to remove the cause of the anxiety as well. • This drug may cause a dry mouth. To reduce this feeling, chew gum or suck on ice chips or hard candy.

Zantac antisecretory

Manufacturer: Glaxo, Inc.
Ingredient: ranitidine
Dosage Form: Tablet: 150 mg (white)
Use: Treatment of duodenal ulcer and hypersecretory conditions
Minor Side Effects: Constipation; decreased sexual ability; depression; diarrhea; dizziness; headache; insomnia; nausea; sedation; stomach upset
Major Side Effects: Agitation; blood disorders; confusion; palpitations; rash; weakness; weak pulse
Contraindications: This drug should not be taken by anyone who is allergic to it.
Warnings: This drug must be used with caution by pregnant and nursing women and elderly people. It should be used with caution by people with liver and kidney diseases. If this drug has been prescribed for you and you fit into any of these categories, consult your physician. • Safety of this drug for use in children has not yet been established. Therefore, it is not recommended for children under 12. • This drug has not been shown to affect the concurrent use

of other medications. However, check with your doctor or pharmacist before taking any other drugs.

Comments: This drug must be taken continuously for as long as your physician prescribes. Stopping therapy early may be a cause of ineffective treatment. • This drug may be used in conjunction with antacids, to relieve pain.

Zepine antihypertensive (Foy Laboratories), see reserpine antihypertensive.

Zide diuretic and antihypertensive (Reid-Provident Labs., Inc.), see hydrochlorothiazide diuretic and antihypertensive.

Zovirax topical antiviral

Manufacturer: Burroughs Wellcome Co.
Ingredient: acyclovir
Dosage Form: Ointment: 5%
Use: Management of genital herpes and herpes infections of the skin
Minor Side Effects: Temporary pain, burning, stinging, itching or rash after application
Major Side Effects: None
Contraindications: This drug should not be used by anyone who is allergic to it. Consult your doctor immediately if this drug has been prescribed for you and you have such an allergy.
Warnings: This drug is intended for use on the skin only and should not be used in the eyes. • This drug should be used cautiously by pregnant women, and only when the benefits outweigh the risks. • Nursing women should also use Zovirax with caution, since it is not known whether or not the drug passes into breast milk.
Comments: This drug will not cure a herpes infection but may relieve pain associated with the viral infection and may shorten its duration. • Apply this drug as soon as possible after symptoms of a herpes infection begin and use a rubber glove to apply the ointment in order to avoid spreading the infection. • To achieve full effect, this drug must be used as prescribed. Continue using it for the prescribed period even if symptoms disappear before that time. • This drug may cause temporary burning, itching, and stinging. Notify your doctor if these symptoms worsen or persist. • This drug should be stored in a cool, dry place.

Zoxaphen analgesic (Mallard, Inc.), see Parafon Forte analgesic.

Zyloprim gout drug

Manufacturer: Burroughs Wellcome Co.
Ingredient: allopurinol
Equivalent Products: allopurinol, various manufacturers; Lopurin, Boots Pharmaceuticals, Inc.
Dosage Form: Tablet: 100 mg (white); 300 mg (peach)
Use: Treatment of gout
Minor Side Effects: Diarrhea; drowsiness; nausea; stomach upset; vomiting

Major Side Effects: Blood disorders; bruising; chills; fatigue; fever; kidney or liver damage; loss of hair; muscle ache; numbness or tingling sensations; paleness; rash; sore throat; visual disturbances

Contraindications: This drug should not be used by children, with the exception of those children with cancer; nursing mothers; or persons who have had a severe reaction to it. Consult your doctor immediately if this drug has been prescribed for you and you fit any of these categories.

Warnings: This drug should be discontinued at the first sign of skin rash or any sign of adverse reaction. Notify your doctor immediately if reactions occur. • This drug should be used with caution by pregnant women; persons with blood disease, liver disease, or kidney disease; or people receiving other gout drugs. Be sure your doctor knows if you fit any of these categories. • Some investigators have reported an increase in gout attacks during the early stages of use of this drug. • Drowsiness may occur as a result of using this drug; avoid tasks that require alertness. • Periodic determination of liver and kidney function and complete blood counts should be performed during therapy with this drug, especially during the first few months of therapy. • Iron salts should not be given simultaneously with this drug. • This drug should be used cautiously in conjunction with ampicillin, azathioprine, cyclophosphamide, mercaptopurine, oral anticoagulants, theophylline, or thiazides. If you are currently taking any drugs of these types, consult your doctor about their use. If you are unsure about the type or contents of your medications, ask your doctor or pharmacist. • Avoid large doses of vitamin C while taking this drug. The combination may increase the risk of kidney stone formation.

Comments: It is common for persons beginning to take this drug to also take colchicine for the first three months. Colchicine helps minimize painful attacks of gout. • If one tablet of this drug is prescribed three times a day, ask your doctor if a single dose (either three 100 mg tablets or one 300 mg tablet) can be taken as a convenience. • The effects of therapy with this drug may not be apparent for at least two weeks. • Drink at least eight glasses of water each day to help minimize the formation of kidney stones. • While you are on this drug, do not drink alcohol without first checking with your doctor. • To lessen stomach upset, take this drug with food. Take each dose with a full glass of water.

Index

A

Accutane acne preparation, 40
acetaminophen with codeine analgesic, 40
Aceta with Codeine analgesic, 41
Achromycin V antibiotic, 41
acne preparation
    Accutane, 40
    Retin-A, 186
Actacin-C expectorant, 41
Actamine-C expectorant, 41
Actifed-C expectorant, 41
acyclovir. *See* Zovirax antiviral
Adapin antidepressant, 42, 194
administration of medicine, 13–18
adrenergic
    methylphenidate hydrochloride, 142
    Ritalin, 187
adrenergic and antihistamine
    Allerfrin, 47
    Amaril "D" Spantab, 47
    Decongestabs, 78
    Naldecon, 148
    Naldelate, 149
    Nalgest, 150
    Sinocon, 194
    Tri-Phen-Chlor, 222
    Tudecon, 222
adrenocorticotropic hormone, 31
Adsorbocarpine ophthalmic solution, 42
adverse reaction, 19
Advil anti-inflammatory, 42
aerosol spray administration, 18
Akarpine ophthalmic solution, 42
AK Sporin H.C. Otic, 42
AK Sporin Ophthalmic Ointment, 42
Ak-Sulf ophthalmic solution and ointment, 42
Alatone diuretic and antihypertensive, 42
Aldactazide diuretic and antihypertensive, 42
Aldactone diuretic and antihypertensive, 44
Aldomet antihypertensive, 44
Aldoril diuretic and antihypertensive, 46
Allerfrin with Codeine, 47
allergy medication, 37
allopurinol. *See* Zyloprim gout drug
Almocarpine ophthalmic solution, 47

alprazolam antianxiety, 47
Alzide diuretic and antihypertensive, 47
Amaril "D" Spantab, 47
Amcap antibiotic, 47
Amcill antibiotic, 47
Amen progesterone hormone, 47
aminophylline bronchodilator, 47
Aminophylline bronchodilator, 48
Amitid antidepressant, 48
Amitril antidepressant, 48
amitriptyline hydrochloride antidepressant, 48
Amoline bronchodilator, 48
amoxicillin antibiotic, 49
Amoxil antibiotic, 49
ampicillin antibiotic, 49
analgesic, 35
    acetaminophen with codeine, 40
    Aceta with Codeine, 41
    Bayapap with Codeine, 57
    Bexophene, 59
    Capital with Codeine, 62
    Chlorofon-F, 66
    Chlorzone Forte, 67
    chlorzoxazone w/APAP, 67
    Codap, 69
    Codoxy, 69
    Darvocet-N, 77
    Darvon Compound-65, 77
    Dolene Compound-65, 86
    Dolobid anti-inflammatory, 86
    Doxaphene, 88
    Emcodeine, 92
    Empirin with Codeine, 99
    Equagesic, 94
    Equazine-M, 95
    Meprogesic Q, 141
    Micrainin, 142
    Norgesic, 155
    Norgesic Forte, 155
    oxycodone hydrochloride, oxycodone terephthalate, and aspirin, 162
    Panadol, 162
    Parafon Forte, 162
    Percodan, 167
    Phenaphen with Codeine, 169
    Phenazodine, 169
    phenazopyridine hydrochloride, 169
    Polyflex, 172
    propoxyphene hydrochloride compound, 180
    Pyridiate, 181
    Pyridium, 181
    Pyridium Plus, 182

CONSUMER GUIDE®

SK-APAP with Codeine, 194
SK-65 Compound, 195
Synalgos, 202
Synalgos-DC, 202
Talwin compound, 205
Talwin Nx, 205
Tranquigesic, 217
Tylenol with Codeine, 223
Zoxaphen, 230
analgesic and sedative
Buff-A-Comp, 61
Butal Compound, 61
Fiorgen PF, 97
Fiorinal, 97
Fiorinal with Codeine, 98
Isollyl, 118
Isollyl with Codeine, 118
Lanorinal, 126
Marnal, 136
oxycodone hydrochloride,
    oxycodone terephthalate, and
    aspirin, 162
Protension, 180
anorectic, 34
Depletite, 79
diethylpropion hydrochloride, 81
Fastin, 96
Ionamin, 118
Obe-Nix, 157
Obephen, 157
Obermine, 157
Obestin-30, 157
phentermine hydrochloride, 172
Phentrol No. 2, 172
Preludin, 176
Tenuate, 207
Tepanil, 208
Unifast Unicelles, 223
Wilpowr, 228
anti-anginal, 27
Calan, 62
Cardizem, 63
Cordilate, 72
Dilitrate SR, 82
diltiazem, 82
dipyridamole, 84
Iso-Bid, 118
Isonate, 119
Isoptin, 119
Isordil, 121
isosorbide dinitrate, 122
Isotrate Timecelles, 122
Klavikordal, 124
N-G-C, 152
Niong, 153
Nitro-Bid, 153
Nitrocap T.D., 154

Nitrodisc, 154
Nitro-Dur, 154
nitroglycerin, 154
Nitroglyn, 154
Nitrol, 154
Nitrolin, 154
Nitro-Long, 154
Nitronet, 154
Nitrong, 154
Nitrospan, 154
Nitrostat SR, 155
Onset-10, 157
Persantine, 158
Procardia, 178
Pyridamole, 181
Sorate, 198
Sorbide T D, 198
Sorbitrate, 198
Transderm-Nitro, 217
Trates Granucaps, 219
anti-arrhythmic, 27
Cin-Quin, 68
Norpace, 156
procainamide hydrochloride, 177
Procan, 177
Promine, 179
Pronestyl, 179
Quinidex Extentabs, 183
quinidine sulfate, 183
Quinora, 184
SK-Quinidine Sulfate, 195
anti-asthmatic
Beclovent, 57
Proventil, 180
Vanceril, 225
See also allergy and congestion
    remedy
antibacterial, 32
Bactrim and Bactrim DS, 56
Bethaprim SS and Bethaprim
    DS, 59
Cotrim and Cotrim DS, 75
Gamazole, 101
Gantanol and Gantanol DS, 101,
    102
Gantrisin, 102
Gulfasin, 103
Lipo Gantrisin, 132
Macrodantin, 136
nitrofurantoin, 154
Septra and Septra DS, 189
SK-Soxazole, 195
SMZ-TMP and SMZ-TMP DS, 197
sulfamethoxazole, 200
Sulfatrim and Sulfatrim DS, 200
sulfisoxazole, 200
Sulfizin, 200

Urobak, 223
antibiotic, 32
  Achromycin V, 41
  Amcap, 47
  Amcill, 47
  amoxicillin, 49
  Amoxil, 49
  ampicillin, 49
  Beepen VK, 57
  Betapen-VK, 59
  Bristamycin, 61
  Ceclor, 65
  cefadroxil, 89
  Cycline-250, 76
  Cyclopar, 76
  D-Amp, 77
  Deltamycin, 78
  Deltapen-VK, 78
  Doxy-Caps, 88
  Doxychel, 88
  doxycycline hyclate, 89
  Doxy-Lemmon, 89
  Doxy-Tabs, 89
  Duricef, 89
  E.E.S., 91
  E-Mycin, 93
  Eramycin, 95
  Eryc, 95
  Erypar, 95
  Ery-Ped, 95
  Ery-Tab, 95
  Erythrocin, 95
  erythromycin, 95
  Ethril, 96
  Ilosone, 113
  Ilotycin, 113
  Keflex, 122
  Larotid, 127
  Ledercillin VK, 128
  M-cillin B 400, 137
  Minocin, 144
  Neomycin Sulfate-Polymyxin B
    Sulfate-Gramicidin Solution, 151
  Neosporin, 151
  nitrofurantoin, 154
  Nor-Tet, 157
  Omnipen, 157
  Panmycin, 162
  Pediamycin, 165
  Penapar VK, 165
  penicillin G, 166
  penicillin potassium
    phenoxymethyl, 166
  Pentids, 167
  Pen-Vee K, 167
  Pfizer-E, 169
  Pfizerpen A, 169
  Pfizerpen G, 169
  Pfizerpen VK, 169
  Polycillin, 172
  Polymox, 172
  Principen, 177
  Repen-VK, 185
  Retet, 186
  Robicillin VK, 188
  Robimycin, 188
  Robitet, 188
  RP-Mycin, 188
  SK-Ampicillin, 194
  SK-Erythromycin, 195
  SK-Penicillin G, 195
  SK-Penicillin VK, 195
  SK-Tetracycline, 195
  Sumox, 201
  Sumycin, 201
  Supen, 201
  Suspen, 201
  Tetra-C, 208
  Tetracap, 208
  tetracycline hydrochloride, 208
  Tetracyn, 209
  Tetralan-250, 209
  Tetralan-500, 209
  Tetram, 209
  Totacillin, 217
  Trimox, 221
  Ultracef, 223
  Unifast Unicelles, 223
  Uticillin VK, 223
  Utimox, 223
  V-Cillin K, 226
  Veetids, 226
  Vibramycin, 226
  Vibra-Tabs, 227
  Wyamycin, 228
  Wymox, 228
anticholinergic, 30
anticholinergic and antispasmodic,
    30
  Diphenatol, 83
  diphenoxylate hydrochloride with
    atropine sulfate, 83
  Enoxa, 94
  Lofene, 132
  Lomotil, 132
  Lonox, 133
  Lo-Trol, 134
  Low-Quel, 134
  Nor-Mil, 156
  SK-Diphenoxylate, 195
anticholinergic and phenothiazine
  Combagen, 70
  Combid Spansule, 70
  Isopro T.D., 119

CONSUMER GUIDE®

Prochlor-Iso, 178
Pro-Iso, 178
anticoagulant, 28
  Coumadin, 75
  Panwarfin, 162
  sodium warfarin anticoagulant,
    197
anticonvulsant, 34
  Dilantin, 81
  Dilantin with Phenobarbital, 82
  Diphenylan Sodium, 83
  Ditan, 84
  phenytoin sodium, 172
  Tegretol, 205
antidepressant, 34
  Adapin, 42
  Amitid, 48
  Amitril, 48
  amitriptyline hydrochloride, 48
  Desyrel, 79
  Elavil, 91
  Emitrip, 92
  Endep, 93
  imipramine hydrochloride, 113
  Janimine, 122
  Limbitrol, 131
  Ludiomil, 134
  Sinequan, 193
  SK-Amitriptyline, 194
  SK-Pramine, 195
  Tipramine, 214
  Tofranil, 214
  Tofranil-PM, 215
  trazodone, 219
antidiabetic, 31
  chlorpropamide, 67
  Diabinese, 79
  insulin, 116
  Oramide, 159
  Orinase, 160
  SK-Tolbutamide, 196
  tolbutamide, 215
  Tolinase, 216
antidiarrheal, 30
  Imodium, 113
  See also anticholinergic and
    antispasmodic
antifungal, 33
  Gyne-Lotrimin, 103
  Korostatin, 125
  Lotrimin, 134
  Monistat 7, 144
  Mycelex, 146
  Mycelex G, 146
  Mycostatin, 147
  Nilstat, 153
  nystatin, 157

antihistamine, 37
  Belix, 57
  Benadryl, 57
  Bendylate, 58
  cyproheptadine hydrochloride, 76
  Diahist, 81
  Diphen, 83
  diphenhydramine hydrochloride,
    83
  Fenylhist, 97
  Periactin, 167
  Phen-Amin, 169
  SK-Diphenhydramine, 195
antihistamine and adrenergic
  Condrin-LA, 72
  Deconade, 78
  Drize, 89
  Neotep, 152
  Orahist, 157
  Oraminic Spancaps, 160
  Ornade Spansule, 161
  Redsaid T.D., 185
  Rhinolar-EX 12, 187
  Tuss-genade, 223
antihistamine and decongestant
  azatadine and pseudoephedrine,
    55
  Bromalix, 61
  Bromophen, 61
  Brompheniramine Compound, 61
  Cordamine-PA Tabs, 72
  Dimalix, 82
  Dimetapp, 82
  Histatapp TD, 105
  Midatap, 143
  Normatane, 156
  pseudoephedrine and azatadine,
    181
  Purebrom TD, 181
  Rotapp, 188
  S/T Decongest, 198
  Tagatap, 204
  Trinalin, 221
  Tri-Phen, 222
  Veltap, 226
  Westapp, 228
antihypertensive, 27
  Aldomet, 44
  Apresoline, 51
  Azaline, 55
  Capoten, 62
  captopril, 63
  Catapres, 64
  hydralazine hydrochloride, 106
  Minipress, 143
  reserpine, 185
  Sandril, 189

Serpalan, 192
Serpanray, 192
Serpasil, 192
Serpate, 192
SK-Reserpine, 195
Zepine, 230
anti-infective, 32–33
  Flagyl, 99
  metronidazole, 142
  Metryl, 142
  Sulfa-Gyn, 200
  Sultrin, 200
  Triple Sulfa, 222
  Trysul, 222
anti-inflammatory, 35
  Advil, 42
  Clinoril, 68
  ibuprofen, 113
  Indocin, 115
  Meclomen, 137
  Motrin, 145
  Nalfon, 149
  Naprosyn, 150
  Nuprin, 157
  Rufen, 189
  Tolectin, 215
antilipidemic, 29
antimicrobial and antiparasitic
  Flagyl, 99
  metronidazole, 142
  Metryl, 142
  Protostat, 180
  Satric, 189
antinauseant, 30
  Antivert, 50
  meclizine hydrochloride, 137
  Tegamide, 205
  T-Gen, 209
  Tigan, 213
  trimethobenzamide, 221
antineoplastic, 32
antiparkinson agent, 34
  Aphen, 51
  Artane, 53
  Cogentin, 69
  Sinemet, 192
  Tremin, 219
  Trihexane, 221
  Trihexidyl, 221
  Trihexy, 221
  trihexyphenidyl hydrochloride, 221
antipsychotic agent, 34
  Haldol, 104
antisecretory
  Tagamet, 204
  Zantac, 229
antispasmodic, 30

Bentyl, 58
Bentyl with phenobarbital, 59
Dibent, 81
dicyclomine hydrochloride, 81
Di-Spaz, 84
See also anticholinergic and
  antispasmodic
antitubercular
  isoniazid, 119
  Laniazid, 126
  Niconyl, 152
  Panazid, 162
  Teebaconin, 205
antitussive, 36
anti-ulcer
  Carafate, 63
  medication, 30
Antivert antinauseant, 50
antiviral, 33
  Zovirax, 230
Anugard-HC
  steroid-hormone-
    containing anorectal product, 51
Anusol HC
  steroid-hormone-
    containing anorectal product, 51
AP Creme steroid hormone and
  anti-infective, 51
Aphen anti-parkinson drug, 51
A-poxide sedative and hypnotic, 51
appetite suppressant. See anorectic
Apresoline antihypertensive, 51
Aprodine-C, expectorant, 52
Aquatensen diuretic and
  antihypertensive, 52
Aquazide H diuretic and
  antihypertensive, 52
Aristocort A steroid hormone, 52
Aristocort steroid hormone (topical),
  53
Armour thyroid hormone, 53
Artane antiparkinson drug, 53
Atarax sedative, 54
atenolol. See Tenormin beta blocker
Ativan sedative and hypnotic, 55
Atozine sedative, 55
Azaline antihypertensive, 55
azatadine and pseudoephrine. See
  Trinalin antihistamine and
  decongestant.

B

Bactrim and Bactrim DS
  antibacterials, 56
Barbita sedative and hypnotic, 56
Barophen sedative and
  anticholinergic, 57

Bayapap with Codeine analgesic, 57
Bay-Ase sedative and
  anticholinergic, 57
BaySporin Otic, 57
beclomethasone dipropionate.
  See Vanceril anti-asthmatic.
Beclovent anti-asthmatic, 57
Beepen VK antibiotic, 57
Belix antihistamine, 57
belladonna alkaloids with
  phenobarbital sedative and
  anticholinergic, 57
Bellalphen sedative and
  anticholinergic, 57
Bellastal sedative and
  anticholinergic, 57
Benadryl antihistamine, 57
Bendylate antihistamine, 58
Bentyl antispasmodic, 58
Bentyl antispasmodic with
  phenobarbital, 59
benztropine mesylate. See Cogentin
  antiparkinson drug
beta blocker, 29
  Blocadren, 59
  Corgard, 72
  Inderal, 113
  Lopressor, 133
  propranolol, 180
  Tenormin, 206
betamethasone valerate. See
  Valisone steroid hormone
Betapen-VK antibiotic, 59
Betatrex steroid hormone, 59
Beta-Val steroid hormone, 59
Bethaprim DS antibacterial, 59
Bethaprin SS antibacterial, 59
Bexophene analgesic, 59
birth control pills. See oral
  contraceptives
Bleph-10 Liquifilm ophthalmic
  solution and ointment, 59
Blocadren beta blocker, 59
blood disorders, drug-induced,
  25-26
blood pressure drug. See
  antihypertensive; diuretic and
  antihypertensive
blood thinner. See anticoagulant
Brethine bronchodilator, 60
Bricanyl bronchodilator, 61
Bristamycin antibiotic, 61
Bromalix antihistamine and
  decongestant, 61
Bromophen antihistamine and
  decongestant, 61
Brompheniramine Compound

antihistamine and
  decongestant, 61
Bronchial expectorant and smooth
  muscle relaxant, 61
bronchodilator, 36
  aminophylline, 47
  Aminophylline, 48
  Amoline, 48
  Brethine, 60
  Bricanyl, 61
  Choledyl, 67
  Constant-T, 72
  Duraphyl, 89
  Elixophyllin SR, 92
  LaBID, 126
  Lixaminol, 132
  Phyllocontin, 172
  Proventil, 180
  Quibron-T/SR, 183
  Respbid, 186
  Slo-Phyllin, 196
  Somophyllin, 197
  Somophyllin-DF, 198
  Sustaire, 201
  Theoclear, 209
  Theo-Dur, 209
  Theophylline, 210
  theophylline SR, 210
  Theostat, 210
  Theo-Time, 210
  Truphylline, 222
  Uniphyl, 223
  Ventolin, 226
  See also allergy and congestion
    remedy; anti-asthmatic
Buff-A-Comp analgesic and
  sedative, 61
Butal Compound analgesic and
  sedative, 61

C

Cafergot migraine remedy, 61
Cafergot P-B migraine remedy, 62
Cafetrate migraine remedy, 62
Calan anti-anginal, 62
Cam-ap-es diuretic and
  antihypertensive, 62
Capital with Codeine analgesic, 62
Capoten, 62
capsule administration, 14
captopril antihypertensive, 63
Caquin steroid hormone and
  anti-infective, 63
Carafate anti-ulcer, 63
carbamazepine. See Tegretol
  anticonvulsant
cardiovascular drugs, 27–29

Cardizem, 63
Carmol HC topical steroid, 64
Catapres antihypertensive, 64
Ceclor antibiotic, 65
cefaclor. See Ceclor antibiotic
cefadroxil. See Duricef antibiotic
Cena-K potassium chloride
replacement, 65
central nervous system drugs,
33–36
central nervous system stimulant
methylphenidate, 142
Ritalin, 187
Centrax sedative and hypnotic, 65
cephalexin. See Keflex antibiotic
Cerespan vasodilator and smooth
muscle relaxant, 66
Cetamide ophthalmic solution and
ointment, 66
chemotherapeutics, 32
Cherapas diuretic and
antihypertensive, 66
chlordiazepoxide hydrochloride
sedative and hypnotic, 66
Chlordinium sedative and
anticholinergic, 66
Chlorofon-F analgesic, 66
Chloroserpine diuretic and
antihypertensive, 66
chlorothiazide diuretic and
antihypertensive, 66
chlorothiazide with reserpine diuretic
and antihypertensive, 67
chlorpromazine hydrochloride
phenothiazine, 67
chlorpropamide oral antidiabetic, 67
chlorthalidone diuretic and
antihypertensive, 67
Chlorzide diuretic and
antihypertensive, 67
Chlorzone Forte analgesic, 67
chlorzoxazone w/APAP analgesic,
67
Choledyl bronchodilator, 67
cimetidine. See Tagamet
antisecretory
Cin-Quin anti-arrhythmic, 68
Circanol vasodilator, 68
circulatory system side effects,
22–23
Clindex sedative and anticholinergic,
68
Clinoril anti-inflammatory, 68
Clinoxide sedative and
anticholinergic, 69
Clipoxide sedative and
anticholinergic, 69

clonidine hydrochloride. See
Catapres antihypertensive
clorazepate dipotassium. See
Tranxene sedative and hypnotic
clotrimazole. See Lotrimin antifungal
agent
Codap analgesic, 69
Codoxy analgesic, 69
Cogentin antiparkinson drug, 69
ColBENEMID uricosuric, 70
cold remedy. See allergy and
congestion remedy;
antihistamine; cough remedy;
expectorant
Combagen anticholinergic and
phenothiazine, 70
Combid Spansule anticholinergic
and phenothiazine, 70
Compazine phenothiazine, 71
Condrin-LA antihistamine and
adrenergic, 72
conjugated estrogens hormone, 72
Constant-T bronchodilator, 72
contraceptive. See oral
contraceptives
contraindications, 39
Cordamine-PA Tabs antihistamine
and decongestant, 72
Cordilate anti-anginal, 72
Corgard beta blocker, 72
Corque steroid hormone and anti-
infective, 73
Cortan steroid hormone, 73
Cortef Acetate topical steroid, 73
Cortef steroid hormone, 73
Cortin steroid hormone and anti-
infective, 73
cortisol steroid hormone, 73
Cortisporin ophthalmic suspension,
73
Cortisporin otic solution/suspension,
74
Cotrim and Cotrim DS antibacterials,
75
Coumadin anticoagulant, 75
Curretab progesterone hormone, 76
Cycline-250 antibiotic, 76
cyclobenzaprine hydrochloride. See
Flexeril muscle relaxant and
analgesic
Cyclopar antibiotic, 76
cyproheptadine hydrochloride
antihistamine, 76

D

Dalmane hypnotic, 76

D-Amp antibiotic, 77
Darvocet-N analgesic, 77
Darvon Compound-65 analgesic, 77
Deapril-ST vasodilator, 78
Deconade antihistamine and
    adrenergic, 78
Decongestabs adrenergic and
    antihistamine, 78
decongestants, 36
Delapav vasodilator and smooth
    muscle relaxant, 78
Deltamycin antibiotic, 78
Deltapen-VK antibiotic, 78
Deltasone steroid hormone, 79
Depletite anorectic, 79
Desyrel antidepressant, 79
diabetic drug. See antidiabetic
Diabinese oral antidiabetic, 79
Diachlor diuretic and
    antihypertensive, 80
Diahist antihistamine, 81
Diaqua diuretic and
    antihypertensive, 81
diazepam. See Valium sedative and
    hypnotic
Dibent antispasmodic, 81
dicyclomine hydrochloride
    antispasmodic, 81
diet aid. See anorectic
diethylpropion hydrochloride
    anorectic, 81
diflunisal. See Dolobid anti-
    inflammatory analgesic
digestive tract side effects, 21–22
digitalis, 28
digoxin heart drug, 81
Dilantin anticonvulsant, 81
Dilantin with Phenobarbital
    anticonvulsant, 82
Dilart vasodilator and smooth
    muscle relaxant, 82
Dilitrate SR anti-anginal, 82
diltiazem anti-anginal, 82
Dimalix antihistamine and
    decongestant, 82
Dimetapp antihistamine and
    decongestant, 82
Diphen antihistamine, 83
Diphenatol anticholinergic and
    antispasmodic, 83
diphenhydramine hydrochloride
    antihistamine, 83
diphenoxylate hydrochloride with
    atropine sulfate anticholinergic
    and antispasmodic, 83
Diphenylan Sodium anticonvulsant,
    83

dipyridamole. See Persantine anti-
    anginal
disopyramide phosphate. See
    Norpace anti-arrhythmic
Di-Spaz antispasmodic, 84
Ditan anticonvulsant, 84
Diupres diuretic and
    antihypertensive, 84
diuretics, 28
diuretic and antihypertensive, 27–28
    Alatone, 42
    Aldactazide, 42
    Aldactone, 44
    Aldoril, 46
    Alzide, 47
    Aquatensen, 52
    Aquazide H, 52
    Cam-ap-es, 62
    Cherapas, 66
    Chloroserpine, 66
    chlorothiazide, 66
    chlorothiazide with reserpine, 67
    chlorthalidone, 67
    Chlorzide, 67
    Diachlor, 80
    Diaqua, 81
    Diupres, 84
    Diuril, 85
    Diu-Scrip, 86
    Dyazide, 89
    Enduron, 93
    Esidrix, 96
    Ethon, 96
    furosemide, 101
    H-H-R, 105
    Hydrap-Es, 106
    Hydro-Chlor, 106
    hydrochlorothiazide, 106
    hydrochlorothiazide, reserpine,
        and hydralazine diuretic and
        antihypertensive, 107
    hydrochlorothiazide with
        reserpine, 107
    HydroDIURIL, 109
    Hydromal, 109
    Hydro Plus, 109
    Hydropres, 110
    Hydroserp, 111
    Hydroserpine, 111
    Hydrosine, 111
    Hydro-T, 111
    Hydrotensin, 111
    Hydro-Z, 111
    Hygroton, 111
    Hylidone, 112
    Hyserp, 112
    Inderide, 114

Lasix, 127
Mallopress, 137
methyclothiazide, 142
metolazone, 142
Mictin, 143
Oretic, 160
Rezide, 187
Ser-A-Gen, 189
Seralazide, 189
Ser-Ap-Es, 189
Serpazide, 192
SK-Chlorothiazide, 194
SK-Furosemide, 195
SK-Hydrochlorothiazide, 195
Spiractazide, 42
Spironazide, 198
spironolactone, 198
spironolactone with
    hydrochlorothiazide, 198
Spirozide, 198
Thalitone, 209
Thiuretic, 210
triamterene with
    hydrochlorothiazide, 219
Tri-Hydroserpine, 221
Unipres, 223
Zide, 230
Diuril diuretic and antihypertensive,
    85
Diu-Scrip diuretic and
    antihypertensive, 86
Dolene Compound 65 analgesic, 86
Dolobid anti-inflammatory analgesic,
    86
Donnamor sedative and
    anticholinergic, 87
Donnapine sedative and
    anticholinergic, 87
Donna-Sed sedative and
    anticholinergic, 87
Donnatal sedative and
    anticholinergic, 87
Doxaphene Compound analgesic,
    88
doxepin hydrochloride. See
    Sinequan antidepressant
Doxy-Caps antibiotic, 88
Doxychel antibiotic, 88
doxycycline hyclate antibiotic, 89
Doxy-Lemmon antibiotic, 89
Doxy-Tabs antibiotic, 89
Drize antihistamine and adrenergic,
    89
drug
    accurate measurement, 13
    administration, 13–18
    storing, 12

Duraphyl bronchodilator, 89
Duricef antibiotic, 89
Durrax sedative, 89
Dyazide diuretic and
    antihypertensive, 89

E

ear medicine, 29
    administration, 15
    See also otic solution; otic
        solution suspension; otic
        suspension
edema, 22–23
E.E.S. antibiotic, 91
Effer-K potassium replacement, 91
Elavil antidepressant, 91
Elixophyllin SR bronchodilator, 92
Emcodeine analgesic, 92
Emitrip antidepressant, 92
Empirin with Codeine analgesic, 92
E-Mycin antibiotic, 93
Endep antidepressant, 93
Enduron diuretic and
    antihypertensive, 93
Enoxa anticholinergic and
    antispasmodic, 94
epilepsy drug. See anticonvulsant
Equagesic analgesic, 94
Equanil sedative and hypnotic, 95
Equazine-M analgesic, 95
Eramycin antibiotic, 95
Ercatab migraine remedy, 95
Ergo-Caff migraine remedy, 95
ergoloid mesylates vasodilator, 95
Eryc antibiotic, 95
Erypar antibiotic, 95
Ery Ped antibiotic, 95
Ery-Tab antibiotic, 95
Erythrocin antibiotic, 95
erythromycin antibiotic, 95
Esidrix diuretic and antihypertensive,
    96
Estrocon estrogen hormone, 96
estrogen, 32
    conjugated, 72
    Estrocon, 96
    Premarin, 177
    Progens, 178
Ethon diuretic and antihypertensive,
    96
Ethril antibiotic, 96
Etrafon phenothiazine and
    antidepressant, 96
expectorant, 36
    Actacin-C, 41
    Actamine-C, 41
    Actifed-C, 41

Allerfrin with Codeine, 47
Aprodine-C, 52
Bronchial, 61
Mallergan, 136
Mallergan VC with Codeine, 137
Phenergan, 169
Phenergan VC, 170
Phenergan VC with Codeine, 170
Phenergan with Codeine, 169
promethazine hydrochloride plain, 178
promethazine hydrochloride VC with Codeine, 179
promethazine hydrochloride with codeine, 179
Prometh VC with Codeine, 179
Prothazine, 180
Prothazine with Codeine, 180
Rofed-C, 188
Triacin C, 219
expectorant and smooth muscle relaxant
Bronchial, 61
Glyceryl-T, 103
Lanophyllin-GG, 126
Quibron, 182
Slo-Phyllin GG, 197
Theocolate, 209
Theolate, 210
eyedrops and ointment
administration, 14–15
types of, 29–30
See also ophthalmic solution/ointment

F

Fastin anorectic, 96
female hormone. See estrogen; oral contraceptives; progesterone
fenoprofen calcium. See Nalfon anti-inflammatory
Fenylhist antihistamine, 97
Fiorgen PF analgesic and sedative, 97
Fiorinal analgesic and sedative, 97
Fiorinal with Codeine analgesic and sedative, 98
Flagyl antimicrobial and antiparasitic, 99
Flexeril muscle relaxant and analgesic, 100
Florvite vitamin and fluoride supplement, 101
fluocinolone acetonide. See Synalar steroid hormone
fluocinonide. See Lidex steroid hormone

Fluonid steroid hormone, 101
flurazepam hydrochloride. See Dalmane hypnotic
Flurosyn steroid hormone, 101
Flutex steroid hormone, 101
furosemide, 101

G

Gamazole antibacterial, 101
gamma benzene hexachloride. See Kwell pediculocide and scabicide
Gantanol antibacterial, 101
Gantanol DS antibacterial, 102
Gantrisin antibacterial, 102
gastrointestinal stimulant
metoclopromide, 142
Reglan, 184
gastrointestinal system
drugs for, 30
side effects affecting, 21
generic drugs, 10–11
Gerimal vasodilator, 103
glucagon, 31
Glyceryl-T expectorant and smooth muscle relaxant, 103
gout remedy
allopurinol, 47
Lopurin, 134
Zyloprim, 230
See also uricosuric
Gulfasin antibacterial, 103
G-well pediculocide and Scabicide, 103
Gyne-Lotrimin antifungal agent, 103

H

Halcion Sedative-hypnotic, 103
Haldol antipsychotic agent, 104
haloperidol. See Haldol antipsychotic agent
HC-Form steroid hormone, 105
heart drugs, 27–29
digoxin, 81
Lanoxin, 126
SK-Digoxin, 194
Hemorrhoidal HC steroid-hormone-containing anorectal product, 105
H-H-R diuretic and antihypertensive, 105
Histatapp TD antihistamine and decongestant, 105
hormone, 31–32
See also estrogen; prednisone; progesterone; steroid; thyroid drug; thyroid hormone

Hydergine vasodilator, 105
hydralazine hydrochloride
 antihypertensive, 106
Hydrap-Es diuretic and
 antihypertensive, 106
Hydro-Chlor diuretic and
 antihypertensive, 106
hydrochlorothiazide diuretic and
 antihypertensive, 106
hydrochlorothiazide, reserpine, and
 hydralazine diuretic and
 antihypertensive, 107
hydrochlorothiazide with reserpine
 diuretic and antihypertensive,
 107
hydrocortisone acetate topical
 steroid, 107
hydrocortisone steroid hormone, 108
hydrocortisone with iodochlorhydroxyquin steroid hormone
 and anti-infective, 109
Hydrocortone steroid hormone, 109
Hydrocorton topical steroid, 109
HydroDIURIL diuretic and
 antihypertensive, 109
Hydroloid-G vasodilator, 109
Hydromal diuretic and
 antihypertensive, 109
Hydro Plus diuretic and
 antihypertensive, 109
Hydropres diuretic and
 antihypertensive, 109
Hydroserp diuretic and
 antihypertensive, 111
Hydroserpine diuretic and
 antihypertensive, 111
Hydrosine diuretic and
 antihypertensive, 111
Hydro-T diuretic and
 antihypertensive, 111
Hydrotensin diuretic and
 antihypertensive, 111
hydroxyzine hydrochloride sedative,
 111
Hydro-Z diuretic and
 antihypertensive, 111
Hygroton diuretic and
 antihypertensive, 111
Hylidone diuretic and
 antihypertensive, 112
Hyosophen sedative and
 anticholinergic, 112
Hy-Pam sedative, 112
hypnotic, 34
 Dalmane, 76
 See also sedative and hypnotic
Hyserp diuretic and

antihypertensive, 112
Hysone steroid hormone and anti-
 infective, 113

I

ibuprofen, 113
Ilosone antibiotic, 113
Ilotycin antibiotic, 113
imipramine hydrochloride
 antidepressant, 113
Imodium antidiarrheal, 113
Inderal beta blocker, 113
Inderide diuretic and
 antihypertensive, 114
Indocin anti-inflammatory, 115
indomethacin. See Indocin anti-
 inflammatory
insulin antidiabetic, 116
Iodocort steroid hormone and anti-
 infective, 117
Ionamin anorectic, 118
Iso-Bid anti-anginal, 118
Isollyl analgesic and sedative, 118
Isollyl with Codeine analgesic and
 sedative, 118
Isonate anti-anginal, 119
isoniazid antitubercular, 119
isonicotinic acid hydrazide. See
 isoniazid antitubercular
Isopro T.D. anticholinergic and
 phenothiazine, 119
Isoptin anti-anginal, 119
Isopto Carpine ophthalmic solution,
 120
Isordil anti-anginal, 121
isosorbide dinitrate anti-anginal, 122
Isotrate Timecelles anti-anginal, 122

J

Janimine antidepressant, 122

K

Kaochlor potassium chloride
 replacement, 122
Kaon potassium chloride
 replacement, 122
Kato potassium chloride
 replacement, 122
Kay Ciel potassium chloride
 replacement, 122
Keflex antibiotic, 122
Kenac steroid hormone, 123
Kenalog steroid hormone, 123
kidney problems, drug-induced, 25
Klavikordal anti-anginal, 124
Klor-Con potassium chloride
 replacement, 124

K-Lor potassium chloride
replacement, 124
Klor potassium chloride
replacement, 124
Klorvess potassium chloride
replacement, 124
Klotrix potassium chloride
replacement, 124
K-Lyte/Cl potassium chloride
replacement, 124
K-Lyte DS potassium replacement,
124
K-Lyte potassium replacement, 124
Kolyum potassium chloride
replacement, 125
Korostatin antifungal agent, 125
K-Tab potassium chloride
replacement, 125
Kwell pediculocide and scabicide,
125
Kwildane pediculocide and
scabicide, 126

L

LaBID bronchodilator, 126
Laniazid antitubercular, 126
Lanophyllin-GG expectorant and
smooth muscle relaxant, 126
Lanorinal analgesic and sedative,
126
Lanoxin heart drug, 126
Lanvisone steroid hormone and anti-
infective, 127
Larotid antibiotic, 127
Lasix diuretic and antihypertensive,
127
Ledercillin VK antibiotic, 128
Levothroid thyroid hormone, 128
levothyroxine sodium, 128
Librax sedative and anticholinergic,
128
Libritabs sedative and hypnotic, 129
Librium sedative and hypnotic, 129
Lidex steroid hormone, 130
Lidox, 131
Limbitrol antidepressant, 131
lindane. See Kwell pediculocide and
scabicide
Lipo Gantrisin antibacterial, 132
Lipoxide sedative and hypnotic, 132
liquid medicine administration, 13
liver problems, drug-induced, 25
Lixaminol bronchodilator, 132
local anesthetic, 36
Lofene anticholinergic and
antispasmodic, 132
Lomotil anticholinergic and

antispasmodic, 132
Lonox anticholinergic and
antispasmodic, 133
loperamide hydrochloride. See
Imodium antidiarrheal
Lopressor beta blocker, 133
Lopurin gout drug, 134
lorazepam sedative and hypnotic,
134
Lotrimin antifungal agent, 134
Lo-Trol anticholinergic and
antispasmodic, 134
Low-Quel anticholinergic and
antispasmodic, 134
Ludiomil antidepressant, 134
Luminal Ovoids sedative and
hypnotic, 135

M

Macrodantin antibacterial, 136
Malatal sedative and anticholinergic,
136
Mallergan expectorant, 136
Mallergan VC with Codeine
expectorant, 137
Mallopress diuretic and
antihypertensive, 137
maprotiline hydrochloride. See
Ludiomil antidepressant
Marnal analgesic and sedative, 137
Materna vitamin-mineral
supplement, 137
M-cillin B 400 antibiotic, 137
meclizine hydrochloride
antinauseant, 137
meclofenamate sodium. See
Meclomen anti-inflammatory
Meclomen anti-inflammatory, 137
Medrol steroid hormone, 138
medroxyprogesterone acetate. See
Provera progesterone hormone
Mellaril phenothiazine, 139
meprobamate sedative and
hypnotic, 140
Meprogesic Q analgesic, 141
Meprospan sedative and hypnotic,
141
methotrexate antimetabolite, 141
methyclothiazide diuretic and
antihypertensive, 142
methyldopa. See Aldomet
antihypertensive
methylphenidate hydrochloride
central nervous system
stimulant, 142
methylprednisolone steroid
hormone, 142

Meticorten steroid hormone, 142
Metoclopromide gastrointestinal
    stimulant, 142
metolazone diuretic and
    antihypertensive, 142
metronidazole antimicrobial and
    antiparasitic, 142
Metryl antimicrobial and
    antiparasitic, 142
Micrainin analgesic, 142
miconazole. See Monistat 7
    antifungal agent
Micro-K potassium chloride
    replacement, 142
Mictin diuretic and antihypertensive,
    143
Midatap antihistamine and
    decongestant, 143
migraine remedy
    Cafergot, 61
    Cafergot P-B, 62
    Cafetrate, 62
    Ercatab, 95
    Ergo-Caff, 95
    Wigraine, 228
Miltown sedative and hypnotic, 143
mineral, 37
Minipress antihypertensive, 143
Minocin antibiotic, 144
minocycline hydrochloride. See
    Minocin antibiotic
Mity-Quin steroid hormone and anti-
    infective, 144
Momatal vitamin-mineral
    supplement, 144
Monistat 7 antifungal agent, 144
monoamine oxidase inhibitor, 34
Motrin anti-inflammatory, 145
Murcil sedative and hypnotic, 146
muscle relaxant, 35
muscle relaxant and analgesic
    Flexeril, 100
Mycelex antifungal agent, 146
Mycelex-G antifungal agent, 146
Mycogen topical steroid hormone
    and anti-infective, 146
Mycolog steroid hormone and anti-
    infective, 146
Mycostatin antifungal agent, 147
Myco Triacet topical steroid
    hormone and anti-infective, 148
Mykacet topical steroid hormone
    and anti-infective, 148
Myobid vasodilator and smooth
    muscle relaxant, 148
Mytrex topical steroid hormone and
    anti-infective, 148

N

nadolol. See Corgard beta blocker.
Naldecon adrenergic and
    antihistamine, 148
Naldelate adrenergic and
    antihistamine, 149
Nalfon anti-inflammatory, 149
Nalgest adrenergic and
    antihistamine, 150
Naprosyn anti-inflammatory, 150
naproxen. See Naprosyn anti-
    inflammatory
narcotic, 35
Nembutal Sodium sedative and
    hypnotic, 151
Neomycin Sulfate-Polymyxin B
    Sulfate-Gramicidin Solution, 151
Neoquess sedative and
    anticholinergic, 151
Neosporin antibiotic ophthalmic
    solution and ointment, 151
Neotep antihistamine and
    adrenergic, 152
nervous system side effects, 23
Neuramate sedative and hypnotic,
    152
Neurate-400 sedative and hypnotic,
    152
N-G-C anti-anginal, 152
N.G.T. topical steroid hormone and
    anti-infective, 152
Niconyl antitubercular, 152
Nicorette smoking deterrent, 152
nicotine resin complex. See
    Nicorette smoking deterrent
nifedipine. See Procardia anti-
    anginal
Nilstat antifungal agent, 153
Niong anti-anginal, 153
Nitro-Bid anti-anginal, 153
Nitrocap T.D. anti-anginal, 154
Nitrodisc anti-anginal, 154
Nitro-Dur anti-anginal, 154
nitrofurantoin antibacterial, 154
nitroglycerin anti-anginal, 154
Nitroglyn anti-anginal, 154
Nitrol anti-anginal, 154
Nitrolin anti-anginal, 154
Nitro-Long anti-anginal, 154
Nitronet anti-anginal, 154
Nitrong anti-anginal, 154
Nitrospan anti-anginal, 154
Nitrostat anti-anginal, 155
Nitrostat SR anti-anginal, 155
Norgesic analgesic, 155
Norgesic Forte analgesic, 155

Normatane antihistamine and
decongestant, 156
Nor-Mil anticholinergic and
antispasmodic, 156
Norpace anti-arrhythmic, 156
Nor-Tet antibiotic, 157
Nuprin anti-inflammatory, 157
nystatin antifungal agent, 157

O

Obe-Nix anorectic, 157
Obephen anorectic, 157
Obermine anorectic, 157
Obestin-30 anorectic, 157
Omnipen antibiotic, 157
Onset-10 anti-anginal, 157
Ophthacet ophthalmic solution and
ointment, 157
ophthalmic solution/ointment
Adsorbocarpine, 42
Akarpine, 42
AK Sporin Ophthalmic Ointment,
42
Ak-Sulf, 42
Almocarpine, 47
Bleph-10, 59
Cetamide, 66
Cortisporin, 73
Isopto Carpine, 120
Neosporin antibiotic, 151
Ophthacet, 157
Pilocar, 172
pilocarpine hydrochloride, 172
Pilocel, 172
Pilomiotin, 172
Piloptic, 172
Sodium Sulamyd, 197
sodium sulfacetamide, 197
Sulf-10, 200
Sulten-10, 200
Timoptic, 213
See also eyedrops and ointments
ophthalmic suspension
Cortisporin, 73
Orahist antihistamine and
adrenergic, 157
oral contraceptives, 158
Oramide oral antidiabetic, 159
Oraminic Spancaps antihistamine
and adrenergic, 160
Orasone steroid hormone, 160
Oretic diuretic and antihypertensive,
160
Orinase oral antidiabetic, 160
Ornade Spansule antihistamine and
adrenergic, 161
Ortega Otic M otic solution, 161

otic solution
Ortega Otic M, 161
Otobione, 162
otic solution/suspension
AK Sporin H.C Otic, 42
BaySporin Otic, 57
Cortisporin, 73
Ortega Otic M, 161
otic suspension
Otobione, 162
See also ear medicine
Otobione otic suspension, 162
over-the-counter (OTC) drug, 10
oxazepam. See Serax sedative and
hypnotic
oxtriphylline. See Choledyl
bronchodilator
oxycodone hydrochloride,
oxycodone terephthalate, and
aspirin analgesic, 162

P

Palbar sedative and anticholinergic,
162
Panadol with Codeine analgesic,
162
Panasol steroid hormone, 162
Panazid antitubercular, 162
Panmycin antibiotic, 162
Panwarfin anticoagulant, 162
Papacon vasodilator and smooth
muscle relaxant, 162
papaverine hydrochloride vasodilator
and smooth muscle relaxant,
162
Parafon Forte analgesic, 162
Pavabid Plateau Caps vasodilator
and smooth muscle relaxant,
163
Pavacap Unicelles vasodilator and
smooth muscle relaxant, 164
Pavacen Cenules vasodilator and
smooth muscle relaxant, 164
Pavadur vasodilator and smooth
muscle relaxant, 164
Pavadyl vasodilator and smooth
muscle relaxant, 164
Pavagen vasodilator and smooth
muscle relaxant, 164
Pava-Par vasodilator and smooth
muscle relaxant, 164
Pava-RX vasodilator and smooth
muscle relaxant, 164
Pavased vasodilator and smooth
muscle relaxant, 164
Pavasule T.D. vasodilator and
smooth muscle relaxant, 164

Pavatine vasodilator and smooth
  muscle relaxant, 164
Pavatym vasodilator and smooth
  muscle relaxant, 164
Paverine Spancaps vasodilator and
  smooth muscle relaxant, 164
Paverolan Lanacaps vasodilator and
  smooth muscle relaxant, 165
PBR/12 sedative and hypnotic, 165
Pediamycin antibiotic, 165
Pedi-Cort V steroid hormone and
  anti-infective, 165
pediculocide and scabicide, 33
  Kwell, 125
  Kwildane, 126
  lindane, 125
  Scabene, 125
Penapar VK antibiotic, 165
penicillin G potassium antibiotic, 165
penicillin potassium phenoxymethyl
  antibiotic, 166
penicillin VK antibiotic, 166
pentazocine hydrochloride. See
  Talwin Nx analgesic
Pentids antibiotic, 167
Pen-Vee K antibiotic, 167
Percodan analgesic, 167
Percodan-Demi analgesic, 167
Periactin antihistamine, 167
Persantine anti-anginal, 168
Pfizer-E antibiotic, 169
Pfizerpen A antibiotic, 169
Pfizerpen G antibiotic, 169
Pfizerpen VK antibiotic, 169
Phen-Amin antihistamine, 169
Phenaphen with Codeine analgesic,
  169
Phenazodine analgesic, 169
phenazopyridine hydrochloride
  analgesic, 169
Phenergan expectorant, 169
Phenergan VC expectorant, 170
Phenergan VC with Codeine
  expectorant, 170
Phenergan with Codeine
  expectorant, 170
phenmetrazine hydrochloride. See
  Preludin anorectic
phenobarbital sedative and hypnotic,
  171
phenothiazine, 34
  Compazine, 71
  Mellaril, 139
  prochlorperazine, 178
  Promapar, 178
  Stelazine, 198
  Thorazine, 211

Thor-Prom, 212
phenothiazine and antidepressant
  Etrafon, 96
  Triavil, 219
phentermine hydrochloride
  anorectic, 172
Phentrol No. 2 anorectic, 172
phenytoin sodium anticonvulsant,
  172
Phyllocontin bronchodilator, 172
Pilocar ophthalmic solution, 172
pilocarpine hydrochloride ophthalmic
  solution, 172
Pilocel ophthalmic solution, 172
Pilomiotin ophthalmic solution, 172
Piloptic ophthalmic solution, 172
Polycillin antibiotic, 172
Polyflex analgesic, 172
Polymox antibiotic, 172
Poly Tabs-F vitamin and fluoride
  supplement, 173
Poly-Vi-Flor vitamin and fluoride
  supplement, 173
Polyvite with Fluoride Drops vitamin
  and fluoride supplement, 173
Potachlor potassium chloride
  replacement, 173
Potage potassium chloride
  replacement, 173
Potasalan potassium chloride
  replacement, 173
Potassine potassium chloride
  replacement, 174
potassium chloride replacement,174
  Cena-K, 65
  Kaochlor, 122
  Kaon, 122
  Kato, 122
  Kay Ciel, 122
  K-Lor, 124
  Klor, 124
  Klor-Con, 124
  Klorvess, 124
  Klotrix, 124
  K-Lyte/Cl, 124
  K-Lyte DS, 124
  Kolyum, 125
  K-Tab, 135
  Micro-K, 142
  Potachlor, 173
  Potage, 173
  Potasalan, 173
  Potassine, 174
  Rum-K, 189
  SK-Potassium Chloride, 195
  Slow-K, 197
potassium replacement, 28

Effer-K, 91
K-Lyte/Cl, 124
K-Lyte DS, 124
potassium-sparing diuretic, 28
prazepam. *See* Centrax sedative
and hypnotic
prazosin hydrochloride. *See*
Minipress antihypertensive
Prednicen-M steroid hormone, 174
prednisone steroid hormone, 175
Preludin anorectic, 176
Premarin estrogen hormone, 177
prescription
abbreviations, 6–7
reading a, 6–8
Principen antibiotic, 177
procainamide hydrochloride anti-
arrhythmic, 177
Procan anti-arrhythmic, 177
Procardia anti-anginal, 178
Prochlor-Iso anticholinergic and
phenothiazine, 178
prochlorperazine phenothiazine, 178
Progens estrogen hormone, 178
progesterone, 32
Amen, 47
Curretab, 76
Provera, 180
Pro-Iso anticholinergic and
phenothiazine, 178
Promapar phenothiazine, 178
promethazine hydrochloride
expectorant plain, 178
promethazine hydrochloride VC
expectorant plain, 178
promethazine hydrochloride VC with
codeine expectorant, 179
promethazine hydrochloride with
codeine expectorant, 179
Prometh VC with Codeine
expectorant, 179
Promine anti-arrhythmic, 179
Pronestyl anti-arrhythmic, 179
propoxyphene hydrochloride
compound analgesic, 180
propranolol and hydrochlorothiazide,
180
propranolol, 180
Protension analgesic and sedative,
180
Prothazine expectorant, 180
Prothazine with Codeine
expectorant, 180
Protostat antimicrobial and
antiparasitic, 180
Proventil anti-asthmatic, 180
Provera progesterone hormone, 180

pseudoephedrine with azatadine,
181
Purebrom TD antihistamine and
decongestant, 81
Pyridamole anti-anginal, 181
Pyridiate analgesic, 181
Pyridium analgesic, 181
Pyridium Plus analgesic, 182

Q

Quibron expectorant and smooth
muscle relaxant, 182
Quibron-T/SR bronchodilator, 183
Quinidex Extentabs anti-arrhythmic,
183
quinidine sulfate anti-arrhythmic,
183
Quinora anti-arrhythmic, 184

R

Racet steroid hormone and anti-
infective, 184
ranitidine. *See* Zantac antisecretory
Rectacort steroid-hormone-
containing anorectal product,
184
rectal suppository administration, 16
Reglan gastrointestinal stimulant,
184
Relaxadon sedative and
anticholinergic, 185
Repen-VK antibiotic, 185
Reposans-10 sedative and hypnotic,
185
Resaid T.D. antihistamine and
adrenergic, 185
reserpine antihypertensive, 185
Respbid bronchodilator, 186
respiratory system
drugs for, 36–37
side effects affecting, 23
See also antihistamine;
antitussive; expectorant
Restoril sedative and hypnotic, 186
Retet antibiotic, 186
Retin-A acne preparation, 186
Rezide diuretic and
antihypertensive, 187
Rhinolar-EX 12 antihistamine and
adrenergic, 187
Ritalin central nervous system
stimulant, 187
Robicillin VK antibiotic, 188
Robimycin antibiotic, 188
Robitet '250' antibiotic, 188
Rofed C expectorant, 188
Rotapp antihistamine and

decongestant, 188
RP-Mycin antibiotic, 188
Rufen anti-inflammatory, 189
Rum-K potassium chloride
  replacement, 189

S

salicylate, 35
Sandril antihypertensive, 189
Satric antimicrobial and antiparasitic,
  189
Scabene pediculocide and
  scabicide, 125
Sedabamate sedative and hypnotic,
  189
sedative, 33–34
  Atarax, 54
  Atozine, 55
  Durrax, 89
  hydroxyzine hydrochloride, 111
  Hy-Pam, 112
  Vistaril, 228
sedative and anticholinergic
  Barophen, 56
  Bay-Ase, 57
  belladonna alkaloids with
    phenobarbital, 57
  Bellalphen, 57
  Bellastal, 57
  Chlordinium, 66
  Clindex, 68
  Clinoxide, 69
  Clipoxide, 69
  Donnamor, 87
  Donnapine, 87
  Donna-Sed, 87
  Donnatal, 87
  Hyosophen, 112
  Librax, 128
  Lidox, 131
  Malatal, 136
  Neoquess, 151
  Palbar, 162
  Relaxadon, 185
  Seds, 189
  Spaslin, 198
  Spasmolin, 198
  Spasmophen, 198
  Spasquid, 198
  Susano, 201
  Vanatal, 225
sedative and hypnotic
  A-poxide, 51
  Ativan, 55
  Barbita, 56
  Centrax, 65
  chlordiazepoxide hydrochloride,

66
diazepam, 224
Equanil, 95
Halcion, 103
Libritabs, 129
Librium, 129
Lipoxide, 132
lorazepam, 55
Luminal Ovoids, 135
meprobamate, 140
Meprospan, 141
Miltown, 143
Murcil, 146
Nembutal Sodium, 151
Neoquess, 151
Neuramate, 152
Neurate-400, 152
PBR/12, 165
phenobarbital, 171
Reposans-10, 185
Restoril, 186
Sedabamate, 189
Sedadrops, 189
Serax, 191
Sereen, 192
SK-Bamate, 194
SK-Lygen, 195
SK-Phenobarbital, 195
Solfoton, 197
Tranmep, 217
Tranxene, 218
triazolam, 221
Valium, 224
Vistaril, 228
Seds sedative and anticholinergic,
  189
Septra and Septra DS antibacterial,
  189
Ser-A-Gen diuretic and
  antihypertensive, 189
Seralazide diuretic and
  antihypertensive, 189
Ser-Ap-Es diuretic and
  antihypertensive, 189
Serax sedative and hypnotic, 191
Sereen sedative and hypnotic, 192
Serpalan antihypertensive, 192
Serpanray antihypertensive, 192
Serpasil antihypertensive, 192
Serpate antihypertensive, 192
Serpazide diuretic and
  antihypertensive, 192
sex hormone, 32
  See also estrogen; progesterone
side effects, 19–26
Sinemet antiparkinson drug, 192
Sinequan antidepressant, 193

Sinocon adrenergic and
    antihistamine, 194
SK-Amitriptyline antidepressant, 194
SK-Ampicillin antibiotic, 194
SK-APAP with Codeine analgesic,
    194
SK-Bamate sedative and hypnotic,
    194
SK-Chlorothiazide diuretic and
    antihypertensive, 194
SK-Digoxin heart drug, 194
SK-Diphenhydramine antihistamine,
    195
SK-Diphenoxylate anticholinergic
    and antispasmodic, 195
SK-Erythromycin antibiotic, 195
SK-Furosemide diuretic and
    antihypertensive, 195
SK-Hydrochlorothiazide diuretic and
    antihypertensive, 195
skin side effects, 24
SK-Lygen sedative and hypnotic,
    195
SK-Penicillin G antibiotic, 195
SK-Penicillin VK antibiotic, 195
SK-Phenobarbital sedative and
    hypnotic, 195
SK-Potassium Chloride potassium
    chloride replacement, 195
SK-Pramine antidepressant, 195
SK-Prednisone steroid hormone,
    195
SK-Quinidine Sulfate anti-
    arrhythmic, 195
SK-Reserpine antihypertensive, 195
SK-65 Compound analgesic, 195
SK-Soxazole antibacterial, 195
SK-Tetracycline antibiotic, 195
SK-Tolbutamide oral antidiabetic,
    196
Slo-Phyllin bronchodilator, 196
Slo-Phyllin GG expectorant and
    smooth muscle relaxant, 197
Slow-K potassium chloride
    replacement, 197
smoking deterrent
    Nicorette, 152
smooth muscle relaxant, 36
SMZ-TMP and SMZ-TMP DS
    antibacterials, 197
Sodium Sulamyd ophthalmic
    solution and ointment, 197
sodium sulfacetamide ophthalmic
    solution and ointment, 197
sodium warfarin anticoagulant, 197
Solfoton sedative and hypnotic, 197
Somophyllin bronchodilator, 197

Somophyllin-DF bronchodilator, 198
Sorate anti-anginal, 198
Sorbide T.D. anti-anginal, 198
Sorbitrate anti-anginal, 198
Spaslin sedative and anticholinergic,
    198
Spasmolin sedative and
    anticholinergic, 198
Spasmophen sedative and
    anticholinergic, 198
Spasquid sedative and
    anticholinergic, 198
Spironazide diuretic and
    antihypertensive, 198
spironolactone diuretic and
    antihypertensive, 198
spironolactone with
    hydrochlorothiazide diuretic and
    antihypertensive, 198
Spiractazide. See Aldactazide
    diuretic and antihypertensive
Spirozide diuretic and
    antihypertensive, 198
S-P-T thyroid hormone, 198
S/T Decongest antihistamine and
    decongestant, 198
Stelazine phenothiazine, 198
steroid, 31
    Anugard-HC anorectal, 51
    Anusol HC anorectal, 51
    Aristocort A, 52
    Aristocort (topical), 53
    betamethasone valerate, 223
    Betatrex, 59
    Beta-Val, 59
    Carmol HC topical, 64
    Cortan, 73
    Cortef Acetate topical, 73
    Cortef steroid hormone, 73
    Cortin steroid hormone, 73
    cortisol steroid hormone, 73
    Deltasone, 79
    fluocinolone acetonide, 201
    Fluonid, 101
    Flurosyn, 101
    Flutex, 101
    HC-Form, 105
    Hemorrhoidal HC anorectal, 105
    hydrocortisone acetate topical,
        107
    hydrocortisone steroid hormone,
        108
    Hydrocorton, 109
    Hydrocortone steroid hormone,
        109
    Kenac, 123
    Kenalog, 123

Lidex, 130
Medrol, 138
methylprednisolone, 142
Meticorten, 142
Orasone, 160
Panasol, 162
Prednicen-M, 174
prednisone, 175
Rectacort, 184
SK-Prednisone, 195
Synalar, 201
Synemol, 203
Triacet, 219
triamcinolone acetonide, 219
Triderm, 221
Trymex, 222
Valisone, 223
Vanceril, 225
steroid and anti-infective
AP Creme, 51
Caquin, 63
Corque, 73
Cortin, 73
hydrocortisone with
iodochlorhydroxyquin, 109
Hysone, 113
Iodocort, 117
Lanvisone, 127
Mity-Quin, 144
Mycogen, 146
Mycolog, 146
Myco Triacet, 148
Mykacet, 148
Mytrex, 148
N.G.T., 152
Pedi-Cort V, 165
Racet, 184
triamcinolone, neomycin,
gramicidin, and nystatin steroid
hormone and anti-infective, 219
Tri-statin, 222
Viodo HC, 227
Vioform-Hydrocortisone, 227
Vioquin-HC, 228
Viotag, 228
storing drugs, 12
Stuartnatal 1 + 1 vitamin-mineral
supplement, 199
sublingual tablets administration, 14
sucralfate, 63
Sulfa-Gyn vaginal anti-infective, 200
sulfamethoxazole. See Gantanol
antibacterial
Sulfatrim and Sulfatrim DS
antibacterials, 200
sulfisoxazole antibacterial, 200
Sulfizin antibacterial, 200

Sulf-10 ophthalmic solution, 200
sulindac. See Clinoril anti-
inflammatory
Sulten-10 ophthalmic solution, 200
Sultrin vaginal anti-infective, 200
Sumox antibiotic, 201
Sumycin antibiotic, 201
Supen antibiotic, 201
suppository administration, 16
Susano sedative and anticholinergic,
201
Suspen antibiotic, 201
Sustaire bronchodilator, 201
Synalar steroid hormone, 201
Synalgos analgesic, 202
Synalgos-DC analgesic, 202
Synemol steroid hormone, 203
Synthroid thyroid hormone, 203
Synthrox thyroid hormone, 204
Syroxine thyroid hormone, 204

T

tablet administration, 14
Tagamet antisecretory, 204
Tagatap antihistamine and
decongestant, 204
Talacen Caplets analgesic, 204
Talwin Compound analgesic, 205
Talwin Nx analgesic, 205
Tandearil anti-inflammatory, 205
Teebaconin antitubercular, 205
Tegamide antinauseant, 205
Tegretol anticonvulsant, 205
temazepam. See Restoril sedative
and hypnotic
Tenormin beta blocker, 206
Tenstan analgesic and sedative, 207
Tenuate anorectic, 207
Tepanil anorectic, 208
terbutaline sulfate. See Brethine
bronchodilator
Tetra-C antibiotic, 208
Tetracap antibiotic, 208
tetracycline hydrochloride antibiotic,
208
Tetracyn antibiotic, 209
Tetralan-250 antibiotic, 209
Tetralan-500 antibiotic, 209
Tetram antibiotic, 209
T-Gen antinauseant, 209
Thalitone diuretic and
antihypertensive, 209
Theoclear bronchodilator, 209
Theocolate expectorant and muscle
relaxant, 209
Theo-Dur bronchodilator, 209
Theolate expectorant and smooth

CONSUMER GUIDE®

muscle relaxant, 210
theophylline. *See* Slo-Phyllin
    bronchodilator
Theophylline bronchodilator, 210
theophylline SR bronchodilator, 210
Theostat bronchodilator, 210
Theo-Time bronchodilator, 210
thiazide diuretic, 28
thioridazine hydrochloride. *See*
    Mellaril phenothiazine
Thiuretic diuretic and
    antihypertensive, 210
Thorazine phenothiazine, 211
Thor-Prom phenothiazine, 212
Thyrar thyroid hormone, 212
thyroid drugs, 31
    Armour, 53
    Levothroid hormone, 128
    levothyroxine sodium, 203
    Noroxine, 158, 204
    S-P-T, 198
    Synthroid, 203
    Synthrox, 204
    Syroxine, 204
    Thyrar, 212
    thyroid hormone, 212
    Thyro-Teric, 213
thyroid hormone, 212
    See also Synthroid thyroid
    hormone
Thyro-Teric thyroid hormone, 213
Tigan antinauseant, 213
timolol maleate. *See* Timoptic
    ophthalmic solution
Timoptic ophthalmic solution, 213
Tipramine antidepressant, 214
Tofranil antidepressant, 214
Tofranil-PM antidepressant, 215
tolazamide. *See* Tolinase oral
    antidiabetic drug
tolbutamide oral antidiabetic, 215
Tolectin anti-inflammatory, 215
Tolinase oral antidiabetic drug, 216
tolmetin sodium. *See* Tolectin anti-
    inflammatory
topical medication, 33
    administration, 17–18
Totacillin antibiotic, 217
Tranquigesic analgesic, 217
tranquilizer, 34
transdermal patches, 18
Transderm-Nitro anti-anginal, 217
Tranxene sedative and hypnotic,
    218
Trates Granucaps anti-anginal, 219
trazodone, 219
Tremin antiparkinson drug, 219

tretinoin. *See* Retin A acne
    preparation
Triacet steroid hormone, 219
Triacin C expectorant, 219
triamcinolone acetonide steroid
    hormone, 219
triamcinolone, neomycin, gramicidin,
    and nystatin steroid hormone,
    and anti-infective, 219
triamterene with hydrochlorothiazide
    diuretic and antihypertensive,
    219
Triavil phenothiazine and
    antidepressant, 219
triazolam sedative and hypnotic, 221
Triderm steroid hormone, 221
Tri-Fed C expectorant, 221
trifluoperazine hydrochloride. *See*
    Stelazine phenothiazine
Trihexane antiparkinson drug, 221
Trihexidyl antiparkinson drug, 221
Trihexy antiparkinson drug, 221
trihexyphenidyl hydrochloride
    antiparkinson drug, 221
Tri-Hydroserpine diuretic and
    antihypertensive, 221
trimethobenzamide antinauseant,
    221
Trimox antibiotic, 221
Trinalin antihistamine and
    decongestant, 221
Tri-Phen antihistamine and
    decongestant, 222
Tri-Phen-Chlor adrenergic and
    antihistamine, 222
Triple Sulfa vaginal anti-infective,
    222
Tri-Statin topical-steroid hormone
    and anti-infective, 222
Truphylline bronchodilator, 222
Trymex steroid hormone, 222
Trysul vaginal anti-infective, 222
Tudecon adrenergic and
    antihistamine, 222
Tuss-genade antihistamine and
    adrenergic, 223
Tylenol with Codeine analgesic, 223

U

Ultracef antibiotic, 223
Unifast Unicelles anorectic, 223
Uniphyl bronchodilator, 223
Unipres diuretic and
    antihypertensive, 223
uricosuric, 35
    Lopurin, 134
    Zyloprim, 230

Urobak, 223
Uticillin VK antibiotic, 223
Utimox antibiotic, 223

V

vaccine, 33
vaginal anti-infective. See anti-
    infective
vaginal medication administration,
    16–17
Valisone steroid hormone, 223
Valium sedative and hypnotic, 224
Vanatal sedative and anticholinergic,
    225
Vanceril anti-asthmatic, 225
Vasocap-150 vasodilator and
    smooth muscle relaxant, 225
vasodilator, 29
    Circanol, 68
    Deapril-ST, 78
    ergoloid mesylates, 95
    Gerimal, 103
    Hydergine, 105
    Hydroloid-G. 109
vasodilator and smooth muscle
    relaxant
    Cerespan, 66
    Delapav, 78
    Dilart, 82
    Myobid, 148
    Papacon, 162
    papaverine hydrochloride, 162
    Pavabid Plateau Caps, 163
    Pavacap Unicelles, 164
    Pavacen Cenules, 164
    Pavadur, 164
    Pavadyl, 164
    Pavagen, 164
    Pava-Par, 164
    Pava-RX, 164
    Pavased, 164
    Pavasule T.D., 164
    Pavatine, 164
    Pavatym, 164
    Paverine Spancaps, 164
    Paverolan Lanacaps, 165
    Vasocap-150, 225
    Vasospan, 225
Vasospan vasodilator and smooth
    muscle relaxant, 225
V-Cillin K antibiotic, 226
Veetids antibiotic, 226

Veltap antihistamine and
    decongestant, 226
Ventolin bronchodilator, 226
verapamil hydrochloride. See Isoptin
    anti-anginal
Vibramycin antibiotic, 226
Vibra-Tabs antibiotic, 227
Viodo HC steroid hormone and anti-
    infective, 227
Vioform-Hydrocortisone steroid
    hormone and anti-infective, 227
Vioquin-HC steroid hormone and
    anti-infective, 228
Viotag steroid hormone and anti-
    infective, 228
Vistaril sedative, 228
vitamin and fluoride supplement
    Florvite, 101
    Poly Tabs-F, 173
    Poly-Vi-Flor, 173
    Polyvite with Fluoride Drops, 173
vitamin-mineral supplement
    Materna, 137
    Momatal, 144
    Stuartnatal 1+1, 199
vitamin supplement, 37

W

warfarin. See Coumadin
    anticoagulant
water pills. See diuretic; diuretic and
    antihypertensive
Westapp antihistamine and
    decongestant, 228
Wigraine migraine remedy, 228
Westhroid thyroid hormone, 213,
    228
Wilpowr anorectic, 228
Wyamycin antibiotic, 228
Wymox antibiotic, 228

X

Xanax anti-anxiety, 229

Z

Zantac antisecretory, 229
Zepine antihypertensive, 230
Zide diuretic and antihypertensive,
    230
Zovirax topical antiviral, 230
Zoxaphen analgesic, 230
Zyloprim gout drug, 230